PENGUIN BOOKS

# BLUE-WATER EMPIRE

Robert Holland is one of the world's leading historians of the Mediterranean and the author of *Britain and the Revolt in Cyprus, 1954–59*, and (with Diana Markides) *The British and the Hellenes: struggles for mastery in the Eastern Mediterranean, 1850–1960*. He holds professorial positions at the Centre for Hellenic Studies in King's College London and the Institute of Commonwealth Studies in the same University.

ROBERT HOLLAND

# Blue-Water Empire

## *The British in the Mediterranean since 1800*

PENGUIN BOOKS

PENGUIN BOOKS

Published by the Penguin Group
Penguin Books Ltd, 80 Strand, London WC2R 0RL, England
Penguin Group (USA) Inc., 375 Hudson Street, New York, New York 10014, USA
Penguin Group (Canada), 90 Eglinton Avenue East, Suite 700, Toronto, Ontario, Canada M4P 2Y3
(a division of Pearson Penguin Canada Inc.)
Penguin Ireland, 25 St Stephen's Green, Dublin 2, Ireland (a division of Penguin Books Ltd)
Penguin Group (Australia), 707 Collins Street, Melbourne, Victoria 3008, Australia
(a division of Pearson Australia Group Pty Ltd)
Penguin Books India Pvt Ltd, 11 Community Centre,
Panchsheel Park, New Delhi – 110 017, India
Penguin Group (NZ), 67 Apollo Drive, Rosedale, Auckland 0632, New Zealand
(a division of Pearson New Zealand Ltd)
Penguin Books (South Africa) (Pty) Ltd, Block D, Rosebank Office Park, 181 Jan Smuts Avenue,
Parktown North, Gauteng 2193, South Africa

Penguin Books Ltd, Registered Offices: 80 Strand, London WC2R 0RL, England

www.penguin.com

First published by Allen Lane 2012
Published in Penguin Books 2013
001



Typeset by Jouve (UK), Milton Keynes
Printed in Great Britain by Clays Ltd, St Ives plc

A CIP catalogue record for this book is available from the British Library

ISBN: 978-0-141-03610-6

www.greenpenguin.co.uk

Penguin Books is committed to a sustainable future for our business, our readers and our planet. This book is made from Forest Stewardship Council™ certified paper.

ALWAYS LEARNING PEARSON

*In Memory of Peter Trevor Holland*

*We must therefore sometimes conquer, and if we are sometimes excluded from the continent of Europe, form for ourselves an insular empire, complete in its parts, and sufficient to itself.*

G. F. Leckie (1808) on Britain in the Mediterranean

*With the English for my friends I can do anything; without their friendship I can do nothing . . . Wherever I turn, they are there to baffle me.*

Mehmet Ali, Viceroy of Egypt (1834)

# *Contents*

# *List of Illustrations*

For their assistance in identifying and obtaining images relating to Cyprus thanks are due to Dr Anastasia Yiangou at the Cyprus Research Centre and to Marina Vryonidou-Yiangou and Christina Christodolou in the Marfin Laiki Bank Cultural Centre in Nicosia.

23. Churchill addresses British Army and Royal Air Force units at Carthage, Tunisia, 9 June 1943 (Imperial War Museum)
24. George VI, accompanied by a parish priest, views the ruins of Senglea, 22 June 1943 (Imperial War Museum)
25. HMS *Formidable* exercising with destroyers in the Strait of Gibraltar, December 1943 (Imperial War Museum)
26. A Spanish worker crosses the frontier into Gibraltar, 1943 (Imperial War Museum)
27. Workers in Gibraltar collect their rations from NAAFI (Imperial War Museum)
28. The Victory Parade for British Forces, Alexandria, July 1945 (Imperial War Museum)
29. Navy House gutted, Port Said, after the British assault on 6 November 1956 (Imperial War Museum)
30. Michael Karaolis emerges under guard from the Nicosia court-house, December 1955 (from Alex Ethyvoulu and Marina Vryonidou-Yiangou's *Cyprus* 100 *Years* / Marfin Laiki Bank Cultural Centre)
31. Anti-British signs in Kingsway, Valletta, 1960 (National Maritime Museum, Greenwich)

# *List of Maps*

1. Europe's southern waters

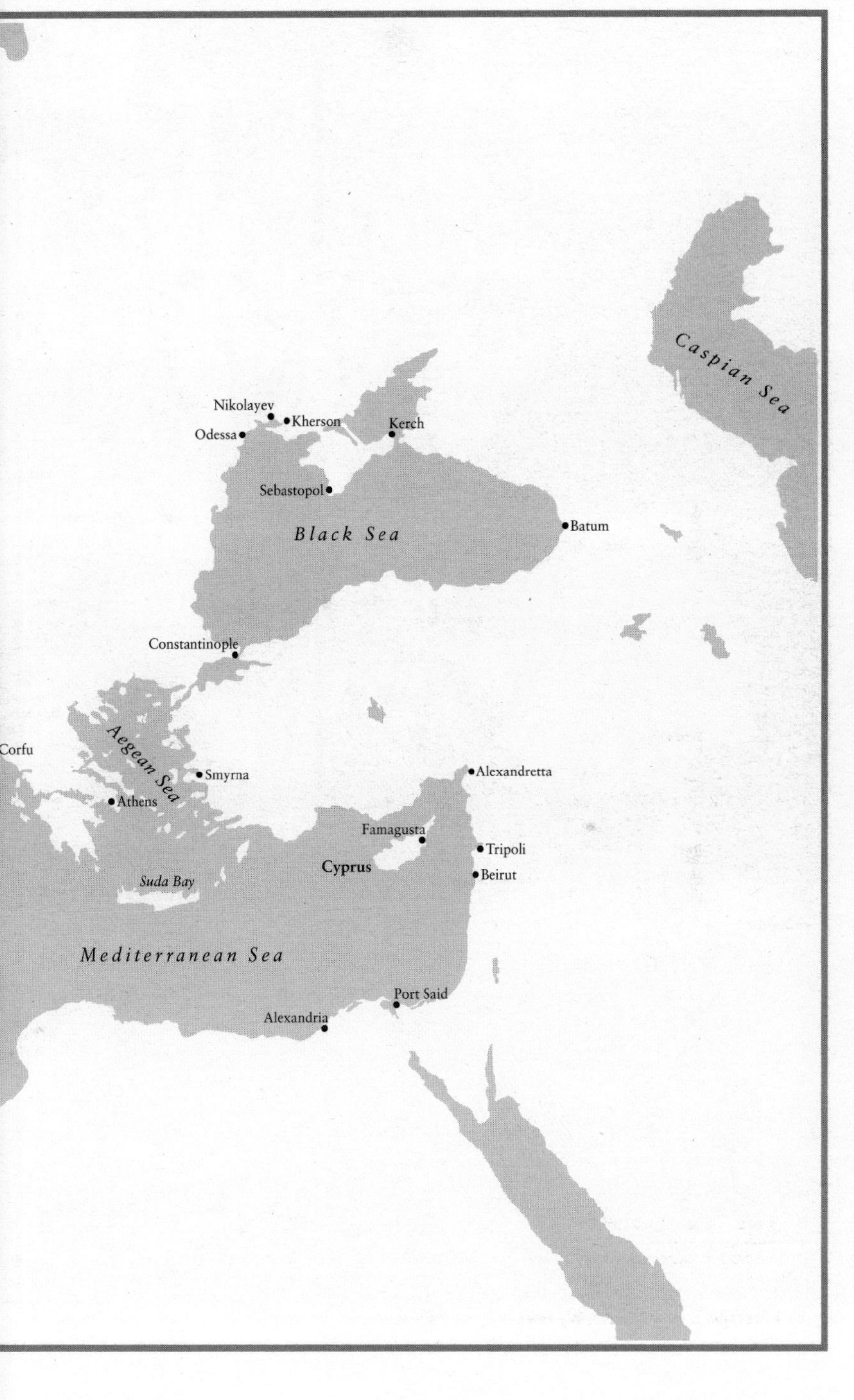
Caspian Sea
Nikolayev
Kherson
Odessa
Kerch
Sebastopol
Black Sea
Batum
Constantinople
Corfu
Aegean Sea
Smyrna
Athens
Alexandretta
Famagusta
Tripoli
Cyprus
Beirut
Suda Bay
Mediterranean Sea
Port Said
Alexandria

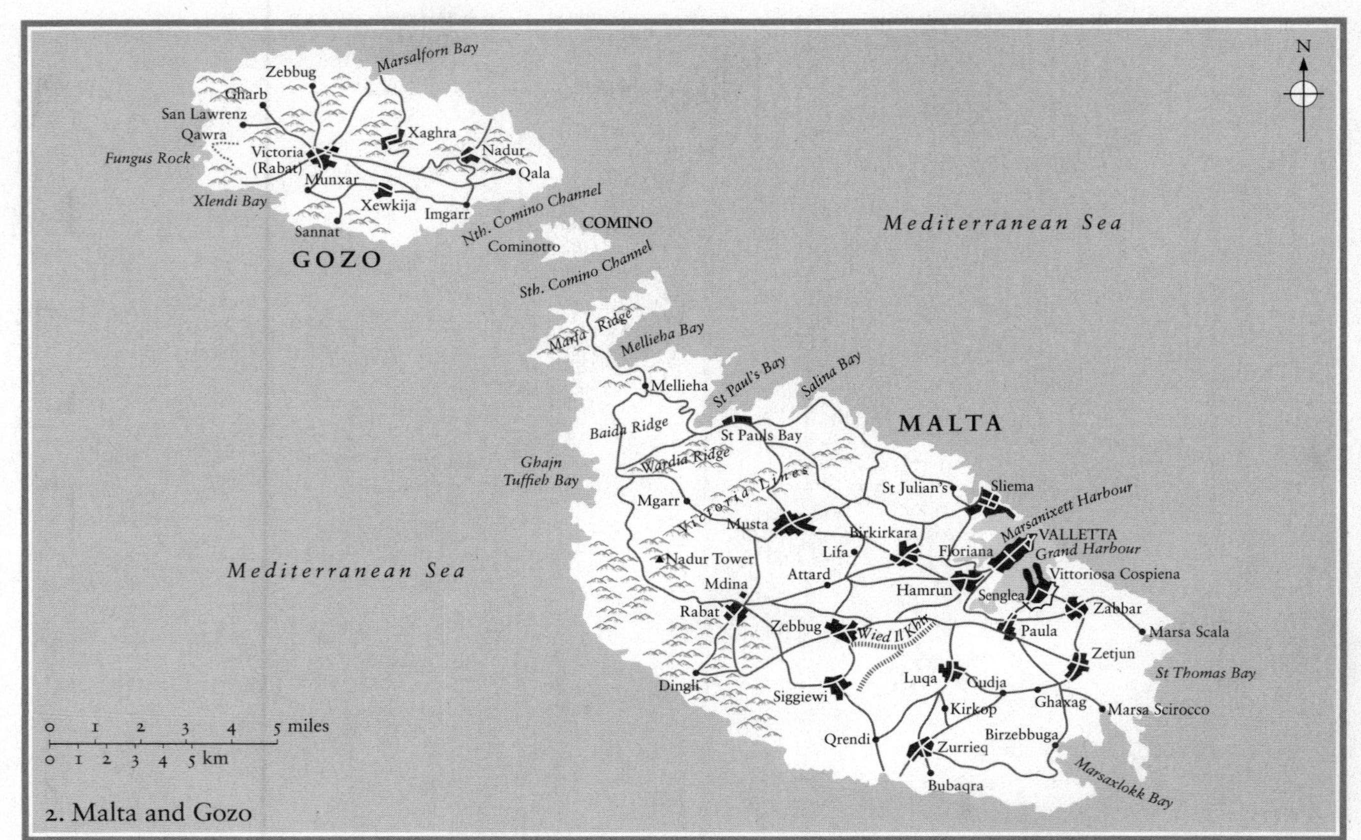

2. Malta and Gozo

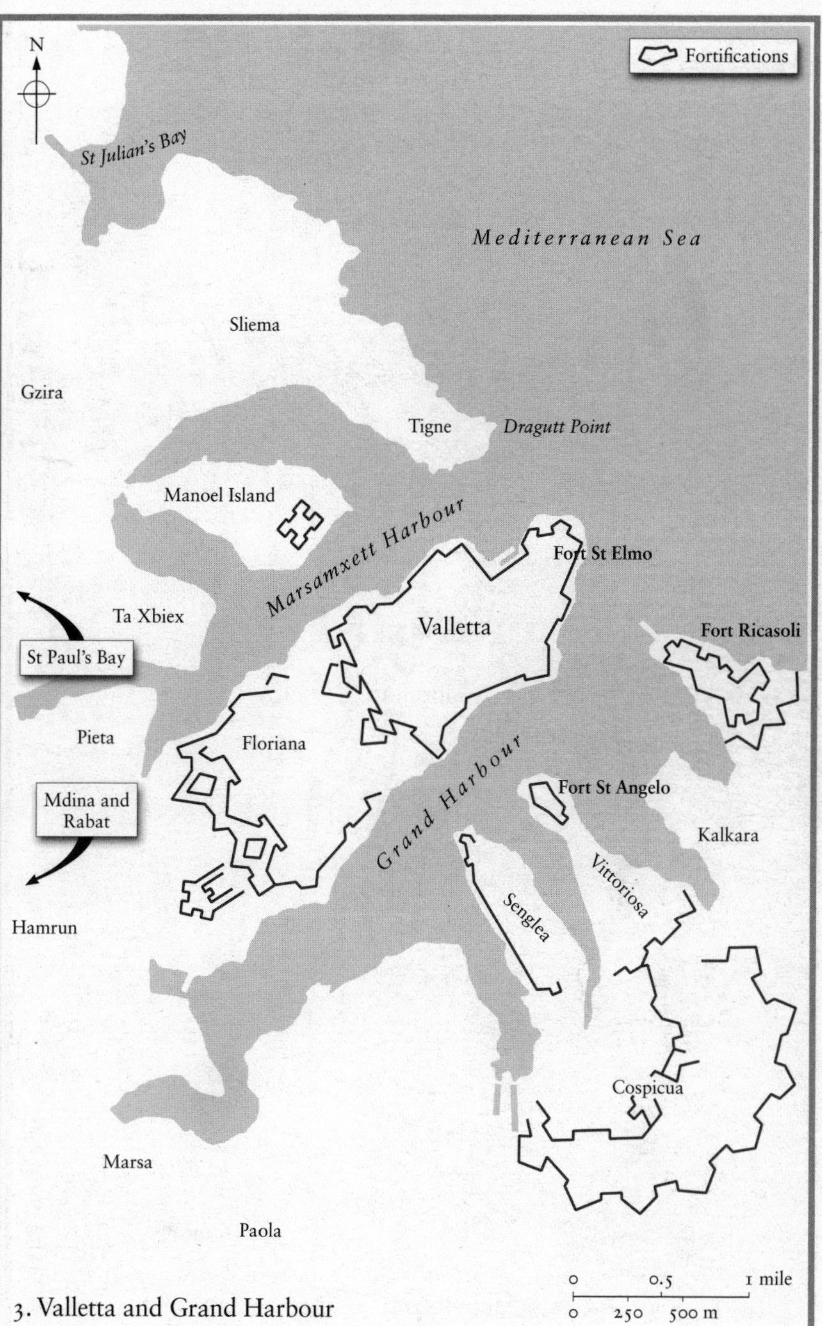


3. Valletta and Grand Harbour

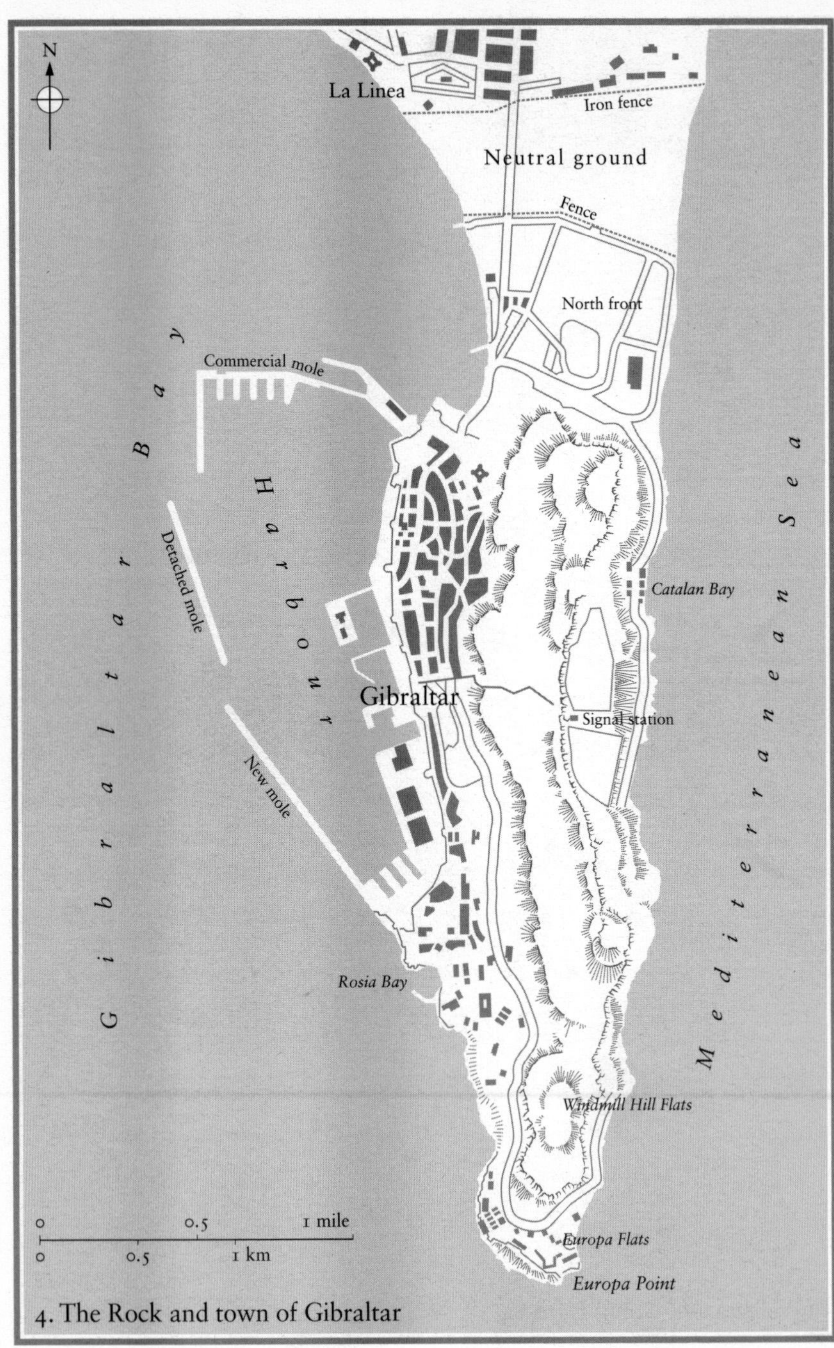

4. The Rock and town of Gibraltar

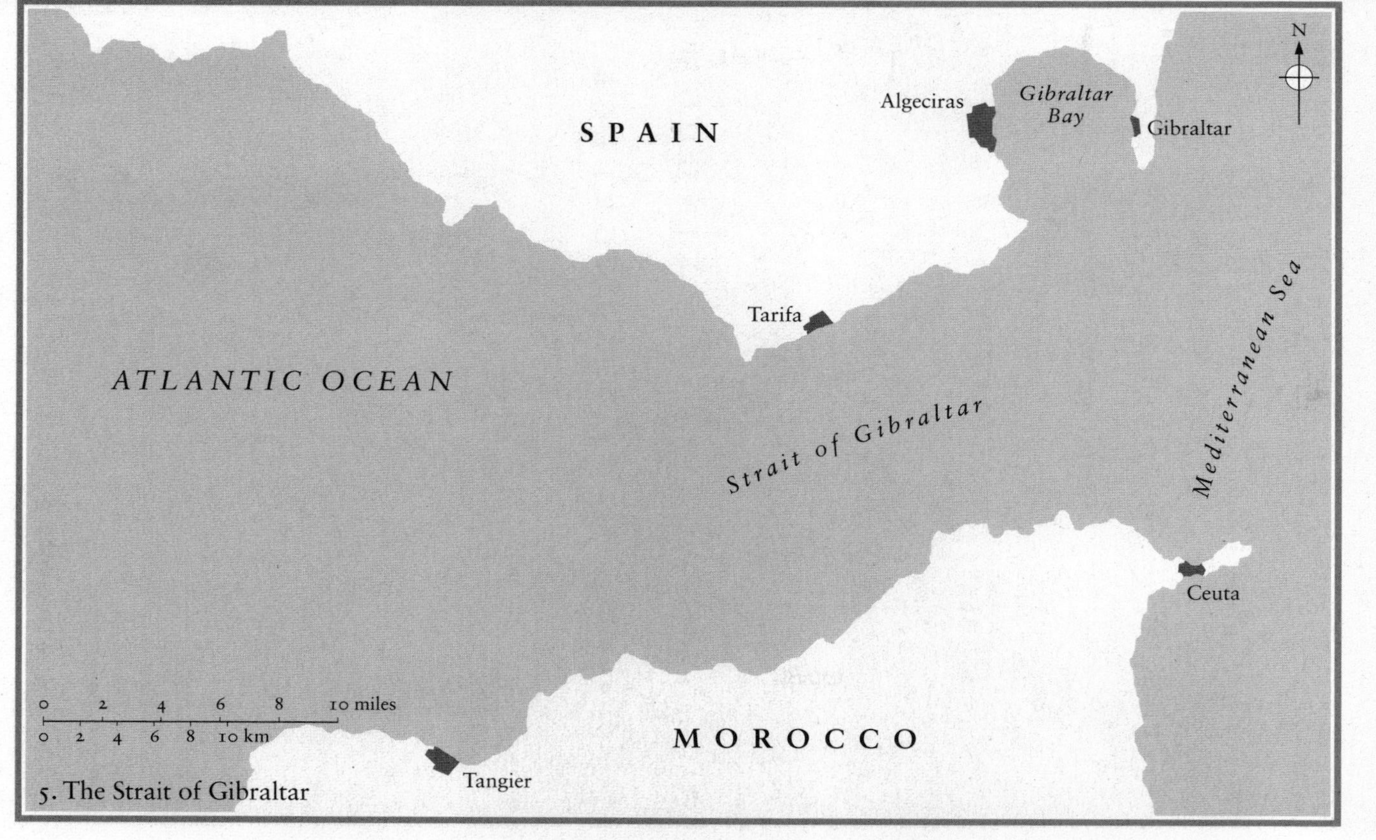


5. The Strait of Gibraltar

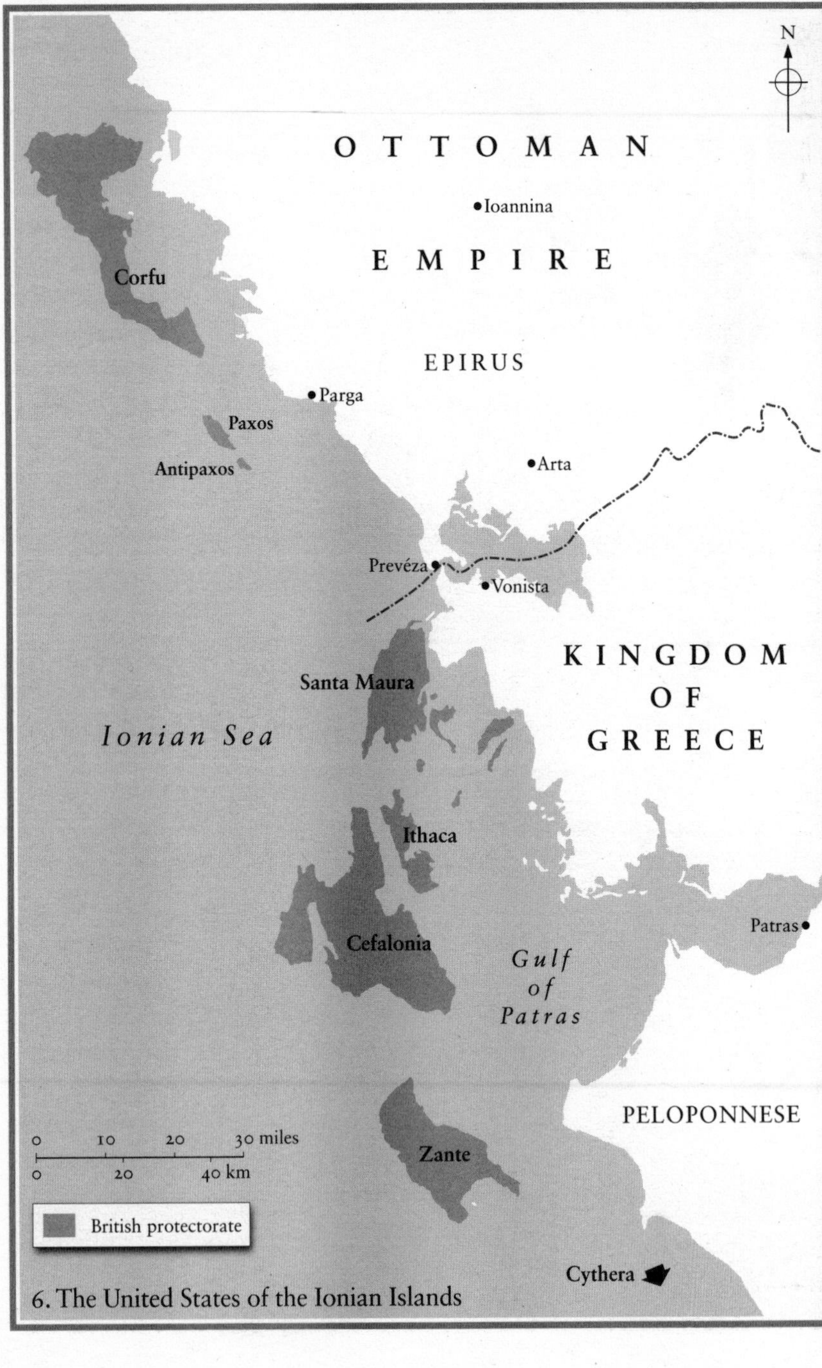


6. The United States of the Ionian Islands

N
MACEDONIA
THRACE
Black Sea
Kavalla
Salonika
Stavros
Dedeagach
Constantinople
Thasos
Samothrace
Marmara
Point Kara
Chalkidlhi Peninsula
Gulf of Orphano
Gallipoli Peninsula
Corfu
EPIRUS
Lemnos
Imbros
Mudros
Tenedos
Paxos
GREECE
Vola
Aegean Sea
TURKEY
ASIA MINOR
Santa Maura
Mytilena
Skyros
Cephalonia
Ithaca
EUBOEA
Salamis
Chalkis
Cape Geroghambo
Argostoli
Patras
Chios
Smyrna
Athens
Zante
Corinth Canal
Stena Channel
Piraeus
PELOPONNESE
Andros
Samos
Skalanova
Ionian Sea
Nikaria
Zea
Tinos
Syra
Forni
Mykonos
Denusa
Pylos
Kalamata
Leros
Sapienza
Naxos
Bodrum
Kalymnos
Milo
Cape Matapan
Cape Melea
Kos
Symi
Cythera
Cerigotto
Rhodes
Suda Bay
Skarpanto
Mediterranean Sea
Crete
0 50 100 miles
0 50 100 km
7. The Aegean

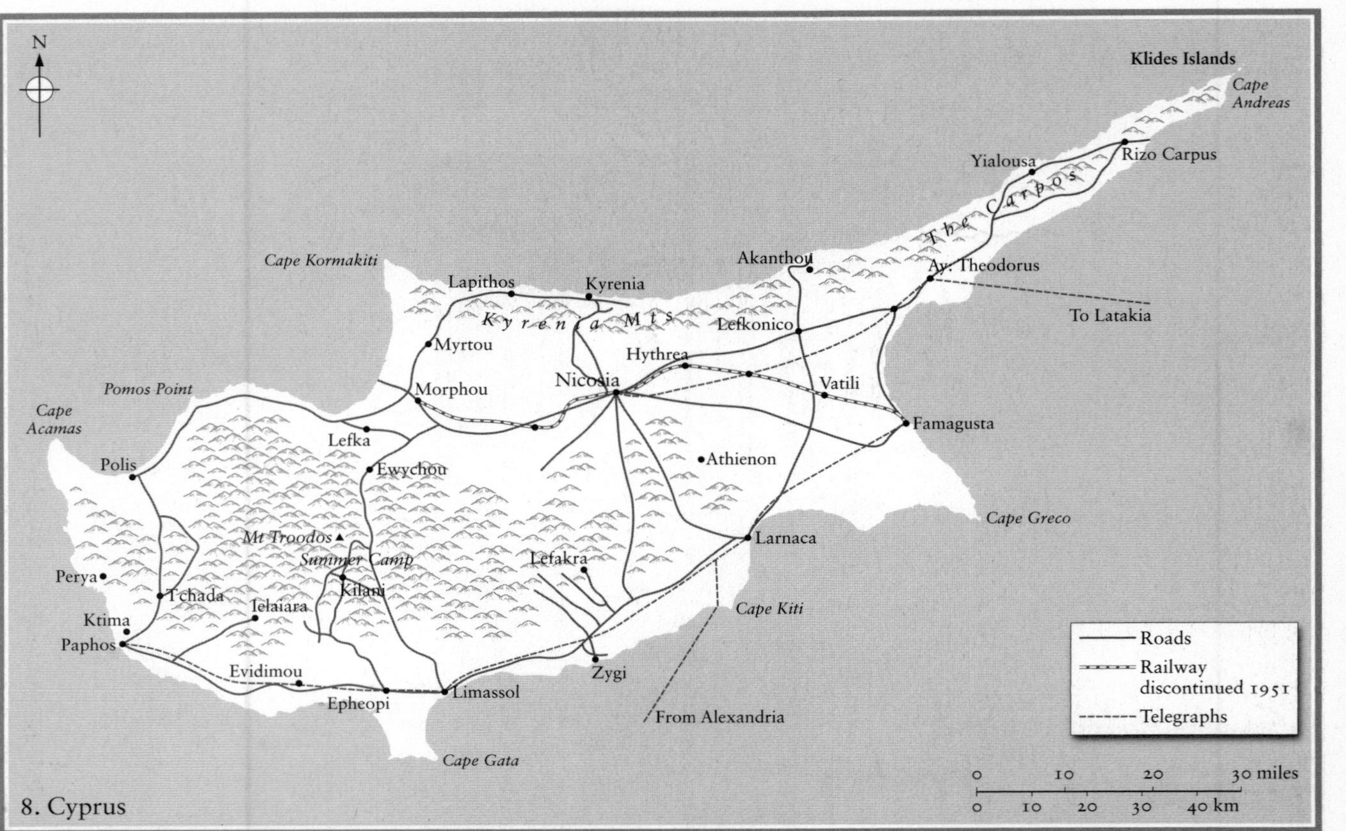
N
Klides Islands
Cape Andreas
Rizo Carpus
Yialousa
The Carpos
Ay. Theodorus
To Latakia
Akanthou
Cape Kormakiti
Lapithos
Kyrenia
Kyrenia Mts
Lefkonico
Myrtou
Hythrea
Nicosia
Vatili
Pomos Point
Morphou
Famagusta
Cape Acamas
Lefka
Polis
Ewychou
Athienon
Cape Greco
Mt Troodos
Larnaca
Summer Camp
Lefakra
Perya
Kilani
Tchada
Telaiara
Cape Kiti
Ktima
Paphos
Evidimou
Zygi
Epheopi
Limassol
From Alexandria
Cape Gata
Roads
Railway discontinued 1951
Telegraphs
0 10 20 30 miles
0 10 20 30 40 km
8. Cyprus

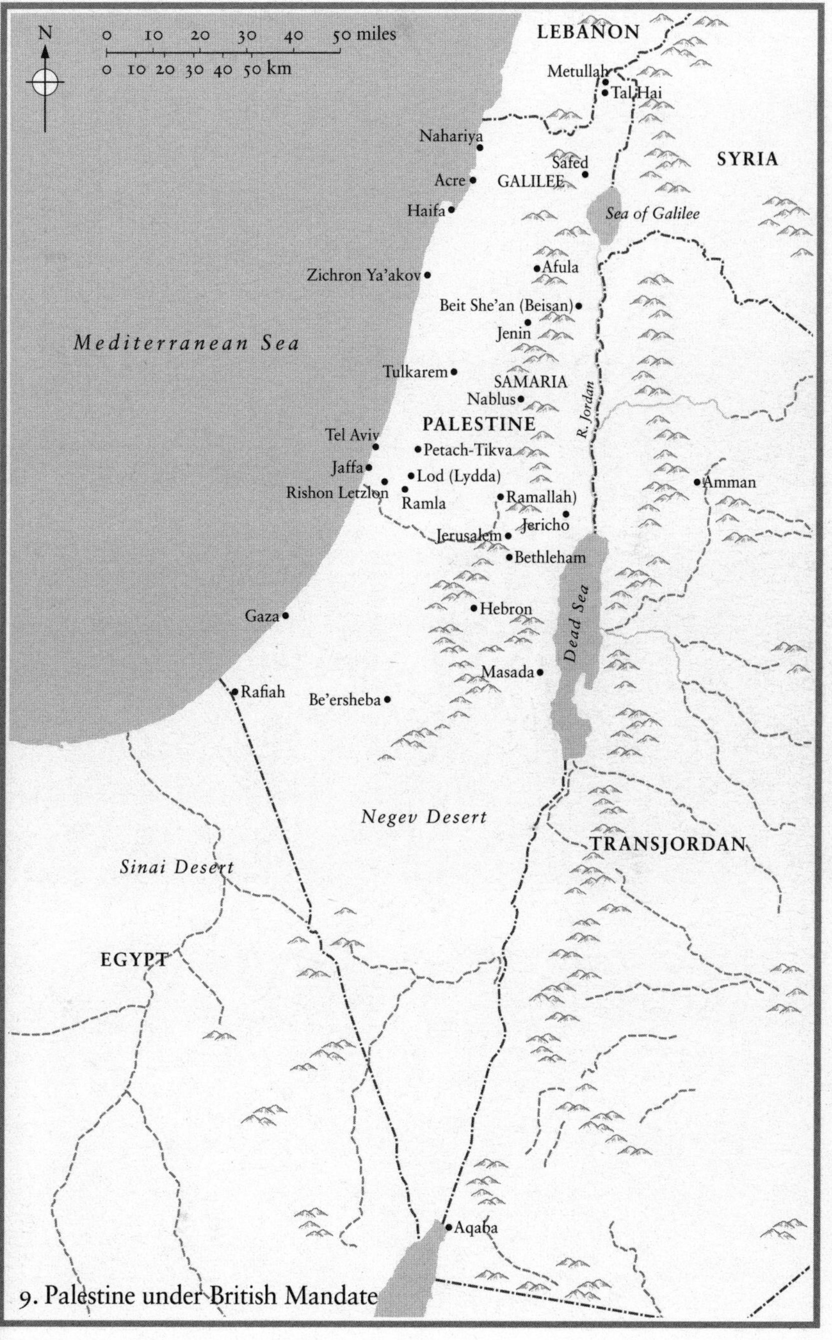

9. Palestine under British Mandate

# Blue-Water Empire

# Introduction: The British and the Mediterranean

A British diplomat, standing on a Greek steamer at the beginning of June 1864 as it passed between the channel separating the Ionian islands of Zante and Cephalonia, and coming within sight of Corfu, felt a strong surge of emotion at a vista which, he said, 'had been dear to so many of our English race' for over half a century.[1] He was going to attend the handing over of those islands by Great Britain to the Kingdom of Greece. An echo of that emotional chord can still be conjured up today by visitors to Corfu Town – architecturally a unique blend of Venetian splendour, early Victorian neoclassicism and modern Greek blight – who take the advice of the *Rough Guide* and visit the botanist's heaven of the British Cemetery, tended in 2011 by the same dedicated local caretaker for over sixty years.

The gravestones are not only of those who died on the island when Corfu was British-ruled after 1817, but go up to the present; they reveal lives – some for many years, some more transiently – bound up with that of Corfu itself. There are many such cemeteries dispersed throughout the Mediterranean, some under the auspices of the Commonwealth War Graves Commission, such as that at Suda Bay containing the memorials of 1,500 soldiers killed during the battle for Crete during May 1941, and millions of tourists will have at one time or another come across them. One of the earliest is Gibraltar's Trafalgar Cemetery, tranquil despite its proximity to bustling Main Street, originally consecrated in June 1798, two months before Admiral Horatio Nelson's triumph at the Battle of the Nile. The graveyards themselves are not static phenomena. During 2005 the bodies of thirty British sailors in the victorious fleet, one in officer's uniform, were discovered on Nelson's Island in Aboukir Bay and reburied with full honours, an Egyptian navy band and British buglers sounding the 'Last Post', at Chatby Military Cemetery in Alexandria.[2]

A historian nicely evoking the passion for British travel to the Mediterranean during the Victorian and Edwardian eras remarks how such visitors 'touched Southern life too lightly to receive its imprint or extract its essence'.[3] This must surely be true of most of those who came and went purely as tourists, however discerning, mostly for short periods, and preoccupied with galleries, museums, churches, piazzas and sometimes beaches. This book, however, is about a more penetrating and tangible subject. From the end of the eighteenth century there emerged, at first tentatively but by the 1830s and 1840s more visibly, a British presence in the Mediterranean – political, administrative, military and strategic – broadly designated by the mid-Victorian generation as the outcome of their maritime supremacy as a nation. For many Britons, indeed, their most acute awareness of the power and authority modern conditions had fortuitously conferred on their homeland came during sojourns in the Mediterranean. During 1882 one visitor to Malta wrote:

> Most Englishmen at home are so far from warlike sights, that they are apt to forget that their country has after all shown herself great in war as in commerce. But no man can forget that fact as he stands here upon the Barecca [Baracca] of Valletta and looks down upon the great forts and the ironclads which sleep securely beneath their walls.[4]

The following pages will refer frequently to the great naval base of Valletta's Grand Harbour, and by extension the Royal Navy will also loom large. My interest will not lie within the 'wooden walls' of that navy, with all the minutiae of its organization and operations, but rather in the interaction between naval power and its general environment. British supremacies were rarely what they seemed. But the British presence was vital and powerful and lasted well beyond the end of the Second World War. To local people it often seemed to have anything but a light and superficial touch. In the process the British left an imprint on the Mediterranean, and the Mediterranean certainly left an imprint on the history of Britain. This book is concerned with those effects, and the complicated and varying relationships bound up with them.

So entrenched did the British become in significant parts of the Mediterranean that their presence became something deeper: a world of its own, though like all such phenomena, one shot through with other worlds, presences and rivalries. I shall focus here on those places, mostly but not exclusively islands, that the British came to rule over, albeit under varying rubrics and circumstances. At one time or another this range of venues comprised Gibraltar, Malta, Corfu and the other Ionian islands, Cyprus, Egypt (that is, Mediterranean Egypt) and Palestine. But so pervasive was the British influence that a much longer list would be required to incorporate those societies where war, revolution or some other disruption led to intervention or some degree of control by Great Britain and her agents.

As this book begins, indeed, Minorca and Corsica were just emerging from such experiences, the first prolonged, the second brief but tempestuous. Sicily had her own 'English decade' after 1806, while as late as 1935 it could be said that 'the Cretans appeared ready to hoist the British flag'[5] (in fact the British did occupy parts of Crete for several years after 1897, and again in the Second World War). Islands that got away entirely in this process were rare and they usually did so only narrowly. Sardinia, which more than any other island excited Nelson's acquisitiveness, was rarely omitted from his Mediterranean dispatches in the early 1800s, although in the end it was never exposed to British rule.[6]

Something should be said at the outset about the Mediterranean as a category. Fernand Braudel in his great work on the history of the Mediterranean treated it as a world, not as a distinct region, since its natural features were open to so many variations and definitions, most popularly the idea of 'below and above the olive line'.[7] The same issues of definition apply in the geopolitical realm. A Maltese historian comments how 'the regionality of the Mediterranean is recognized more by external actors with alleged "vital interests" than by the indigenous states [themselves]. In itself this follows directly from the last [nineteenth] century when Mediterranean regionality was largely brought about by the British-Russian contest for hegemony.'[8] That contest for hegemony, of course, included competing powers other than Britain and Russia, most obviously France, but certainly it has been pressures bearing down from a number of external sources which have given a coherence to the Mediterranean that it otherwise lacks. This was pre-eminently true with regard to the actions of the United Kingdom, and if there has in modern times been a predominant instrument for integrating the Mediterranean as a single theatre it was the British, together with the responses and challenges, both international and within the societies themselves, that its ubiquity often precipitated. It was the British presence in the Mediterranean, and the stability it provided, which made the region what an eminent historian writing in 1904 encapsulated as the 'keyboard of Europe': if that was shaken, everything else would shake too.[9] When progressively after 1945 the international system was reshaped in the image of two superpowers, the United States and the Soviet Union, for whom the region was purely a supplementary theatre for their own mutual contests, the Mediterranean relapsed into something less than the sum of its parts. As a result, nothing has quite replaced the Anglo-Mediterranean order; and although every so often calls are made, usually by Presidents of France, for a more unified Mediterranean, they always fall flat.

Over the decades after 1800 the British brought to the forefront of the Mediterranean stage their ambition, instinct for domination, penny-pinching ways, grating superiority and many other such traits; but they also brought much-needed protection against other predators and would-be successors to regional primacy, more secure food supplies, hopes of prosperity, apprehensions of a wider world beyond constraining parochialism and accelerating social change – in sum, modernity. It is the shifting boundaries between these powerful forces that make the subject so interesting. This book is not exclusively or even principally about the place of the Mediterranean in the larger and more systemic framework of Britain's foreign policy, strategy and empire, though by its nature this has to enter into discussion. Readers with tastes for the global not the local must look elsewhere. The interest here is in something inherently subtle, indefinable and ultimately, perhaps, more absorbing: the British experience of the Mediterranean, and the Mediterranean experience of the British.

# 1
# The Origins of an Anglo-Mediterranean Order, 1800–1814

On 27 August 1800 the French warships *Diana* and *La Justice* (both survivors of Nelson's smashing victory at the Battle of the Nile two years earlier) made a sudden dash out of the spacious harbour of Valletta, Malta's baroque capital. The island's light summer airs had given way to a strong breeze, providing a sudden opportunity to escape from a close two-year British blockade of the French-held island. It was an attempt the blockaders had been waiting for. *La Justice* made it to the open sea and back to France; *Diana* was raked with shot, dismasted and escorted by HMS *Superb* to the harbour mouth, where the British squadron was concentrated. From dispatches found aboard the *Diana* it was confirmed that the prolonged resistance of the French garrison was about to crack.

On 5 September General Charles Henri Vaubois and Admiral Pierre Charles de Villeneuve (later Nelson's adversary at Trafalgar) capitulated.[1] Immediately redcoats occupied the forts held tenaciously by the French ever since a Maltese rebellion had broken out on receipt of the news of the destruction of Napoleon's fleet in Egyptian waters. The Royal Navy now took over Valletta's grand anchorage. Valletta became its greatest overseas base and it was not to leave for 178 years. Captain Alexander Ball, who had been sent ashore by Nelson in October 1798 to liaise with Maltese forces, made a formal entry into the city, retracing the steps along the elegant Strada Reale where Napoleon himself had briefly resided en route to his Egyptian adventure. A *Te Deum* was sung amid the magnificence of St John's Church, and the gates of Valletta swung open to admit the general population, though, as Vaubois had insisted, no armed persons were allowed among them.[2] On 8 September the French garrison, its semi-starvation eased by British military rations, was evacuated. It did so with honour, drums beating, colours flying, accompanied to the rear by two-pound cannon with matches alight.

Yet wherever the British occupied Mediterranean territory, a degree of misunderstanding invariably prevailed. Malta's inhabitants, who under Ball's command had been besieging the French from the landward side, welcomed the British occupying force and wanted it to stay. A British presence offered protection, and guarantees of food when war had brought acute deprivation. The last thing desired was any return of the feudal Knights of St John who, before Napoleon's abrupt intrusion, had lorded it over the island for hundreds of years. Yet at the same time the Maltese believed that their own fighters had played the main role in defeating the French, and that the British (without losing a single soldier in the siege) had simply delivered the *coup de grâce*. This belief – according to which Malta became British by a 'deed of gift' on the part of the inhabitants and not by conquest – ultimately came to form the bedrock of an evolving Maltese political consciousness.

The British held to their own version of events. More than 100 sailors had died in blockading duties. Inspection showed that the artillery of the Maltese irregular militia had done very little damage to the fortifications of Valletta. The British therefore contended that the French garrison had in the end only been reduced by an acute shortage of supplies, that is by the blockade, as Vaubois himself confessed.[3] The laurels of victory therefore lay, it was argued, with the British Navy, and Malta's liberation from French arms (and French looting) became a mere coda to Nelson's successes.[4] The British Commander-in-Chief, General Henry Pigot, saw to it that the Union Jack was raised over the fortress and harbour, paying no heed to other claimants – especially Sicilian and Russian – to lordship over the island. The Anglo-Maltese relationship, while in many ways unusually intimate in colonial terms, was also to be incorrigibly quarrelsome, and such differences of interpretation went back to these earliest moments of British occupation.

In fact, an incipient British Empire in the Mediterranean was far from taking shape in September 1800. Contemporaries would have regarded any such idea as highly improbable. For much of the eighteenth century the British had possessed a weak and fluctuating influence there; 'experimental . . . almost fumbling', according to one historian.[5] Great Britain had acquired two vantage points in the western Mediterranean under the Treaty of Utrecht in 1714: Minorca and Gibraltar. Minorca, however, was repeatedly lost in wartime, having to be reconquered on four separate occasions (it was eventually ceded to Spain in 1802, though British warships continued to winter there for the rest of the war against France). Admiral Rooke's capture of Gibraltar in 1704 and the exploits of its garrison in successfully resisting the Spaniards during the Great Siege of 1782–4 both entered British folklore, but throughout the eighteenth century doubts persisted as to the colony's true worth. George III was all for giving it away to Madrid as an unnecessary irritant.[6] British trade in the Mediterranean, too, was anything but vibrant, and was dwindling as the 1790s opened. The Levant Company (holding by royal authority a monopoly in British commerce over much of the area) required a state subsidy to keep going, and the British consulate in Alexandria was actually closed down for want of activity.[7]

This partly explains why on the outbreak of war with revolutionary France during February 1793, Royal Navy warships in the Mediterranean were depleted and dispersed. The key concern in the Mediterranean was to bottle up the French fleet in Toulon. In that great port a major opportunity soon presented itself following a French royalist revolt, and British troops were put ashore to take control, especially of the dockyard. Surrounded by high ground, and with a partly hostile population, Toulon was difficult to hold. It became impossible when a French republican militia arrived with a young officer, Napoleon Bonaparte, in its ranks. It was in Toulon that Napoleon and Nelson came physically closest in careers that for the next few years were tempestuously entwined. A hasty exit by British forces and thousands of destitute royalist refugees followed in mid-December 1793. The British Commander-in-Chief in the Mediterranean, Admiral Samuel Hood, fell back on Corsica as an alternative base. There the fortresses of Bastia and Calvi were successively besieged and conquered. It was when assaulting the latter on 12 July 1794 that Nelson lost the sight of one eye – an engraved French inscription on a rock still marks the spot.[8] For a short but rumbustious interval Corsica, indeed, became more than simply a base, since what was designated the 'Anglo-Corsican Kingdom' had a British Viceroy in the form of Sir Gilbert Elliot. This curious polity was a further premonition – already foreshadowed in Minorca and Gibraltar – of an Anglo-Mediterranean order in the making.[9]

Elliot's viceregal authority, however, was highly precarious. He had to cope with fierce rivalries between British sailors and soldiers – Nelson was at loggerheads there with Colonel Sir John Moore, also destined to be a fallen hero at the Battle of Corunna in January 1809 – and between warring Corsican factions. Nor were ministers in London especially bothered about Corsica's fate; one admitted that news from the island felt like that from the moon.[10] This chaos was ended by the arrival of a French expeditionary force from Leghorn on 19 October 1796. As the French progressed inland many of the local inhabitants who had rallied to the British flag now deserted it. Nelson personally supervised an unavoidable evacuation, being, he assured his wife, 'absolutely the last man who quitted'.[11] With the balance of power shifting, and Spain now allied with France, the government of William Pitt felt under so much pressure that they had to pull British warships out of the Mediterranean altogether during October 1796. The West Indies suddenly seemed to promise easier and safer acquisitions. The little Italian island of Elba briefly remained under British occupation, but once that feeble toehold was given up, only the guard-post of Gibraltar remained. This was very far, therefore, from an era of British mastery in the Mediterranean.

The decision to send a British squadron back into the Mediterranean under Nelson's command in May 1798 did not necessarily presage fundamental change. The intention was not to counter the preparations at Toulon for Napoleon's looming eastern campaign, culminating in his invasion of Egypt two months later. Ministers in London knew nothing for some while about this visionary expedition. The object of re-entry into the Mediterranean was to meet the urgent plea of Britain's ally Austria to protect the Neapolitan Kingdom (the 'Two Sicilies'), and so counter the rapidly spreading French domination of Italy. Critics were poised to pour scorn on the rather frenzied movements of Nelson's ships – his 'unfortunate cruise', as one put it.[12] As it happened, Nelson proved extraordinarily fortunate. After chasing the French fleet back and forth around Sardinia and Sicily, to his intense relief Nelson found his prey at anchor in Aboukir Bay off Alexandria. His ships then destroyed the French formation in one brutal assault on 1 August 1798. The shocking violence of the explosion that tore apart the French flagship, *L'Orient*, provided a talking point all over Europe, and was graphically portrayed in innumerable journals.[13] 'Victory is not a name strong enough for such a scene,' Nelson remarked on the immediate aftermath; seven years later his own coffin was to be made from the shattered mast of *L'Orient*. When news of the triumph reached Gibraltar, the Governor ordered a twenty-one-gun salute, though he first politely forewarned the Spanish authorities (as we shall see, there was always a tradition of Anglo-Hispanic manners surrounding the Rock). Once the information was hurried to London, theatres in celebration added 'Rule, Britannia' to their nightly performances.

The Battle of Aboukir Bay heralded a critically important strategic shift, restoring Britain's leading role in the Mediterranean for the rest of the war against France.[14] Yet in the short term its effects wore off all too rapidly. Napoleon himself was trapped in Egypt but he and his army had not been evicted; its eastern advance was only stemmed by the Anglo-Turkish defence of Acre in Syria in mid-1799. Nelson himself had gone straight to Naples, where amid all the hubris he became fatally entangled in the affairs of the Neapolitan Court. In particular, he renewed a previously passing acquaintance with the British Minister, Sir William Hamilton, his much younger wife, Emma, and with Emma's patron, Maria Caroline, Queen of the Two Sicilies (that is, Naples and Sicily combined). An outraged and vengeful royalism in a ruptured Mediterranean society was to mark ensuing events. It was with Nelson's encouragement that the Neapolitan army was dispatched to bar the French republican advance at Rome, only to meet headlong defeat. The Bourbon court, with Emma in its entourage, was forced to retreat with a now infatuated Nelson and his fleet to Sicily. One of the Queen's young sons died in Emma's arms on the troubled voyage.

At this point the British military presence in the region was still thinly scattered between Gibraltar, Sicily and Malta; nor could localized naval superiority easily match French predominance on land, above all in Italy, where Napoleon, now back in Europe and having seized dictatorial power, went on to win a smashing victory at Marengo on 14 June 1800. When the Royal Navy took Valletta's Grand Harbour, therefore, it was in some degree a compensation for difficulties and defeats elsewhere. Overall, the British presence in the Mediterranean remained wavering and by no means set to be permanent.

Much of the naval contest in the Mediterranean, as in the West Indies, revolved less around the permanent seizure of bases or colonies than around the acquisition of prizes to be traded for a profit at some future peace conference. This was not so much the shock of the new, or the lineaments of a newly possessive colonialism, but good old-fashioned eighteenth-century warfare and territorial diplomacy. Still, the question took shape within Pitt's wartime government as to whether the British aim in the Mediterranean was simply to restore the *status quo ante bellum*, as Pitt himself preferred, or whether a more lasting commitment was being hammered into place. The British seizure of Malta did not resolve this matter. In raising the British flag on the island, General Pigot made no explicit claim to British sovereignty. He was punctilious in confirming the Maltese, and not least the Roman Catholic Church, in all their ancient privileges, while outside Valletta itself the Sicilian flag flew on the island, since King Ferdinand of Naples had provided the Maltese rising with arms and money. Nor was the military value of Malta quite apparent. For Napoleon it had just been a convenient stop on the way to Alexandria, with the added bonus of booty. Its smallness meant there was no strategic depth by which an occupying force could find security, as the French forces Napoleon left there found out. Nelson considered Malta 'a useless and enormous expense',[15] and his successor as Commander-in-Chief of the Mediterranean Fleet, Admiral Lord Collingwood, shared the prejudice, calling Malta on one occasion 'the most gossiping, gourmandizing place I ever heard of'.[16] More important for Pitt was the belief that hanging on to Malta was not worth the price of undermining peace negotiations to end an exhausting war. Under Article 10 of the Treaty of Amiens (25 March 1802) the British Government agreed to withdraw from the island and to its retrocession to the Knights – almost the last thing wanted by the Maltese themselves, whose deputation to London protested at the injustice done to them.[17]

The fierce reaction to the decision in influential British circles, however, indicated that the parameters of Mediterranean policy were moving. This reaction was political as much as naval, despite the advantages as a centre for refitting and repair that Malta offered to warships. When Nelson himself spoke in the Lords, he gave no indication that he wanted to keep Malta or Minorca.[18] Practising politicians, mostly Tories, however, attacked the giving up of Malta as 'disgraceful, humiliating and pregnant with danger'.[19] This sentiment offered a convenient rallying point for all those opposed to the Peace of Amiens. Throughout the uneasy period of peace following the treaty, the British in fact kept the strength of the Mediterranean Fleet at a high level and dragged their feet over leaving Malta. When Napoleon sought to pin responsibility for the renewal of conflict on the British, he put their refusal to leave Malta in the forefront, stating – according to one of London's negotiators in Paris – that 'he [Napoleon] would rather see us in possession of the Faubourg St. Antoine' than remaining on the island.[20] Yet Bonaparte's motives were as supple as those of the proponents of a 'British' Malta, since he saw advantage in luring Britain into peripheral and burdensome Mediterranean commitments liable to weaken their resistance to the cross-Channel invasion taking shape in his mind. Once war was renewed with even more devastating violence, the Opposition leader in Westminster, Charles James Fox, lamented that the fresh conflict was seemingly for 'plain bare, wretched Malta', unconnected, as he saw it, with any real British interest. The allegation drew this retort from a Government defender: 'We are at war for Malta, but not for Malta only, but for Egypt, and not for Egypt only, but for India, but not for India only, for the integrity of the British Empire.'[21]

This kind of high strategic determinism, blurring places and military logic, underlines a persistent difficulty in explaining Great Britain's role in the Mediterranean. Partisanship invariably generated a fuzzy imperial rhetoric, masking more practical aims. Mention of India became a habitual sign of this tendency, as some contemporaries noted.[22] In reality Egypt came to matter to the British, in a mirror-image of Napoleon's own fascination, not as a stepping stone to India but as a useful element in the struggle to gain leverage over the future of the Ottoman Empire. Before the Treaty of Amiens the French army had been finally prised from Egypt, when a British expedition was landed under General Sir Ralph Abercromby close to Aboukir Bay in

March 1801. Abercromby himself was soon killed – his body taken for burial to Fort St Elmo on Malta – but in early September a force of Grenadiers and Guards had occupied Alexandria. Many British agents in the Levant viewed this enthusiastically as the harbinger of a permanent presence. But it was nothing of the kind. Having got the French out, British officers scarcely had time to play tourist at the Pyramids before they had been evacuated themselves, with some 7,000 troops going to Malta.[23] Only a static garrison was left, and even that was withdrawn at the peace of 1802.

Napoleon's adventure in Egypt, in fact, had left a deeper and more lasting mark on Egyptian affairs than Abercromby's men,[24] and after the renewal of war the British never stopped worrying that the French would make another attempt with a view to reviving France's wider influence on the Ottoman Empire. This explains Nelson's growing concern with eastern Mediterranean waters once he went back as Commander-in-Chief to supervise the new hostilities.[25] When French influence over Turkey showed signs of revival, a British army, 6,000-strong, under General Henry Fox was dispatched again to Egypt in mid-1806, this time with explicit instructions to occupy Alexandria directly. This was successfully accomplished. Food was in short supply in the city, however, and the decision was taken to extend the occupation to Rosetta. The detachment entering that town found themselves engaged in desperate street fighting with local militia, and it was virtually annihilated in retreating.[26] Alexandria was retained for a while, but in 1807 the remaining troops were withdrawn. British experience in Egypt would always be mixed. The occupations of 1801–2 and 1806–7 not only kept the French out, they underpinned the foundation of a continuing British stake, including a commercial interest. A full-time British consulate was re-established at Alexandria in 1810, and when in 1816 the post was upgraded to a consul-generalship the expanded remit of the job was to keep in close touch with His Majesty's Minister at Naples, the British Resident at Corfu, the Governor of Malta and the Commander-in-Chief of the Mediterranean Fleet. In fits and starts Egypt had come to be viewed by the British as an integral part of politics and strategy in the Mediterranean.[27]

Part of the significance of Egypt during the war after 1803 lay in control over its corn exports. This was only one aspect of a tightening of British control over Mediterranean trade. During the eighteenth century English products had been eclipsed by superior French competition in both Mediterranean and Levantine markets. But revolution and war after 1789 badly affected French manufacturing and gave Britain a new opening. After 1798 the British gradually imposed a quasi-monopoly of their own, assisted by the subordination of those secondary powers and city-states hitherto so prominent in Mediterranean affairs. As more and more enemy ships of all kinds were taken to Malta as prizes, so their crews, along with their skills and experience, became entangled with British military and commercial operations rather than those of Venice, Ragusa or Genoa.[28]

Here was the cosmopolitanism, flexibility and absorptive capacity behind an incipient British Mediterranean phenomenon. Nelson's smashing of the main French battle fleet at Trafalgar on 21 October 1805, by clearing the sea for British commerce, gave an enormous boost to this process. There was, nevertheless, a vital distinction between the operation of land and sea power. Trafalgar conquered water but not territory and wealth, in contrast to Napoleon's virtually simultaneous triumphs in central Europe at Ulm and Austerlitz.[29] The latter provided Napoleon with the inspiration for an attempt to strangle Britain's commerce with Europe (the 'Continental System') begun by the Berlin Decree of November 1806. Yet water held its own key to commercial sway, and ironically the French Emperor's continentalized vision served only to bring an unparalleled boom to Mediterranean ports and hinterlands under British oversight. Nor was this reversed when he imposed peace terms on Russia at his meeting with Tsar Alexander I at Tilsit on 7 July 1807. This represented the height of Napoleon's diplomatic power, and he subsequently failed to exert a similar grip over the Ottoman Porte. From then onwards it was largely as a vent into Turkey and back into Europe through many circuitous but profitable channels that a new Mediterranean emporium for British industrial output took shape.

Meanwhile retaliatory British Orders-in-Council forbidding all trade with the enemy were made ruthlessly effective by Royal Navy captains. Paying for, and distributing, the supplies required by the 30,000 British troops now deployed in the Mediterranean theatre compounded this effectiveness. British merchant houses in Alexandria funnelled vital

Egyptian wheat for the garrisons on various islands, including Sicily after the latter's occupation during February 1806. The biggest supply system, however, was that required by another British army (eventually more than 40,000 strong) in the Iberian peninsula assisting the Spanish revolt against French invasion from mid-1808 onwards. By 1812 Egyptian warehouses were said to be 'stuffed with British goods' in payment for local produce, reflecting a trade that helped fuel Britain's own industrial transformation.[30] Paradoxically, the rise to power in Egyptian politics of the Albanian warlord Mehmet Ali, later to become such a *bête noire* of English policy in the Levant, was greased by the profits generated from this commerce.

Malta, helped by having the best lazaretto, or place of quarantine, in the Mediterranean, offered the most striking example of a bubble of war-driven commercialism under British auspices. Respectable English merchants flocked to Valletta to establish branches, encouraged by administrative and legal stability (including an Admiralty Prize Court) presided over by Sir Alexander Ball, who had returned to the island knighted as Civil Commissioner in 1803. In 1808, 12.2 per cent of all British exports went to the island, most for onward transmission. What this meant in terms of employment and cash circulation in a desperately poor and overpopulated island can easily be imagined. 'In the poorest home of the most distant *casal* [village],' wrote Samuel Taylor Coleridge, the poet, who in an opium-filled interlude served as Public Secretary in the administration of Malta, 'two rude paintings were sure to be found: a picture of the Virgin and Child and a portrait of Sir Alexander Ball.'[31] Here Coleridge's Tory Romanticism, suggestively developed under Mediterranean conditions, assumed an exaggerated conceit featuring in his regular journal *The Friend*.

But when Ball died in harness at San Anton Palace on 25 October 1809 the public mourning touched some kind of popular chord, despite criticisms – for example, of corrupt appointments – occasionally levelled at him by some on the island.[32] Open subscription paid for his imposing neoclassical memorial in the Lower Barracca Gardens overlooking the spectacular harbour. Though by the time of his death the British presence in Malta was not absolutely secured, it was well on the way to being so.[33] Ball had executed an essential aim of British policy, which was to give the Maltese themselves a vested interest in the new regime.[34] His memory, however, could not escape being absorbed into the incurable disputatiousness of Anglo-Maltese relations, so that his record was still sufficiently contested to be the subject of lively letters to the *Times of Malta* on the bicentenary of his death in October 2009.[35]

The wartime prosperity easing Ball's administration in Malta, however, had an underside from the start. Local traders felt threatened by newcomers attracted to such a honeypot. Besides the English, these included an influx of allegedly 'bad characters', including rowdy Sicilians, Albanians, Genoese, and Jews from Gibraltar. Local reactions to Greeks were most hostile, because the interaction between Roman Catholicism (so dominant in Malta) and those practising Eastern Orthodoxy was sometimes fraught. In 1805 the first 'popular' demonstrations by a Maltese crowd hinged on protests against undesirable immigrants. Simultaneously, inflation eroded the salaries of public officials, who became conscious of the growing number and higher remuneration of their British counterparts. Ball clashed with his superiors in London on the use of Malta as 'a nest for home patronage', though this was not easily stemmed.[36] Although the old nobility had hoped that they would come into their own after both the Knights and the French had been got rid of, they found that they began to lose their footing in this brave, brash and materialistic world. Other English-occupied territories in the area shared similar discontents. In Gibraltar, for example, British military control grew tighter. In the early 1800s armed sentries began to be posted beyond the Rock proper, in what became British Neutral Ground on the isthmus. The Spanish were not in a position to resist this encroachment. Tensions also existed within the garrison and town. There was a mutiny among some of the troops in 1802 against the harshness of the Duke of Kent as Governor, while the latter was at odds with merchants over a crackdown on the taverns that had long brought big profits to local bar-keepers and suppliers.[37] In short, an incipient British Mediterranean world sometimes brought external protection and material betterment, but also nagging uncertainty about unsettling change and a considerable chafing with established customs.

Meanwhile the meeting between the French and Russian emperors at Tilsit had strategic as well as economic effects. It gave a fillip to the last spasm of Napoleon's eastern ambitions, and included in its effects the further integration of the Mediterranean as a theatre. It was in blocking this movement, too, that the British got pulled further into the Mediterranean mainstream. Napoleon's prime aim was to force Russian complicity in his dream of reducing the Ottoman Empire to satellite status. Behind this lay a profound geopolitical shift first unleashed from the 1770s when Empress Catherine II oversaw a drive to extend the southern borderlands of Moscow's power. The Black Sea was brought back into a pan-European commercial network from which it had been partly cut off since the demise of the Italian trading colonies in the fifteenth century.[38] By the turn of the nineteenth century that sea was no longer, as a Sultan had once expressed it, 'a virgin shut up in a harem',[39] but was now open to other contenders. British fear that Napoleon would succeed in subordinating Sultan Selim III to his will and so gain entry to Constantinople led to the dispatch of a fleet under Admiral Sir John Duckworth in February 1807. Here, too, was a test of the technical capacity of the Royal Navy. The British fleet could sink rival fleets when they were tempted into battle at sea, as they had at Trafalgar. But could it reverse Nelson's old dictum that anybody who thought wooden ships could triumph over stone forts was a fool? This was a question that was to come up again and again under Mediterranean conditions.

In this case, Admiral Duckworth's squadron of eight warships successfully navigated a passage through the Dardanelles on 19 February and moored off Constantinople, which they threatened to bombard unless the Turkish fleet surrendered. Ten days later, however, no reply had come. Meanwhile Napoleon's special envoy in the Levant, François Sebastiani, was directing the Turks to bring their armaments to bear along the line of retreat. Duckworth decided to pass quickly back through the Straits while he could, losing one of his ships on the way.[40] The whole expedition had been miscalculated. After this failure, diplomacy had necessarily to fill the breach, and a political mission was sent instead to the Ottoman court. After laborious negotiations Britain's chief negotiator, the young Stratford Canning, brokered a Russo-Turkish Treaty, signed at Bucharest (1810), barring further French progress. Arguably, this would be the finest achievement of a diplomat who was to figure prominently in Mediterranean affairs for decades.

In its wake the newly installed Sultan Mahmud II became, according to a French diplomat, 'plus Anglaise ques les Anglais mêmes'.[41] All this meant was that he understood how British sea power might intrude less damagingly on the Ottoman world than rival land powers, and if skilfully managed might even provide a protective screen for Turkey itself. In this lay the genesis of the Eastern Question and Britain's part in it. Furthermore, the embassy at Constantinople, which had long been of largely commercial significance, emerged as the critical vantage point, 'the sentinel upon the bridge',[42] for British interests across much of the Mediterranean.

The Franco-Russian deal at Tilsit had yet another consequence. It brought the Greek provinces of the Ottoman Empire within the active margins of European conflict. This was initially achieved through the swift eviction by more than 13,000 French troops of the Russian forces which had taken Corfu and the other Ionian islands opposite Albania and the Peloponnese in 1799. The Russians had then set up a Septinsular Republic under effective Russian protection, drawing on fellow Orthodox feeling. After Napoleon had taken possession, Corfu displaced all other Mediterranean islands in his vision as offering 'the key to the Adriatic', and a potential route back into the Ottoman world.[43] Stretched in manpower and other resources, the British Government strove to obstruct this advance as cheaply as possible. It appointed a Consul in the Morea, leading to the first calls for a British 'protectorate' among local Christians eager for possible means of escape from Turkish rule. Political feelers and weapons were sent to Ali Pasha of Ioannina, already portrayed by some as a model of the wily Oriental despot, but trumpeted in British circles as offering 'the keystone of Greece'.[44] The easiest way of gaining a Greek stake, however, was by acquisitions in the adjoining Ionian archipelago, offering 'an observatory on the whole of European Turkey'.[45] In October 1809 a force of 1,700 troops was sent to capture the southern Ionian island of Zante. Britain's modern engagement with Hellenic affairs started here.

With the bulk of French troops concentrated further north in Corfu, the small garrison on Zante surrendered almost as soon as British warships appeared. The islands of Cephalonia, Ithaca and Cerigo followed in their wake. General John Oswald, commanding this operation, made clear that these occupations were expected to be purely temporary.

Conscious of the growing cult of Ionian nationalism,[46] with its strong Greek identification, Oswald discreetly raised, not the British flag, but that of the Septinsular Republic, hoping to ensure a warmer welcome. As in Malta, the seeds of confusion underlying British occupation were immediately present. Nonetheless, Britain's stake remained limited so long as the prize of Corfu remained beyond its grasp. The French Imperial Commissioner, Matthieu de Lesseps (father of the future constructor of the Suez Canal) set about improving Corfu's fortifications, while Napoleon's instruction was to defend the island to the last. The British never seriously contemplated any assault on such a heavily fortified location (so determined, indeed, was the French garrison to resist that when peace came a special delegation had to be sent from the new regime in Paris to persuade them it was time to give up). Admiral Collingwood at the head of the Mediterranean Fleet sought at this stage only to 'act defensively' while the really decisive campaigns unfolded across Spain and, to a much greater extent following Napoleon's invasion of Russia in 1812, along the Vistula.[47]

Meanwhile the pitfalls in British interaction with local populations in the Mediterranean during these dying phases of the struggle with Napoleon were exhibited most tellingly, perhaps, in Sicily. The purpose of the British garrison kept in that island from February 1806 was to stop the French breaking out of the Italian peninsula. The trouble was, as always, that for Britain the holding of Mediterranean islands could prove a drain as much as an asset. The defence of Sicily, with some 17,000 troops stationed there, shackled British military resources in the Mediterranean throughout the remainder of the war.[48] If the British had been able to make effective use of Sicilian and Neapolitan forces for their own purposes, things would have been different, but their estimation of the worth of these forces declined as the war dragged on. In Sicily, social conditions were so brittle, and food in such short supply, that preventing an internal explosion became an end in itself. The resulting frustration showed in the disillusionment of local British commanders in the island.

Just as the Maltese had welcomed the British in 1800 as salvation from the French, so the Sicilians had enthusiastically greeted them as providing a potential escape from Bourbon misrule. Sicilian reformers rallied to the British presence as offering a short cut to constitutional liberty. Such hopefulness was the essence of an Anglomania taking root in various branches of an emerging southern European bourgeoisie.[49] This phenomenon, however, was intrinsically unstable and always subject to erosion and reversals. Such a roller-coaster experience unfolded after Lord William Bentinck was appointed in 1811 to the dual post of principal British agent in Sicily and Commander-in-Chief of the British Army in the Mediterranean.[50] Impatient to get things done, he introduced a new English-style constitution in 1812. This afforded him popularity in some quarters, but he also imposed new taxes, ignored local institutions as excessively corrupt and veered towards military autocracy whenever an obstacle blocked his own path. His main trouble was with the refugee Bourbon Court in Palermo (once so beloved of Nelson) and above all its Queen, Maria Caroline. For the latter, the British had only one use: that of getting her family back onto its Neapolitan throne occupied by the Bonapartist, Joachim Murat. But this was far from Bentinck's thoughts. As a fervent Whig, he aspired to promote Italian liberalism, albeit on distinctively English lines, and to consign Bourbon absolutism to the past. The sister of Marie Antoinette, executed Queen of France, Maria Caroline once bitterly remarked that 'when she saw an Englishman she felt the guillotine on her neck', and finally pronounced herself to be 'entirely disanglomanized'.[51]

In the end, Bentinck used force to get rid of the Queen. Three battalions of infantry and a cavalry squadron presided over her departure from Messina in June 1813, aboard a British warship (a conveyance for many Mediterranean royals and celebrities, on the way up or down, in the following decades) to Venice. Thereafter Bentinck declared an Emergency and assumed full powers of government. The results were very mixed. The imposition of direct British administration alienated inhabitants used to less intrusive ways, while the Government back in London disliked the responsibilities and expenses involved. The British Foreign Secretary, Lord Castlereagh, grumbled about Bentinck's 'frequent acts of undisguised power' and before long recalled him.[52] The latter left Sicily denouncing it as 'the rotten galley to which he seemed chained', and his dream of that island as 'the Queen of our Colonies' proved a phantasm. Yet as was often the case even a brief if intense British involvement left a mark. Progressive liberals in both Sicily and mainland Italian states held up the constitution of 1812 as a beacon of hope in the dark days of post-war reaction well into the age of the Risorgimento.

Castlereagh's irritation with Bentinck's Sicilian venture coincided with a natural impulse against fresh Mediterranean commitments as the finale to the long years of warfare approached. Nonetheless these years witnessed a huge extension of British power in the region.[53] Theorists of a new British Mediterranean imperium sought to give it doctrinal respectability. The most influential example was *An Historical Survey of the Foreign Affairs of Great Britain* (1808) by G. F. Leckie, a long-standing British landowner in Sicily closely connected with army commanders in the island. His argument was that Britain should construct 'an insular empire throughout the Mediterranean', since, he asserted, an 'Empire of the Sea will always balance that of Land'. By seizing Mediterranean islands the British could progressively draw trade and political influence in the region to themselves.[54] Leckie's ideas were those, as one critic expressed it, of an 'extreme dispersionist',[55] and the influence to which he pointed was by its nature partial, fluctuating, evanescent. But his theorizing pointed to a flexibility that was to underpin the operation of British power, and, crucially, make it at least tolerable to other powers who might otherwise have fought it tooth and nail.

The strategic debates concerning the effectiveness of Britain's Mediterranean warfare during the Napoleonic age touched on issues that were to run deeply in British affairs for well over a century. Prime Minister Pitt had laid down the principle in 1805 that there should be no major military effort in the Mediterranean proper, and that all the vital points were nearer home.[56] This principle held throughout the conflict. The problem was that an insular and naval strategy or a territorial empire in the Mediterranean necessitated garrisoning by troops taken away from other fronts. Napoleon himself in his exile expressed contempt for the 'pygmy combinations' behind British operations in the Mediterranean,[57] reserving his most sweeping remarks for the value of Britain's so-called fortresses. 'Things suited us as it was' the ex-Emperor said when he was asked why he had never attacked the Rock. 'Gibraltar is of no value to Britain. It defends nothing. It intercepts nothing.

It is simply an object of national pride.'[58] Sir John Fortescue's influential *History of the British Army*, appearing in 1905 at a time of reaction against purely peripheral commitments, took aim at the habit 'of frittering away' England's limited forces against Napoleon, instead of 'keeping it united at a single [continental] point'.[59] Yet against this were strategic protagonists at the time like Leckie, and many latter-day commentators, often reflecting the experience of the Second World War, who have applauded the 'defensive success' in the Mediterranean in the years after 1803 which contained Napoleon within mainland Europe, keeping commerce flowing to Britain's advantage, while installing her authority in islands that might, or might not, ultimately be retained. Such contested views were never to be far from the overall conduct of British policy in the Mediterranean in the decades ahead.

In the conditions of early 1814, however, Castlereagh, as the dominant figure in British diplomacy, was bent on adjusting the balance of British efforts away from the Mediterranean.[60] He wanted to reinsert Britain into the foreground of the continental European politics from which Napoleon had banned her for so long. This marginality was epitomized when Tsar Alexander I and the King of Prussia finally entered Paris on 31 March 1814 at the head of the Allied forces but with no senior British military or political figure alongside them. One of Castlereagh's chief tasks in the peacemaking ahead was to deflect the other European powers' suspicions of British motives. One source of such suspicion was a perceived British tendency to sacrifice continental stability if it ever conflicted with her own aggrandizement in the Mediterranean – just as, allegedly, the British had once plunged the world into fresh torments for the sake of keeping Malta. During the struggle against Napoleon a trans-Mediterranean world had been integrated and in various ways mobilized, with the British lodged at crucial points in and around it. Once Nelson had destroyed the remnants of the French fleet at Trafalgar, the Royal Navy's control in these waters had been again assured; and during the Hundred Days following Napoleon's escape from Elba during March 1815 even Marseilles was occupied by Sir Hudson Lowe and his Corsican Rangers.[61] Yet it was still unclear whether the British were merely birds of passage in the Mediterranean or would be a permanent factor in its affairs. There was no certainty that the reassertion of peacetime normality would not relegate them back to the margins they had occupied before 1793.

By the time of Napoleon's downfall, a British cadre – naval, military and civil, including their families who sometimes accompanied them – had been intensely exposed to Mediterranean life.

Sir Hudson Lowe, already mentioned, and soon to be Napoleon's jailer on St Helena, had, for example, served as a volunteer in Gibraltar as far back as 1785–6. He took part in the siege of Toulon in 1793, and served in the British administrations of Corsica and Elba. In 1801 he led a corps in the occupation of Alexandria, and had done several stints in Malta and Sicily. His Mediterranean service ended with responsibility for various Ionian islands. His failure after April 1816 to strike up a good relationship with the ex-Emperor on St Helena was sometimes ascribed to his long association with the Corsican Rangers, which Napoleon – as a Corsican himself – always regarded bitterly as 'a collection of renegades and deserters'.[62] Lowe's experience of the Mediterranean as an English officer was clearly outstanding, but it was not unique. This particular cohort of leadership, with its lasting imprint of a war spread across the Mediterranean, did not fade away in British life until the 1840s and 1850s.

As for Mediterranean populations themselves, it was true that the British were often welcomed during the revolutionary and Napoleonic struggles because they were seen as providing protection in a predatory age. The ecstatic crowds who greeted the British when they arrived to annex Corsica in 1793 set a pattern later repeated in other locales. 'Viva Nelson!' a heaving mass of Neapolitans – aware that English victory at Aboukir Bay made them safe from French invasion for a while at least – shouted in September 1798 as the triumphant Admiral was paraded with Lady Hamilton around the city in a carriage.[63] But not all Neapolitans felt the same about the English hero with his Bourbon friends after June 1799 when, with the city split by civil conflict, he cancelled a safe conduct given to local Jacobins. Some were imprisoned and tried on Nelson's flagship, HMS *Foudroyant*, before being hauled off for execution. One British officer present confirmed that Emma Hamilton's hand, guided by Queen Maria Caroline, added names to the condemned list.[64] First and most eminent of these was Admiral Prince Francesco Caracciolo, head of the small Neapolitan navy, who was liked even in local British circles. Like many of the aristocratic intelligentsia in Naples, the Admiral had given up on the corrupt Court and supported the French. Brought on board in chains, his plea to be shot rather than hanged was denied.[65] Accusations that Lady Hamilton was rowed around the *Foudroyant* to gloat over Caracciolo's body hanging from the yardarm are unlikely to be true, but their circulation shows how quickly anything British could become absorbed into the pattern of Neapolitan life.[66] The affair, in the estimation of one British diplomat, left 'a stain of blood upon our character' that took years to fade.[67] Nelson's tangled involvement in Neapolitan affairs carried an unusual intensity both for personal reasons, and because of political complexities that went beyond his own experience and expertise. But through its very extremity it illustrated certain underlying dilemmas in Britain's deepened engagement with Mediterranean affairs. Strict aloofness, married to a concentration on narrow British interests, carried costs and penalties. But then so did the temptation to enter into the intense rivalries of Mediterranean societies, with all their distorting effects. This thin line between intervention and non-intervention would permanently bedevil Anglo-Mediterranean relationships.

# 2

# The Formation of a 'British Lake', 1815–1841

The making of the ensuing peace settlement was protracted. It began with the Allied negotiations at Châtillon during March 1814 and then the convening of the Congress of Vienna the following November, with its narcotic combination of glittering society and salon power-mongering, only to be interrupted by the interlude of Napoleon's return to France and ensuing defeat at Waterloo. The climax came with the signature of the Treaty of Paris in November 1815. Throughout the dominant British figure was the Foreign Secretary, Lord Castlereagh, whose achievement has been lauded as 'half a century of cheap security'.[1] The Great Powers – a category now for the first time endowed with a distinct identity – were torn between a collective desire to restore the pre-Napoleonic order, and a crude temptation to grab individual spoils. This was particularly true of Great Britain in the Mediterranean.

The security craved by the British Government led by Lord Liverpool was essentially maritime. A key concern was the neutralization of those continental dockyards and arsenals that had stretched British resistance so thinly after 1793, and the threat from which had still not entirely disappeared by the end of the conflict.[2] The fate of Antwerp was important, and it was only once this point was clarified satisfactorily by the Allied decision to erect a kingdom of the Netherlands[3] – that is, a state sufficiently viable not to fall back into dependency on France – under de facto British sponsorship that Castlereagh turned his attention elsewhere. A situation like that of 1797, when danger in the Channel panicked Britain into clearing her warships from the Mediterranean, had been guarded against for the foreseeable future.

The future of Venice was resolved by handing the port, along with the ships and material Napoleon had crammed into it, as well as the surrounding territory to Austria.[4] This suited Britain because the Habsburg Empire was not a seagoing power and from its geography seemingly unlikely ever to become one. The fate of Genoa, critical to Napoleon's Italian campaigns, loomed large too.[5] Here Britain was also in a position to exert leverage, having occupied the town at the end of the war. It was added to the Kingdom of Sardinia, bolstering a southern barrier to any new French expansion. The huge stocks of timber there were taken to docks in Britain. The logistics within the Mediterranean of any putative challenge to British predominance were therefore also dismantled.

Geopolitically, the fate of the rest of the Italian peninsula crucially affected British interests in the region. While in Sicily, Bentinck had dreamed of creating a unified and 'national' Italy under British patronage. Castlereagh firmly ruled out something that would require continued upheaval. 'It is not insurrection we now want in Italy or elsewhere,' he had said; 'we want disciplined force under sovereigns we can trust.'[6] The disciplined force was to come from Austria, reinforced by Habsburg Grand Duchies in Tuscany and Modena, and capped by the eviction of Joachim Murat from Naples in early May 1815 (he was then executed as a Bonapartist who could plausibly try a comeback). The Bourbon Ferdinand IV was duly restored to the throne of the Two Sicilies, giving Bentinck's old rival, Queen Maria Caroline, a triumph from the grave. Ironically, given how large a part Naples had played in the Mediterranean campaigns of Nelson between the battles of Aboukir Bay and Trafalgar, the British contribution to this outcome was limited to a naval demonstration in the bay and a few marines put ashore. In Castlereagh's eyes, like those of all true conservatives, Austria was destined to be 'the guardian of the Mediterranean against France'.[7] Here was the basis of a continuing Anglo-Austrian tie which, though subject to ups and down, was still not entirely dead even as late as 1914.

As for Britain's island conquests in the Mediterranean during the war, Castlereagh stuck faithfully to his Pittite belief in regarding such conquests as essentially secondary. They were to be 'held in reserve as a control over the conclusions of peace',[8] and bargained away if the necessity arose, as Malta had in theory been yielded at Amiens in 1802. But times had changed since then, and some of Castlereagh's colleagues no longer shared such restraint or old-fashioned views. This was true, for example, of the Secretary of State for War and the Colonies, Lord Bathurst, who developed a taste for expanding frontiers. He pointed out to Cabinet colleagues that the later stages of the war 'have occasioned a material change in the actual value of Malta', and underlined the premium attached to having a permanent station in the Mediterranean. He went on: 'As a Military Post, as a secure Place of Depot for British merchants, there appears no spot in the south of Europe so well calculated to fix the influence and extend the interests of Great Britain as the Island of Malta.'[9]

Situated so as to command the central Mediterranean narrows between Sicily and Cape Bon on the northern tip of Tunisia, the value of the island was clear enough,[10] though even in 1815 the full implications of its centrality in the Mediterranean were still only vaguely apprehended. British rulers in Malta since its occupation in 1800 had continued to be called 'Civil Commissioners', but in 1813 it had been decided to appoint a fully fledged Governor. The post had gone to a hard-bitten Scottish soldier and ex-Governor of Ceylon, Sir Thomas Maitland. Arriving in Valletta on 30 October that year, he had issued a proclamation annexing the island to the British Crown. The armorial bearings and assorted emblems of the old order of the Knights of St John had been definitively removed from all public buildings and replaced by the British Royal Arms.[11] By the time that British possession was recognized at the Treaty of Paris British rule was already firmly in place.[12]

One of the tasks imposed by his colleagues on Castlereagh in Vienna was to get this formal British takeover recognized by the other powers. The rather bereft representatives of the Knights lodged a formal protest, but, as one writer states, 'they could have spared themselves the bother'.[13] But there was still a price to be paid in the irritation caused to other European states. Prime Minister Liverpool captured something of this when remarking that Britain's allies had no choice but to accept her pocketing of Malta, but that doing the same with Sicily 'could not fail greatly to revolt them'.[14] The temptation to keep the latter, where after all many more British troops had been stationed in the recent war than in Malta, and which possessed the considerable fortress of Messina, was ultimately resisted. European distaste boiled down to resentment that Great Britain, while having its own strongly expressed views on continental questions, was disinclined to listen to anybody else when maritime and colonial topics were discussed. Britain had the unique advantage in 1815 of being a military and naval power, as well as being the paymaster of the winning coalition. But paymasters are rarely popular. Over coming decades the not unreasonable feeling that Britain invariably exploited the main chance in the Mediterranean at other people's expense became widespread. This sentiment – typified in the phrase 'perfidious Albion' – was tangible in the post-Napoleonic settlement, and became more overt in the following years.

British relations with Russia in particular became fragile. 'You must make up your mind to watch him [Tsar Alexander],' Castlereagh warned Liverpool from Vienna, 'and to resist him as another Bonaparte.'[15] One Bonaparte-like trait in Russian policy was a desire to make things difficult for the British in the Mediterranean. Nelson's fierce dislike of the Russian Fleet when it ventured anywhere near warm water had been second only to his hatred of the French,[16] and this feeling still existed in the British Fleet in 1815. Although the Russians had forsaken the Mediterranean after Tilsit, Tsar Alexander's sniping at British 'maritime rights' at the Congress of Vienna suggested a desire not to forgo all influence there. This Anglo-Russian tension found one vent in the unresolved question of what was to be done with the Ionian Islands, where British occupation still only had shallow roots.

Initially these Islands had been earmarked as compensation for King Ferdinand, should he not be restored in Naples and Palermo. As it turned out, he was, but there was no chance the Ionians would be added to the Bourbon estates. Castlereagh was determined to keep 'control' over this element in the reconstruction of outer Europe, his own preference again being to hand the archipelago to Austria, so bottling up the Adriatic in a way compatible with British interests. But it became clear that the Tsar would not tolerate any further Habsburg advance towards the Balkans. His chief adviser on Mediterranean questions, Ioannis Kapodistrias, was a Corfiote noble himself. Of the latter it was once said that he 'hated England like an Ionian', though, it might be added, like an Ionian who had taken Russian employment.

But since in 1815 the British were already installed in most of the Islands, Kapodistrias saw some advantage in letting them stay there. They would be easier to winkle out at some future point than the obstinate Austrians, with their big armies. But to this there was a crucial Russian caveat: the Islands should not be a colony, but only under British protection. This meant that the liberties secured amid the revolutionary euphoria after the Venetian departure from the Islands in 1800 should continue in some form, providing scope for stirring up trouble for the British when it might be convenient to do so.

Lord Liverpool's Cabinet in London, having confirmed their grip on Malta, were in any case bent on making good their Ionian claim. Possession of the archipelago offered a cheap and easy means of watching and if necessary guiding developments in European Turkey. Ministers were at first reluctant to accept the proposed Russian limitation on how British authority might operate. Castlereagh persuaded them to do so on the grounds that 'the substance of power remained',[17] while any guarantees of the old Ionian constitution, including a Senate dominated by the nobility, were scrupulously avoided. On 5 November 1815 the Islands passed by treaty under British control. The first article declared that they constituted 'a single, free and independent state', but the rest of the document made no mention of constitutional rights. However, the fact that the British Protectorate in the Ionian Islands was negotiated in this way, and derived its legitimacy through a European agreement, was to be important in making British Protection in the Ionian Islands a more vulnerable phenomenon than it would otherwise have been.

There was one other matter discussed at the Congress of Vienna with a Mediterranean dimension: slavery. For the first time at an international level this included the question of captive Europeans ('white slaves') held by Barbary corsairs from North Africa. From the late eighteenth century there had been calls for the leading states to set aside their petty rivalries – so astutely manipulated by the Barbary regents – and form a 'universal league' to suppress North African piracy and bondage. Bonaparte had latched on to a seemingly idealistic cause with potential for advancing territorial interests.[18] Nelson had no such large ideas, but he had been enraged whenever North African privateers preyed on British shipping in the Mediterranean seaways.[19] He never possessed the strength in frigates – able to go close inshore – to inflict punishment on the Barbary states. There was even a degree of dependence on the latter. As late as 1814 the food supply of Gibraltar hinged on their co-operation. A desire to end this situation once the necessities of war eased was part of a heightened sense of British power in the region. It was a British admiral, Sir William Sydney Smith, who at Vienna convened a 'Society of the Knights Liberator of the Slaves in Africa' calling for an end to all forms of servitude, but especially the purging of 'Turkish pirates'.

A special edge to the issue came also from the United States navy, which had recently obtained special privileges from the Dey of Tripoli for American traders. A United States squadron had threatened to bomb that port to smithereens if their demands were refused. In the Royal Navy this touched a nerve. It had not enjoyed any spectacular victories of its own since Trafalgar and its prestige relative to the British army had waned. In the War of 1812 against the United States, too, the navy had generally come off worst in encounters. The Admiralty were on the lookout for some means of reasserting the prestige of its flag. A display of British power in the Mediterranean, furthermore, would send a message to various quarters, including the Americans, whose fleet in the region was to remain more of a concern to Britain than that of France for much of the 1820s.

Bathurst oversaw the assembling of a powerful fleet for action against Algiers during September 1815.[20] It was put under an experienced commander, Lord Exmouth. At the last minute it was held back because the Ionians were thought less likely to accept subjection to Britain if their own fear of North African corsairs was suddenly lifted. Such security was for them, as it was for the Maltese, a major advantage of the new Mediterranean order.[21] Instead, in January 1816 a detailed reconnaissance was made by HMS *Banterer* of the defences of Algiers: the flanking batteries of its harbour, the number of sea-facing guns, the height of the walls, and the position of the Dey's palace.[22] This delay held pitfalls. Continental opinion saw a crusade against Barbary as a mask for another extension of an English presence, and it was possible that some other power, or combination of powers, might act first.[23] In July 1816 Exmouth's fleet sailed, and after linking up with a Dutch squadron in Gibraltar, and fine-tuning their combined artillery, the allied force (including nineteen ships of the line) appeared off Algiers on 26 August. The Dey was duly presented with an ultimatum (with a one-hour deadline) including demands for trading privileges, the freeing of slaves held in the town, and recognition of British Protection over the Ionian Islands. Acceptance was neither expected nor particularly desired.

A vicious fight followed. An Algerine flotilla of galleys and gunboats sped from harbour to attack the Anglo-Dutch ships, only to meet a shower of Congreve rockets. Exmouth's flagship, HMS *Charlotte*, trained its big cannon on the town. 'Like two bare-knuckle fighters,' a historian of this episode records, 'the opponents . . . fought each other to a standstill', with the Algerines crowding back into harbour. But the Allied warships had themselves been hurt, and Exmouth ordered them to cut their cables and get out of range of shore artillery. The Allied losses were considerable: 141 dead and 742 badly wounded. Still, the marine section of Algiers had been cut to pieces. 'Lord Exmouth', the American Consul, whose own residence had been reduced to rubble, declared, 'holds the fate of Algiers in his hands.'[24] The Dey accepted the terms, and the European slaves were assembled on the harbour front for transport to the waiting ships. According to an eyewitness, this ragged but elated group (some 1,200 Neapolitans, Sicilians and Sardinians, but with a sprinkling of Spaniards, Greeks, French and English) clambered aboard the rowing boats crying (at least apocryphally), 'Long Live England and the English Admiral'.

It was to require further bombardments of Barbary ports, not just by the Royal Navy, during the 1820s to curtail most of their piracy, marking a critical step in the creation of a free-flowing, more integrated Mediterranean marketplace, and also one increasingly open to intrusion by powerful outsiders. For the present the stricken town of Algiers offered a graphic example of what could happen to those who did not respect the White Ensign of the Royal Navy. Exmouth's biographer shortly afterwards wrote: 'The battle of Algiers forms a class by itself among naval victories. It was a new thing to place a fleet in a position surrounded by such strong batteries. Bold, breathtaking and original in conception, it was brilliant and complete in execution.'[25] At Algiers the Royal Navy seemed to have done what it had failed to do at Constantinople in 1807, and had not risked at Corfu after 1813:

batter a fortified Mediterranean bastion into compliance. But even here the issue was not clear-cut. The Dey, at the height of the battle, had reportedly marched up and down the battlements shouting 'We are not vanquished!'[26] and within three months the fortifications were restored (though the Dey himself was soon deposed in a coup and executed). Wherever the British came up against physical resistance in the Mediterranean, punishment was rarely one-sided. Still, when Exmouth returned to London in October 1816 he met with an ecstatic welcome, receiving both a vote of thanks from Parliament and a viscountcy. The episode entered into popular consciousness. The three-act opera *The Fall of Algiers* was one of many theatrical reconstructions. An implicit message was that the British, far from making a purely transitory appearance as a Mediterranean power, had every intention of becoming a permanent fixture.

In becoming entrenched, however, there was always a risk of being compromised. The embarrassment attending the eviction of the Christian population from the coastal town of Parga, in the west of modern Greece, offered an early instance of pitfalls ahead. Ali Pasha of Ioannina had long wanted to get possession of Parga, but the Pargiotes had eluded his grasp, first by calling in Russian help, and then by securing French protection. Napoleon's local commander remained adamant that he would not sully his flag by giving up Parga to the Pasha's revenge.[27] By contrast, ministers in London saw the small port as fair game for Ali.[28] Even so, the Pargiotes felt secure when Parga was finally occupied by British troops on 22 March 1814. The British commanding officer, General Sir James Campbell, showed every sign of ensuring their safety. But the omission of any reference to Parga, in theory an Ionian dependency, in the treaty transferring these states to British protection suggested something different. That treaty invited the Ottoman Sultan to signify his agreement to its provisions, and under encouragement from Ali Pasha the Sultan made Parga his price for doing so. In late 1816 the British Ambassador in Constantinople was instructed to authorize a handover to the Pasha's troops.

By this point Sir Thomas Maitland, already Governor of Malta, had also been appointed as Lord High Commissioner in the Ionian Islands (a suitably portentous title for the job). The fragility of British authority in the Mediterranean was reflected in the combination of these posts in the hands of an administrator known for toughness. Maitland assured the Pargiotes that they would be compensated by Ali for being dispossessed, and receive new homes in nearby islands, but that if they did not co-operate they would be left to an unfortunate fate. It was typical of what one writer termed Maitland's 'savage, Swift-like cynicism', however, that in gifting the town to the Pasha, he did so as if tossing a bone to a snarling dog.[29]

The senior British military officer on the spot, Colonel C. P. de Bosset, wholly sympathized with the townspeople's plight. With the Pargiotes in a state of panic, he protested to Maitland, but swiftly found himself recalled.[30] On 24 April the nerves of the population broke, and 4,000 of them took what goods and mementoes they could and crossed over to Corfu and Paxos. The Pasha, however, had still not come up with the compensation, though when meeting Maitland in early May he tantalizingly showed him several sacks of hard currency. Shortly afterwards the coinage arrived in the town on a donkey-train, and the British force duly departed with the money, suspiciously guarding their rear as they did so. But any hope in London that this shady transaction could be effected without publicity was disappointed. The matter was raised in Parliament and bitter exchanges were aired in the *Edinburgh Review*. Castlereagh had to resort to government slush money to shut up critics.[31] Especially damaging use was made of the Parga episode in Europe to mock British claims to moral superiority – poets and artists featured pathetic scenes of the Pargiote flight, most vividly in Italy, where the episode was taken as a touching echo of the plight of Italian refugees fleeing Austrian tyranny. Most lasting was the bitterness of the Pargiote exiles in the Islands, many living for decades in a shanty outside Corfu Town. As long as Protection lasted, they were a thorn in the side of the British.[32] This episode is worth recalling because, coming at an early stage in British Mediterranean experience, it highlighted the clash between political imperatives and their moral fallout. There were quite a few Pargas during the years ahead.

But if the change the British brought with them into the post-war Mediterranean was bad for the Pargiotes, for others it was to prove more beneficial, though often ambivalently so. Maitland himself embodied the paradox. He was described by an otherwise friendly subordinate as 'a rough old despot',[33] and by his fierce Radical critic in the Westminster Parliament, Joseph Hume, as 'a disgrace to England'.[34] Glaswegian irascibility, a heavy consumption of liquor and not much interest in his personal appearance were part of the alleged disgrace. He was later to be criticized for spending too much time in the Ionians, which he preferred to knightly, more refined Valletta (a packet service from Malta to Corfu Town was not established until the 1830s, so communication was poor). But the crucial point was that while Malta could be controlled from Corfu, Corfu and the Islands – inherently unstable – could not be controlled from Malta.[35]

When Maitland had first arrived in Malta in 1813, the island was above all in need of protection from plague. Disease had followed the supplies and shipping criss-crossing the Mediterranean with increasing intensity during the war years. The new Governor had immediately cordoned off all towns into districts, stopped movement between them, scoured and disinfected all houses, confined the infected to the lazaretto and effectively reduced Valletta to a prison.[36] Such abrasive measures were novel and not always welcomed by those whose interests were affected. By September 1814, however, it had been possible to relax these restrictions, even when the plague was still raging in Gibraltar and elsewhere. Out of a population of 116,000, fatalities had totalled 4,500 (the British garrison being relatively unscathed). Maitland's taming of the plague in Malta earned him a gratitude that few other achievements could have done. His personal authority when peace came and the Ionians took him away to other duties was partly secure for this reason.

Poverty, however, was a more continuous threat to Malta than disease. Overpopulation, above all relative to food resources, was aggravated by the rapid ebbing of the artificial prosperity of the war. The restoration of the old pattern of Mediterranean trade brought recovery to Leghorn and Genoa, but the reverse for Malta (and to some extent for Gibraltar). Maitland struggled to persuade the Colonial Office to provide some financial aid, encourage local cotton production and assist migration, with limited results. In the Ionian Islands conditions were generally better. Greater fertility and spare land meant fewer shortages. Nevertheless, the Ionian peasant led a hard life, often paying usurious rates of interest to urban creditors. Maitland began tentatively to legislate on this matter, sought to disseminate agricultural skills and, with the advice of the renowned civil engineer Thomas Telford, instituted a road-building programme. British administrators were able to get around the Ionian Islands in a way their Venetian predecessors had never done.[37] Just as importantly, marketable goods were transported more efficiently. In both Malta and the Ionians, then, British rule, whatever its disadvantages, offered a prop to shore up economic activity during an unstable post-war adjustment.

These Mediterranean societies shared one pressing need in equal measure: institutional reform, particularly of the judiciary. In Malta, the legal system was a morass of tradition in which the ordinary person might sink without trace. Maitland abolished outdated tribunals, insisted on the reading of sentences in open court, eliminated torture, paid judges by fixed salaries rather than fees and introduced the separation of powers (but characteristically left them fused at the top in the Supreme Council of Justice as a control device). The codification and improved transparency of laws had to wait until the 1830s and 1840s, but Maitland's innovations improved procedures. Such changes meant there was a risk of colliding with such hallowed props of the old order as the Catholic Church in Malta or the Greek Church in the Ionian Islands. Maitland was careful to avoid doing so. In Malta, he focused on preventing Church premises being used as sanctuary from the law, but generally adhered closely to the assurances to the Roman faith 'as by law established' given at the outset of British administration. Maitland accorded to the Catholic Archbishop a precedence second only to the Governor, while the long-standing claim of the great Church of St John's in Valletta to equality with the Cathedral in the ancient capital of Notabile was granted in 1816, winning favour with the clergy. In the Ionian Islands the Greek Orthodox faith was elevated above the Roman Catholicism privileged by the Venetians. The fact that, as he put it, 'the two hagiologies were at daggers drawn' in both Malta and Corfu allowed Maitland to play them off against each other.[38] In Corfu, the biggest annual event – the festivity of the patron saint, Spyridon – was scrupulously respected, and British officers even walked in the procession behind the Saint's revered relic.[39]

There was no surer way to popularity in Malta than to reduce the price of bread. Maitland intervened in the opaque working of the grain monopoly (the *università*) without going the whole hog of privatization. He had an instinct for when to reform, and how far to go. He left the hospitals, a bastion of the old order, largely untouched, as had Ball before him. Maitland was especially conscious that to attempt to squeeze out local revenues for British military purposes would be disastrous for good relations and resisted Colonial Office pressure to do so; and he blocked what he contemptuously called 'ordnance cocks' in the garrison who called for expensive but unnecessary schemes for new fortifications.[40] Too much fraternizing between British soldiers and locals was also something Maitland believed could cause trouble, so on first arriving in Corfu he arranged for the garrison there – *in situ* for several years – to be exchanged with that in Malta. All in all, measures to eradicate plague, shore up commerce, humanize the law, improve institutions and cushion the impact of a British presence defined the essential paradox of Maitland, whereby a domineering style coexisted with a fierce ambition to pull societies out of what he saw as backward feudalism. Although there is some truth in the portrayal of him as the archetypal precursor of a new British imperial proconsularism after 1815,[41] Maitland's record in these possessions also reflected an older enlightened absolutism in distinctive southern European form.[42]

Yet a 'rough old despot' Maitland always remained. Like most British rulers in the Mediterranean before and after him, he could see only the vices in those subject to his authority. 'It is impossible for any man who has not seen it', he reported from Corfu, 'to believe the extent of duplicity, chicanery and want of principle that uniformly prevail here.'[43] His view of the Maltese was not more charitable. He believed that fear and interest were the sole factors to be played upon. 'Interest' above all meant jobs, and it was the essence of Maitland's system that public positions were given to those who espoused loyalty to the new regime. Patronage was ruthlessly employed to suborn the faction in Corfu connected with Ioannis Kapodistrias (who remained influential at the Russian court until his liberal views led him in 1822 to retire to Geneva), Maitland noting with satisfaction that 'it has been a race which of them could run fastest into our arms'.[44] It was one of his many contradictions that although he affected to despise the 'fawning and cringing' he saw as a Mediterranean trait, Maitland cracked down hard when anybody expressed an opinion opposite to his own. One means of binding local elites to British rule was to reinvent those cheap recognitions of rank and chivalry used by the Knights. Maitland established the Order of St Michael and St George, the 'big Shewy Star' of which might dazzle aspiring Maltese and Ionians.[45] In Malta, the Order was inaugurated by a banquet in the Grand Master's Palace, now appropriated as the Governor's residence, the ceremony climaxing in a salvo from the fleet in the harbour. Both Maltese and Ionian aristocracies were not slow to take whatever marks of status were dangled before them, but the political advantage gained was subject to diminishing returns. The response of many older 'notables' was to retreat into their villas. There was to be no more corrupting element in Anglo-Mediterranean relationships than a sense of depreciation.

For the moment, Maitland's goal of squashing opposition to British administration in Malta was achieved with relative ease. Plague, the peacemaking in Europe and commercial depression turned attention in other directions. Political discontent only revived gradually in the wake of the Neapolitan revolution in 1820. The latter was the first blow to post-war stability in southern Europe. It was suppressed by Austria; on the occasion it was said of Castlereagh that 'he wishes to applaud, but he dare not', since an association with European reaction did not go down well in Britain.[46] The Neapolitan liberals who fled to Malta were the first of what was to prove a steady flow of refugees from autocratic Italian states, with considerable cultural repercussions in the island. The Catholic Church, however, scarcely welcomed an influx of anti-clerical radicals, and the modus vivendi between Maitland's regime and the Catholic hierarchy was assisted by a shared suspicion of incoming troublemakers. This pattern was to be repeated many times under different labels and in different permutations.

Maitland faced a bigger challenge in the Ionian Islands. The threat of Russian meddling meant that the prestige of the Lord High Commissioner was never quite that of a colonial Governor in Malta, where no such external complication operated. There was also the pressure flowing from a new constitution, or 'Chart', presented by an Ionian delegation to the Prince Regent at the Royal Pavilion, Brighton, on 26 August 1817. Even the Lord Chancellor had to ask for a summary in plain English so he could get the hang of it.[47] In fact it had been framed in such a way that Maitland could do what he liked anyway. His contempt for the legislature was never concealed. In his early days in the Islands the upper chamber, or Senate, used to meet in a drawing room adjacent to Maitland's bedroom. One morning, disturbed by the assembling of the members, he appeared in the doorway still wearing his nightclothes, and declared to the administrating officer, 'Damn them, Secretary. Tell them to go to hell.'[48] But at least the Ionians had a constitution, whereas the Maltese had to wait some time and even when they got one, as we shall see, it never really worked.

Conditions in the Ionian Islands varied enormously. Although the British had never conquered Corfu, their presence took a firmer root there than in the southern islands. Corfiotes were used to foreign rulers – Venetian, Russian and French – and knew how to twist them to their own purposes (and indeed the British themselves were hardly unknown, since English merchants had been prominent in the Ionian export trade for two hundred years). The British troops, concentrated in Corfu, spent more money than previous occupiers simply because they were wealthier. Money helped to forge an Anglo-Corfiote rapport, which explains why one British administrator could believe that the leading classes there were 'essentially English' in disposition.[49] The other islands, especially the largest, Cephalonia, had more primitive social conditions and susceptibility to disorder. Here Maitland left the chief British officials, or Residents, to govern according to their own whims. The result was petty fiefdoms where corruption and poverty flourished. From the outset of British Protection, the possibility of violence could not be excluded, which was why Maitland complained of 'living on top of a volcano'.[50] This was very different from relatively stable, if boisterous, Malta.

Maitland soon faced a more or less permanent emergency originating in the mainland Greek revolt against hated Turkish rule. This revolt erupted during February 1821 in the Ottoman Danubian provinces, where it was speedily crushed, only to recur in the Peloponnese, fanned by a communal massacre of Muslims. The origins of the revolution were sometimes attributed to the inspiration afforded by the recent affirmation of constitutional liberty in the Ionians. That such a declaration as the one decreed in the Brighton Pavilion could be the precursor of such a coping stone of nineteenth-century nationalism may seem curious, but liberty is always relative. Crucially, Ionian 'independence' had been recognized by Europe, and it was Europe's help that Greek rebels knew they would need to survive. Maitland's reading was more cynical, claiming that the explosion proceeded 'upon a fixed and settled plan of which Kapodistrias is the Head', operating through Ionian agents placed in the Greek provinces.[51] This was exaggerated, but the most reliable information about the fluctuating struggle was always culled from correspondence intercepted by the Ionian authorities, which was why the British Government always knew more about what was happening than other European governments.[52]

Maitland's overriding task in relation to the revolution in Greece was to maintain strict Ionian neutrality.[53] This reflected his prejudices. He disliked Turks, but liked the Balkan Greeks even less, and considered their aspirations to statehood ridiculous.[54] Yet, prejudice apart, political interest dictated that safety for British Protection lay in sealing itself off from such tumultuous events. British shipping and stores required protection from the piracy that was now enjoying a last golden age amid insurrectionary turmoil. But since Greek privateers were rampant, it was against them that the Royal Navy directed their efforts, creating a sense of bias. The large reductions in British naval spending after 1815, enforced by the scrapping of income tax, meant that the number of warships in the Mediterranean had been cut, making Maitland's job all the harder. The need to guard the Ionian coast began a gradual revival in the British Mediterranean Fleet during the 1820s.

Maitland cracked down hard on Hellenic enthusiasm in the Islands. This included any British officials displaying such inclinations. Colonel Charles Napier, the Resident of Cephalonia, was at odds with Maitland on this and various other matters. Later the conqueror of the Sind provinces in India (memorialized on his statue in Trafalgar Square), Napier once said that he would give them all away for his beloved Cephalonia. While he had governed that island, however, Maitland forced him to shave off the long moustache which signified sympathy with Greek revolutionary ideals long before it became a British Victorian fashion-statement. Much more difficult was to stem the flow of armed Greeks to the mainland. The volunteer Ionian Regiment was one of the few effective semi-regular formations in the provisional Greek army. A series of ordinances legalized interdiction of volunteers by the Protectorate authorities, but in the process much goodwill was lost. A watershed was passed in October 1821 when Greek ships drove a Turkish brig ashore on Zante, and British troops intervened to protect the stranded Ottomans. In the resulting fracas a British soldier was killed, 'as if . . . jumped upon and battered with a big stone'.[55] Martial law was decreed and five Zantiotes were executed. Yet another side to Maitland was evoked when Sultan Mahmud sent his forces crashing into western Greece. Maitland proceeded to open the small island of Kalamas as a refuge for fleeing Christians. He did this, as he informed the Colonial Office, 'to soften the bitterness of that Fate which now inevitably attends the unfortunate Greeks, no longer to be considered as insurgents . . . but as mere Fellow Creatures . . . which demand consideration'.[56] Kalamas was still serving this humanitarian end as late as August 1829. Under these conditions Ionian Protection was often real enough.

By then Maitland had been dead for some time. In late December 1823 he took possession of the new and impressive Palace of St Michael and St George, built to give future Lord High Commissioners a residence to compare with the knightly edifices surrounding Governors of Malta. He then left for Valletta, and on 17 January suffered a massive stroke on a rare visit to the army chaplain's house and died that night. His body lay solemnly in the main hall of the great palace, surrounded by lighted tapers and constantly attended. He was buried in the Upper Barracca Gardens overlooking Grand Harbour. An elegant rotunda was erected in his name on the esplanade of Corfu Town, still a landmark today. Testifying to how Mediterranean affairs often reflected ideological differences among the British themselves, Maitland's reputation afterwards became something of a football for those of more liberal and 'Whiggish' beliefs at home. '[H]is system', one critic noted, 'of driving and kicking Mankind into obedience is, in the long run, mischievous and absurd.'[57] It certainly seemed so by the 1830s, when in the wake of the Reform Act Maitland's style of Toryism seemed outdated. But at the time the British Government had needed a hard and unyielding administrator to entrench a still wavering British presence. Maitland may have acted on the principle that 'our [British] partisans are our bayonets and our people in office – we have no other',[58] but when he died he had overseen the successful institutionalization of British rule in Malta, even if the same could not altogether be said of the Ionians.[59]

The revolution in Greece had far wider implications for Great Britain than merely its effect on the Ionian Islands themselves. It threatened massive instability across the east. As the historian and long-time resident of Athens George Finlay noted, only partly facetiously, the British Government 'viewed the outbreak with more aversion than any other Christian government'.[60] Unlike recently suppressed protests in Spain and Naples, this revolution was transparently national and popular. But it was also religious, and provided Russia with plenty of scope for intervention under the mantle of fellow Orthodoxy. An Austrian diplomat in London captured British reactions in reporting that even those sympathetic to the Greeks 'are not prepared to see the liberty of Greece bought at the price of Russian supremacy in the Mediterranean'. This ambivalence towards the Greek struggle was never to disappear.

Just as Maitland enforced neutrality in the Ionians, so Castlereagh translated it into broader diplomacy. But neutrality was capable of strong bias. The 'violently pro-Turk' views of Lord Strangford, British Ambassador in Constantinople, were evident following a key event in the drama: on Easter Sunday 1821 the Ecumenical Patriarch of Constantinople, Gregory V, was pulled from his Cathedral and hanged in his vestments from the main gate of the Phanar.[61] Strangford immediately wrote an impassioned defence of Sultan Mahmud, arguing that the attacks on Greek churchmen were no more savage than the anti-papal Gordon Riots in Britain during the 1780s, and that while the Patriarch's death was deplorable he 'felt bound in conscience and in honour' to point out that many of the bishops and priests slaughtered alongside him were indeed guilty of conspiracy.[62]

But such views were one end of a wide spectrum. Greek affairs were supercharged by intense and conflicting currents in post-Napoleonic Europe. Philhellenism had evolved in recent decades as an enthusiasm of everyone from poets, architects and essayists to those like Lord Elgin, who took up the game of acquiring ancient marble artefacts.[63] The lyrical outpourings of Lord Byron – whose immensely successful

*Childe Harold's Pilgrimage* (1812) was followed by other poems with a Greek background – perfected the displaced (usually aristocratic) figure who 'embodied a culturally alienated anti-hero, bearing within a dark secret . . . '.[64] Such a theme resonated in the deeply insecure and troubled world left in the wake of Napoleon's fall. The insurrection in Greece triggered a philhellenic response that became a political force capable of drawing in people normally outside the realm of public debate. In this mobilizing capacity it resembled the contemporary movement for the abolition of slavery.

Byron was as much a European as a British icon, a new 'celebrity', and the initial flood of philhellenic volunteers to fight alongside Greek insurgents were French, German and Swiss – often drawn from the great pool of unemployed military officers – rather than British. French philhellenism bonded together royalists, old Bonapartists and Orleanists, and one thing they often shared was a desire to see the British taken down a peg or two in the Mediterranean. In fact, it is the relative slowness of the British philhellenic reaction that stands out.[65] For some while the London Greek Committee organizing aid to the insurgents remained a preserve of Whigs and doctrinaire Radicals seeking to use the question as a weapon against the Tory government. Levant Company merchants and other 'respectable' elements kept clear. The ministry of Lord Liverpool hoped that by fixing a diplomatic and domestic blanket over the revolutionary outbreak, time might be bought and Sultan Mahmud given the space to asphyxiate a rebellion with many unwanted complications.

Yet Liverpool's government, its popularity eroded by post-war repression, was evolving a kind of 'disguised liberalism' at home and abroad as a roundabout way of survival.[66] George Canning, Foreign Secretary after Castlereagh's suicide in August 1822, moved in this direction. He was before long faced with humiliating defeat when the Bourbon regime in France, ignoring British opposition, invaded Spain and extinguished the new constitutional regime in that country. This was the first significant French action after 1815, breaching the guidelines set by the victor powers. But it was especially jarring with opinion in Britain, where Wellington's Iberian triumphs had led to an assumption that British influence was paramount in determining Spain's future. Canning had little choice but to accept the fait accompli in

Madrid – he did not, after all, have an army to send back into the peninsula – but he published a warning that he was 'an enthusiast for national independence'. This rhetoric subsequently took solid form in his recognition of the South American republics liberated from Spanish rule, by which he claimed – in one of the great diplomatic phrases by a British leader in the nineteenth century – to balance the Old World by bringing in the New. But another testimony to this shift was Canning's recognition of the Greeks as 'belligerents' by virtue of their having survived Ottoman pacification, with the rights in international law that such status carried with it. In fact Canning was not concerned with Greek welfare as such any more than Castlereagh; though a notable classical scholar, he himself harboured no traces of philhellenism. 'There is no denying', he once said of the Greeks, 'that they are a most rascally set.'[67] Still, the Greek Question offered a laboratory within which Canning could experiment with a more flexible foreign policy, though the basic aim of that policy for Canning, as an old Pittite, remained familiar: to fend off any threat, French or Russian, to British naval power in the Mediterranean.

Lord Byron, too, had no romantic illusions about contemporary, or indeed ancient, Greece.[68] Prematurely aged, weakened by sexual scandal, ceaselessly itinerant, and agitated that life had slipped by, the poet contemplated going off to fight in Spain or Mexico before Greece popped back into his vision; even then the prospect 'appealed to him mainly as a fight for liberty, not as a fight for Greeks as such'.[69] He was in Genoa when he first came under pressure to take up that banner – 'your presence [there] will operate as a talisman', the leading philhellene, Edward Blaquiere, wrote on 5 April 1823, 'and the field is too glorious . . .'[70] Byron finally departed to Cephalonia during August as a stepping stone to the mainland. But there, in the little village of Metaxata, he hovered, his indecision reinforced by obscurity surrounding the real state of affairs in Greece, where the fighting sporadically flared up and subsided without any apparent resolution of the conflict.

Byron's immobility witnessed a fundamental gulf between European impulses and Greek realities. The philhellenes (a growing proportion of them British after 1823, including a large Celtic minority) were closely connected with the 'Western Greeks', a designation referring to their cultural orientation to Europe, and who often came from outside Greece itself. This group espoused progressive political ideals and Hellenic regeneration. The key figure was Alexandros Mavrocordatos, whose conception of Greek revolution was very compatible with that of Byron, that is, he stressed the importance of constitutional and centralized government, underpinned by a keen awareness that foreign help would be required to guide events to a successful conclusion.[71] Byron waited for some evidence that such a scenario was credible before exposing himself to the full force of Greek events, massacres and all.

Yet Mavrocordatos's version of Greek affairs was partial, contradicted by the way that the insurgents fell into a submerged civil war. Most of the fighting against the Turks was 'hit and run', carried out by Peloponnesian warlords like Kolokotronis – once a resident of the Ionian Islands – who despised oversight by foreign powers, had minimal sense of western culture and wished Greece to be 'competent to her own liberation'.[72] He had certainly never read a single canto by Byron. Had Byron gone, as he first intended, to the Peloponnese, he would have had to come to terms with the raw instincts of Kolokotronis; as it was, when he took the jump and went across to the mainland, his destination was Missolonghi, the key to western, not central, Greece, and where the more supple westernized Greeks and their philhellenic allies were holding out against a Turkish siege. Byron, clad in military scarlet, arrived in the harbour of the marsh-fringed town on 4 January 1824, his little boat greeted with a salvo by every Greek vessel as it went by. The malarial virus he had first picked up in Greece during the summer of 1810, however, now suddenly returned with frightening force, and he died amid bouts of delirium on 18 April. All the shops in Missolonghi closed and Easter festivities were suspended for the funeral; the foreign onlookers were mostly Germans. The leading oration was made by Spyridon Trikoupis, founder of the most powerful of Greece's political dynasties in the nineteenth century. It was intensely ironic, and also an apt comment on the revolution, that the ship *Florida*, which arrived on 28 June to take Byron's body back to England, brought the first tranche of hard currency raised by the London Greek Committee. Control of this money soon provided a key to coming out on top in the visceral politics of the struggle. But in the

Greek Revolution the pedestrian and the heroic went inextricably together. Byron's death at Missolonghi not only capped the second greatest literary reputation in the English language after Shakespeare, it also gave birth to the most poignant British legend in the Mediterranean. No Briton was ever to make himself such a touchstone of a foreign people's freedom as Byron did in Greece; and there are few large towns in the Greek-speaking world today which do not have a memorial to Byron in one form or another.

Byron's death gave European philhellenism a boost that lasted till the end of the Revolution, undiminished by the disillusionment of returnees. But it coincided with darkening days for the insurgents. Mehmet Ali, still Pasha of Egypt, now came to the aid of the Sultan who was his nominal suzerain. The Pasha had invested huge sums in an Egyptian fleet, and started the conversion of Alexandria into a military port, much to Britain's later benefit. By early 1824 his son, Ibrahim, had crushed the Christian rebels in Crete. Delayed by the threat of Greek fire-ships, he finally landed with more than 10,000 troops in the Morea, and overwhelmed Missolonghi in late April 1826. Ibrahim then strangled the insurgency, in the ruins of which the remaining philhellenes died (and during which the only physical relic of Byron remaining in Greece, his lung, disappeared). Ibrahim averted the wholesale slaughter which had marked the earlier phases of the conflict. But Greeks were taken off as slaves to Africa, and the rumour took hold that a large-scale population transfer was under way, in which Christians would be replaced by incoming Arab settlers.

These developments forged what proved a lasting connection between British strategic necessities and ultimate Greek survival. The British feared that Tsar Nicholas I (who succeeded Alexander I in 1825) would take the opportunity to make that war on Turkey that British diplomacy had been straining to avoid. Meanwhile even non-western Greeks like Kolokotronis realized that they needed saving – dressed up as 'mediation' – by somebody more powerful than themselves. They much preferred to be saved by England than by Russia. This was not because they trusted the British. But others were likely to disappoint them more. Russia as a land power had many continental ambitions. Once let in, they might not go away. By contrast, Great Britain's aims were largely maritime, and therefore more compatible with Greek aspirations. Such thoughts lay behind the Greek Provisional Government's call for British Protection, expressed in an Act of Submission, during the summer of 1825. Great Britain emerged as the 'authorized pleader for the Greeks',[73] and in January 1826 Stratford Canning (nephew of the Foreign Secretary) was dispatched on another mission to St Petersburg. He went via Corfu and Hydra, where Mavrocordatos signalled for the first time that the Greeks were prepared to accept an outcome short of full independence.

Ibrahim's alleged plan for a transfer of population prompted George Canning to declare that there was to be 'no new Barbary state in Europe'. But by framing intervention along these moral lines any agenda of philhellenism, and redrawing of borders, was kept to a minimum. The ensuing St Petersburg Protocol (April 1826) consisted of an Anglo-Russian call for an armistice leading to an autonomous state under formal Ottoman sovereignty, while the powers themselves abjured any territorial claims for themselves. But this remained suspended as long as the Sultan refused to swallow the pill of formal Greek statehood, even in this form. In the interim all the British could do was to strengthen the Mediterranean Fleet as a counter to the ominous build-up of Russian troops along the Danube, while the final extinction of Greek rebellion seemed imminent with the fall of the Athenian Acropolis on 6 June 1827. The remaining garrison there, under the Anglo-Irish soldier Sir Richard Church as Commander-in-Chief, was allowed by Ibrahim to march out with honours of war.

The fall of the Acropolis crystallized the necessity for European intervention to ensure some variant of a 'free' Greece. Scrambling not to be left behind, a resentful and marginalized France adhered to the tripartite Treaty of London (July 1827), authorizing the signatories to interpose their forces if necessary to keep the belligerents apart, and impose an armistice. Such action could only be naval, and that meant it had to be under British leadership. Admiral Sir Edward Codrington, Commander-in-Chief of the Mediterranean Fleet, was instructed to cut off Ibrahim's forces from supplies and reinforcements in Asia Minor and Egypt. He collected his warships in Valletta harbour, the first truly strategic use of Malta by the Royal Navy. On 19 August the Admiral received emergency instructions from Stratford Canning in Constantinople to enforce an armistice in the Morea, 'by cannon-shot if necessary'. Joined by French and Russian squadrons, on 14 October 1827 the fleet arrived off Navarino Bay in the Ionian Sea, where Turco-Egyptian shipping was concentrated. Codrington's force barred Ibrahim's naval commanders from venturing out to combat the Greek privateers harassing them. The burning villages and fields on the mainland – where Ibrahim's troops were reduced to scavenging for food – were plainly visible from the decks. Codrington then took the fateful decision that the approaching winter made sustained blockade impossible, necessitating an immediate entry into Navarino harbour.

The Admiral was insistent that this action was conceived as merely a show of force. But the orders to his captains to anchor close alongside the Ottoman vessels meant that a battle was inevitable. The Royal Navy's patience with the slow grind of policing Ionian neutrality had run its course. The Admiralty wanted a decisive resolution to the Greek affair. When Codrington's twenty-two powerful warships penetrated the harbour, they headed straight for the Turkish ships, and, when a nervous warning shot issued from one of the latter, a series of devastating cannonades were unleashed. Three-quarters of Ibrahim's fleet were sunk, and approximately 4,000 Turco-Egyptian sailors killed (including some French mercenaries). Allied fatalities were 181. It was the last great battle of sail, and passed into naval legend. It also reasserted British strategic leadership in the approaches to the eastern Mediterranean.

Navarino opened the way to Greek statehood, certainly in so far as Ibrahim's army had been the only hope of continuing the Turkish struggle in Greece itself. Yet the battle touches on one of the underlying themes of this book: the effectiveness, but also the constraints, of British navalism in the region. Though the latter could often dictate immediate outcomes, it could not fully control how those outcomes evolved. Ibrahim's army was compelled to evacuate, but its departure had to be overseen by a French force, since Britain did not have the troops to do the job itself. More significantly still, what ultimately broke the Sultan's will over the Greeks was not the naval defeat of Navarino but the land war which the Tsar fought against Turkey during 1828–9, bringing his troops within 40 miles of Constantinople. Under the Treaty of Adrianople (September 1829) not only did the Sultan concede an autonomous Greece, but he conceded key gains to

Russia in the Caucasus. This treaty crucially set many of the terms of the emerging Eastern Question. It was not a question which the British were likely to find easily conformable with their interests.

This explains why on the British side enthusiasm for a new Greek polity soon faded. The Duke of Wellington (who had become Prime Minister on Canning's sudden death in August 1827) had always feared that a 'free' Greece would make British Protection in the adjoining Ionians impossible. He also considered Navarino 'mere humbug' given the enormous disparity of fire-power involved. He disliked the political ramifications even more. When news of the battle reached Constantinople, the allied embassies had immediately been surrounded by military patrols, and their staff had to make an undignified exit. Stratford Canning and his wife walked through the eerie streets at night to a waiting frigate. Measures of protection were also required for Europeans in Muslim Alexandria.[74] Against this background British official attitudes began to shift their position. When Parliament opened in January 1828, the Prime Minister referred to the battle as 'an untoward event'. Subsequently Codrington was recalled, and found an icy welcome waiting for him at home. In the endgame of the Greek Revolution there were two guiding British principles: to ensure that the Ottoman Empire received no further humiliations, and that the new Greece should be as small as possible.

Presentiment that a Greek state would be 'if not wholly under the influence of Russia, then at least sufficiently so to be irrevocably hostile to England' was the nightmare in London.[75] The Government there turned against the idea of 'autonomy' under Ottoman sovereignty, fearing that the reality – as in the Danubian provinces – was likely to be Russian domination. Instead, Wellington insisted on full independence, since an independent but weak Greece would be more susceptible to British naval pressure. As for size, the British premier's preference was that the country should 'comprise nothing north of the Isthmus of Corinth',[76] and he was insistent that Crete should be excluded despite arguments (with which he would have happily concurred) that Greece without that island would remain poor and unstable. The Protocol of Poros (December 1828) established procedures for fixing the frontiers of the new state broadly in line with Wellington's preferences. This process took some time, and Greek independence did not gain a formal European blessing until the Treaty of London (7 May 1832), under which – after a messy 'presidency' under Kapodistrias that was ended by the latter's assassination – a monarchical form of government was prescribed. A Bavarian prince was duly selected for the throne, and King Otto eventually arrived in the Greek capital of Nauplion aboard HMS *Madagascar* on 30 January 1833. The scene of allied squadrons in the harbour and the waving of various flags on the forts strongly suggested that Ottoman sovereignty had been replaced by another form of foreign tutelage.[77] Maintaining that tutelage under primarily British oversight, however, was to prove not at all easy.

The disorders of Greece throughout the 1820s had meant widespread disruption for trade and commerce in the Mediterranean. Constraints on responding to the challenges this brought led the British Government to revoke the old Tudor monopoly of the Levant Company in 1825. Damage to trade stemming from the Greek troubles hurt Malta, where a pattern in which war brought prosperity but peace led to the return of depression was already becoming ingrained. A British resident of Valletta wrote home in 1828 of the rural situation of Malta: 'Figure to yourself crowds of human beings . . . some in a state of absolute nudity, with all the others in rags, pouring in from the country to implore a single morsel of bread . . . No picture of fictitious distress conveys anything like an adequate idea of the real misery of the unfortunate Maltese.'[78]

Maitland's successor, Viscount Hastings,[79] had appointed a committee to assess the extent of misery, but he had little means at his disposal to relieve it, though some help came with the expenditures associated with the Navarino campaign. Migration to North Africa, where the Maltese increasingly filled the interstices between 'native' traders and European merchants, also afforded modest relief. For reasons of culture and pride, migration was not an option for the approximately 2,000 Maltese families in the professional and landed classes. The adult males scrambled for salaried positions, though there were never enough of these to go round. One British resident was able to talk of the 'intense hatred' with which some Maltese regarded the English who appropriated the best jobs.[80] Economic recovery did come gradually. By 1830 there were double the number of vessels calling at Malta than in the plague year of 1813, and the greater use of

Valletta harbour by the Royal Navy during the following decade meant more cash and employment. By 1840, it has been judged, the island was 'a little happier, a little less distressed than the Malta of the two previous decades'.[81] But things were improving only slowly and differentially between classes and groups, and not on a scale sufficient to ward off discontent with British rule.

Material conditions remained better in the Ionian archipelago. They were assisted by the reduction of British domestic tariffs on the import of olives and currants. British consumption of these products rose rapidly, and what became the classic Victorian 'pudding' was often stuffed with Mediterranean, including Ionian, ingredients. During the 1830s Austrian Lloyd steamers included the Ionians on their Levant routes, and the islands – each a world to itself – became linked by government-owned ships. Increasingly an entrepôt for regional commerce, the Ionians ceased to be confined within a 'narrow-sea' Adriatic economy, and instead functioned within a broader British-led trading system.[82] Land reform was too sensitive for any Lord High Commissioner to attempt, and without that the rural economy remained trapped. In 1839 the Ionian Bank (one of the first British 'overseas banks') was set up to improve agricultural credit, but it quickly became remote from poorer farmers, and made profits by lending to an always cash-strapped government. There were signs, however, of a new prosperity. The second Lord High Commissioner, Sir Frederick Adam, built the palace of Mon Repos – later a favourite residence of Greek royalty, and the birthplace of the Duke of Edinburgh – as the country residence for Lord High Commissioners. General Sir Howard Douglas after 1835 oversaw a new prison, a lunatic asylum, a hospital and finally a new commercial exchange in Corfu Town. Through all these innovations the British essentially created a new town.[83] By 1840, however, the economic stimulus deriving from the early phases of British Protection was wearing off.

As we have seen, the mainland Greek troubles during the 1820s meant that British rule in the islands had got off to a rocky political start. Maitland's successors tried to deflect trouble by drawing on the financial reserves left by the parsimonious Scot, creating more jobs for the Ionian elite. But the scope for buying off trouble was limited by the fiscal constraints of government. Douglas diagnosed the underlying problem to be that the Protectorate was 'a sort of middle state between a colony and a perfectly independent country, without in some respects the advantages of either'.[84] In the history of British dependencies, indeed, such hybrids – not full colonies, but not truly self-governing – often proved the most troublesome. Douglas, like other High Commissioners, retreated into reliance on the *camarilla*, a close-knit but already fraying group of Corfiote conservatives attached to the British flag.[85] By the end of the 1830s the British administration faced a movement of *rizapastoi* (radicals), albeit focusing on practical grievances rather than calling openly for union with the Kingdom of Greece. Douglas met this challenge by sporadic imprisonments, banishments of allegedly seditious individuals and prorogations of the Assembly. This did not yet mean that British Protection was doomed. The banquet held when the commercial exchange building was inaugurated in 1841, celebrated by prosperous local merchants, members of the intelligentsia, British traders, the Lord High Commissioner and his Lady, the President of the Assembly and various members of the Italianate nobility, epitomized the polity in its most durable form. But the system this represented always lacked a firm social basis.[86]

Reform politics in Britain itself during the first half of the 1830s largely passed the Ionians by. That this was not true of Malta shows how the island was now more closely related to the metropole. The downturn in military and naval expenditure once the Greek crisis passed, coupled with British refusal to undertake administrative reforms, led to a spate of protests in the early 1830s. In 1836 a Royal Commission, composed of John Austin, an academic lawyer, and George Cornewell Lewis, a political economist, was sent from London to report on the causes and possible solutions. Lewis likened the administration of colonial Malta to Austrian rule in Lombardy, a comparison which at the time was the most scathing comparison imaginable for anyone of a liberal disposition. But as in absolutist Europe, aspiration to reform came cheap; executing it was not so easy. Austin and Lewis enjoyed the 'full tide' of popularity greeting their arrival, acclaimed by crowds as if they came 'with Magna Carta in their pockets',[87] but they were all too aware that their recommendations were bound to be more modest than local expectations hoped.

Lewis's own condescension and caustic cynicism marked the limits of the English progressive imagination under Mediterranean conditions. He commented that the chief spokesman of Maltese protest, George Mitrovich, 'might be bought body and soul for two hundred pounds a year. The people, of course, think him a giant.'[88] Even the practical reforms advised by the Commission after two years' labour, including a tentative start down the road towards a free press and an encouragement of education through the medium of Maltese, were attacked in Westminster. The aged Duke of Wellington, in his most provocative style, remarked that 'we might as well think of planting a free press in the foredeck of the Admiral's flagship, or in the *casernes* of the batteries of Gibraltar . . . as of establishing it in Malta'.[89] Here was the seminal definition of Malta's future as a military fortress under British rule, and in one form or another it was to be repeated many times thereafter.

There was one weak point in these British Mediterranean possessions that showed up early on: interaction between British officialdom and local social hierarchies tended to taper off. When the young and dandyfied Benjamin Disraeli visited Malta in 1830 he remarked that (as in Gibraltar) the British military 'do nothing but play rackets, billiards and cards, race and smoke', while the local Club was as smart and snobbish as anything in Pall Mall.[90] English residents nipped across to Naples on small, fast boats (*speroni*) to attend the San Carlos opera and hobnob with its super-fashionable clientele. When Austin and Lewis came in 1836 they identified English isolation as a harmful trait (though the process worked both ways, since upper-class Maltese, with a patrician Italianism, sometimes looked down on the common and pedestrian English). Austin's wife, Sarah, a noted translator of German literature, tried to remedy this by visiting villages, propagating universal education and inviting Maltese to parties at her residence in the Auberge d'Aragon; one Maltese remarked that Sarah ('la signora commissionaria') was 'a mother to us all'.[91] Much the same process was played out in the Ionians. In Corfu, the racetrack for some while provided a cosmopolitan meeting-point. Sir Frederick Adam married into the Corfiote aristocracy, and similar unions were not unknown. The most sympathetic figure in straddling Anglo-Ionian lines was Lord Guilford (son of the eighteenth-century

Prime Minister Lord North), whose philhellenism extended to dressing like an ancient Greek 'with a gold band around his mad pate and flowering drapes of a purple hue'. Guilford set up the Ionian Academy, the first modern Greek-language university, in the old Venetian Provveditore Generale in Corfu Town, bequeathing its library 10,000 volumes.[92] To improve the quality of university recruitment Guilford encouraged the spread of schools using the economical Lancastrian method of teaching; these spread even to the southernmost Ionian island of Kythera. Sometimes ridiculed in England, Guilford was revered by a generation of Greek men of letters. People like Sarah Austin and Guilford, however, were not the norm in local 'British' society, though there were always to be others, often more obscure but of similar disposition, to blur lines of division.

Just as dangerous as social exclusivity was when the British presence got entangled in a toxic mix of religion, culture and language. The first two proved the most sensitive in the Ionians; the last was not a problem, as in this period Italian was uniformly accepted as the official language of the Protectorate. A watershed was the separation of Ionian Orthodoxy from patriarchal authority in Constantinople in 1833. Subsequently the British tried to institute a control of their own by ensuring senior Church appointees were loyal to the Protection. This led to friction, and in 1834 there was a minor riot when British soldiers were said to have shown disrespect to the revered St Spyridon. During the 1830s the London Missionary Society sent proselytizers to the Islands, often setting up schools of their own. Under the Venetians, the Orthodox Church had been subordinated to Roman Catholicism; its clergy had no intention of letting the Protestants take over under the British. The Colonial Office back in London was only too well aware of the dangers of getting mixed up in religious matters,[93] but they were not so easy to avoid for those actually charged with the government of a society where Church and faith were so central.

English Protestant missionaries to the Ionians came in the first instance from their base in Malta. The latter location was seen as one from which English influence might radiate culturally as well as politically. Lord Bathurst in 1813 had looked forward to 'the Diffusion of the English language among the inhabitants [of Malta] and the promotion of every method by which the English language may be brought to supersede the Italian tongue'.[94] Maitland cannily avoided such matters, and as Mediterranean trade reverted to pre-war patterns, Italian reasserted itself over English in commerce. A Chair of Italian was established at the university, while *italianità* dominated lower schooling under the supervision of the clergy, who despised English as 'a short-cut to Protestantism'.[95] Yet the new reality of Malta made the medium of English a valuable commodity. It was the language of government at the top, if not lower down. The expanding employment linked to the Royal Navy and the British garrison necessitated facility in English, so that its popularity spread among workers while being studiously avoided by Maltese country gentry and a professional middle class. It is quite conceivable that if the usage of English, Italian and indigenous Maltese (which everybody spoke, but which still had no written form) had been left to freely adjust from their separate bastions in law, salon, bank, shipping agency, dockyard and farmyard, a workable equilibrium might have emerged over time. But in 1840 Governor Henry Bouverie introduced a legal code with the ruling that English should henceforth be 'the authoritative text'. Here were the first glimmerings of a struggle over language that was to define a great deal of Maltese politics.

Even at this stage in Malta, then, there were the perceptible outlines of an island caught between the opportunities of a better life that having the British planted in their midst – with their warships, cash and modern ways – brought with them, and the displacements and misunderstandings that were also part of the process. On the one hand there were occasions like nights at the opera house in Valletta ending in a brawl between English and Maltese, the legs allegedly being ripped off the chair in the naval Commander-in-Chief's box as a weapon.[96] On the other hand, there were dignified occasions like that when Queen Adelaide, the widow of William IV, visited Valletta in 1838 to inaugurate the Anglican Cathedral of St Paul's. At this celebration the Catholic Archbishop and representatives of Maltese society attended receptions in her honour, the colourful military parades enjoyed by large, animated and 'loyal' crowds.[97] This was the start of a tie between the island and British royalty that encapsulates the ambivalence of the island's development.

*

A change in the status of Gibraltar was not discussed during the post-Napoleonic settlement. It could be argued that it was a missed opportunity to resolve Anglo-Spanish differences rooted in the Treaty of Utrecht, but this was always unlikely.[98] Britain held Gibraltar 'by long continued hostile possession ... against Spain',[99] and nothing much had changed that reality. Ferdinand VII, restored to his throne in Madrid, was keen to make a gesture as a Spanish patriot. He ordered the reconstruction of the fortifications at the Spanish end of the isthmus, which the British had blown up in 1810 to prevent their use by the French. But this building ceased once the British expressed strong disapproval, and relations between the acting Governor, Sir George Don, and the Spanish Commandant of the surrounding *campo* do not seem to have suffered as a result.[100]

With Spain exhausted after recent struggles, the British were able to recommence their surreptitious advance of Gibraltar's frontier, using when necessary an old legal justification that jurisdiction on the Rock extended within a radius defined by the garrison's artillery. In this way the Neutral Ground between Gibraltar and Spain attained what proved to be its maximum physical extent during the 1820s and 1830s. Endless disputes were to hinge on the exercise of rights within this space. In fact, Sir George Don himself mostly lived on the other side of the frontier, in San Roque, the village where the original inhabitants of the Rock had retired in 1704. Movement to and fro gathered pace, with poor Andalusians seeking employment in Gibraltar. By the end of the 1830s the nucleus of La Linea de la Conceptión (in effect, what was to function as the working-class suburb of Gibraltar) had become visible on the Spanish side. This transition in the character of the land frontier from a barrier to a permeable zone of exchange was to be of fundamental importance in the growth of Gibraltar's development as a civil society in the nineteenth century.[101] The extent of coexistence between the various authorities was shown when in 1828 Gibraltar suffered an epidemic of yellow fever and emergency flour cargoes were sent from Spain, matching aid that had occasionally flowed in the other direction under similar circumstances.[102]

This permeability, however, had a distinctive and not always entirely respectable character. Ferdinand VII's regime instituted a number of customs posts opposite Gibraltar in the hope of securing revenue. One effect was to keep legitimate Spanish trade, lost by Cadiz to Gibraltar during the war years, with the former port. What replaced it was a pervasive and growing contraband trade beyond the reach of Spanish authority. A large proportion of Gibraltar's civilian population of 17,000 in 1830 – including some 1,400 Britons, the rest a medley of Jews, Greeks, Maltese, Spanish, Portuguese and Genoese – depended on the smuggling of such dutiable goods as textiles and tobacco. Domestic Spanish industry was inevitably undermined, later embodied in the grimy Seville cigarette factory featuring in Bizet's opera *Carmen* (the bandits Carmen famously goes off with are smugglers from Gibraltar). Contraband was taken in small boats from the Rock and landed across Algeciras Bay and then inland, often using the old wartime tracks of *guerrilleros*. Ferdinand sent a horde of civil servants to stamp out a network fatal for Spanish revenues, but bribery and the scale of the task ensured failure. So long as Andalusia remained a province of vast underexploited *latifundia*, a black-market economy run from the Rock provided the only feasible livelihood for many on both sides of the frontier.[103] Only the emergence of a different role for Gibraltar as a transit port in the 1840s, as steam passenger liners first began to use its bunkering facilities, altered the balance between legal and illegal occupations that sustained the tiny colony's economy.

This seediness led to rather critical appreciations of Gibraltar by outsiders, and although the nature of the critique has fluctuated over time, it has never altogether disappeared. An English visitor in 1830 found the town so squalid that he thought the only thing to do was to pull it down.[104] Poor sanitation made it even unhealthier than Valletta. Partly for this reason, but also for others, the civilian and military sections lived very much apart. At the outset of the 1820s possible civil unrest within Gibraltar had still been a factor in the garrison's organization.[105] Ten years later this was no longer really the case. A civil police force was established in 1830, the first such institution in Britain's overseas empire, and the Rock became essentially a Crown Colony proper. First and foremost an army bastion, however, it had no prospect of constitutional development. The prevailing tone was no longer quite so rough and tinged with alcoholic excess as it had once been. Officers could use the Garrison Library, still an important feature of Gibraltar's cultural life today, and by 1836 a garrison church, where Sir George Don was buried, had been properly consecrated, giving a stronger focus to Anglican activity in an overwhelmingly Catholic setting.[106] A new equilibrium in the life of the Rock was taking shape.

One symbol of that equilibrium, relating both to garrison ritual and an interaction with the surrounding environment, merits special mention. This was the Calpe Hunt, composed of hounds brought out during the final years of the Napoleonic conflict, and which soon became an exclusively military event.[107] The officers would jog out past the saluting batteries, weaving their way through the packed cosmopolitan streets of Gibraltar, before passing by Government House ('The Convent') and out into the cork woods and olive groves of the surrounding countryside. The local farmers had first allowed these sportsmen in their extravagant uniforms access to their estates as a mark of solidarity in the wake of the struggle against Napoleon, but this practice continued, eased by small subsidies and the fact that Spanish army officers also sometimes took part. The 'meets' were always advertised in the messes of the Spanish garrisons at Algeciras and San Roque, the local military governor being only too pleased to permit his officers a diversion from the boredom of garrison life, even if it enraged politicians in Madrid. Their British counterparts had to be back in Gibraltar by the sunset gun, but this usually allowed a meal to be enjoyed with a landlord's family and neighbours along the route. The Calpe Hunt captured in cameo an Anglo-Spanish social world, encapsulating the ways in which a British, but always very diverse, Gibraltar adapted to its special circumstances.

There was one major change in the western Mediterranean during these years: the seizure of Algiers by France in 1830. France after 1815 remained conscious that any new eastward movement in the Mediterranean had Napoleonic overtones and was likely to trigger intervention by Great Britain. But such a reaction was less likely if a measured French expansion took place in the west and not unduly close to the Strait of Gibraltar. An alleged insult to the French consul in Algiers by one of the Dey's officials provided a suitable pretext. An expedition was assembled in Toulon during early 1830, and on 25 May a force of 350 vessels and 35,000 troops set off for North Africa. A British naval patrol dashed from Malta to check on it. But the French had been careful that this expedition was in no sense a battle fleet, but rather a collection of troopships.[108] The British did nothing to stop its progress, and by 5 July the Dey capitulated to the French force put ashore. The Bourbon flag, the fleur-de-lys, was hoisted over the Casbah. The lowered standard of the Dey is still displayed in the Victor Hugo Museum in Paris.

Charles X was not a beneficiary, since later that month he was deposed in a revolution by the chief of the Orléans clan, Louis Philippe. Yet French troops were not recalled from Algiers. A European power in North Africa marked a fresh departure, and one that Lord Palmerston, Foreign Secretary in the Whig government following the foundering of Wellington's Tory ministry, soon regretted having tolerated. For Palmerston, what mattered now was that the French did not expand outside the frontiers of Algeria; any movement into Morocco, for example, would have had implications for Gibraltar. In fact, there was little risk of this for many years, since the French writ at first scarcely extended beyond Algiers itself. More than 100,000 French troops were engaged in the pacification of the territory by the end of the 1830s. Such an absorption of French resources helps to explain why, despite the gradual renewal of Anglo-French rivalry in the Mediterranean and elsewhere, a confrontation between them was avoided. But that Palmerston's long if sporadically interrupted incumbency at the helm of British foreign policy started with a setback in the Mediterranean helps to explain his sustained preoccupation with the balance of power in that region.

Indeed, Palmerston's anxiety that Britain's position remained fragile was underlined by uncertainty over Spain's future. After October 1833 a bitter struggle in that country broke out between the Queen Regent, Maria Christina, and her rival, the reactionary and absolutist Don Carlos.[109] An opportunity of 'helping the Spanish people to drive out a priest-blighted despotism' fitted with Palmerston's as yet tentative credo of liberal intervention.[110] On this issue the British and the French, whose shared liberalism marked them off from the conservative powers in Europe, were theoretically on the same side, though King Louis Philippe let supplies leak across the Pyrenees to the Carlists to keep the struggle going, albeit feebly. Palmerston would have liked to suppress the conflict by sending an expedition of his own, arguing that his aim was not an Austrian (that is, Habsburg–Bourbon) Spain or a French Spain, but a Spanish Spain; though by this he really meant a Spain with an English tint.[111] There was no way, however, that such an expensive measure could be got through a penny-pinching Parliament. Palmerston did, however, manage to secure the suspension of the Foreign Enlistment Act in June 1835 to allow the dispatch of a volunteer force. The British Legion was 10,000 strong, composed mostly of unemployed soldiers, many of them Irish (a comparable profile to philhellenic recruits in the Greek Revolution). British opinion, including Palmerston and soon the newly enthroned Queen Victoria, thereafter waited for news of the Legion with baited breath.[112]

The Legion had a bumpy experience. Members falling into Carlist hands were often executed on grounds that they were not covered by the Convention (July 1835) brokered by British intermediaries that set constraints on a vicious conflict. This agreement had some importance in the evolution of the laws of war. Critics of the Legion, often Tories with Carlist sympathies, painted a picture of a shambling militia, accompanied by 800 baggage mules and 500 prostitutes, and not actually fighting anybody.[113] As in the 1930s, so a century earlier Spain provided a laboratory within which British ideological divisions played themselves out. Predictably, British intervention did not always prove welcome even to those it was intended to help. An early historian of the Legion remarked that 'there was always a coldness, a jealousy and an injustice on the part of successive governments in Madrid' towards the force.[114] It was finally dissolved in May 1837, having suffered more than 460 fatalities. Meanwhile the Royal Navy was busy maintaining the Queen Regent's authority along the coasts, and British naval pressure helped finally bring about the end of the conflict by the Convention of Bergara (August 1839). By then Palmerston had not been able (in the words of the British Ambassador in Madrid) to 'Portugalize' Spain, meaning bring it under preponderant guidance from London;[115] and when Queen Christina eventually gave up and went into exile, taking a large part of the Madrid treasury with her, she chose to go to France. Nevertheless, Palmerston ensured that the tenuous Spanish compromise that emerged was one not positively hostile to England. This met what was always the essential British requirement with regard to Spain.

It was in the Near East, however, that Palmerston's determination to keep regional affairs from slipping out of control met its most powerful challenge. After Egyptian troops had been evacuated from Greece during 1828, the British had wondered where Mehmet Ali, always restless, might seek to recoup his losses. It was known he was spending vast sums on armaments. When Mehmet finally struck, it was north into Ottoman Syria and deep into Asia Minor against his own nominal suzerain, the Sultan Mahmud. His army defeated the Turks at the Battle of Konieh on 21 December 1832. This threatened a major redrawing of Mediterranean boundaries. Yet when the Sultan appealed to Great Britain for support, Palmerston could not persuade his Cabinet colleagues to act. Mehmet Ali chose his moment carefully. The British Fleet was numerically depleted; reform politics at home had gone hand in hand with reduced expenditure on the army and navy. There was also a sizeable body of opinion, including a ring of British merchant houses in Cairo and Alexandria, who thought Great Britain should side with the Pasha against the Sultan on the grounds that the former represented the better bet for the future.[116] Frustrated, the Sultan turned to Russia, and the price of the latter's help was the Treaty of Unkiar Skelessi (8 July 1833). This laid down a 'shadow' Russian protectorate over Turkey. As such, it was the biggest diplomatic defeat Palmerston ever incurred, and he vowed never again to be caught out in the same way.

Behind this defeat lay what had been a key Russo-Turkish understanding: in peacetime no foreign warship was in future to be allowed to pass through the Dardanelles. Whoever controlled the Straits could bar any rival coming down from the north, or entering from the south.[117] This was what made Constantinople in the eyes of many strategists then and later the first strategic position in the world. Russian leverage there now meant that her fleets would be able to dash into the Mediterranean and inflict punishment on an enemy, and get back again to total safety before anybody could react. Unkiar Skelessi therefore mortgaged the eastern Mediterranean to Russian power.

From the moment of its signature Palmerston settled on its reversal as the touchstone of his foreign policy. To do this the Sultan had to be weaned from Russia and provided with incontrovertible proof that Great Britain was 'a safer and more acceptable shield' against the Egyptians. This was the paradox of Mahmud II: defeated even within the Ottoman realm, he still made himself the arbiter of Great Power rivalry, and drew the British onto his side as a means of reducing his dependence on Russia. For Palmerston, Mehmet Ali, as the Sultan's chastiser, became an obsession. 'For my part, I hate Mehmet Ali,' Palmerston remarked, and the force of this emotion puts it in a long tradition of British leaders' monomaniac preoccupations with eastern potentates, framed in their minds purely as threats to British interests and therefore international peace.[118]

Diplomacy alone, however, was not likely to see Mehmet Ali put back in his place. A Navarino-like exercise in naval power was bound to be called for sooner or later. King William IV (the 'Sailor King') had for some time pressed his government to pile British warships into the region, and after 1834 Palmerston added his weight. The Mediterranean Fleet was progressively reinforced and kept in a constant state of readiness. It was in and out of Valletta harbour with unprecedented frequency. Work got under way to improve and expand Malta's dockyard facilities. The numbers of British naval personnel there rose sharply. The island became a more important place for another reason. In the pre-telegraph age, the British Fleet in an emergency would be reduced to impotence if it had to await instructions from London before it could even begin to move. Speed and decisiveness were essential. The British Government therefore reluctantly gave joint contingent powers – the 'last trump of whist', as it was called[119] – to Ambassador Ponsonby at Constantinople and the Commander-in-Chief of the Mediterranean Fleet in Valletta to send British warships rushing to the Dardanelles if the necessity arose. This meant that events of potentially immense cost to Britain – involving huge sums of money and perhaps many lives – might in effect be triggered, not from Downing Street, but from the embassy in Constantinople and naval headquarters in South Street, Valletta. It was this political power inherent in British naval leadership in the Mediterranean which helped to set it apart for much of the nineteenth century.

For five years after Unkiar Skelessi these tendencies in the Levant took shape under an armed peace on all sides. The British fretted anxiously about the reliability of the Sultan, Mehmet Ali's intentions, his connections with the French, as well as recurrent Russian naval manoeuvres. Ponsonby's role in Constantinople was to ensure that the floundering Sultan was kept up to the mark, and did not try to cut a separate deal with Mehmet Ali. Finally, in June 1838 Mehmet dispatched his armies into Asia Minor once more. The Egyptian ruler knew very well that he was pitting himself into a decisive struggle in which British sea power would be highly dangerous to him. In all probability, he calculated that time was against him, and that it was better to gamble while he still had a chance. On 24 June 1839 the Egyptians defeated the Ottomans again at the Battle of Nezib. Almost simultaneously the Turkish fleet defected by sailing to Alexandria, and on 1 July 1839 Mahmud died. Turkey had lost a battle, an army, a fleet and a Sultan more or less simultaneously. It was a moment in which the configuration of power in the eastern Mediterranean hung in the balance.

Palmerston's actions to assert Britain's regional position became the classic exposition of his methods. When the crisis first erupted, the British fleet under Admiral Sir Robert Stopford and its French counterpart were both sent by their governments rushing towards the Dardanelles. At that point the general expectation in the British squadron was that the joint Anglo-French force would smash their common Russian rival.[120] The aims of the ministry in Paris led by Adolphe Thiers are essential in evaluating Palmerston's subsequent coup. There is no evidence that Thiers and his colleagues were scheming to bring about an Egyptian triumph over the Ottomans under their own patronage.[121] What Thiers did hope to achieve, however, was a collective European settlement in which French leverage was maximized through their capacity to mediate with Cairo. But French mediation as the key to stabilizing the Levant was one thing that Palmerston wanted to avoid. He needed a triumph, not a negotiation. Far from taking the opportunity to smash the Russians, Palmerston therefore did a somersault and went into diplomatic harness with them, rushing through a Four Power Convention on 15 July 1840 that laid out humiliating terms for Mehmet Ali. France was left abandoned on the sidelines. The containment of French power was essential to Palmerston's Mediterranean vision, and circumstances had arisen in which this could be decisively imposed. Russia – bigger fry altogether – could be left to another time.

Stopford's squadron, including Austrian and Turkish as well as British warships, was meanwhile dispatched to the Syrian coast to carry out a naval attack against the Egyptian occupation. Palmerston was careful to defend this operation by saying it was conducted in the name of the new Sultan, Abdulmecid I, though this was open to allegations of hypocrisy in Europe. On 9 September 1840 Beirut was bombarded, and Sidon shortly afterwards. Stopford was able to pin down Mehmet Ali's troops on the coast, interrupt their supplies, and reduce them to impotence by continual harassment. Such a demonstration of the Royal Navy's ability to disrupt almost any military activity subject to British disapproval would be one of the defining features of its Mediterranean prestige. The climax came when Stopford was ordered to reduce Acre, a resonant name in the ears of the British public because of its association with Napoleonic campaigns. Eight ships of the line pounded the town during the afternoon of 3 November for three hours. Eventually the powder magazine in the fort exploded. The tremor was so great that even the British ships were shaken to their keels. Twelve hundred died under the rubble. A British eyewitness stated afterwards: 'The town and walls [of Acre] present a mass of ruin beyond conception; but what place could withstand the fire of more than 400 cannon, directed with a precision and rapidity unknown in any former warfare?'[122]

HMS *Charlotte* delivered 4,500 32-pound cannonballs. British losses were light: eighteen killed and forty-one wounded. The reduction of Acre has been described as 'the high water mark of naval gunnery during the age of sail'.[123] It served as a crushing example to those in Europe who doubted Britain's preparedness to act against those who threatened Mediterranean stability *à l'anglaise*. The lesson struck home in Paris, with a hard-pressed army in Algeria whose supply was at risk if the British ever chose to cut it. The Thiers ministry fell after a tempestuous debate in the Chamber, in which he was attacked for having put France dangerously at odds once again with other Great Powers. In London, even those Cabinet colleagues who had jibbed at being pulled along in Palmerston's wake fell in behind him.

But, as so often in demonstrations of invincibility, a close examination indicates more nuanced realities. British warships might intimidate towns and forts ashore, and even destroy them as technology improved, but could they hold them for any length of time? And could their projection of power be sustained behind as well as along extended coastlines? During the Syrian war British marines had been put ashore at Beirut, but after only a few days they had to be taken off in a state of some confusion.[124] Palmerston dispatched Stopford's deputy, Commodore Charles Napier, to Alexandria, where the local population panicked that the town 'was about to be beaten about their ears'.[125] Yet Alexandria's defences were not so flimsy as those of Acre. Napier went ashore, and like others before him, fell under Mehmet Ali's charm before deciding to sail off. Simultaneously the main British fleet was driven away from the Syrian coast by stormy weather. If Mehmet had wanted to, he could have reoccupied much of the area. Instead he left Syria and Lebanon to their troubles, and evacuated his troops back to Egypt. Acre nonetheless left an indelible impression, and – along with the assault on Algiers in 1816 – was later to be quoted as a precedent for forceful naval action against the Crimean fortress of Sevastopol. A good few lives were to be wasted as a consequence.[126]

Yet for now Palmerston was in a diplomatic position to enforce his will. The French Government had little choice but to participate in a Near Eastern concert on British terms. Those terms were inevitably harsh on Mehmet Ali. The 'three wretched Pashaliks', as Thiers termed the Syrian provinces, were restored to the Sultan. Palmerston insisted that Crete, under Egyptian administration for some years during which it had thrived, be returned to Ottoman rule (after which it certainly did not).[127] The coping stone of the Near Eastern settlement was the Straits Convention (13 July 1841). One of the foundations of the nineteenth-century international order, this agreement denied passage through the Straits to all foreign warships during peacetime. It therefore guaranteed Russia against foreign navies battering their way through the Dardanelles. But equally, Tsar Nicholas gave up the 'right of attack' in the Mediterranean.[128] The Ottoman Empire was not to be an exclusive Russian protectorate, but came under the collective oversight of the Great Powers, and the outcome of the crisis strongly suggested that the centre of gravity of that supervision would be in London. Finally, Palmerston remained adamant that in an emergency the Sultan had the right to summon the British Fleet to Constantinople, even though others saw this as patently against the letter and spirit of the Convention.

The settlement over the Straits marked Palmerston's greatest overseas triumph, just as Unkiar Skelessi had been his biggest defeat. It slotted into place a vital component of Britain's preponderance in the Mediterranean. Henceforth Great Britain could to a large degree control entrance into and exit from the Mediterranean at both ends, that is, through the Strait of Gibraltar and at the Dardanelles (hence the common metaphor of a ' British Lake'). Malta provided a central base from which the Royal Navy could move quickly in any direction. Italy still remained subject to a friendly power in Austria. Spain had been at least partially 'Portugalized'. French dreams of Mediterranean revival had been scuppered in the east, and carefully regulated in the west. In reducing Mehmet Ali to his Egyptian patrimony, the British had seen off what a historian still writing in the age of empire called 'the last oriental attempt to found a power on the shores of the Mediterranean'.[129] It was true that British maritime reach had its limits. But Palmerston, despite his natural belligerence, was never interested in territorial gain, and had a realistic grasp of diplomacy as the art of the possible. He typically said of the Italian disturbances, for example, that 'what he tried to do was to make sure that each side took British opposition into account so as to reinforce the desire for general peace'.[130] This 'general peace', of course, was to have a strongly British imprint. Britain's Mediterranean mastery depended on its acceptability to others, and on not pressing its claims too far. In pursuing this modus operandi the British did not make themselves loved in the Mediterranean, or in Europe generally, but it made them respected and above all heeded in the things that really mattered to them.

By 1841, then, a durable equilibrium had come into being in the Mediterranean, incorporating a much more confident and stable British presence than in 1815. This presence was subtle and pervasive, underpinned by an expanding British trade with southern Europe.

It was policed from Gibraltar, Malta and (to a somewhat lesser extent) Corfu. These were no longer depots of fluctuating safety as they had still been at the end of the long wars against France, but rather imperial fortresses. The established principle had emerged that the garrisons lodged in these strongpoints should not be less than 2,500 in Gibraltar, 3,000 in Malta and 3,000 in the Ionian Islands. In 1840 there were 9,000 regular British troops stationed in the Mediterranean, or 20 per cent of all British forces serving overseas.[131] These places were never quite as strategically indispensable or as impregnable as the British public supposed, but the imagery itself was influential in shaping conceptions of the Mediterranean and Britain's place in it.

During 1830, on the trip to the Mediterranean that helped shape his exotic political imagination, the youthful Disraeli wrote how he revelled in the 'increased activity and vitality and expansion of my blood' engendered by such an intoxicating experience.[132] A decade later improving communications and spreading wealth meant that a new and more varied generation of British visitors were arriving on shiny new steamers in Gibraltar, Trieste or Brindisi, carrying the ubiquitous Murray *Handbooks*, those British bibles of Mediterranean travel. In the mid-Victorian age the centrality of the Mediterranean and its shores to the British world-view was to become even more pronounced. But the societies in the region were themselves experiencing an increased activity and vitality, including in their politics, and this transformational energy was to confront Britain with challenge after challenge.

# 3
# The British *Pax* in the Mediterranean, 1841–1878

The public gaze of early and mid-Victorian Britain came to be progressively fixed overseas. The pre-eminent historian of that culture, G. M. Young, remarked: 'the soldier, the emigrant, and the explorer, the plots of Napoleon III and the redshirt of Garibaldi take and fill the imagination.'[1] That Young's list veered towards the Mediterranean was appropriate, since much of Britain's influence and activity came to be exercised there. The visit of Garibaldi, the Italian revolutionary hero, to London in 1864 was one of the great events of the age, the vast crowds who welcomed him presaging a new era of movement in British politics that would culminate in the age of electoral democracy introduced by the Second Reform Act of 1867.[2] The post-Crimea era, too, was one in which Great Britain's limited leverage over continental issues was becoming plain. A senior minister described her as 'a spectator of events' during the crisis over the fate of the Duchies of Schleswig and Holstein, when, much as Palmerston wished to meet a treaty obligation to Denmark when attacked by Austria and Prussia in February 1864, no practical means existed to bring pressure to bear on the German powers.[3] This humiliation highlighted the Mediterranean as a better prospect for effective British intervention because there the Royal Navy was in its element. Yet these years also witnessed grave instability within the Mediterranean state system itself. Whether British preponderance would be able to survive the resulting turbulence was by no means clear.

British fears of French plots remained constant after 1841. Neither Louis Philippe nor his supplanter, Napoleon III, had any real intention of sliding into outright confrontation with the British, but it was still axiomatic that France should retain sufficient naval power to threaten a *guerre de course* – that is, a policy of targeted disruption – in Mediterranean waters.[4] Conversely, British policy-makers debated whether their purposes were best met by maintaining a rough par there between their own Fleet and the French marine, or whether a significant margin of safety was required. Successive panics as to the insidious successes of French diplomacy were the natural accompaniment. 'In Greece,' Admiral Sir William Parker, Mediterranean Commander-in-Chief, wrote to a correspondent in Beirut in late 1846, 'France has established her ascendancy. In Egypt the same. She is fast advancing at Tripoli and Tunis, and now in Spain also.'[5] Perceptions of 'plots' worked both ways, so that the French believed that Abd-el-Kader, the Islamic warlord resisting pacification in Algeria, was supplied with guns by merchants from Gibraltar.[6] On most Mediterranean questions Britain and France had a looking-glass perception of the other's triumphs and strategic goals.

The uncertainties of technological change fed this rivalry. Because the initial generation of steamships could not yet challenge sail on the long Cape route, innovation was principally tested on shorter Mediterranean journeys carrying growing trade volumes.[7] But French steam packets retained a virtual monopoly well into the 1840s. Only subsequently did the Peninsula and Oriental come to compete with the Marseilles-based Compagnie des Services Maritimes des Messageries Impériale, most effectively on luxury steam travel to Egypt. The P&O ship *Oriental* was equipped with the cold showers, ice houses, wine cellar and bakery required by Mr Thomas Cook's increasingly discerning customers.[8] It took even longer for steam to transform fighting navies. The Admiralty in London clung to sail as a tested medium of British skills; 'the introduction of steam', one of its commissions asserted after a visit to Malta, 'is calculated to strike a vital blow to the naval supremacy of the British Empire.'[9] Steam vessels played a vital role in Royal Navy operations during the Crimean War, but fighting ships were still under canvas; only the experience of that conflict provided the stimulus for an ironclad, propeller-driven, all-steam Fleet in the Mediterranean. The construction of such a fleet in the 1860s finally confirmed that steam had in fact clinched, not undermined, Britain's Mediterranean power.[10]

Greece provided a leading venue for Anglo-French jostling from the early 1840s. This was convenient, since war was never likely to arise while diplomatic points could be notched up by one side or the other. Simultaneously, however, the British began to learn the lesson that there was a price to pay for preponderance. Because English merchants were most prominent in the foreign trade of Greece, more disputes and therefore more friction arose.[11] In Athens (that still small and dusty town having replaced Nauplion as the country's capital), it sometimes seemed that whereas other European powers wanted *influence*, the British expected *domination*.[12] The British Ambassador in Greece, Admiral Sir Edmund Lyons, epitomized the sort of raw swagger we have already noted in Sir Thomas Maitland's rule over Mediterranean islands. Lyons, a naval hero of the war against Napoleon whose promotions were said to owe something to a noted physical resemblance to Nelson, acted as if King Otto of Greece and his ministers were at the beck and call of his embassy. There soon arose a personal feud between Lyons and the King, so that the Admiral's reports from Greece 'read simply as accounts of pillage, murder, and persecution under his [King Otto's] tyrannical regime'.[13] But behind the denigration lay something more. King Otto, in Palmerston's mind and that of his local agents like Lyons, became the symbol of resistance to the advance of a liberal and moderate political civilization for which England offered the true exemplar. Disseminating and occasionally imposing these values became central to Palmerstonian politics in the Mediterranean.

What precise role, if any, English instigation played in the Greek Revolution of 1843 is unclear, though the leader of the 'English party', and veteran of the 1820s insurrection, Sir Richard Church, took the insurgents' demands to the Royal Palace. The pro-British and avowedly 'moderate' politician Alexandros Mavrocordatos was rushed from Constantinople back to Athens in a British warship to guide developments. But these events provided a perturbing example of how Mediterranean revolutions were no easier to nudge in the right direction than they had ever been. The man who came out on top of the Greek struggle was Ioannis Kolettis, who had a noted sympathy for France. Kolettis presided over the unveiling of a dangerously 'advanced' constitution and a new foreign policy, the latter incorporating ideas of a 'Greater Greece' at odds with the settlement of 1830–32.

Much of this was shadow-play. Beneath the hubbub, Greek politics was reducing its dependence on competing foreign sponsors, though its vulnerability to outside interference always remained. Yet for Palmerston Greece emerged in the 1840s, as Spain had done in the 1830s, as a key measure of Britain's position, though with a cruder edge. Stratford Canning in the Ottoman capital mused that one day 'a knife will walk into Otto and Kolettis'.[14] In fact Kolettis did die suddenly in September 1847, though Canning lamented that it came 'too late to check the progress of evil in Greece'. Otto remained the obstacle, and it was with a view to removing the King, or at least reducing him to compliance, that evidence was collected on a range of issues to be used at some point as the pretext for intervention – unless, as many expected, a knife walked into him first. This process was to frame one of the defining political episodes in mid-Victorian Britain.

Meanwhile the revolution in Athens tipped the odds against being able to keep Protection in the Ionian Islands running on the old Maitland lines. Wellington, who knew a good deal about how Mediterranean politics worked, believed that once an independent Greek state came into being on the mainland, that Protectorate – with its Hellenic identity and loyalties – would sooner or later be ungovernable by the British. It was the advent of constitutionalism in Greece after 1843, however, which brought this closer. Lord Seaton had arrived as a new Lord High Commissioner just months before. Seaton's experience of the Mediterranean also went back to the great war against France; and just as Sir Edmund Lyons was likened to Nelson, Seaton was widely compared by contemporaries to Wellington as the 'beau ideal of the English gentleman' allied to a keen political judgement. But whereas Wellington ended up a crusty Tory, turbulent colonial experience – he had just put down a revolt by French-Canadians – made Seaton into what he called a 'reasonable conservative'.[15] Seaton elaborated on this by saying that he could boast of being a conservative in every country 'where there are institutions worth preserving'. Quite how soon he came to the conclusion that this was not the case in the Ionian Islands remains unclear. For five years Seaton muddled along by reducing, if he could not wholly abolish, reliance on what he contemptuously termed methods of 'Austrian espionage', and by giving more senior jobs to Ionians (increasing numbers of whom were streaming back from universities in France and Italy).[16] He encouraged municipal self-government and built public works through deficit financing frowned upon by London – the latter tendency always a ploy of British rulers under pressure in the Mediterranean.

The moment of truth in the Islands as elsewhere came with the revolution in France in February 1848. The Orleanist throne imploded and after a brief interregnum a Napoleon came again into power in Paris. It rocked Europe, and indeed was the precursor of a revolutionary 'springtime of peoples'. Its full force was felt in north-central Europe, but the effects radiated out to the southern margins of the continent. Guiding and shaping this instability when it erupted in and around Britain's Mediterranean sphere was to be a critical challenge.

More than either Gibraltar or even Malta, Ionian politics were closely interwoven with European politics. Seaton's job was to stay in the saddle during what seemed likely to be tumultuous times. As a soldier himself, he could have decided, with a garrison of 3,000 troops at his disposal and the ability to call upon the British Mediterranean Fleet, to stick to the tried and tested ways of the Maitland system. This is what some senior Protectorate officials wanted him to do. Instead in a 'bold stroke of policy', he advocated freedom of the press, the control of extraordinary expenditure by the Ionian Assembly, and finally a simplified and enlarged electorate.[17] Ministers in London might have dismissed the Lord High Commissioner's call for change. But they, too, had become increasingly irritated by Ionian problems. It was embarrassing for them to advocate England as a model for European governance, only to elicit sneers in Paris, Vienna or St Petersburg that the Ionian Protectorate was a dressed-up despotism belying all their claims to superiority. Seaton's programme got the go-ahead. 'On 1 May 1849,' a discontented British official afterwards characterized the change, 'the Lord High Commissioner had more power than Queen Elizabeth; on 10 May he was left with less than Queen Victoria.'[18] This was a gross exaggeration. But Seaton's volte-face still bears an uncanny resemblance to the 'leap in the dark' that Disraeli made in British politics nearly twenty years later when ramming home political reform. Seaton's motives, like Disraeli's, however, were good Tory ones; that is, not to sink a system – not, in this case, to find a way to end Protection – but to explore a fresh basis for its survival.

Seaton's risky experiment, however, was fatally wounded by insurrection, though the challenge had to be faced by his successor, Sir John Ward. During August 1849 a brief but intense jacquerie brought chaos to Cephalonia. Gentry with close English connections had to scramble onto boats for safety in Corfu. Troops took six weeks to restore order, assisted by martial law. Twenty-one found guilty of violent acts were executed. Somewhat belatedly, a squadron under Admiral Parker as Commander-in-Chief of the Mediterranean Fleet arrived on the scene. The Fleet always had a calming, or at least a cowing, effect on disturbed populations. Whether or not Parker's marines put ashore used the infamous 'cat-o'-nine-tails' – for some years banned in the Royal Navy – to administer floggings was a matter raised in the House of Commons (the answer remained unclear).[19] The debate indicated, however, that Ionian problems had become morally and politically sensitive in Britain, as issues relating to Greek-speaking populations often did. The degree to which the Victorian ruling class was itself steeped in conceptions of ancient Greek civilization had something to do with this.[20]

The causes of the Cephalonian rebellion were hotly debated. Peasant violence had been directed at the landlords (the *signori*) as well as the British. What was undeniable was that the insurgents sported emblems of Hellenic nationalism: the Christian Cross and the Greek flag. Whatever hope Protectorate officials retained that Ionians could ever be made 'loyal' took a hit; as Sir John Ward said in implicit criticism of his predecessor's reform, there were 'no English habits, objects or symptoms to appeal to'.[21] Reformism now disappeared. Henceforth the Assembly was repeatedly prorogued, the 'Senate' was packed with cronies, and corruption became more endemic than ever. These were Austrian-style tactics; but then amid upheaval in Europe typically Austrian solutions – a firm reimposition of the status quo – had their attraction. Even a liberally inclined Colonial Secretary in Whitehall, Lord Grey, thought it best to 'let Ward play out the game in his own way' in the Ionians. By the early 1850s the legitimacy of British Protection, and the political support it could garner in London, was visibly slipping.

It was one thing for the British Government to face crises at either end of the Mediterranean in, say, Greece or Spain and their immediate environs. When trouble spread to the central Mediterranean – the middle parts of the Middle Sea – the issues became very serious. This above all meant Italy, where the original Napoleon had caused such havoc. Parker's fleet rushed to Sicily, still under the rule of Bourbon Naples, when the outbursts in Europe got under way during early 1848. Our 'good shire', as the Admiral referred to Sicily, echoing the lordship of a Sicilian shire once conferred on Nelson, was on the verge of complete chaos.[22] In assessing the instability he found ashore, Parker speculated that Sicily would be either 'a republic or a British province in a fortnight'. If the island had begun a final slide into a radical republic – as happened subsequently in Milan, Venice and Rome – an occupation like that after 1806 might have occurred. But Palmerston, no more than Castlereagh earlier, did not actually want to rule Sicily. What mattered was to stop it becoming republican, anti-English or pro-French (and possibly all three at once). Parker was therefore under clear instructions to remain above local struggles, encouraging 'the blessings of a free constitution established if possible by legitimate means'. This was a clearly intentional echo of the defunct but never forgotten 'English constitution' in Sicily of 1812. Whether such shibboleths, with their resonances of Britain's experience in 1688, could have relevance for Italian states fractured by social, religious and national enmity lay at the heart of ambivalent British responses to the 'springtime' of 1848–9.

Events testified to Great Britain's special role in Mediterranean politics. Contending Italian factions vied for British patronage, and sought to predict Britain's actions. This became more pronounced the further south one went and the closer to the sea. In such brittle conditions the mere appearance of a British warship might intensify existing conflicts by arousing expectations among those who thought it would tell in their favour – expectations that Parker was keenly aware he might only disappoint.[23] This was true in Italian states under Austrian rule, but again had particular relevance in Bourbon Sicily, where the rebel forces (designating themselves a 'provisional government') strove to avoid having to negotiate with the Viceroy from Naples. Parker was furious when naval officers from his squadron went ashore in Palermo with revolutionary tricolours tucked into their waistbands. He insisted that any signs of sympathy be abandoned. Mediterranean questions aroused deep and contrary feelings among the British themselves, some favouring republican liberty, others the continuance of the order symbolized by the Habsburgs and the Bourbons. Meanwhile Parker hoped to avoid the moment when he might have to 'deceive' (or disappoint) Sicilian revolutionists, desperately clinging to the memory of Lord William Bentinck as the embodiment of liberal and English salvation from absolutist oppression.

On the wider Italian scene, Palmerston's goal at the head of British foreign policy was to avoid a general war. This remained the abiding English interest in the Mediterranean. The widespread feeling that Palmerston was playing the Austrian game was by no means fair.[24] Such accusations were the inevitable result of his seeking to mediate between Austria and the monarchy of Piedmont rather than simply supporting the latter in its self-declared role of incubator of a new national order. Yet mediation provided the pause during which Austria could ready its forces for a decisive blow. These forces, under the redoubtable General Radetzky, went on the offensive, defeating the Piedmontese at Custozza during July 1848, and again decisively at the Battle of Novara in March of the following year.

Habsburg victories in the north were matched by Bourbon revival in the south. In Sicily, the increasingly beleaguered insurgents sought to activate Parker's help by signalling their loyalty to the British connection. But the Admiral stood by, and continued to do so when King Ferdinand, freed from fear of disorder in Naples itself, dispatched an expedition of 20,000 troops to the island in September 1848. A ferocious bombardment began on Messina (earning the King his lasting pejorative nickname among European, including British, liberals of 'Bomba'). HMS *Gladiator* took off 1,500 frightened women and children from the shore. Even pleas from the *Gladiator*'s captain, however, did not persuade Parker to impose an armistice; a ceasefire only came on 8 October after the commander of the French squadron in the vicinity, Admiral Baudain, warned that he might act alone.[25] An uneasy calm held into the New Year, but in March 1849 Ferdinand ordered a fresh offensive. Catania was razed, and Neapolitan forces advanced towards Palermo, leaving burning villages in their wake. To save the capital from the fate of other towns, the rebels finally capitulated, at which point Parker allowed some of their leaders to avoid execution by scrambling aboard the British warships.

Variants of the climax of 1849 were played out in the other revolutionary republics on the Italian mainland; and if the British were not always so closely engaged as in Sicily, they could not avoid involvement and the compromises this led to. Rome was the pivot, its radical government led by Giuseppe Mazzini ruthlessly crushed when Louis Napoleon sent an army under General Oudinot to restore papal authority, and, crucially, win favour for his new regime in Paris among French clerics.[26] Oudinot purged any Roman rebel he could lay hands on. Around 500, including Mazzini, were said by some to owe their escape to the British Consul, Mr Freeborn, who handed out emergency visas.[27] This earned Freeborn a rebuke from Palmerston.[28] There was, as Palmerston knew, a sizeable slice of British opinion which would have been happy to hear that Mazzini had ended up in front of a French firing-squad; and afterwards Mazzini himself, despite the years of his subsequent exile in London and love of English ways, could never quite 'reconcile the irreconcilable: Anglophilia and revolutionary zeal'.[29] Yet whatever the evasions of the British in 1849, they had not – like the French in Rome – come down decisively on the side of order and reaction; and later on many English progressives came to see the Roman Republic as the precursor of Britain's own emergence as a mass democracy.[30] The events of the revolutionary drama and its apparent nemesis, indeed, when suitably airbrushed over the next few years, 'left Englishmen the only notable defenders of civil liberty surviving in Europe'.[31] William Gladstone's celebrated pamphlet in 1850 attacking prosecutions and prisons in Naples (his scathing description of Bourbon rule as 'the negation of God erected into a system of Government' resounded throughout the Continent) marked the consolidation of a constitutional and liberal distinctness fundamental to British national identity.[32] This 'distinctness' had become defined, in part, by the impact of Mediterranean events.

Another underlying shift concerned Anglo-French relations. Early on in the crisis a clash between the two sides had been feared. The Admiralty ordered the Mediterranean Fleet to concentrate and 'look to Malta', now the instinctive response to any spike in regional tension. As the drama unfolded, and navies dashed from one hotspot to another, there was the possibility of a chance misunderstanding between British and French commanders escalating. Yet the opposite happened. The respective Admirals found themselves co-operating, as they eventually did over the shaky Sicilian armistice. Whatever differences lay between London and Paris, the sheer scale of disruption in Europe emphasized the shared interests of the two liberal powers, however inconsistent their rather different forms of liberalism might be. Above all, this unexpected congruence was becoming defined by a rejuvenated suspicion of Russia. During the spring of 1848 Stratford Canning had initiated a series of warnings from Constantinople on the Russian naval build-up in the Black Sea.[33] Fearing a new Russian descent on Turkey, Canning exercised his authority to summon Parker's squadron to the Straits. This fresh eastern frisson passed away and Parker's ships were stood down. But the nightmare that, if some new convulsion shook Europe, the Russians would sooner or later take advantage of British distraction to come crashing down into the Mediterranean remained vivid. Here were the first tremors of what was later to become the Anglo-French alliance in the Crimea.

After settling Canning's nerves in Constantinople, there was a bit of unfinished business in the area for Parker's fleet: dealing with King Otto of Greece. This denouement hinged on a running dispute surrounding the claims in the Greek courts of Don Pacifico, a Portuguese Jew whose property had suffered some damage during anti-Semitic riots in Athens at Easter 1848. The fact that Don Pacifico had been born in Gibraltar gave him a technical claim to British citizenship, and when his claim for compensation got stuck in a legal logjam he used this claim to appeal to Palmerston.[34] The latter was quick to give it. Parker was ordered to go straight to the Bay of Salamis, where he arrived in mid-January 1850. Palmerston instructed the British minister in Athens that the ultimatum to Otto regarding Don Pacifico's reimbursment be measured 'by days – perhaps by some very small number of hours'; if Otto did not then submit, Parker was to strike.[35] Speed being of the utmost importance, the Admiral used the occasion of a dinner held by Otto in his honour on 18 January at the Royal Palace, 'a most singular party', as Parker called it afterwards. He left the ultimatum on his host's in-tray when leaving. Otto refused the demand, and the British Fleet duly struck. It entered Piraeus harbour with guns primed. Greek Government ships were seized, and then local merchantmen, all laid out in 'arrest' across the Bay. Damage was not all one-sided. On 31 January a huge snowstorm descended, bringing down the yardarms on the British warships. Ten sailors were killed. Eventually Palmerston extracted the financial compensation demanded. But the transparent subordination of the Greek King was the crux. In Europe, Russian accusations that this was an abuse of naval superiority struck a chord, and all the more so because Don Pacifico's credibility was questionable. Confronted with a résumé of the latter's business dealings, Parker admitted: 'I always knew our Moses was cheating.'[36]

Early Victorian political culture, shaped by the Reform politics of the 1830s, however, was uneasy with vulgar displays of power. Palmerston's triumphalism in the Near East in 1840–41 had not been shared by all, even in England. During what became known as the Don Pacifico affair, domestic political opponents set out to nail him for the shoddy bullying of a small country. In a tense parliamentary debate Palmerston nonetheless succeeded in turning the tables, highlighting his actions – and those of Parker – as a defence of the rights of British nationals in foreign lands. At the climax of his address on 9 July 1850 he famously stated it to be a fundamental principle of British foreign policy that, just as 'the Roman . . . in days of old held himself free from indignity when he could say "Civis Romanus sum", so also a British subject, in whatever land he may be, should feel confident that the watchful eye and strong arm of England will protect him against injustice and wrong'. This was what the British trading classes of the day wanted to hear, and one historian writing as late as the 1920s could still say that 'the idea to which he [Palmerston] gave form has since never left English politics'.[37] Afterwards there was some speculation that Palmerston's actions had made Otto, temporarily at least, more popular among Greeks than he would otherwise have been, adding years to his reign.[38] For our purposes, it is most striking that what came to be widely interpreted as the definitive statement of British power overseas in the mid-Victorian age turned on an exercise of naval supremacy in Mediterranean waters.

After its harassment of Otto, the Mediterranean Fleet wintered quietly in Malta. The island could not be wholly unaffected by recent turbulence. During the 1840s it had become a haven for displaced radicals from Italian states.[39] An edgy and secular Italianism in some classes interacted with growing irritation about the continuing stream of British military governors. The appointment of a civilian and Catholic official, Sir Richard More O'Ferrall, as Governor in October 1847 was an attempt to damp down such grievances. There were echoes here of Seaton's soothing role in the Ionians. Like Seaton, O'Ferrall put more locals into senior government jobs, so that by the end of the 1840s five of the eight most important departments had Maltese heads.[40] He also inaugurated administrative reforms and undertook public works to boost employment, including a new commercial port and more bonded warehouses. With advanced constitutions springing up throughout Europe, some sort of elected element in Malta's government could not be put off any longer. Such a system was approved in May 1849, with lively elections taking place the following August, though the electorate remained very small (3,767 voters in Malta and Gozo combined).

But just as Seaton's Ionian experiment had been derailed by Cephalonian disorder, so O'Ferrall's attempts in Malta were compromised by the arrival of more Italian refugees fleeing from resurgent absolutism. Some 800 came to Valletta on Parker's ships from Sicily, and on vessels from Rome's Civitavecchia. These people were destitute and anticlerical, and on both counts O'Ferrall would have barred them if he could; Malta was, in his view, in no position to be generous. The Governor drew the line when a French steamer tried to dock with 200 more 'paupers and democrats'.[41] Their exclusion reduced the French captain to apoplexy, and even the Foreign Office in London regretted that 'the common law of hospitality' was denied.[42] Maltese radicals, already critical of the Governor's habit of riding roughshod over elected members with the help of the official majority in the Council, were handed a weapon with which to beat him, and they made full use of it. Escalating bitterness led to the Governor's resignation in frustration during 1851. The experience of both Seaton and O'Ferrall exhibited a paradox that was often to be played out in the British Mediterranean. What seemed to London and its agents to be conciliatory and liberal concessions, far from being enthusiastically and gratefully embraced, frequently met with a hail of brickbats from local opponents.[43]

Malta and the Ionian Islands, however, differed in one key respect.

The significance of the former in British naval strategy was on the rise, while that of the latter was on the wane. During the 1820s and 1830s more money was spent on the fortifications of Corfu – and at times more military engineers kept there – than on either Malta or Gibraltar. Indeed, the extraction of a military contribution was a prime Ionian complaint. But during the 1840s this began to change. The growing British stake in the eastern Mediterranean meant that the centrality of Malta gained an extra premium as a place for the preparation and launch of expeditions, underpinned by the British possessing no lodgement in or adjacent to the Levant.

This process received a boost in the period leading up to Anglo-French hostilities against Russia. Ostensibly the Crimean War had Mediterranean roots in arguments about religious rights in Jerusalem's Holy Places, but the disputes were organically connected to diplomatic rivalries.[44] Intense British suspicions of Napoleon III had initially fed the possibility of an Anglo-Russian deal at French expense. But fear that Russia was promoting a protector role over Turkey's Orthodox population to regain her old leverage over Constantinople proved stronger. In London, the feeling took hold that matters had to be brought to a head. On 23 March 1853, therefore, Lord Clarendon (Foreign Secretary in a ministry led for the first time by Palmerston as Prime Minister) suddenly terminated talks with Tsar Nicholas in which a likely carve-up of Turkey had earlier been contemplated. An Anglo-French alliance was clinched when their Mediterranean navies were ordered on 7 June to head for the Dardanelles. Parker's successor as Commander-in-Chief, Sir William Dundas, issued his instructions that evening, and the leading vessel, HMS *Arethusa*, eased out of Malta's Grand Harbour and turned to the east.[45] From that moment the odds on war shortened considerably.

Even after Dundas's force reached Besika Bay, near the mouth of the Dardanelles, however, the issue of war hung in the balance for some time. During this interval extra troops and shipping poured into Malta. On 30 November a Russian squadron made a dash across the Black Sea and annihilated the Turkish fleet at Sinope, the last naval battle fought completely under sail in the Mediterranean region. At the time it tipped the balance in British public opinion by seeming to prove the likelihood that the Russian navy could emerge from its

Black Sea base of Sevastopol, rush the Bosporus and enter the Mediterranean proper before anybody could block its path.[46] But now it is clear that Tsar Nicholas never harboured any such idea. Russian power could hardly exert full control over the north shore of the Black Sea, let alone control the approach to the Straits. After Sinope, indeed, the Russian vessels had returned to their home-port. What the Russian action – 'a contempt and defiance of our flag' as the First Lord of the Admiralty, Sir James Graham, described it[47] – did was to frame and legitimize a war fought to keep the Russians as far away from the Mediterranean as possible.[48]

The critical British objective in subsequent operations was the destruction of the Russian fleet and arsenal at Sevastopol. This was, Graham stated grimly, the only way 'to leave our mark in the Black Sea this time' (as opposed to previous occasions when the fleet had been sent through the Dardanelles but withdrawn without further action).[49] This was a political as much as a military imperative; and just as Palmerston had been irritated by Admiral Stopford's caution in Syria in 1840, so there was anxiety about Dundas's alleged timidity. A more 'political' seaman was required on station, and to meet the need Sir Edmund Lyons, having left his diplomatic post at Athens, was made Dundas's deputy. Relations between the two men were frosty.[50] Although the first necessity after the outbreak of hostilities at the end of March 1854 was to counter the Russian land threat to Constantinople, this was soon taken care of when the Ottoman army barred the Russian advance at Silistria in Bulgaria. This allowed a British expedition (already ravaged by plague) to be despatched post-haste towards the Crimean peninsula in the company of their French allies. The attack by six British and six French warships on the naval installations at Odessa on 22 June began the Crimean War proper.[51]

The fighting proceeded in a sequence of ferocious land encounters, with the battles of Alma on 20 September 1854 and Inkerman the following 5 November most prominent. The initial object was to seize Sevastopol directly, but when this failed, what followed was an investment rather than a siege proper, since the city remained open to the north for supplies. The Russians blocked the approaches to Sevastopol by sinking seven of their own warships in the harbour, not only destroying any hope of an Anglo-French naval victory on the open sea but making a close bombardment of the defences more hazardous. Whereas the allied Commander-in-Chief, Lord Raglan, and Dundas remained wary of any rash attacks,[52] Lyons – Raglan's 'evil genius' according to one critical account[53] – successfully pressed for the full-scale assault desired by ministers at home. As we touched on before, much was now made of the examples of Algiers in 1816 and Acre in 1840 to prove that naval gunfire could destroy stone forts. A Crimean fortification made of hard steppe limestone, however, was somewhat more resistant than anything Algiers or Acre had been able to offer. The assault on 17 October 1854 was a fiasco in which more than 300 British sailors died. The siege of the city had to be prolonged through the following winter, with dire results for the allies, who had dwindling supplies and mounting sickness. Not only was the Royal Navy now reduced to what officers resented as 'perfect inaction',[54] but gradually the French army was reinforced till it outstripped its wilting British counterpart.

This was not at all what had been expected. Newspapers in London attacked the competence of the military command. For the Royal Navy, relegated to the margins in the climax of 1815, to be sidelined in the war of 1854–5 was especially galling. Lyons agitated for, and finally won, authorization for an amphibious operation in the Sea of Azov (the French pulled out at the last minute). This, however, was just a 'sink and burn' exercise.[55] 'We spare nothing at all,' one British sailor wrote home; 'pigs, sheep, duck, geese, fowls, and every mortal thing I can put my hands on.'[56] At Kerch, dominating the opening into Azov waters, the town's museum with its fine collection of Hellenistic art was smashed to bits. Following the razing of Taganrog, the *Illustrated London News* eulogized on 14 July 1855 that it would 'spread the terror of the British navy beyond the confines of Europe'. A mark was left on the Black Sea, though to what real military purpose was unclear and there was scepticism even within the British ranks.

Plague more than anything else finally choked off the war. Sevastopol eventually fell on 11 September 1855, though most Russian troops had left beforehand anyway. Admiral Lyons wanted to go on and devastate Odessa, with all its commercial wealth. The politicians and public at home, however, had begun to lose interest and patience. The expeditionary force endured one more cold and famished winter.

When a peace settlement was concluded after laborious negotiations at Paris on 16 April 1856 what remained of the Russian Black Sea Fleet was dismantled, along with coastal fortifications and arsenals. The Black Sea was declared a neutral zone and warships prohibited. British public opinion did not find that this neutralization fitted very easily with what they thought the war had been all about. Nevertheless, it gave Great Britain a guarantee of safety from any attack emanating from Black Sea ports, ending recurrent fears from the 1830s onwards. To that extent the war was a considerable success, with British domination in the Mediterranean confirmed and much reinforced, albeit at a high cost.

After the Crimea there was a 'back to basics' in British strategy, and this meant a concentration in the Mediterranean proper on established positions. Heavy British guns evacuated from the Crimea and some captured artillery were dropped off at Malta and Gibraltar instead of being taken back to England; slim imperial Russian cannons from that time continue to stand guard today in front of the Almeida Botanical Gardens on the Rock. Malta in particular had received a boost. It had been the de facto rear base for the expedition to the Crimea. In spring 1854 there had been three regiments of Guards, the Rifle Brigade, four infantry line regiments, substantial numbers of Zouaves from Algeria, plus the combined Anglo-French naval presence crammed into the harbour and island. If the war was bad for many, it was excellent for most Maltese. The activity triggered a boom to compare with that following Napoleon's continental blockade of British trade after 1806. When troopships left for the eastern battlefront, excited crowds lined the harbour.[57] 'The time of Crimea' passed into Maltese folklore as a time of plenty. Not surprisingly, political discontents ebbed away.

Although peace as always brought with it a certain economic relapse, the push to create an all-steam, ironclad fleet based on the lessons of the recent war carried with it a fresh focus on the improvement of Valletta's dockyards. Technology in ships, guns and fortifications generally was about to inaugurate an era of great military bases in a modern sense, and Malta was to be Britain's prime Mediterranean exemplar. Malta now uncoupled its old economic links with North Africa, although Maltese migrant labour continued to head there. The island definitively assumed a more stable though always contested identity as a British imperial island.[58] New forms of modernity came with it. Valletta's streets were gas-lit from 1857. Suburbs spread outwards from the baroque capital, especially towards Sliema, the first part of the island 'to adopt an Anglicized style and subculture'.[59] It is worth dwelling on a picture-postcard description of 'British' Malta as seen in the early 1860s by a young naval officer:

> Then there is the Naval Commander-in-Chief, who has a house in *Strada Mezzodi* [South Street] . . . and lives on shore in the winter; the Dockyard Admiral; and the officers of the ships, with a number of wives and families. The military also [have] a general commanding the troops, engineers, artillery, and two or three line regiments, with a great many wives and families. Besides these there is the Colonial Secretary; the Maltese Nobility, who . . . are generally not Maltese at all, but old Spanish, Italian and Sicilian families who have settled in Malta. Lastly, there are minor officials, elected Members of Council, etc., etc. As unless the ships are in the sailors have little to do, and the soldiers . . . comparatively nothing, there are a great many entertainments, and everybody meets everybody else at least twice a day.[60]

Here was a more refined atmosphere than had prevailed since the rougher days of Alexander Ball and Thomas Maitland. The rawness of occupation had taken many years to fade, but by *circa* 1860 an Anglo-Maltese brawl around the opera house was an unlikely event. But although this was becoming an identifiably British colonial society, it was also one that remained distinctively Latin. This complexity was to define Maltese political culture for decades ahead.

A very different trajectory was being played out in the Ionian Islands. The islands played no strategic role in the Crimean War. Where many Maltese cheered allied troopships steaming out of Grand Harbour, Ionians actually celebrated news of allied setbacks against what they regarded as fellow Orthodox Russia (in fact, when Sevastopol had fallen, one of the few enemy detachments arrested by the allies was a band of Ionian volunteers).[61] At a time, too, when the British were promoting themselves as the champion of moderate constitutionalism in Europe, the grubby reality of the Protection became more than ever an embarrassment. A newly installed Lord High Commissioner, Sir

John Young, caught this mood in 1854 when stating that 'the truth is that no permanent benefit to England, or real satisfaction to the Ionians, can occur. England is in a false position here, and the Islands are too widely separated geographically, and their interests too distinct, ever to form a homogeneous whole under foreign auspices.'[62] Young did see one way out. This was to integrate Corfu and nearby Paxos fully into the British Empire, and to let the other islands, including Cephalonia, join Greece. The Ionian classes closest to the British connection were, after all, Corfiote. What Young saw as a moment of opportunity in the post-Crimean lull to effect such a solution, however, slipped away. His suggestion was rejected in London on the grounds that, whereas annexing African Hottentots might be straightforward enough, annexing Greeks was altogether a more awkward proposition.[63] It is nevertheless an intriguing thought that had Young's recommendation caught on, Corfu might still have had a future ahead of it as the Malta of the Adriatic.

That England was in a false position in the Ionian Islands – in other words, that she had too little local support to lay any credible claim to legitimacy – was painfully obvious to ministers. Some of them were more than happy to dispose of the islands.[64] How to do so, however, was not at all clear. Where once the Islands might have been handed over to Austria, what was perceived as treacherous Habsburg neutrality during the Crimean War made this unthinkable. Giving the Islands to a Greece still ruled by Otto was also out of the question; the Greek King had infuriated Palmerston again during the crisis of 1854 by invading Thessaly, seeking to stick a knife in the back of Britain's ally Turkey. By this time Palmerston felt that putting Otto on the Greek throne in 1833 had been the worst thing he ever did. By the late summer of 1858 the only alternative in the drifting Protectorate was to buy a bit of time by trying some more reform. But this time the attempt could not be left to an isolated figure like Seaton. The Conservative Government of Lord Derby thought it held a key to the puzzle when it persuaded William Gladstone to go out to the Islands as Extraordinary Lord High Commissioner (the 'Extraordinary' was both to entice a reluctant Gladstone into the role, and to dazzle the Ionian political class with his aristocratic prestige). After all, what could evoke co-operation from the latter more certainly than the coaxings of the most Hellenic of English politicians, whose voluminous translation of Homer's great work had just appeared in print?

This was to be William Gladstone's only experience of direct responsibility overseas. On 31 December 1858 he wrote in his diary: 'It may seem strange but so it is that my time and thoughts are as closely occupied and absorbed in the affairs of these little islands as they have been at almost any period in Parliamentary business . . . The complexity of the case is inversely (so to speak) as the extent of the sphere.' This reflection summed up why the problems of Mediterranean island societies so often fascinated British statesmen, scholars and writers then and since. In setting out on his mission, Gladstone had firm preconceptions on Ionian affairs. These hinged on their subordination to the higher necessities of regional statecraft, defining the circumstances as 'the narrow corner of a very great question . . . the political reconstruction of all political society in south-eastern Europe'.[65] Viewed from such an angle, and reified by reference to an emerging Public Law of Europe, Gladstone argued that the Islands could not be absorbed into Greece in any foreseeable future. To do so would only stimulate Christian aspirations in adjoining Ottoman provinces, and possibly lead to uprisings in Macedonia, Thessaly and Crete. On arrival in Corfu Town, accompanied by his wife and daughter, on 24 November 1858 Gladstone was well aware that he would not be able to meet the expressed wishes of Ionians, and that his main task was to sweeten the pill of 'undeceiving' them as to their prospects of throwing off English rule and finally joining Greece.

In conveying to Ionian opinion this unwelcome constraint, however, Gladstone was careful to display his cultural empathy for Hellenic aspirations and – so crucial in his own world-view – Greek religion. In doing so he took risks with opinion at home, where Protestant zealotry was at a peak. When he kissed the hand of the Orthodox Archbishop of Corfu a storm broke out in some London papers. The psychological pitfalls were considerable, encapsulated in the anecdote that when Gladstone met the Bishop of Paxos, both bowing to acknowledge the dignity of the other, their two heads banged together. True or false, Lawrence Durrell found the story still circulating in Corfu seventy years later.[66] When Gladstone left for the southern islands, he came up against more physically demonstrative elements demanding union with Greece. In Cephalonia, an enthusiastic crowd briefly hijacked his carriage as it approached Argostoli, taking him to the town centre, though not before haranguing him with Hellenic slogans. In Zante, the atmosphere took on a darker tone, armed British troops having to clear the Residency of protesters against continued Protection. Gladstone brought with him into these situations an immense respect for Greek heritage, as well as a respect for modern-day Greek culture that was much more rare among his own countrymen by the end of the 1850s. His mission, however, was to show that expressions of respect and sympathy did not go very far in Mediterranean politics.

On one matter Gladstone shared the views of most politically inclined Ionians: the Protectorate was currently an 'engine of corruption', a conviction which explained why Gladstone was not popular with the Corfu garrison.[67] The plan of reform he drew up was designed to cleanse the regime of its failings, and to make the legislature constitutionally 'responsible'. Yet here was arguably the basic flaw of the mission: there was not any real desire among Ionians for British-style colonial government, however liberal it might be. Gladstone's reform proposals were soon rejected in the Ionian Parliament, though by then Gladstone had set off back to England because of problems in his Oxford constituency, disillusioned with 'the Greeks in general and the Ionians in particular'.[68] What he claimed to have done, however, was to restore by his proffered reform the 'policy and character of England'.[69] Although this was not very credible to most Ionians, the real audience aimed at by the mission was the European Great Powers. With some poison drawn from the Ionian abscess, a less extraordinary Lord High Commissioner was appointed to keep the Protection ticking over. This was General Sir Henry Storks, whose competence had been shown in helping to manage the evacuation of British forces from the Crimea. At least time had been bought, though how much was to depend on events beyond the Islands themselves.

On their journey back to England from Corfu the Gladstones witnessed demonstrations in Tuscany heralding the outbreak of a new upheaval in Italy. As during the events of 1848–9, British interests in the region were bound to be closely involved. Regime-change in the peninsula remained as forbidding as ever because it could cut in so many different directions. The Prime Minister of Piedmont, Count Camillo Cavour, grasped this English hesitation, and turned instead to Napoleon III as his collaborator in ejecting the Austrians from the region. At Plombières (July 1858), the two made a secret agreement aimed at ending Habsburg rule once and for all. The Franco-Piedmontese war against Austria starting in March 1859, and Napoleon III's entry into Milan alongside King Victor Emmanuel after the Battle of Magenta (4 June) seemed likely to let let loose forces over which the British had little if any influence. The outstanding feature of the founding drama of modern Italy was indeed that nobody was in control of events.

The likely effects on the Neapolitan Kingdom in particular remained a preoccupation of the British, with their eye as ever on Sicily. As in 1848, so in early 1859, a British squadron quickly arrived off the island, this time under Admiral Rodney Mundy as Mediterranean Commander-in-Chief. When the British ships entered the port of Catania large and enthusiastic crowds in a strongly anti-Bourbon town lined the shoreline. The more respectable families were allowed to come aboard, bands played in the evenings and naval officers danced with the daughters of local merchants.[70] Like Parker earlier, Mundy was conscious of being caught between the deep suspicion of the Bourbon authorities and the habitual 'expectation' of liberals and radicals aching to throw off a hated despotism.

But by 1859 Great Britain was a country whose sense of its own growing power had become entwined in a particular version of liberal constitutional belief. In June 1859 Lord Palmerston became Prime Minister again, this time at the head of a newly formed Liberal Party. Gladstone later claimed that it was because the new Cabinet was more sympathetic to Italian aspirations that, after years of wavering, he agreed to nail his own colours to a Liberal mast by becoming Chancellor of the Exchequer. Here was one of the vital instances where Mediterranean questions powerfully interacted with political change in Britain itself. Yet this is not to say that at this point Palmerston, Lord John Russell as Foreign Secretary or Gladstone himself was in favour of Italian unification from Alpine tip to Calabrian toe. Not even Cavour yet thought in these terms. The most essential British aim remained the avoidance of a general European war. Next to this absolute necessity was an inclination towards an integrated and stable North Italian entity under Victor Emmanuel's crown capable of acting as a counterpoise to French expansion.[71] Preferred outcomes further south were more fluid, since the spectre of social war in Rome and Naples was frightening; the classic English formula of moderate reform could not easily be applied there. In Sicily, the British response was to keep all options open, including an independent state, since such a country would naturally gravitate – temporarily or perhaps even permanently – towards the strongest naval power.

Palmerston and Russell needed time to coax things along in safe directions. But the dynamics of Italian affairs meant that they did not have this luxury. In January 1860 Cavour renewed an understanding with the Emperor Napoleon by ceding Nice and Savoy to France. In a fresh offensive against the Habsburgs, the bulk of central Italy was consolidated under Piedmontese rule. But not only had the cession of Nice and Savoy set off another surge in English belief 'that the [French] Second Empire was dishonest',[72] but such views were given an acute edge by anxiety that Cavour's bartering might prove unstoppable. If Savoy and Nice were to be ceded in this way, why not Sardinia or Elba, or even worse, Sicily? Against this background, the significance of the invasion of Sicily by the insurgent leader Giuseppe Garibaldi and his red-shirted 'Thousand' on 11 May 1860 may be grasped. In English eyes, after all, Garibaldi had one great recommendation: not only was he not French, but he detested Cavour for letting the French Emperor into Italy 'through the back-door' of Savoy.[73]

In continental Europe the mystery of Garibaldi's triumph against all the numerical odds was sometimes held to be 'wrapped in English banknotes', that conveniently catch-all explanation for a good many events in the contemporary Mediterranean.[74] Allegations that the English intended to seize the island were rife, with reports in *The Times* of Sicilian demonstrators shouting 'Long Live Victoria and Annexation to England'.[75] In truth, such language arose more out of a desire to win English support for their own aims than anything else. What is undoubted, however, is that the British were determined to control Sicily's fate, and not be caught out again as they had been over Nice and Savoy.[76] Garibaldi's presence in the island was a possible lever. This was why a British warship had stood nonchalantly by while Garibaldi's expedition, having embarked from Genoa, got safely ashore at the little Sicilian harbour of Marsala. With unexpected rapidity, the Neapolitan defences within the island collapsed. Mundy refused the pleas of the Bourbon Royal Commissioner, General Ferdinando Lanza, desperate to gain time somehow to mediate, and warned him not to bombard Palermo as Messina had been in 1849. There was, Mundy said, 'a vast difference between the indiscriminate destruction of the edifice of a great city, and the use of artillery against a people in revolt'.[77]

On 27 May 1860, however, Lanza ignored this warning and attacked the city. The British Consul in Palermo remained in his Residence, into which hundreds of local women and children were crammed for refuge. The marina of the port was riddled with shells. Insurgents and royal troops fought for control of the city. But the Neapolitan Government forces were overwhelmed as rebels flooded in from the countryside. By now Mundy was the only mutually acceptable arbitrator. Much haggling ensued over how the Neapolitan representatives were to be conveyed to HMS *Hannibal* under the protection of a Union Jack. A naval officer, Captain Wilmot, was simultaneously dispatched to Garibaldi's encampment. Wilmot afterwards described the devastation he saw along the way, the balconies full of frightened people, desperately asking as he passed 'if the British Admiral was going to stop the bombardment'.[78]

In effect the post-Bourbon dispensation for Sicily was sealed on board HMS *Hannibal*, and according to Mundy's rules. These rules favoured Garibaldi, and the latter was well aware what he owed to the Royal Navy. The following day the Admiral went ashore and travelled across the city. He felt moved by the scenes of destruction. Mundy reported that he

> had driven for miles into the country . . . and whether in the midst of royalists or rebels, patriots or priests, *squadre* or red-shirted *Garibaldini*, he had always been received with respect and civility. I was proud to believe that the prestige and moral power of the British flag had exacted the willing homage from bodies of men who had not been tutored by their governments to look favourably on England.[79]

Mundy's account is a classic evocation of what came to be denoted the *Pax Britannica* in its southern European form. The essence of this semi-mythological conception lay in the mental and moral sway of the British flag under naval auspices, capable of straddling bitter divisions in local society, and bringing a rough-and-ready peace that protected ordinary people caught in the middle of strife. Of course, Mundy's version of events was all smoke and mirrors, but among the frightened inhabitants of Palermo it had at least some reality.

The orderly evacuation of 15,000 Bourbon troops to Naples took place under British supervision (many Royalists left for Malta, where shelter was provided). For the British, however, the most vital decision during the great Italian crisis now loomed. Garibaldi made no secret of his intention to take his Red Shirts to Naples and finish off the Bourbons once and for all. Napoleon III pressed the British Government to instruct its fleet to join with his own in stopping any revolutionary attempt to cross the Strait of Messina. Palmerston and Russell refused to do so, though according to Risorgimento legend Cavour's envoy had to plead with Lord John Russell in his own home up to the last minute to let Garibaldi's flotilla proceed unmolested.[80] On 19 August the Red Shirt brigades crossed the Strait and landed in Calabria. The ensuing climax of Italian unification continued to arouse deeply contending sentiments even among the British themselves. Sir Henry Elliot, British Minister in Naples, felt there was not a 'shred of character' among the Garibaldians, and reserved his keenest contempt for Garibaldi's English Legion – the 'Excursionists', as he called them – whose loutish behaviour terrified Naples (the same Tory revulsion that had been levelled against the British Legion in Spain during the 1830s).[81] At the same time, a contemporary diarist in the city recorded the pursuit of Garibaldi by English fans, some women tracking him down to the Hôtel d'Angleterre in order to snip off wisps of hair, an operation to which the insurgent hero submitted politely.[82]

Such differences were suggestive, but what mattered was the British Government's fundamental decision that its best interest was now served by liquidating the Neapolitan state, once so beloved by Nelson, and by repositioning its territories, including Sicily, under the national Italian crown of Victor Emmanuel. This was the consummation that the British Mediterranean Fleet under Mundy helped to guide into being. The latter helped ensure stability in Naples until the new authorities were in place. Victor Emmanuel himself soon came, though in arriving in the south it was as though he was entering an unknown and primitive world. Again, Mundy's account, in describing the gigantic arches and decorations made for the King's entry, highlighted a theme in the understanding of the British and at least some Italians of what had happened:

> At the summit of one of the pyramids, as a compliment to the great nation, the moral influence of which had been so steadily exerted for the benefit of Italy, and against which not the shadow of suspicion existed of interested motives, two large ... Union Jacks of Great Britain, were suspended on lofty staffs, and billowing out firmly in the breeze, were objects conspicuous to many quarters in the town.[83]

Here was an airbrushed vision of a distinctive British role in the Mediterranean, helping to guide into the paths of liberty and moderation a new apprentice-state. Most important, however, was the immediate practical necessity to make sure that Garibaldi did not now make a dash to Rome to finish the job of unification and so, as Mundy and Elliot impressed on Garibaldi aboard HMS *Hannibal*, risk triggering a counter-revolution in clerical Europe.[84] Garibaldi shortly left, not for Rome but, under pressure from many sides, for his little home island of Caprera, where it was hoped he would remain in a dignified but passive retirement. His last action in Naples was to pay a farewell visit to Mundy, without whom he knew he would never have got as far as he had.

Throughout the course of the great Italian crisis, the British had in fact been as confused, and thrown back on improvisation, as everybody else. Beyond limiting any destabilizing effects on the wider European system, preventing the Italian peninsula becoming a French satellite, and keeping Sicily under close inspection, they did not know what they really wanted until towards the very end. Yet British actions crucially shaped events, as much by blocking the interventions of others, as by acting themselves.[85] The most important Mediterranean regime-change in the nineteenth century, therefore, was navigated without any serious damage to English interests and indeed some advantage compared to rivals. A largely unified Italian peninsula, capable of guarding itself, and surrounded by seas in which the Royal Navy preponderated, was to be for some time a further guarantee for the security of the British Mediterranean order. Just as Russia had been shut out of its eastern approaches, so both the French and the Habsburgs had been removed as real or potential threats in much of Italy.

There were other varieties of Mediterranean regime-transformation the British had to steer a path through. If they had got their way, the Suez Canal linking the Mediterranean to the Red Sea would never have been built. The project had been speculated about since the 1830s. Once the idea gained traction under French control Palmerston opposed it during the 1850s as 'one of those bubble schemes'.[86] Anxiety that the waterway would make Egypt a more independent actor, less susceptible to pressure exerted through Constantinople, and that towns on the projected route would be little more than French colonies, sustained British obstruction well after work began in April 1859. Such obstruction included encouraging the Sultan's hesitations in issuing the necessary *firmans*, and the orchestration of opposition on humanitarian grounds. The latter campaign was not without point: 20,000 worker-peasants were to die in forced labour, shifting the vast quantities of sand and soil required for the Canal.

Egyptian transport, however, proved even less amenable to British influence than Italian politics. Not even Palmerston could head off the passionate commitment and energy of Ferdinand de Lesseps, the French diplomat-turned-engineer. De Lesseps was able to persuade the Khedive Said (ruled 1854–63) to buy up the stock of the Compagnie Universelle du Canal Maritime de Suez when it looked as if the commercial flotation might sink; for Said, the Canal promised to restore Egypt to the great days of Mehmet Ali. But over and above everything else was the sheer commercial exuberance and technology carrying the project along. By 1862–3 a saltwater canal flowed from Port Said into Lake Timsah, and a freshwater section between Timsah and Suez was inaugurated. When the British Ambassador in Constantinople inspected the works he was impressed and told ministers in London that, since the canal would certainly be built, it was in British interests to accept enthusiastically what could not now be stopped by subterfuge.[87] Admittedly, the French flavour of the achievement could not be eradicated. 'The Queen of England has opened Holborn Viaduct,' the *Saturday Review* sarcastically remarked in November 1869, 'and the Empress of the French is going to open the Suez Canal.'[88] Empress Eugénie (a cousin of Ferdinand de Lesseps) did so on the 16th of that month, leading a convoy of ships through the waterway, joined by a galaxy of European sovereigns and princes, but with no similar British representative. Nevertheless, the first commercial passage was made by a P&O liner. *The Economist* predicted that the Suez Canal had been 'cut by French energy and Egyptian money for British advantage'.[89] In some respects the effect of the new waterway on Britain's Mediterranean interests should not be exaggerated. Military reliefs to India continued to be sent for the most part by the longer Cape route, and the Victoria Military Hospital at Suez was actually shut down in 1871 due to its limited use.[90] Yet over time the Canal was to become of prime commercial and strategic value. In the process the weight of the British stake in the Mediterranean shifted steadily eastwards.

Over such issues as Italy and Suez, Anglo-French tensions, however brittle, were kept under control. But they nearly imploded over Syria. This was partly due to the resonances of 1840–41, but also because they touched an older Napoleonic neurosis in English psychology. Under Napoleon III, France had emerged as the champion of Latin Christianity in the Levant, with its heartland on the Lebanese 'Mountain'; indeed, the role had allowed her gradually to recuperate from earlier setbacks in the area.[91] When a massacre of local Christians occurred in June–July 1860, spreading to Damascus, French opinion was duly outraged. The Emperor set out to offer protection, claiming a duty to do so under Article IX of the 1856 Treaty of Paris relating to the rights of Ottoman Christians. British ministers could only sit and watch a French force 'partant pour la Syrie' (the phrase became famous), landing in Beirut and fanning out through the hinterland, though they discreetly refrained from entering Damascus as a holy centre of Islam. For Palmerston the tricolour being carried into the Syrian interior took the shine off fond memories of past triumph.

The efficacy of French intervention was hotly debated. The British claimed that the expedition only arrived when the bloodletting was over, and that its presence made things worse by wounding Muslim susceptibilities. To French opinion, an alleged willingness ('le défiance anglaise') to sit back while the Druze, with whom English influence was closely connected, perpetrated massacres of Christians generated allegations of debased British diplomacy in the Levant.[92] If the British thought the Second Empire of Napoleon was dishonest in the Mediterranean, the French believed that the British had blood on their hands. Palmerston had one overriding priority: to get the French troops out. The only way to do so was to exhort the Ottoman authorities to provide proof that they were punishing their own delinquents. Sultan Abdulaziz was hectored into sending a mission to the Syrian provinces. One hundred and eleven of those found guilty after rushed legal proceedings were executed.[93] After this show of restoring order, an international commission was set up to consider the causes of the outbreak and how to avoid any recurrence. Its subsequent work marked a watershed in the evolution of international humanitarian law, though more immediately it provided a lesson in the development of Ottoman skill at playing off the European powers against each other.

The work of the commission led to a new inter-communal 'constitution' for Mount Lebanon, inaugurating a complex system of power-sharing (including an Ottoman Christian as Governor-General) the tangled legacy of which is still with us today. This compromise left little excuse for the continued presence of the French army, which finally evacuated Syria in June 1861, while French commentators wrote sarcastically about British policy-makers clinging to a Turkey that was little changed from the days of Suleiman the Magnificent.[94] In fact one consequence of what had happened was that it shunted British views away from Palmerston's old blanket defence of the Ottoman status quo. Instead, British preferences turned towards the idea of quasi-autonomous *vilayets* as a better formula for introducing and (even more difficult) sustaining a stable reform programme. This was to define a great deal of Levantine diplomacy up to 1914. Meanwhile, Syria in 1860–61 constituted the last of the classic 'panics' in Anglo-French rivalry in the Mediterranean after 1815, though this did not mean at all that the rivalry itself was dead.

By this time Palmerston was entering his final phase as Prime Minister (he died in 1865), but he had one last major political gratification: he saw the back of King Otto of Greece. Otto was swept aside by a revolution in mid-October 1862. It was symptomatic of the complexity of their relations with the British that, despite mutual bitterness, the King and Queen had arrived in Greece on Royal Navy warships twenty-nine years before, and now they both escaped with their lives on one following a mutiny in the Greek marine (a number of royalist officers had been hanged from yardarms, and it was feared that the same might happen to the royal couple). They were taken safely to Corfu, where ex-Queen Amalia vented her fury to High Commissioner Storks about being let down by British actions over the years. Storks was sympathetic about their plight, though reporting home that 'he [Otto] had little love for us, and was mixed up in a good deal of the intrigue that has been going on so long in the Ionian Islands'.[95]

Palmerston understandably relished the political demise of his old *bête noire*. But where Greece was concerned one always had to be careful what one wished for. A successor was needed, but there was no guarantee that the person chosen would be any better than Otto, and might even be worse. The Greeks themselves wanted the second son of Queen Victoria, Prince Alfred: they even held a plebiscite on the matter resulting in an overwhelming plurality. This was a token of the special standing Great Britain, and especially her flag and throne, had acquired in the eastern Mediterranean by the mid-1860s. But Victoria was adamantly opposed to putting one of her own family on such a rickety throne. Palmerston and Russell had to set off in search of a safe alternative, and eventually found one in Prince William of Schleswig-Holstein, seventeen-year-old brother of Alexandra of Denmark, recently betrothed to the Prince of Wales. The Greeks and the Danes were persuaded to proclaim this youth 'King George I of the Hellenes' at a ceremony at Christiansborg Castle in Copenhagen on 3 April 1863. After a delay, he was packed off to Athens, where the long interregnum had led to violence between competing factions. Royal Navy marines protected the gold hoard in the Bank of Greece (the security of bullion always being a key priority) and kept armed gangs out of the city centre. King George I arrived in Athens on 30 October and addressed his new subjects in the Cathedral, offering a vision of Greece as a 'model state in the East'. The very phrase, in fact, was Palmerstonian. Implicitly, this model was to be the very opposite of Otto's rule, and *ipso facto* the one the British had hoped for unavailingly since 1832. At last it had a chance of becoming a reality.

The slotting into place of Prince William of Schleswig-Holstein-Sonderburg-Glücksburg in Greece was therefore essentially a British-managed process, albeit one still requiring a European imprimatur. But if this new Greece was to be a model state, it had to be given some model advantages. Palmerston and Russell had one boon at their disposal to get George I off to a good start: the gift of the Ionian Islands. George's selection had been lubricated along the way by an announcement that the British Government would be willing to cede all the Islands, Corfu included, to Greece providing that nothing happened to upset the transition within that country. This willingness reflected the reality that the strategic value of the Islands for Britain was now very small, though even to the end some military experts contended the opposite. The fact was that, in the age of the Risorgimento, the Protection had become a political and a moral liability, as well as a strategic nullity. Events in Greece provided a convenient opportunity to ditch it, and cream off some advantage at the same time.

This was hard luck on Storks in Corfu Town. He had striven hard to clean up the Protectorate in the wake of Gladstone's mission. He had travelled widely in the Islands, encouraged moderation wherever he found it and purged corruption. The trouble with such 'improvement', as so often, was that instead of gaining support, even more of it was lost. '[A]re there not friends of the Protectorate', one Colonial Office minister in London asked on one occasion, 'on whose assistance Sir Henry Storks can rely?'[96] The High Commissioner could not provide any such reassurances. What Storks himself most resented was not the sniping of those who had always been enemies of the Protection, but increasingly the defection of those families who had received British patronage ever since 1817. Nor, when Palmerston and Russell decided that time was up, did Storks even have the courtesy of some advance notice. Inevitably, the last few shreds of his authority in the Islands disintegrated. He could not even rely on the local police – the *reductio ad absurdum* of any colonial regime – and had to request the co-operation of the Archbishop of Corfu to keep order (Maitland would have turned in his grave). Fear that the Protectorate might come to an end with some violent clash between British troops and local people, and so compromise what Gladstone had called the 'policy and character of England', dogged Storks for what remained of his time in Corfu. The chances of such an encounter were enhanced by the partial destruction, at London's insistence, of Corfu's fortifications, on the grounds that this was required to ensure that no future possessor made the island a base for aggression against Turkey. To Edward Lear, the British poet-artist resident in Corfu, the demolition was 'a most singular folly, done ... simply to aggravate and vex an impressionable people'.[97] Even the most senior British army engineer present thought it entirely uncalled for.[98]

When the handover to Greece arrived on 2 June 1864, nonetheless, Storks' fears proved groundless. He gave a farewell address to Ionian public functionaries in the throne room of the palace in fluent Italian; as two historians comment, 'this ceremony marked the end of that special Anglo-Italian-Hellenic blend which had characterized leading Ionian society for a considerable period'.[99] He then left for the harbour, the famous Esplanade – henceforth to be safe for respectable Corfiote women to promenade at night with English tars no longer cruising the harbour-front[100] – crammed with boisterous and good-natured crowds. 'It required all one's *sang-froid*', Storks wrote immediately afterwards, 'not to break down completely.' But although there was a tendency on all sides to ensure that the occasion went off in a friendly spirit, nothing could efface the fact that the Protectorate had never really gelled. When, ahead of transfer, a party of Royal Engineers took down the Royal Arms from the frontage of the Palace of St Michael and St George, and sold them off as a curiosity for the best price going, it was because their officers knew that otherwise they would be prised off anyway thereafter.[101] 'In the eyes of the Ionians,' all this was cryptically summed up in the *Saturday Review*, 'nothing in our Protectorate has become us like our leaving of it.'[102]

Although, on balance, it served British interests to have put the wearying Ionian experience behind it, the dream of a model Greek state faded all too quickly. For the British, the modern Greeks were all too often a disappointment (the disillusionment was mutual). One senior minister in London in 1865 predicted with unconcealed ill will that 'so rude and primitive a state as Greece' would in the end 'split up into little communities, each with an interest and policy of their own – Athens and Sparta, minus the slaves and the literature'.[103] In Whitehall, it was devoutly hoped that the Ionian Islands was to be the last enlargement of

Greece. The apparent attempts of that country to get bigger still by exciting a rebellion in Ottoman-ruled Crete from mid-1866 caused a new flurry of criticism. The British even encouraged the Sultan to send a military expedition to crush the Cretan rebels.[104] When the French and Russian navies took off distressed refugees from Cretan shores, British captains were under instructions not to do the same, since any assistance would only prolong an unwise struggle.[105] It provided more grist to the mill of Britain's critics that when her own interests were at stake, the veneer of liberalism and moderation soon slid away.

In the end the rebellion in Crete fizzled out, helped by the Sultan's edict applying an organic statute to the island replicating elements in the recent Lebanese settlement. Its provisions included greater Christian rights, and in particular the installation of an Ottoman Christian as Governor-General. The British Consul played a leading part in cobbling together an agreement. This was a measure of growing British influence, despite the prevarications of their own policy. The binding fact was that no other power could concentrate naval force around the island to the same degree. Some local Christians even began calling for the island to become a British Protectorate as a way out of the current impasse. In Europe, rumours of English ambitions to take Crete – long circulating – increased. They had some foundation. Combined with a growing scepticism as to Turkey's future, a feeling grew that sooner or later the British needed a possession of their own in the eastern Mediterranean – nearer than Malta – from which to react quickly to events in the Levant. In the Admiralty and War Office officials were already looking at maps for just such a lodgement, and Crete was one – though only one – of the possibilities. Lord Salisbury, as Conservative Foreign Secretary, for example, was to raise the matter of Crete in Cabinet during 1876. But by the end of the 1860s such a move remained as yet a scent in the air rather than an immediate prospect.

In Europe, much larger developments were afoot. At their heart was the growth of Prussian power. Austria had been crushed at the Battle of Sadowa (3 July 1866) and from then onwards France in particular feared for its safety along the Rhine. A side effect was that any risk of a sudden French attack on British possessions in the Mediterranean greatly eased. The Prussian Chancellor, Count Otto von

Bismarck, eventually chose a Spanish pretext – a Hohenzollern candidacy for the throne in Madrid[106] – to engineer a war with France in July 1870, leading to Napoleon III's defeat and capture at the Battle of Sedan on 3 September. After the humiliating settlement imposed on France by Bismarck in 1871, Britain enjoyed a 'peace dividend' for the rest of the decade, able both to maintain an unrivalled dominance in the Mediterranean and to keep naval spending down. But there was also something sinister in the outcome of the wars. The Franco-Prussian conflict proved that the stakes of Great Power rivalry had increased, while the Prussian bombardment of Paris provided a startling illustration of what the new artillery could do. The Mediterranean was not immune to the implications. Indeed, Bismarck always saw the region as one where he could set Britain and France against each other if and when it suited him.[107] From this arose a heightened emphasis on the value of Britain's fortresses in the Mediterranean as points of strength, but also the necessity to ensure that they were equipped with the most up-to-date defences.

This applied especially to Malta, the centrality of which had been underlined by its role in allowing naval oversight of recent Mediterranean emergencies. It became axiomatic that if England herself was ever attacked, this would be preceded by aggression against one of her Mediterranean vantage points. It followed that there had to be a sufficient force *in situ* since under such circumstances rapid reinforcement would not be possible.[108] 'Malta is more important for us now,' the First Lord of the Admiralty remarked, 'and our whole strength must be concentrated there.'[109] This meant more extensive dockyards to meet the needs of the all-ironclad fleet, and bigger and better guns. The later 1860s and first half of the 1870s witnessed the modernization of Malta's facilities as a great naval and imperial base.[110] The Admiralty took over French Creek, an indentation of Grand Harbour, opening Somerset Dock in 1871; Valletta at this point provided more space than the naval dockyards at Portsmouth. A new commercial harbour was built at Marsa, just in time to allow the island to cope with the boost to activity generated by the Suez Canal.

These installations, and Grand Harbour itself, needed fresh layers of defence in an age of hardening military power. Here there were two main considerations. The first was the scale of modern naval gunnery, so that an enemy fleet might cause severe damage to Grand Harbour from a considerable distance out to sea. The second was the recrudescence of what had been the fear of Grand Masters before 1800, that is, an attack overland by hostile forces coming ashore elsewhere on the island. The latter threat was met by the construction of the Victoria Lines and associated fortifications lying across the centre of the island (today they offer an interesting walking trail for energetic tourists). Enhanced danger from out to sea was catered for by a new series of forts with thoroughly modern armament. The first of these was the Sliema Point Battery, a fan-shaped structure allowing artillery to cover both Grand Harbour and the Three Cities. Subsequently Rinella and Cambridge Forts were constructed, the former half-sunk into the ground for better protection, and housing a 100-ton muzzle-loading Armstrong capable of firing a one-ton explosive up to a distance of 8 miles. Commanding the entrance to Grand Harbour, this monster weapon still draws admiring visitors as 'The World's Largest Cannon'. When a War Office inspector visited in February 1878, he stated that, in contrast to Gibraltar, essentially still a small and open roadstead, Malta now provided

> a secure and safe point for the largest ships and extensive refitting and repair establishments, without which ... it would be impossible to maintain the British fleet in the Mediterranean unless its place were supplied through an alliance with one of the maritime powers. He considered it essential ... that the defence of Malta should be self-contained so that the fleet could be free to act [in other directions].[111]

The reference here to self-containment suggested an inclination to isolation entering profoundly into British political psychology. Arising from the heightened pace and risks of European rivalry, this ideal was one that could never really be attained. But in so far as it could, keeping and if necessary extending Britain's stake on the margins of southern Europe, that is, in and around the Mediterranean, was absolutely essential. From their accustomed haunts there, the British could watch events, control their exposure to any major war in Europe, and bring their influence to bear when they really needed to. Embedded in this was a central truth: that the Mediterranean crucially defined both British power and its limits. This geopolitical insight, and not the primacy of any 'route to India', was why the Mediterranean and the British place in it were to emerge in future decades as a basic problem of British survival in Great Power conflict.

The military refurbishment of Malta after 1870 also set off local political vibrations. Increased 'imperial' spending encouraged British officialdom to ride roughshod over any obstacles that got in their way. In 1864, amid the Risorgimento afterglow, a Liberal Colonial Secretary in London, Lord Cardwell, had laid down the rule in Maltese administration that in domestic matters the opinions of elected members of the Governor's Council should be given special weight. Indeed, Sir Henry Storks, after ceasing to be High Commissioner in the Ionian Islands, had been sent to Malta as Governor to bring to bear his experience of handling fickle Mediterranean opinion. Storks followed Cardwell's guidelines in paying close attention to Maltese views on public affairs. But his successors after May 1867, General Sir Patrick Grant to May 1872, and then Sir Charles Thomas van Straubenzee to May 1878, proved much less responsive. Legislation such as that to extend drainage schemes in Valletta's expanding suburbs ('improvements' that Maltese politicians by no means supported, because of the expense involved) were rammed through by official majority in the legislature. The Cardwell principle ceased in practice to function. As such, a period of a liberalized British approach to Malta's governance had faded away, replaced by a more self-consciously imperial supervision.[112]

Such an assertive tendency interacted with shifts in Maltese politics. Just as the creation of an independent Greek state had earlier stimulated Hellenic consciousness in the Ionian archipelago, so there was a subdued version in Malta whereby the Risorgimento underpinned a revival of *italianità*. Whereas in the Ionians, however, the British had never been able to shape any local cadres in their own cultural image, in Malta such a transformation got under way, centred above all in the dockyards. A series of commissions sent from England in the mid-1870s looked at taxation, the public service and education, pressing forward a 'reform' programme. Tension and division invariably arose from fresh tampering with established interests. The Rowell Commission on taxation in Malta, for example, sought to broaden the range of taxes paid by the population, while seeking economy by reducing the pension rights of local civil servants. As a result, 2,000 protesters gathered in Valletta, carrying placards vilifying Rowell himself, and, having smashed the windows, they invaded the Council Chamber.[113] A heightened emphasis on the Anglicization of Maltese life gained highly controversial expression in the report on education, completed in June 1879. The principle of parity between the English and Italian languages was laid out. Given the social and imperial dynamics of the island, however, Italian might in practice all too easily lose its place. From this point the language question occupied the centre ground of Maltese politics.[114] Yet behind these anxieties there was something larger: a contest between two opposing conceptions of the island. One was a Latin Mediterranean vision with a cultural, if not political, loyalty to *italianità* as a key identifier. The other was defined by an imperial orientation linked to a military *raison d'être* and the distinctively 'modern' Anglo-Maltese society encrusted around it.[115] Meanwhile the everyday spoken medium of the island was neither English nor Italian, but Maltese. At this stage, however, the latter lacked a written form, and only years later did it find its own place in the tangled language politics of the island.

Still, any such fissures were easily enough covered over so long as Royal Navy ships gathered in strength in Grand Harbour, embodying British power and guaranteeing Maltese living standards. From mid-1875 the Mediterranean Fleet was concentrated there in force, following a rebellion in Bosnia. This outbreak triggered a new phase of Ottoman disintegration. For the first time the British Cabinet actively discussed the desirability of occupying a vantage point closer to the scene: Crete, Rhodes and Egypt were again among the potential targets.[116] In late January 1877, with Russia and Turkey at war yet again, the Mediterranean Fleet under Admiral Sir Geoffrey Phipps Hornby was dispatched from Valletta to the Dardanelles. This was the usual sign of crisis ahead, and the squadron was shortly reinforced further. At this stage the Royal Navy had a clear preponderance in overall fleet strength in the Mediterranean, with the number of warships on station usually around eighteen, though as ever it remained true that the geography and strategy of the sea meant that aggregate strength did not always mean that such preponderance could be brought to bear at the critical point and at the right time.[117]

The traditional view in military circles that the place to defend the Ottoman Empire was in Constantinople itself still prevailed in many quarters. Admiral Hornby himself was later convinced that if this assessment had been stuck to much damage would have been avoided. But Gladstone's great opponent, Benjamin Disraeli, Prime Minister since 1874, was not a traditionalist; he was an opportunist who wanted to make sure that if Turkey was knocked over, the British got their fair share of the pickings. Military planners in London were already checking where these might be. Alexandretta, conveniently close to Syria, entered the reckoning, but it was in Asia Minor, where the difficulty of drawing a neat line around any mainland base was obvious.[118] Alexandria was another possibility, with the attraction of an existing British commercial presence, but it would involve going deeper into Egypt, and would antagonize the French. Crete offered a splendid harbour at Suda; and in fact the British consulate in Canea already enjoyed a kind of 'quiet hegemony' over Cretan affairs.[119] But taking over full responsibility for a place where religious and ethnic violence was so endemic did not bode well. In short, all these places had considerable advantages, but also notable deficiencies.

An urgent need to act one way or another, however, was precipitated once a European Congress was called to adjust the harsh peace treaty imposed by Russia (their troops within sight of Constantinople) on Sultan Abdul Hamid by the Treaty of San Stefano in March 1878. The fact that this Congress was to be convened by Chancellor Bismarck in Berlin was proof of a fundamental reconfiguration in the European balance of power. It was during these deliberations that a novel possibility slipped in through the back door: Cyprus. Admittedly not much was known about an otherwise quite obscure island, one the Ottomans themselves had never made into a military base. But this rather eased things than otherwise. Relations between Christians (the majority) and Muslims were said to be generally harmonious.[120] The fact that the inhabitants were Greek-speaking was a matter for concern from the outset, given the problems experienced in trying to govern the Ionian Islands. This was smoothed over with the suggestion they were not really Greek at all, their 'only connecting link' in that regard being shared Orthodoxy.[121] It was true that perennially isolated Cyprus did not have a good port. But there were several wide bays dotting the coast, especially at Famagusta, which Hornby – whose initial scepticism about the strategic merits of holding the island evaporated once he grasped which way the diplomatic wind was blowing – said 'could be made capable of sheltering more ironclads than the Grand Harbour of Malta'.[122] Finally, Cyprus appeared to those few British observers who knew it as surprisingly prosperous, and therefore able, as Hornby revealingly put it, to offer Britain 'a large tribute' in cash if required.[123] In these ways a persuasive public narrative for the selection of Cyprus was developed.

The public arguments, however, were not the most interesting or compelling motivations. The reasons behind the taking of Cyprus were as much political as military. Disraeli was under enormous pressure to make unmistakably clear to his domestic critics (some of whom thought he had not defended Turkey enough, and some, like Gladstone, that he had gone too far in the other direction) that he was in control of events. The announcement in Parliament during late April 1878 that 10,000 Indian troops had been moved to Malta marked the critical point at which decisive British action in the Mediterranean loomed. The acute sensitivities this raised were symbolized by the abrupt resignation of the Foreign Secretary, Lord Derby, for whom Disraeli's desire for spoils in the Levant was 'mere buccaneering' and 'an absolute violation of international law and right'.[124] Derby's successor, Lord Salisbury, with his formidable intellect mixed with brutal realpolitik, was less choosy. He was also more alert to how Disraeli's mind worked. He noted how unstable the conduct of foreign policy was becoming in the new democracy unleashed by the Reform Act of 1867, but added that the people 'will cling to any military post occupied by England as tenaciously as it had clung to Gibraltar'.[125] A Gibraltar in the east was what, rhetorically as well as strategically, Cyprus provided; and it was no accident that afterwards in British debates on Cyprus the analogy of Gibraltar was never far away.[126] This continued, indeed, right up until independence in 1960.

Yet if for these various reasons Cyprus was to be acquired, it could not with any decency be seized, though both Disraeli and Salisbury were prepared to do so as a last resort.[127] Rather, the young Sultan had to be bullied into agreeing to yield the island by apparent agreement. Bullied Abdul Hamid certainly was, and his relations with the

British, and not least with Salisbury, were never really to recover. He did not give in until the Berlin Congress was well under way. The delayed announcement of the 'secret' Anglo-Turkish convention on Cyprus at the conference caused a sensation; Disraeli's defence that his aim was to consolidate and protect Turkey being considered by other negotiators in Berlin as 'a frigid jest . . . in rather bad taste'.[128]

On the day of the imperial signature (1 July 1878) an English representative from the embassy in Constantinople and a leading Turkish official left the Ottoman capital for Cyprus with the imperial *firman*. At the same time Admiral Sir John Hay in HMS *Minotaur* was ordered to take his squadron from Crete into Cypriot waters. He arrived off Larnaca four days later, and spent some time observing movements ashore, since there was no certainty even at this stage that the Ottoman forces on the island would not offer resistance.

Once Hay was reassured that Larnaca Fort only contained some rusty Venetian cannon and a minuscule garrison, 100 British marines and bluejackets were landed. On a coastal strip denuded of trees, their biggest hazard was the searing heat. Swift control of the capital being essential, the Admiral left his force huddled under canvas and hurried to Nicosia in a wagonette, protected only by a small guard. He entered Nicosia, a largely Muslim town, by the Famagusta Gate, accompanied by a train of mules loaded with sacks of coin, tangible proof that the British would meet their astute promise to pay off all the customary arrears of Turkish officials.[129] Just as in Palermo during 1860, British naval authority ensured that the outgoing regime was treated with punctilious respect. The Sultan's flag was lowered with decorum, and no Ottoman official was required to be present when the Union Jack was raised. Although Turkish troops were speedily evacuated, the previous administrators were given a decent interval before having to pack their bags. By the time that one of the most prestigious British soldiers of the day, General Sir Garnet Wolseley, arrived aboard HMS *Himalaya* on 22 July to be the first High Commissioner (not 'Governor', since in theory the Sultan continued to enjoy residual sovereignty) a bloodless transition occurred. Wolseley was effusively greeted in Larnaca by a throng of enthusiastic Christians led by the local Orthodox Archbishop, who, according to Greek-Cypriot political legend, added the telling caveat that his flock looked forward to their island being ceded by liberal Great Britain to the true Motherland of Greece, as the Ionian Islands had been before.[130] Meanwhile, with the Treaty of Berlin concluded, Disraeli had arrived back in London at Charing Cross to a cheering throng of 'jingoes' – the term was coined at this time – who acclaimed him on the way to Downing Street as 'the Duke of Cyprus' for having secured not only the island but Peace with Honour.[131] Here was a totemic moment in British politics, the imagery and rhetoric of which were to last a long time, and which like a good few others was framed in Mediterranean terms.

The acquisition of Cyprus sealed the identity of Britain as a pan-Mediterranean power with a permanent reach from the Strait of Gibraltar to the Levant. This command no longer fluctuated with events, prone to successive panics, but had become embedded in the life of the region. It was a reflection of growing power and occasionally direct imposition, but the picture of Sicilians calling for British succour in 1848–9 and again in 1860, Maltese crowding Valletta's battlements to view the comings and goings of a British Fleet embodying their own hopes of employment and freedom from deprivation, Cretans hailing an English Protectorate as a possible way out of their miseries, or Cypriots welcoming General Wolseley in Larnaca as an end to Ottoman rule, suggested something deeper. In such cases British intervention was part of the shock of the new and the hopefulness that went with it, deceived though subsequent expectations often were.

British domination in the Mediterranean might easily have come unstuck in the series of upheavals during the 1850s and 1860s, most obviously in the crisis of the Risorgimento. But instead these tumultuous events had only confirmed the solidity of an Anglo-Mediterranean order. The ruin of imperial France in 1870–71 meant, as Gladstone observed, that 'never was there less danger or likelihood of our being overpowered in the Mediterranean'.[132] In the western part of the Mediterranean a few warships were now usually enough to damp down potential troubles. At its other end the pressures were greater, but the outcome of the eastern crisis of 1877–8 was taken to confirm British primacy. Admiral Hornby encapsulated 'jingo' sentiment when he remarked that the Russians could have taken Constantinople had they been prepared to do so, but they had seen 'that "little black cloud" in the shape of English-men-of war . . . on the horizon, and they dared not face the storm'.[133] Here was arguably the high point of British maritime pride – or arrogance – in the nineteenth century. But these were dangerous times, and getting more so. Sooner or later some power, or group of powers, might indeed dare to face a British storm in the Mediterranean. Such a fear was about to become far more real.

# 4
# Messages from the Mediterranean, 1878–1914

A few weeks after a delirious crowd had cheered Benjamin Disraeli's return from the Congress of Berlin with Cyprus in his pocket, Londoners were able to gaze with wonder at a new token of how Britain in the Mediterranean had followed in the footsteps of the ancients. On 12 September 1878 the obelisk known as Cleopatra's Needle was unveiled on the Victoria Embankment, to much popular fascination. This imposing object had first been erected in Heliopolis in 1500 BC by Rameses the Great, and relocated on the seashore of Cleopatra's Royal City of Alexandria in 12 BC. In 1819 the Viceroy of Egypt, Mehmet Ali, had granted it to Great Britain to commemorate Nelson's earlier triumph at the Battle of Aboukir Bay. No attempt to convey the obelisk to England, however, was made till 21 September 1877 when, having been installed in a protective cylinder, its transport vessel – inevitably, the *Cleopatra* – set sail. Hit by a fierce storm in the Bay of Biscay on 15 October, the ship capsized with the loss of six lives, though the cylinder was recovered and taken to the Spanish port of Ferrol, and finally on to London. The names of the fatalities can still be seen on the bronze plaque at the foot of the Needle's mounting stone. The obelisk's troubled passage might have been a metaphor for the travails of the Anglo-Egyptian relationship after Britain's occupation of Egypt in 1882. The occupation was always to have its core in the Delta abutting the Mediterranean, and cosmopolitan, rowdy Alexandria had a special significance in its development for both commercial and strategic reasons.

The British themselves were scarcely newcomers in the country. They had, as we saw, occupied patches of the Mediterranean coastline for short periods in 1801–2 and again in 1806. Britons, too, had joined the influx of expatriates drawn by the great cotton boom of the 1860s that led to Alexandria being characterized as 'the Klondike on the Nile', though the majority were Greeks, Italians and French (in that order). Alexandria had boomed from the 1850s as the outlet for an expanding export economy and had already taken on a European aspect, 'with its water fountains, gas lights, and pavements and its façades all the more depressing for their cheap imitation of some fashionable square in Paris or Rome'.[1] 'Alexandria was a colonial city,' one writer states, 'before Egypt was a colony.'[2] Disraeli's acquisition of half of the Suez Canal Company's shares in November 1875, one of the great flourishes of his career, raised the British stake in the eastern Mediterranean. In the event they had taken Cyprus. The bankruptcy of Khedive Ismail's regime had led to a veiled but intensifying Anglo-French domination of Egyptian affairs through financial supervision. Neither Britain nor France trusted the other enough to let them undertake this task alone. A stream of salaried Europeans employed within the so-called Dual Control became a flood; there were already 1,300 of them by the end of the 1870s. They offered a focus for Egyptian resentment against the continuing payment of crushing interest payments to European bondholders ('the coupon'). When the Khedive Ismail proved resistant, he was deposed and replaced by his more pliable son, Tewfik. The coupon was paid, but the effect from early 1879 was to generate an authentic 'national' movement with roots in the army. Its leader was Colonel Arabi Pasha, a prototype in the long line of allegedly fanatical and revolutionary opponents of the British Empire in what a later generation was to term the Middle East.[3]

Few episodes in British imperial history have been so minutely scrutinized as the occupation of Egypt. One of the most sustained controversies in British historiography has concerned its role as the trigger for the ensuing 'Scramble for Africa', and therefore in shaping the worldwide imperialism of the late nineteenth and twentieth centuries.[4] It was sometimes suggested that the occupation might have been avoided if the British had struck their own deal with Arabi Pasha rather than choosing to 'work in' with the French. Gladstone, Prime Minister after the May 1880 election in Britain, had no natural desire to invade Egypt; indeed, rather the reverse. He had attacked Disraeli's purchase of the Suez Canal Company shares as 'the almost certain egg of a

North African Empire'. Egyptians had anxiously noted the French occupation of Tunis in March 1881, described by Gladstone's Foreign Secretary, Lord Granville, as a recrudescence of French ambitions in the Mediterranean;[5] but since at the Berlin Congress the British acquisition of Cyprus had been eased by promising the French a mortgage on Tunis, there was nothing to be done when Paris decided to cash the cheque. This was to have a lasting effect in the international politics of the Mediterranean. Italy for the first time began to feel like a dissatisfied power, having got nothing herself at the Berlin share-out. More immediately, Arabi Pasha and his followers suspected that Egypt was next in line for the Tunis treatment. The Anglo-French Joint Note of January 1882 was widely taken to mean that this was imminent. 'Let them come,' Arabi Pasha, now Minister of War, warned Sir Alexander Malet, the British Agent in Cairo; 'every man and child in Egypt will fight them.'[6] Egyptian military engineers set about strengthening the fortifications of Alexandria, where any invaders were likely to come ashore.

In the event it was the British, not the French, who became locked into a showdown with the forces for whom the Pasha was the inspiration and leader. This was not only because there was a change of ministry in Paris, from one led by the assertive Léon Gambetta to the more pacific Charles Freycinet. Ultimately the British had more at stake in the geopolitics of the eastern Mediterranean. Suddenly deprived of wholehearted French co-operation, the British hope that Turkey might be a replacement was also disappointed, since the youthful Sultan Abdul Hamid was in no mood to help Britain when the latter had just filched Cyprus from his empire. Meanwhile in Alexandria local feeling against Europeans, brittle from the start of the crisis, began to intensify. The Cabinet in London was immediately faced with the question of whether to send a naval squadron in case the situation deteriorated further. Malet warned ministers that under present Alexandrian conditions it would be counter-productive since 'the fleet is a menace likely to lead to disturbances and not to protection'.[7] But ministers had to do something, and the easiest thing was to send the ships, if only to cover themselves if things went wrong and a speedy evacuation should prove necessary. Reinforcements had already been dispatched to Malta. On 20 May three Royal Navy vessels led by

HMS *Invincible* under Admiral Sir Frederick Beauchamp Seymour arrived off Alexandria in the company of an equivalent French force, though the latter were there to keep an eye on Seymour as much as to intimidate the Egyptians.

At this point Europeans in the city began to get out, but events gave them little time. In a city where altercations between expatriate minorities and native Alexandrians were a daily occurrence, the spark was always likely to be a banal one. On 11 June a Maltese worker thumped an Arab donkey-boy in a dispute over a fare; Egyptian passers-by got involved; a Greek weighed in to help the Maltese; then some Europeans in panic started firing guns from their balconies in rue Ibrahim Pacha. A riot soon became a massacre. Both the British and French consuls were wounded trying to intervene. Most European fatalities were incurred in the harbour area, where many gathered in hope of rescue. They were disappointed. British naval personnel ashore passed news of trouble to the ships, but the latter carried few marines and did nothing. Around fifty Europeans were killed in the city, and some others outside. More than a hundred Egyptians lost their lives. Some 20,000 Alexandrians of all nationalities fled for safety to the European ships.[8]

French versions of this outburst tended to stress that it had been spontaneous. British reports emphasized the complicity of the local Egyptian authorities, and of Arabi in particular. It was noted how the Egyptian police had kept to their barracks, and the army made no appearance till the early evening, when order was swiftly restored (the usual behaviour of local authorities in such circumstances). What evidence there was suggested that the regular Egyptian troops behaved well under impossible conditions. If there was any Egyptian responsibility for encouraging the explosion it did not lie with Arabi, who was struggling to avoid giving the British any motive for intervention, but with the Khedive Tewfik.[9] Genuine evidence, however, was not the point. Once the news of the massacre reached London, the Egyptian issue was framed as a confrontation between civilization and barbarism, and as such just as likely in London to sweep along radicals and liberals as jingo Tories.

These strong emotions got caught up in the drafting of instructions to Seymour, now with fifteen British ironclads and a clutch of gunboats under his command. Some claimed that the Admiral's own determination to exact revenge arose from the death of his manservant in the trouble. Revenge without doubt intruded into the House of Commons. 'They certainly want to kill somebody,' the Liberal MP Charles Dilke wrote in his diary of fellow parliamentarians after one debate on Egypt. 'They [just] don't know who.' Gladstone still hoped that any action would be in concert with the French, if only to help clear up the mess afterwards. On 6 July, however, the French ships slipped anchor and sailed away. Gladstone then tried to limit Seymour's instruction to a demand that the new artillery installed in the main forts protecting Alexandria be dismantled, but his Cabinet colleagues backed Seymour's insistence that the forts should be surrendered. In so far as the British Government was undecided, the Admiral settled the issue for them.[10] A call to surrender the forts was dispatched to Arabi on 10 July, by which date most local Europeans left in the city had been evacuated, while Tewfik had fled for safety to one of Seymour's vessels. The ultimatum was ignored, and the ironclads commenced their bombardment at 7.00 a.m. on the following day.

The British fleet concentrated its fire on the string of low-lying, and therefore exposed, fortifications along the isthmus, and by 5.30 p.m. the Egyptian reply had been silenced at a cost of six British fatalities.[11] The bombardment continued into a second day, after which Seymour reported an 'immense conflagration' consuming the city.[12] On 13 July, after two battalions had been transferred from Cyprus, 800 troops were landed. A civilian who accompanied the first detachment of marines described the devastation and danger posed by the collapsed buildings of the town:

> Then there were the dead bodies, telegraph wires and miscellaneous objects broken and thrown away. In some places the houses were still on fire and smouldering, and the thin columns of smoke curled up the blackened walls . . . To one who had been really attached to Alexandria, it was infinitely painful to see the ruins. The Grand Square, which had been a source of pride, was now almost completely destroyed. The French and Italian Consulates had a few walls left standing, so had the British, but absolutely gutted.[13]

Captain Charles Beresford (later to command the Mediterranean Fleet) was responsible for setting up 'drumhead courts', where some of those found guilty of involvement in the depredations were tied up against acacia trees in the main square and shot.[14] 'The bombardment of Alexandria,' Dilke remarked to a Liberal colleague in Westminster, 'like all butchery is popular', and the popularity alone made it likely that intervention, once under way, would, as Gladstone feared, ineluctably become full-scale occupation. On 18 July the Gladstone Cabinet finally took this fateful decision, in which the rationale of a threat to the Suez Canal was prominent, though in truth 'it was the bombardment of Alexandria which created a threat to the Canal, not a threat to the Canal which made the bombardment necessary'.[15] So it was that crucial issues of causation and motive in the most important of all African 'scrambles', one triggered by the British Fleet off a Mediterranean port, and the genesis of which involved a Maltese disputant over a donkey-fare, disappeared beneath evasive reasoning and calculated dissimulation.

General Sir Garnet Wolseley was put in command of the expeditionary force now sent post-haste to Egypt, ostensibly 'to restore the authority of the Khedive'. Wolseley's strategy was to ensure that the Egyptian army was pinned down outside Alexandria, while the Canal was seized and the main British force drove on quickly to Cairo. On 20 August, 40,000 British and Indian troops were disembarked and made the Canal secure. According to one account, Ferdinand de Lesseps personally obstructed the landing-stage, announcing that 'no one should land except over his dead body', only to be edged aside by a British bluejacket who politely remarked, 'We don't want any dead bodies about here, sir; all you've got to do is to step back a bit.'[16] Apocryphal or not, by imposing a British grip on the Suez waterway, the British were making not only de Lesseps stand back a bit, but France and the rest of Europe. On the night of 12 September Wolseley's force launched a night attack at Tel-el-Kebir, close to the Canal on the road between Cairo and Ismailia, and routed the Egyptian army with a loss of only fifty-seven killed. Three days later Wolseley entered Cairo with a force of Guards, and shortly held a military review to show who was boss, pinning suitably gaudy decorations on those Egyptian dignitaries who quickly transferred their loyalty to the British. Arabi Pasha was promptly put on trial, though since no proof over the Alexandrian massacre could be found, on being found guilty he was not hanged but during December 1882 packed off to a prolonged exile in Ceylon.[17]

The occupation of Egypt was to have profound consequences. That it offended Gladstone's distaste for Tory imperialism was sincere enough; but it is equally the case that he was carried along by imperatives flowing from the logic of Britain's position in the Mediterranean. Gladstone endlessly reiterated that his government's intention was to restore order and get out as quickly as possible. But somehow the British never left, not least because the invasion of 1882 destroyed the only forces on which a stable Egyptian government could have been based. The possibilities of evacuation were severely reduced with the annihilation of General William Hicks's army by the Mahdi's jihadist forces in the wastes of Sudan during November 1883. Since there was no saying what kind of Islamist regime might one day sweep into Cairo and Alexandria – the places that really mattered to the British – the risks of getting out were all the greater.[18] Malet's successor as British Agent, Sir Evelyn Baring, eventually elevated as Lord Cromer, had no intention of easing himself out of a job suiting perfectly his proconsular personality ('Over-Baring' was one of the sobriquets that got attached to him in Cairo). Ministers in London remained committed to evacuating Egypt if political stability, orderly administration and the payment of debts could be guaranteed. Sir Henry Drummond Wolff was sent to Constantinople to negotiate a convention on these lines, and a draft Convention was signed in May 1887. It asserted freedom of passage through the Suez Canal, and made provision for a British military departure from Egypt in three years if conditions permitted. The Constantinople Convention, however, still needed to be promulgated by the Sultan, and to push this through the British needed the support of the ambassadors of the other powers. In fact the powers were quite happy to see the British bogged down in an Egyptian quagmire, and the Convention never saw the light of day. This was scarcely disappointing to Baring in Cairo, who remarked that the French and Russian ambassadors in the Ottoman capital should be given the Grand Cross of the Order of the Bath, since the failure of any agreement provided the British with a perfect excuse for avoiding all future negotiation on Egyptian affairs.[19] This episode was an important moment in the development of the Near Eastern question. It further soured Anglo-Ottoman relations, and allowed Baring to get on with the job of governing Egypt. But it also left Britain subject to the 'policy of pinpricks' adopted by successive French ministries and deftly exploited by Germany, in punishment for Britain's lingering Egyptian sin. The resulting friction was to be a consistent feature of the European diplomatic system in the following years.

Meanwhile during the days after Admiral Seymour's attack on Alexandria, 3,530 British and Ottoman refugees from Egypt had arrived in Cyprus, where they were housed and fed by private donations. The Egyptian campaign of 1882 therefore showed the value of the island to Britain. It proved moderately useful as a routing centre for a number of British battalions, as a source of provisions and as a sanatorium for wounded soldiers.[20] But no attempt had been made since 1878 to convert Cyprus into a genuine *place d'armes*, whereas Malta remained indispensable to the logistics of Egyptian occupation. Furthermore, once Alexandria passed under British control, the potential of Cyprus as a strategic stake in the eastern Mediterranean receded further still, since the former provided the sort of facilities Cyprus signally lacked (though the silting of Alexandria's harbour was always to cause problems). Such a setback to the rationale behind the British seizure of Cyprus always underpinned the lingering sense of bereftness attached to it as a possession, reflected in the commonplace tags thereafter of 'anomalous', 'peculiar', 'orphan' and 'Cinderella'. Dilke later called it 'the whitest of white elephants'.[21]

One reason why Cyprus – where according to the 1881 census there were 137,631 Greek Orthodox inhabitants and 45,458 Muslim Turks – saw so little development after the British arrived was that the terms of the original Convention with the Porte were unusually vague so as to lessen the insult to Ottoman dignity. Herbert Kitchener, whose first independent mission as a young army officer was the mapping of the island, had visions of Cyprus' possibilities once it was put into 'the hand of the capitalist'.[22] But entrepreneurs steered clear of a poor, remote and malarial island with an ambiguous status. Although Wolseley's occupying troops brought in their wake the usual band of property speculators, most went home. This was not to say that no improvements were made. A number of bridges were built, and Paphos linked by a road to Limassol; but their maintenance proved very difficult after a senior Colonial Office official came in 1883 and advised against further investment. Collecting as much revenue as possible and minimizing expenditure became the guiding principle of British administration in Cyprus.

There was one financial clause in the 1878 Convention which proved crippling. This prescribed the continued payment of the annual Tribute of £92,000 to the Ottoman Sultan; and when, shortly afterwards, the Porte defaulted on interest payable under the 1855 Crimean War Loan, these monies were diverted instead directly to the British Treasury. In fact most of the cash then got passed on to French bondholders. Keeping the latter sweet made an essential contribution to pacifying Parisian resentment over what had happened in Egypt, and being able to do so at Cypriot expense was long seen in the Treasury as 'heaven-sent relief'.[23] This recurring appropriation, however, deprived the island of any fiscal surplus. An astute English visitor early in the occupation remarked that the effect was to 'completely paralyze the good intentions of English government'.[24] Cypriot resentment deepened over time, and proved one matter on which Greeks and Turks, as well as the small Armenian and Maronite communities, were all fully agreed. Sir William Haynes-Smith, High Commissioner in 1901, warned the Colonial Office that the Tribute 'was the constant thought of all classes. They speak of it on every occasion; they dream of it; and I believe never refer to it without a curse in their hearts.'[25] The British administration shared the complaint, not least because inadequate revenue was one reason why the island never paid the high salaries enjoyed by expatriate advisers in Egypt. The poor quality of British staff in Cyprus became a perennial – though perhaps not entirely justified – complaint. Yet pleas for the alleviation of the Tribute burden, not least from frustrated High Commissioners, always got short shrift; and one irony was that although the island was not a real British colony, the Tribute meant that metropolitan control over its finances was closer than most territories which were.

Although the Colonial Office was responsible for Cyprus from 1882 (unlike Egypt, which always remained a Foreign Office responsibility), its government was a ramshackle affair. General Sir Garnet Wolseley as first High Commissioner said he felt 'little better than a Turkish Pasha',[26] and in many ways the British just stepped into Ottoman shoes. There was to be no grand palace for High Commissioners, as there was in Malta and had been in the Ionian Islands. In Cyprus they continued to live in a prefabricated wooden building that had been en route to Egypt at the time of occupation and got diverted for this unexpected purpose. One later occupant at first mistook it for the stables (this building was to play a curiously significant part in the history of the island[27]). Nevertheless, in a stuttering way there was an attempt to ensure the bare outlines of a territory under de facto British governance. A new government secretariat was built outside the Ottoman walled town with its insalubrious quarters. This was always to remain a focus of British rule. Military music was important in setting a tone, so that the Royal Sussex Regiment played at such annual functions as Queen Victoria's birthday celebration and the Nicosia races. The Gilbert and Sullivan operettas were especially popular on such occasions.[28] An Anglican cathedral, St Paul's, was built in Nicosia during 1895, when both Greek Orthodox and Muslim dignitaries attended (it still remains very active in the Anglican Diocese of Cyprus and the Gulf). Just as the Ionian Protectorate had been a special blend of Greek and Venetian elements with a British finish, so Cyprus was developing something comparable, but with a Turkish rather than Venetian supplement.

Although not a Crown Colony proper, Cyprus from 1882 did have a colonial-type constitution, if only to appease liberal and radical critics still unhappy with the acquisition. Under these arrangements – which only got into any kind of stride during the 1890s – there were twelve elected members and six 'officials', with the latter always able to combine with the Turkish element to overrule the Greeks. In fact a vocal part of British opinion was never appeased by such innovations; for them knocking anything to do with Cyprus was always a neat way to scrawl graffiti on Disraeli's memory (he died in 1881). 'The Cyprus constitution was a sham gift,' one contributor to the *Edinburgh Review* stated acidly in 1891. 'And the gift had the fate of all shams. It had made the giver contemptible and the receiver ungrateful.'[29] The allegedly sham character of British-designed constitutions in the Mediterranean – not only in Cyprus, but also in Malta and Egypt – was to remain a constant in all discussions.

Introducing a constitution into a Greek-speaking island was certainly a risky enterprise, given previous Ionian experience. One British observer recommended the establishment thereafter of English-language schools since otherwise the population 'will naturally gravitate towards Greece through the simple medium of a mother-tongue'.[30] But the British approach to education in Cyprus remained laissez-faire, largely because there were no funds to do anything else, control being left in the hands of local committees rooted in separate ethnic and religious communities. Nevertheless, Governor Sir Walter Sendall during the 1890s became that rare breed, a British High Commissioner mildly popular with Cypriots, because he took an interest in such matters as primary education. An 'English School' was finally set up by an Anglican canon in 1900 to educate children of the elite for jobs in government; and if any institution during the era of British rule came to embody the ideal of governing Cyprus by uniting, not by dividing, it was indeed the English School. Its role in Cypriot education, including between communities, continues to excite controversy in the twenty-first century.

Inevitably, a crucial variable from the outset concerned relations with the Greek Church. Reflecting an anti-Hellenism discernible in some British opinion from the 1860s onwards, Wolseley harboured a strong distaste for what he called 'these dirty and very ignorant but grasping churchmen of the Greek faith' (Gladstone would have been appalled).[31] Early tensions were summed up by the fate of a Greek priest who was arrested for a minor felony in Famagusta and had his head shaved.[32] The Ottomans might have beheaded bishops in occasional moments of crisis, but in normal times they would never have done such a thing, let alone tax ecclesiastical income as the British started to try to do. Yet it was impossible to administer Cyprus for long without some agreement with the Church, just as the Church's interest decreed that it should rub along with the new secular power. Sendall, when travelling about the island in the 1890s, made a point of visiting the monasteries, and became especially friendly with the Abbot of Kykko; a meeting of the Legislative Council was even hosted by the Abbot at that remote location to discuss the important matter of irrigation. But social and cultural 'distance' was always to remain, and Kykko – where the son of a goatherd, Michael Mouskos, later famous as Archbishop Makarios III, was before many years to arrive as a novice – was to become a hotbed of anti-British feeling.

Crucially, however real and widespread the sentiment for *Enosis* ('Union') with Greece may have been, it did not yet constitute a movement. In the Legislative Council it was the question of the Tribute that aroused the most passion, though from the 1880s there were periodic 'memorials' addressed to the Colonial Office in which the desire for union featured among other things. In 1887 some Greeks boycotted Queen Victoria's Golden Jubilee partly on these grounds. Ten years later during a Graeco-Turkish war young Greek-Cypriot men went off to fight as volunteers, blessed on the quayside by patriotic clergy. Sendall felt that the British garrison was far too small to try to stop them. Greek military defeats at Turkish hands, as in 1897, however, always had a dousing effect on such enthusiasms. They reinforced what for some time remained a key restraint on demands for *Enosis*: fear that if the British ever did leave Cyprus the island would not be handed over to Greece, but given back to the Sultan. This was why Greek-Cypriots were so agitated when most of the few British troops were moved to Malta as Near Eastern tensions peaked again after 1896. Rumours were rife that the British were about to evacuate altogether. The fact, as Sendall complained to Joseph Chamberlain, the Colonial Secretary, that a British warship had not been seen for a year did not help.[33] Although the British had no intention of leaving, playing on the contradictions of Greek-Cypriot expectations and fears provided a useful policy, though not one likely to promote warm relations.

By 1900, however, retrocession of Cyprus to Turkey was losing credibility. Abdul Hamid's reputation in Europe, following massacres of his Armenian subjects during the previous decade, was too dire for a British Government ever to hand Cypriot Christians into his charge. Greek-Cypriot politicians sensed this shift, and the greater room for manoeuvre it gave them. During June 1902 the aspiration for *Enosis* was raised for the first time inside the Legislative Council. Alarm bells began to ring, and the British started to contemplate the possibility of some kind of violent outbreak in the island, perhaps triggered by Christian–Muslim clashes. The simultaneous descent into chaos in Ottoman Macedonia illustrated the familiar pattern yet again. When Haynes-Smith retired as High Commissioner in 1904 his final recommendation was that the Cyprus garrison – then no more than 200 men – should be increased.[34] The police were a largely Muslim force, and the prospect of being reliant on them in a crisis was not relished. A quarter of a century after occupation British control over Cyprus was more than vestigial, then, but it remained rather tenuous and, in the all too probable context of a regional upheaval, quite possibly transient.[35]

The situation in Malta – where by 1900, with the Boer War raging in South Africa, approximately 12,000 troops were stationed – was quite different. At a time of vigorous Maltese integration into the British system, there was a danger of political hubris, exemplified by talk in the Colonial Office of a thoroughgoing Anglicization, to prevent 'the *Italia Irredenta* party obtaining a foothold in the country'.[36] In fact any desire for political union with Italy was always superficial, a vital difference from Hellenic attachment in Cyprus. The leader of the *italianità*, or *anti-reformisti*, faction, Fortunato Mizzi, repeatedly emphasized that the pro-Italian inclination of many Maltese was a matter purely of political aesthetics, not a programme of action. Whereas before 1880 the 'Italian party' had been principally concerned with gaining a public voice, 'after it became a struggle to defend their *individualista nazionale*, their *propria lingua* and their *propria religione*'.[37] As Governors of Malta were frequently to point out, this did not imply any hostility towards, let alone intention to sabotage, British rule as such. But it was not easy to cordon off politics and culture completely. The *Malta Times* during March 1884 referred to a 'nauseating partiality' for all things Italian gaining ground, and the phenomenon was one that grated in the British garrison and community. Friction grew, and in 1895 the Government intervened in a legal case involving a British army officer to ensure the option of having proceedings conducted in English. This opened up a sensitive topic in the sparring that was part and parcel of Maltese society.

The working of the constitution inevitably got caught up in this process. Elected members in the Council of Government complained in 1882 that Malta was still ruled 'like the deck of a man-of-war'.[38] Few Britons then (or indeed much later) thought that anything else was feasible. Governor Sir John Simmons was typical in his belief, laid down in 1885, that the island 'had always to be regarded as in a state of siege'.[39] Of course, if Malta were ever to be in a state of siege, the co-operation of the local population was absolutely essential. It was to guarantee such co-operation that a new, slightly expanded constitution was introduced into Malta in 1887, designed to involve elected members more closely in formulating the details of financial legislation. To this extent it built on the 'Cardwell principle', introduced by Lord Cardwell back in the 1860s. Yet this constitution never worked from the start. What elected members wanted was to be able to decide, or at least participate in deciding, money matters, and this was not at all the official intention. A cycle became established through the 1890s whereby deadlock gripped the Council of Government; elected members resigned when they felt their views were held in contempt; new elections were held – usually after prolonged delays – in which the *anti-reformisti*, or *partito nazional* and *partito populare* as these factions became labelled, were returned, often without contest; and government was subsequently carried on under the Governor's prerogative. In this manner, 'the ghost of the official majority' never really went away,[40] while a sense of paralysis came to surround the constitutional machinery.[41] One effect was to lead many Maltese to see no point in voting at all, so that although anti-Government candidates invariably won elections, they did so on the basis of very depleted polls. Deciphering what the Maltese really wanted for themselves was to remain an enigma, for the Maltese themselves as well as the British, right up to the 1960s.

These issues came gradually to a head under Joseph Chamberlain's prolonged Colonial Secretaryship after 1895. In March 1899, in what one historian describes as 'a spark applied to the powder magazine', the *Government Gazette* in Valletta announced that in fifteen years' time English would replace Italian in Malta's law courts.[42] This created a storm not only in Malta, but also in the Italian Parliament, which hitherto had steered discreetly clear of Maltese questions: an attempt was being made, it was alleged, to eradicate Italian in the only British colony where it was widely used.[43] Chamberlain's subsequent visit to the Mediterranean did not soothe matters. He arrived on HMS *Caesar* on 18 November 1900, with British warships illuminated in Grand Harbour. Chamberlain's horse-carriage – the first motor cars were yet to appear in the island – took him along the Esplanade, lined with crowds seeking to catch a glimpse of the imperial statesman, and finally through the Porta Reale into Valletta itself.[44]

Amid his busy schedule, including the inspection of new harbour works and torpedo defences, and attending a *Te Deum* in St John's Cathedral, the Colonial Secretary allocated a brief space to a meeting with the elected members of Council. Chamberlain proceeded to tell Fortunato Mizzi and his colleagues that he could unfortunately hold out no expectation that their aspirations could ever be met and that the language ordinance would stay. Mizzi ended by saying that what had been said was very painful, and that the Maltese felt themselves to be slaves. The Colonial Secretary, fixing a glance on Mizzi's highly polished and portly figure, then said that he did not look much like a slave to him. So it was that the English and their Maltese opponents habitually sniped at each other.

Subsequently matters turned more in Mizzi's favour when the Maltese language ordinance attracted criticism at Westminster and was discreetly withdrawn in the King's Speech on 28 January 1902. But Chamberlain's climb-down over language did not solve the constitutional matter. The Colonial Secretary was bent on suspending outright the system introduced in 1887, though he felt such an action might have the optimal effect 'by coming on them [the Mizzi faction] unawares'.[45] Afterwards an intention was formed to make a sudden announcement of the closure of the constitution. This could not be done before the new King, Edward VII, made his planned visit to Malta in April 1903 – the first of those Mediterranean tours, usually aboard the royal yacht *Victoria and Albert*, that were to be a feature of the new reign. Large crowds turned out in welcome, and the King opened a new breakwater across Grand Harbour. The following June the Colonial Secretary announced the abolition of the constitution on the grounds of inoperability. Malta was left essentially in the status it had last occupied in 1849. In what became an oft-quoted dispatch to Governor Grenfell, Chamberlain stated that henceforth as a matter of principle 'the island was held primarily as a great fortress'.[46]

This Anglo and imperialized vision of Malta was by no means divorced from realities. When a French writer, René Pichon, published a survey of the British Mediterranean in 1904, he observed that if the British left Malta the following day they would leave nothing behind except for some forts, a racecourse and a few tennis courts.[47] But this was very far from being true even then. Pichon's biting sarcasm towards British aloofness was characteristic of a Gallic critique throughout much of the Mediterranean. In fact one-third of wage-earners in Malta were directly employed by the British and many more indirectly, and any British departure would have affected these people deeply. By the early 1900s an English imprint was to be found at many levels of Maltese society, and royal visitations and nomenclature provided a means of expressing that attachment. The growth of what became a unique Maltese institution, the band club, and of colourful *feste partiti* in towns and villages, testifies to this. The 'La Stella' club changed its name in 1893 to the 'Prince of Wales', and later on to 'The King's Own', and it became common for such clubs to adopt royal British titles, still extant in the twenty-first century. Although these often reflected a tendency to oppose established authority, the particular establishment targeted was generally not British and colonial, but those local elites who wore their bourgeois Italianism on their sleeve.[48] It was already possible for a rising young politician, Gerald (later Baron) Strickland – the son of a Maltese noblewoman and a Royal Navy captain – to make his way expressing the belief that the Maltese should become as thoroughly English as possible. Strickland's increasing vitriol along these lines, stoking up controversy, led the Colonial Office to lure him away for some years to the West Indies and Australia as a colonial Governor, though he was to have a long and stormy career ahead of him in Maltese politics. Since French assessments of the British in the Mediterranean usually had at least a glimmer of truth, René Pichon nonetheless caught something by pinpointing the mobility of sentiment among the Maltese during the war in South Africa. He observed that the relief of the siege of Ladysmith (February 1900) could be greeted with genuinely popular and even 'imperial' enthusiasm, but that whenever more British soldiers and sailors crammed into the island tensions – the result of what even the British Admiralty called 'an overdose'[49] – would rise to the surface.

For more than two decades after 1880 the Mediterranean basin provided the principal theatre for international rivalry. As the Bismarckian system of alliances consolidated Germany's position in the continental heartland, other powers were pushed south in the search for compensation.[50] It was an integral part of Bismarck's diplomatic system that rivals should be coaxed into mutual antagonisms over spoils around Europe's southern margins, about which he himself cared little, though not to the point of war, since actual conflict might too easily spread. An immediate effect was the intensification of Franco-Italian tension, renewed by resentments in Rome that in the carving-up of North African territories they had got nothing. Competition to build more and bigger ironclads (the Italian *Duilio* class was the largest to date) threatened to overturn the Mediterranean naval balance. The British Government responded by passing a Naval Defence Act in 1888, inscribing a new Two-Power Standard. According to this principle, British numerical strength should be equal, in effect, to that of France plus the next largest power. Yet whereas in the mid-nineteenth century a British reassertion of maritime leadership would have calmed everybody down, on the grounds that this primacy guaranteed a broadly acceptable status quo, now British spending helped to accelerate an arms race among the competing Mediterranean nation-states.

What heightened the danger of this phenomenon was its link to the new tendency for alliance-formation. In May 1882 Italy joined Germany and Austria-Hungary in a Triple Alliance which one way or another was to continue until 1914. Four years later Lord Salisbury helped engineer a coalition between Great Britain, Italy and Austria-Hungary pledged to protect the status quo in the Mediterranean, Adriatic and Black Sea. The agreements meant that Britain was therefore for a while associated with the Triple Alliance. These overlapping alignments were essentially aimed against the reviving Mediterranean ambition of France, symbolized by the plan to develop the Tunisian port of Bizerta. This initiative provided a North African base conveniently, if roughly, opposite Toulon; and although the statement that France had now 'seized the Mediterranean by the throat' was overblown, the language was characteristic of the chauvinist atmosphere.[51] Instead of being intimidated by Salisbury's warnings, France veered towards Russia. A French fleet visited the Russian port of Kronstadt in July 1891, yielding the remarkable image of a Tsar (Alexander II) standing to attention on the deck of a French republican warship while a band played the revolutionary anthem of 'La Marseillaise'. Though a formal treaty was only belatedly signed, the rest of

Europe came to sense that France and Russia were in concert. For the British in the Mediterranean, this had always been the nightmare combination.

As a result of these grand diplomatic machinations, British strategists began to weigh up unpalatable prospects. Could Britain afford in any crisis to carry out the traditional Admiralty principle of concentrating the Mediterranean squadron at Malta to await further developments, when at any moment the fleets of Toulon or Bizerta might make a dash for the Strait of Gibraltar before the news even reached Valletta? But if the British moved their own centre of gravity westwards to Gibraltar, would it not become impossible to repeat the feat of 1878, when the Fleet moved in time – if only just in time – to forestall a Russian *coup de main* in Constantinople? This was the dilemma summed up in the contemporary principle that for Britain the road to Constantinople 'lay across the ruins of the French fleet', since no rush to the Dardanelles could be risked unless the force at Toulon had already been destroyed. Yet whether British maritime power was sufficient to pull off a Trafalgar-type triumph had also become problematical. If war were declared the next day, Joseph Chamberlain told the House of Commons in December 1893, the Royal Navy in the Mediterranean 'would have to cut and run – if it could run'.[52]

Such anxiety was the background to a new naval 'panic' gripping British opinion. This tremor became acute because on 17 July 1893 there occurred the greatest single disaster yet to befall the Mediterranean Fleet. Leading combined fleet manoeuvres off Tripoli on the Syrian coast, HMS *Victoria* collided with another British ironclad and sank with 383 fatalities, including the Commander-in-Chief, Sir George Tryon. This was a crushing blow to the prestige of the Fleet itself, and it led some to ask radical questions. Prominent among these was the naval correspondent of *The Times*, W. L. Clowes, whose previous reports had highlighted the transformation of Toulon. He was the most articulate advocate of the view that the time had come for the British to get out of the Mediterranean as it had in 1796 when last confronted with a combined (in that case, Franco-Spanish) threat. Clowes argued that the British position had become 'a comedy', and that Malta, Cyprus and Egypt were merely held on the sufferance of others:

> It is absurd to suggest that our interests in the Mediterranean are paramount to those of France, Italy, or of Spain. It is ridiculous to assert that our occupation of the Mediterranean brings us any corresponding benefit of a substantial kind. But it is true that our attempt to hold the Mediterranean as we do is terribly perilous and may be fatal. Let us then be merely visitors, like the Americans or the Danes . . .[53]

The continuation of this logic was that if a major war came to the Mediterranean, any attempt to hold the British position would only waste scarce resources. The best that could be done was to 'bolt the two narrow doorways of this long [Mediterranean] passage' at Gibraltar and Suez, and fight the war elsewhere. Clowes was not alone in such contentions. 'This is not the scream of an alarmist,' one commentator concluded after having stated that British possessions in the area merely presented a gratuitous temptation to France and Italy. 'It is the message of the Mediterranean.'[54] It was not a message most people in Britain found congenial or persuasive, and least of all those in the Mediterranean Fleet, one of whose distinguishing traits in this period was its sheer bellicosity.[55] When after 1899 Sir John Fisher as Commander-in-Chief set about root-and-branch reforms of its operations, the aim was to make it a bit smaller but also tougher and more efficient. In truth, the time had gone by when the British could be 'merely visitors' in the region. The British presence may have originated in the accidents of the war with revolutionary France, but their presence had since become too entrenched and even instinctive.

That Italy might be tempted to strike at Britain in the Mediterranean showed that something significant had changed since the heyday of the Risorgimento. After 1890 governments in Rome had pressed London for a real alliance, one that could protect them against the French threat of bombardment of their coastal cities, but they got nowhere. In 1896 Italy's attempt to find a 'soft' spot to commence her own overseas expansion ended in embarrassing defeat in Abyssinia, and thereafter her naval resources waned for a while. Salisbury often gave the wounding impression of regarding Italy as simply of little consequence.[56] The accumulating sense of being abandoned by Britain, for which the argument over language in Malta was just one very minor sign, eroded a tradition of regarding England as Italy's 'most sincere friend'. Those holding such a view did not disappear from Italian public life but they had to fight for their place within a wider spectrum of visions of Italy's own best interests.

Given the general sense of flux throughout the Mediterranean, it is not surprising that Gibraltar became an issue. From the 1850s it had sometimes been regarded as a declining asset, a 'port of call' rather than either a commercial entrepôt or an indispensable military base. By 1900 – when the civilian population had grown to 20,355 – such assessments of Gibraltar were again being reversed, as it emerged as the most logical place for the Mediterranean Fleet to be concentrated at the outset of any war. There it could easily be reinforced from the Home Fleet, venturing out into central and eastern waters if that was required; equally, the western exit from the sea could be closed off. The Rock itself had developed considerably over the preceding years, though still remaining very much a garrison town. There was still no local constitution as in Malta and Cyprus. But civilian residents had begun to exercise limited collective responsibilities through such institutions as a Sanitary Commission established in the 1860s, and to express views through an Exchange Committee. In 1890 ordinances afforded a precise legal standing to 'native-born' in the tiny colony for the first time, a landmark on the way to the formation of a Gibraltarian identity.

During the next few years money was spent on improving coaling and dock facilities, drawing in skilled workers from Britain, many of them looking for jobs after the completion of the Manchester Ship Canal in 1893. But the number of Spanish migrants was even more pronounced, so that the curious synthesis of local society and language – including the Anglo-Spanish patois known as *yannitos* – received a further boost. Yet it was an identity that asserted with growing conviction a strong British loyalty. Here, too, royal visits played an important role. Gibraltar was the first British Mediterranean possession visited by Edward VII in 1903, when local Spanish-language newspapers were no less welcoming than the *Gibraltar Chronicle*.[57] From the outside this could seem baffling, so that Fortunato Mizzi once declared in Valletta that the Maltese 'would never submit to the status of Gibraltar, where the natives were prisoners in their own land'.[58] But then the Rock only made sense in terms of its own unique history. Had Mizzi compared the advantages Gibraltar offered its dominant merchant class to conditions in Andalusia or Morocco he might have understood the paradox a bit more clearly.

As more money was invested in Gibraltar's infrastructure the British began to worry again about its defensibility. During the 1890s anxiety grew that should the Spanish ever pull a few modern guns up to the heights of adjacent Algeciras, the famed impregnability of Gibraltar would disappear. By 1901 a running 'scare' was under way that the Rock was vulnerable to such an attack.[59] Like most scares, this missed the point. Some pointed out that the Rock's real security lay in the certainty that, if such a danger emerged, British troops would occupy the interior, cut the railway line and isolate southern Andalusia from any contact with Madrid.[60] In 1898 Spain received a devastating blow in losing her American colonies as well as her navy in a war with the United States. Gibraltar's true impregnability continued to lie in the weakness of Spain itself. But in the changing world of the 1900s calculations of strength and weakness were constantly shifting, and passing anxiety sometimes bore only a loose relationship to the real world.

The imponderables of politics and strategy were still more unstable in the eastern Mediterranean than they were in the west or centre. The 1890s witnessed a succession of Near Eastern crises during which a bitter rivalry set in between Salisbury and Abdul Hamid. This rivalry was reminiscent of that between Palmerston and Mehmet Ali in the 1840s, except that it had an extra edge stemming from an intense clash of religiosity. Salisbury's High Anglicanism was pitted against the Sultan's Islamic revivalism, something neither Palmerston nor Mehmet Ali, for all their differences, would have had much time for.[61] The contest got mixed up in the bloody struggle over the future of Crete after a new Christian rebellion against Ottoman rule broke out in 1895. Following a clumsy intervention by Greece during 1897, a European peacekeeping mission was dispatched to the island. In this very fragile enterprise Great Britain became responsible for the protection and welfare of the remaining frightened Muslim population gathered together in the port of Heraklion. A force of Sutherland Highlanders under Colonel Herbert Chermside, an officer with long experience of Egyptian campaigns, kept the lid with difficulty on a town filled with destitute refugees evicted by Christian militia from their homes in the interior.

On 6 September 1898 this situation reached crisis point. A heated meeting of Muslims, including many refugees, took place in the centre of Heraklion, which a group of beys tried and failed to control.[62] When the crowd surged towards the harbour gates, a British platoon tried to stop them. Three of the soldiers were killed, though the platoon succeeded in closing the harbour gates. The Muslim demonstrators then turned their firearms on local Christians, some of the latter seeking refuge in the cathedral; around 800, however, were massacred. The British encampment on the western edge of the town also came under fire. Only a sustained bombardment by British warships pacified the trouble. Seventeen British sailors and marines were killed and thirty-nine severely wounded (two Victoria Crosses were awarded). The burning to death of Britain's Vice-Consul and his family in their home attracted much attention in the press at home. Queen Victoria called personally for drastic action, and Salisbury pressed forward the rushed military trials – occurring under the guns of HMS *Revenge* looming in the harbour – of those alleged to have been directly involved in the debacle. Those Muslim civilians found guilty were hanged on the walls of Heraklion. Soon afterwards the official Ottoman presence in Crete was liquidated under British supervision. One description states that the whole process of exit 'suggested the workings of an eviction on a grand scale. Here and there some soldier lingered; a minor official attempted to parley, but to no purpose . . . [Ottoman rule] was cast unceremoniously out of the island.'[63] This bore a strong resemblance to what had happened in Cyprus, and if Crete was ever to become a British possession this was the moment. There was indeed talk of Chermside being made Governor. Had the British not already taken Egypt, it is very likely this would have happened. But Salisbury ruled it out on the grounds that it would horrify the other powers. Instead, a new autonomous regime under a Greek prince was decreed, though again, as in Cyprus, the Sultan's vestigial sovereignty remained. During this transformation British officers treated their Ottoman counterparts with punctilious courtesy, but there was no concealing the depth of the humiliation that had been administered. By the end of the century, then, the Anglo-Turkish tie forged in the age of

Palmerston was breaking apart. Any British fleet that rushed up to the Dardanelles in future might be far from welcome. In this context it has been argued – perhaps slightly prematurely – that British policy-makers had now given up on Constantinople and fallen back on Egypt as the crucial line of defence in the eastern Mediterranean.[64]

By striking coincidence, more or less simultaneously with these events the British occupation of Egypt had at last been made safe against external threat after years of nagging uncertainty. At the Battle of Omdurman on 2 September 1898, General Kitchener finally brought to a climax the reconquest of the Sudan, with even fewer casualties than in Crete. This also had a wider significance. Omdurman provided the backdrop to the ensuing stand-off between British and French soldiers at Fashoda on a remote stretch of the Upper Nile, bringing Britain and France to the verge of war through the early autumn of 1898. Yet this was above all a Mediterranean crisis, played out in an African swamp, because it was in the Mediterranean that the impending conflict would have to be fought. British naval squadrons were readied to unleash crushing blows on Bizerta and Algerian ports; the French had plans to mobilize their troops in North Africa to seize whatever British possessions in the region came to hand. Yet the threat of a full-scale Anglo-French clash in these waters quickly petered out: the stakes in Africa were simply too low to merit such a cataclysmic result. It was to be the end of an era. With the British lead in naval armaments re-established after the mid-1890s, the French blinked first.[65] Both countries, however, peered over the abyss and recognized that, if they battered each other in their respective Mediterranean bastions, the victors would probably not be either of themselves but their still more dangerous rivals.

Increasingly this meant Germany. Signs of the Triple Alliance extending its activities in the Mediterranean were not welcome in either London or Paris. Kaiser Wilhelm II's visit to the Ottoman Empire in November 1898 was a case in point. In Constantinople, the Kaiser tried to stir up the Turks about British intentions in Crete, while during his visit to Palestine he famously entered Jerusalem through the Jaffa Gate on a white horse, a sign of Germany's determination to spread her influence more widely through the Ottoman world.[66] The Reichstag's Naval Law of 1900 underlined such ambitions, and in so doing triggered reactions ultimately expressed in the Anglo-French *entente cordiale*. A portent came on 15 April 1903 when British warships saluted the President of the French Republic en route to Algeria; it was followed in May by Edward VII's visit to Paris. Crucially, the *entente* was from the first conceived in Mediterranean terms. A German diplomat in London later recalled a soirée at Marlborough House where he saw Joseph Chamberlain and the French Ambassador, Joseph Cambon, disappear into the billiard room for an animated talk. Their full conversation could not be caught except for two words: 'Egypt' and 'Morocco'.[67] The Anglo-French understanding thrashed out by the diplomats had a natural logic. At its heart lay France's unqualified recognition at long last of British primacy at one end of North Africa, and Great Britain's acceptance of France's position at the other. But in Berlin, where since Bismarck's heyday the Mediterranean had provided exquisite possibilities for setting the British and French at odds with each other, it was a heavy blow to see that German meddling might actually bring them together.

It had always been seen as inconceivable that any French government would abandon its Egyptian grudge against the British. But by the start of the twentieth century the quarrel served little point. Lord Cromer had managed to stabilize Egyptian finance despite the constraints of continuing international oversight. This was his greatest achievement. British personnel had entrenched themselves as a self-confident administrative elite eulogized in Alfred Milner's best-selling *England in Egypt* (1892). After Tewfik had died in 1892, his successor, Abbas Hilmi, briefly tried to flirt with an anti-British line, but Cromer soon sat heavily on 'my poor little Khedive', as he patronizingly put it, and the royal house was reduced to a cipher (though it long remained to irritate the British).[68] Since there was nothing Cromer detested more than a 'Gallicized Egyptian', the French presence in education and law was progressively squeezed out, though the more cultural Francophilia of the Egyptian intelligentsia never went away completely.[69] In sum, by the early 1900s British control in Egypt had bedded down to such an extent that chafing against it was not really worth the effort. This insight led the French Foreign Minister, Théophile Delcassé, to summon up the nerve required to yield claims that went back to the great Napoleon.

The British had to make their own sacrifice over Morocco. Palmerston's regret over letting the French into Algiers in the first place seemed now a very distant memory. It had taken a long time, and a lot of Foreign Legionnaires, but the writ of the French Government finally ran through the vast territory, a writ progressively extended to Tunis after 1878. By the turn of the twentieth century, therefore, it was the fate of Morocco that posed the critical question in the western corner of North Africa. By 1904 it was becoming clear that somebody would grab that prize, and from a British perspective the French were probably more reliable than other protagonists. Even so, the British laid down strict terms to conserve their essential interests in the western Mediterranean basin. There was to be no formal annexation of territory by France; no fortification of any port on the Mediterranean coast of Morocco; and, crucially, the area directly opposite Gibraltar was earmarked for 'harmless' Spain as and when the rule of the Sultan of Morocco might founder altogether.

Palming off the Spanish – who had wanted a much larger portion – with this crumb was not without side effects. Yet Madrid had little choice in the matter. Spain was beset with enough problems keeping hold of what possessions she still had, and needed British goodwill to do so. In an age when dynastic politics was reviving, driven by wider rivalries, King Alfonso XIII set about chasing a connection to the British Crown. He was spurned by the Princess of Connaught, but eventually accepted by Princess Victoria Eugenie of Battenberg, who had been brought up in Queen Victoria's household at Osborne. Eugenie (or Ena, as she was generally known as Queen Consort of Spain) was married to Alfonso at the Royal Monastery of San Geronimo in Madrid on 31 May 1906. It was not a happy day, since an attempted bomb assassination on the way back to the Royal Palace left the bride spattered with the blood of a decapitated cavalry guard. Nor did it prove a happy marriage. Spanish popular feeling never warmed to having an English Queen.[70] Nevertheless, in diplomatic and strategic terms the royal link between Great Britain and Spain was significant, consolidated by King Edward's visit to Cartagena in April 1907 to sign an agreement to maintain the Mediterranean status quo. On that occasion, however, on the insistence of security advisers the British monarch did not go ashore.[71] A weak and friendly Spain was a useful element in both Moroccan crises and more generally for Britain's Mediterranean security.

The Anglo-French *entente* of 1904 not only markedly reduced the old dangers of mutual conflict in the Mediterranean, but also deterred others from making trouble. Its effects were felt at many levels. Wherever factions agitated against British rule – as in Egypt, and even, in some degree, in Malta – the wind was taken out of their sails.[72] This did not mean that the British gave up all suspicion of their old Mediterranean rival (or vice versa). But their suspicions became much more muted. Other factors, too, worked in Britain's favour. The Russian naval defeat in the Far East against Japan in May 1905 meant that the threat from that quarter fell away; and although the Tsar's Black Sea Fleet was unimpaired in numbers, its effectiveness was certainly lessened in the wake of the mutiny that would be famously mythologized in Sergei Eisenstein's film *Battleship Potemkin*. By contrast, Sir John Fisher's reforms as Commander-in-Chief meant that his successor, Admiral Lord Charles Beresford, inherited a British Mediterranean Fleet at the peak of its fighting efficiency. Morale was high when the moment came to celebrate the centenary of Trafalgar. For Beresford's force this was a celebration heavy with meaning. As the squadron with its new combination of black hulls and yellow funnels assembled off Malta's Grand Harbour to celebrate the victory and the loss of Great Britain's revered hero, the Admiral later recalled, 'flags were half-masted. At half-past four o'clock [the time of Nelson's death] ... the colours of Her Majesty's Ships were dipped slowly and reverentially; the band played the Dead March, and at its conclusion the colours were slowly rehoisted.'[73]

Yet paradoxically the following period witnessed the beginning of a process in which the Mediterranean's place in the Royal Navy's fleet distributions was relegated, essentially in relation to the North Sea. Always full of contradictions, Sir John Fisher, criticized for being 'unable to see beyond Mediterranean possibilities' while he was Commander-in-Chief,[74] once elevated in October 1904 to First Sea Lord became the pugnacious advocate of the argument for reducing the squadrons there by half.[75] Fiscal pressure – a revolt by British taxpayers against the recent burdens of the conflict in South Africa – meant that choices had to be made; and the reconfiguration of threats meant that the Mediterranean provided scope for savings.[76]

The strategic environment was also critically affected by the Europe-wide crisis centred on Morocco triggered by Kaiser Wilhelm's visit to Tangier on 31 March 1905, another of the Emperor's fateful Mediterranean jaunts against the backdrop of his love-hate obsession with the Royal Navy. His speech on this occasion was an implicit challenge to the *entente*'s Moroccan dispensation. The ensuing crisis came to a head at the Algeciras Conference (16 January–7 April 1906), where the aim of the Kaiser's Chancellor, Prince von Bülow, was to drive the French Foreign Secretary from office. Although he succeeded, the effect was not to crack the *entente cordiale* apart, but to give it fresh impetus. For the first time Anglo-French military talks began, just as a new Liberal Government was taking over in London with Sir Edward Grey as Foreign Secretary. The Moroccan crisis ended in a compromise by which France retained her claim to preponderance. But the British began to digest the fact that the most likely large-scale conflict involving their own most vital interests lay not in warm southern waters, but closer to home. The resulting logic was to take shape only slowly, involving the progressive redeployment of warships to Channel waters and the rundown of the Mediterranean 'stations'. This was to meet with stiff resistance by those who clung to the notion that Britain's stake in the Mediterranean was too important to risk, but for some years that doctrine was to be on the back burner.

British capacity to guide events in the region was in any case beginning to be questioned. Gone were the days when – as in the crisis with Russia in 1878 – the Royal Navy could turn up at the Golden Horn and lay down the law. A measure of this was the vexed matter of reform in Turkey's Macedonian provinces, where Austria and Russia were taking the lead. Edward VII's rather clumsy suggestion when meeting the Tsar at Reval in June 1908 that the Cretan model of autonomy should be applied in Macedonia, rumours of which spread rapidly, helped to spark revolution in Turkey the following month. An event presaged for so many years produced euphoric fraternization among the various sections of Ottoman society, above all in Constantinople. Greeks, Turks, Armenians, Kurds and Jews 'were all to be equal under the same blue sky'. Such an outcome had long been encouraged by British governments, and ostensibly afforded an opportunity to reverse the growing leverage of Germany in the Ottoman capital. Foreign Secretary Grey was especially determined that the Turks 'should have every chance' to advance down the path represented by a liberal constitution, and to do so if possible under British patronage.[77]

By a 'chance' for Turkey, Grey meant without having territory ripped away by others greedy for expansion. In fact, the Turks got no chance at all, since in October Austria formally annexed Bosnia. The Greek Cretans had recently rebelled and only desisted after British reinforcements had been reluctantly sent to the island; now their leaders, including one Eleutherios Venizelos, proclaimed full union of the island with Greece. The Mediterranean Fleet scrambled to do what it could to stem an Ottoman implosion. A squadron paraded off Salonica to warn against an Austro-Hungarian grab at that city, while another was dispatched to ensure that the Cretan declaration remained a dead letter. What could not be controlled were the effects in Turkish politics. In April 1909 Abdul Hamid was overthrown altogether in an army coup bringing a Committee of Union and Progress (the CUP, or 'Young Turks') to power. The British might long have wanted to see the back of the Sultan, but during the latter's final days in the Yildiz Palace the embassy realized that this was yet another case of being careful what you wished for. For one thing, the Young Turks did not want to liberalize the Empire so much as to Turkify it; and whereas the old Sultan had found any attempt to proffer British 'guidance' distasteful, the Young Turks came to reject it wholesale. Some years later it became commonplace to believe that the British embassy was responsible for turning the new regime progressively back into Germany's camp by a disdainful attitude towards Constantinople's uncouth new rulers. The truth was that British actions had forfeited Ottoman sympathies over a long period, dating at least from Disraeli's seizure of Cyprus.[78]

That the Bosnian affair in late 1908 marked a turning point was obvious at the time. One of its consequences was the rapid expansion of both the Austrian and Italian fleets in the Mediterranean. Traditionally the Austrian navy was very small. Subsequently it was understood that its expansion was the covert price paid for the support given by

The destruction of *L'Orient,* the French flagship, at the Battle of the Nile, 1 August 1798. Nelson's own coffin was made from a fragment of *L'Orient*'s recovered mast.

(*left*) HMS *Britannia* off the coast of Malta, *circa* 1835. The Mediterranean Fleet rapidly expanded in that decade.

(*below*) A British mounted patrol emerges from the Old Fortress of Corfu, *circa* 1850.

(*top*) Troops and stores being landed at Larnaca during the British occupation of Cyprus, July 1878.

(*bottom*) HMS *Himalaya* anchored off Limassol in August 1878 after taking the first High Commissioner of Cyprus, General Sir Garnet Wolseley, to the island.

(*top*) A parade of British troops in the Troodos hills, Cyprus, 1889.

(*bottom*) A district court in Cyprus, 1899. 'Chief among the gifts of British rule,' it was said of the island in *The Queen's Empire* 'is the substitution of just and honest courts for the Turkish tribunals.'

(*top*) British Monitor-class warships leaving Malta, 28 April 1915.

(*bottom*) Men of the London Regiment bathing on the Palestine coast, February 1917.

(*top*) Arabs with their British captors near Gaza, April 1917.

(*bottom*) The Allied fleet fires a 'victory salute' after arriving off Constantinople, 13 November 1918.

Review of the 33rd Artillery Division by Field-Marshal Allenby in Alexandria, December 1918.

(*top*) British soldiers relaxing at a café in Gallipoli, 1919.

(*bottom*) British sailors keeping a close watch over Constantinople, 1920.

Germany over the Bosnian transgression.[79] Italy, with its claims to unfinished business of the Risorgimento in the Habsburg-ruled Tyrol, reacted predictably. The first Italian dreadnought, the newest and most powerful class of battleship, was laid down in June 1909. The fact that these powers both belonged to the Triple Alliance mattered little since they were clearly building against each other. Nonetheless this Italo-Austrian 'race' undermined a brittle naval equilibrium. Since the 1890s the British had coped with the changing numerical strength and dispersion of rival navies. After 1908 the heightened threat-level emerging from the Adriatic, ready in an at least theoretical co-ordination of the Italian and Austrian fleets to burst at any moment into the middle of the Mediterranean proper, shattered existing calculations, and directly prejudiced the security of Malta and even Alexandria. That these pressures came just when the British Admiralty was being forced more and more to concentrate its warships in home waters was the essence of its Mediterranean dilemma.

Redeployment of fleets ran alongside those of garrisons. That in Malta was reduced to below 6,000 after 1906, while the one in Cyprus was in any case very small. In July 1909 British troops were finally withdrawn from Crete as the European peacekeeping role there was wound down. Overall, the British army in the Mediterranean had to make less go further, despite the growing strategic risks. A more unified command structure to improve co-ordination and efficiency was necessary. The War Minister in Herbert Asquith's Liberal government, Lord Haldane, established a new army post of 'Commander-in-Chief, Mediterranean', with headquarters in Malta (the last person to occupy such a position had been Lord William Bentinck in 1816). The problem was to convince a senior military man to take it on. Having to sit in Malta playing second fiddle to admirals, presiding over dispersed tinpot garrisons, was not very attractive. The Duke of Connaught agreed reluctantly, but soon gave it up. King Edward and Lord Haldane then pressed Kitchener to take the position. The King admitted that the Mediterranean was a 'rotten little billet', but the perks in the form of pleasurable travel were glowingly stressed.[80] Kitchener was looking for something more prestigious, and turned it down. The position was finally accepted by General Sir Ian Hamilton in October 1910, drawn by various inducements, including occupancy of San

Anton Palace in Malta, much to the disgust of the Governor, who had to give it up (today it is the residence of the President of Malta).[81] In the next couple of years the organization of Mediterranean garrisons was tightened up, exemplified by practice mobilizations in Gibraltar and Malta in April 1912. But in strictly military terms the British Mediterranean remained fragmented, under-strength and potentially vulnerable.

These shifts and alterations impacted on relationships within the British Mediterranean. Soldiers and sailors were more assertive about their prerogatives, and apt to get impatient with obstructions. In Malta, San Anton Palace was not the only historic edifice the military laid their hands on, to the displeasure of local opinion. For Maltese it was bad enough having fewer Royal Navy warships in harbour, and therefore less money circulating in the local economy.[82] Inevitably, the classic garrison-colony, Gibraltar, felt the same vibrations. The Governor after 1910, General Sir Archibald Hunter, considered that the times made it necessary to be a soldier first and a Governor very much second. He disregarded local views when trying to improve Gibraltar's efficiency as a military outpost, with the result that on the Rock he is still considered one of the worst Governors ever sent there.[83] Attempts were made to pacify bruised feelings. When Edward VII visited Malta again in 1909 he conferred the KCVO on Archbishop Pace; Governor Sir Leslie Rundle managed to get back some of the buildings appropriated by the army; and a Royal Commission was sent to the island in 1912 to begin to see how it could be made less dependent on military expenditure. But in both Malta and Gibraltar during the years before 1914 there was an edgy irritation about economic prospects and an often aloof administration.

In the eastern Mediterranean matters were potentially more combustible. In Egypt, a pall had settled over the last years of Cromer's long rule as Consul-General. As it drew to a close an event happened that was to resonate to the very end of British occupation. This was the Denshaiwai incident in June 1906, when a British soldier died of injuries in obscure circumstances on a flag-showing patrol. After a hasty trial four villagers had been executed with the other inhabitants made to look on. It became a cause célèbre which George Bernard Shaw made scathing reference to in his preface to *John Bull's Other*

*Island*. This sort of arbitrary and incompetent behaviour showed the limits and pitfalls of British rule. Few expatriate officials had any real contact with Egyptians. When Cromer finally left Cairo on 4 May 1907, he did so at night partly to prevent a hostile crowd gathering. His successor, John Gorst, in stark contrast set out 'to render our rule in Egypt more sympathetic'.[84] But what followed only illustrated – like Gladstone in the Ionian Islands some fifty years before – the pitfalls in making the attempt. He cut out dead wood among British personnel; took legal action against corruption in the speculative practices of expatriate businessmen; revived the defunct Legislative Council; and mingled easily, as Cromer had never done, in the polyglot society of Alexandria and Cairo. Gorst even drove his own motor car instead of being surrounded by habitual pomp. Yet his only reward was a whispering campaign against him in the British community, without eliciting any approbation from the Egyptians themselves. By the time he finally went home on leave, stricken by cancer, Gorst's strategy was in tatters. In the days before his death in Wiltshire on 12 July 1911 the only public person who visited his bedside was the Khedive Abbas Hilmi.

In tune with the mood-music of the times, there was a feeling that what Egypt needed after Gorst was a strong man. This was what the country got with the appointment of Field-Marshal Sir Herbert Kitchener, hero of Omdurman and Fashoda. Lord Grey assured Parliament that in making this choice there would be no change 'from civil and administrative reform to military policy', but no informed person could be taken in by that.[85] For one thing, there was apprehension that in any European war Egypt would probably be cut off from the main fleet – always the key to protecting British interests – and exposed to attack by Turkey. After Kitchener's arrival in Cairo in September 1911, the British garrison was increased to more than 8,000 and the existing constitution was withdrawn. The Consul-General's travels through the country became semi-royal progresses, with huge banners in English and Arabic hung across the larger villages on the route reading 'Welcome to Lord Kitchener, the Friend of the Fellah'.[86] In all this there was more than a touch of cliché, but it was from cliché that the Kitchener myth – subsequently so important in recruiting volunteers in Britain after August 1914 – drew its power. Meanwhile 'British' Egypt was edging its way towards a dead end.

A pale version of this process was detectable in Cyprus. By the early 1900s fear of sedition – of a kind highly unlikely in Malta, and inconceivable in Gibraltar – had entered into British psychology. Attempts were made in the next few years to damp down discontent as cheaply as possible. A new High Commissioner, Sir Charles King-Harman, came to Cyprus in 1905 with a Treasury grant to soften resentment about the payment of Tribute, though there was no chance of that burden being lifted entirely. When Winston Churchill visited on a Mediterranean tour in 1907 he made a speech recognizing that union with Greece was something that Greek-Cypriots regarded as 'an ideal to be earnestly, devoutly and fervently cherished', although his report to the Colonial Office vitiated this recognition by adding that any such transfer was impossible so long as Cypriot Muslims looked to Britain for protection. Churchill's stay in the island entered Greek political folklore, which epitomized the developing conundrum of Anglo-Cypriot relationships, in which an ideal image of British liberalism mingled with an intensifying frustration.[87] For the moment the British administration enjoyed one stroke of good fortune in that the focus of local politics, always inherently introspective, became preoccupied with a struggle over the succession to the Orthodox archbishopric. King-Harman even felt in 1910 that 'the bitter ill-feeling between people and government' was being gradually effaced,[88] although he immediately hedged his bets: 'I know the temper of the Greek-Cypriots,' he warned the Colonial Office, 'and I do not underrate their capacity for agitation and disturbance.'[89] Both the ending of the dispute over a new Archbishop and wider regional instability, for reasons we are about to see, meant that his successor, Sir Hamilton Goold-Adams, faced more challenges.

It was in the western Mediterranean, however, that the road, or rather one of the many converging paths, led towards the outcome of war. This happened through a reignition of the Moroccan question. In a classic playing out of European 'scramble', a descent into disorder within the Sultanate was followed first by a French occupation of the interior and then the Spanish seizure of Tetuan. But what then happened was unpredictable. At the outset of June 1911 a German gunboat, the *Panther*, arrived at the Moroccan port of Agadir. There was no personal appearance by the Kaiser, as previously at Jerusalem and Tangier, but the mere hint of German intervention at this end of the Mediterranean, relatively close to the Strait of Gibraltar, had profound implications. It was said of Alfred von Kiderlen-Wachter, the German Foreign Minister, that he 'did not realize the British danger until it was upon him'.[90] Perhaps the full sensitivity of the action at Agadir had escaped Berlin. But the result was on ominous display in the speech of the Chancellor of the Exchequer, David Lloyd George, on 21 July 1911 at the Mansion House, in which for the first time an implied threat of war with Germany – Lloyd George's celebrated 'warning shot' – was made.[91] Again, vagueness prevails as to whether in doing so Lloyd George was himself prompted by general considerations of foreign policy or to safeguard distinctively British interests in the Mediterranean.[92] But fine distinctions were already getting lost in the diplomatic crisis. Meanwhile Berlin discreetly withdrew the offending gunboat, and a compromise was cobbled together. Germany received almost worthless compensation in the Congo (a proverbial million miles from Gibraltar), French primacy over the bulk of Morocco was recognized, while Spain was bullied by Britain and France into accepting another crumb. But a line had been crossed, and it was at this point that a detailed plan to ferry a British expeditionary force across the English Channel was drawn up.

There was, however, a more immediate consequence in the Mediterranean of major significance for the future. Italy was not prepared to be dissatisfied any longer. Rome had for some time fixed its ambition on the Ottoman provinces of Tripolitania and Cyrenaica (today's Libya). As the southern shores of the Mediterranean were carved up in the west, it was felt in the Italian capital that the moment had arrived to act. On 20 September 1911 the Italian fleet was mobilized, and war was declared on Turkey a few days later. Tripoli was bombarded on 3 October and occupied by Italian marines.[93] When this met with continuing resistance, Italy decided in April 1912 to go for broke and also occupy Rhodes and soon afterwards all the Dodecanese.[94] For the first time another power had a potential naval base east of Malta. In London, it was reckoned that the Italo-Turkish war 'revolutionized' the Mediterranean situation. One way it did so was by threatening an ethnic-religious explosion in the east. An exodus of the remaining Muslims in Crete, their fear of extermination little assuaged by assurances of British naval captains from warships hovering offshore, got under way again. In Cyprus, Greeks started calling Muslims '"dogs of Turks" . . . and generally gloating over Italian successes in the Aegean Sea'.[95] The first serious inter-communal clashes since 1878 broke out in the island, which the small garrison struggled to contain for several days. There was even trouble in Alexandria.[96] The era of *pax*, British or otherwise, seemed to be fading fast. Most fundamentally, however, the Mediterranean appeared to be heading for a new bout of regime-change. This time, unlike the 1860s, the British and their fleet were unlikely to be able to control its direction.

Winston Churchill as First Lord of the Admiralty drew radical conclusions. The crisis unleashed by the German gunboat at Agadir had instigated him to write a sweeping paper for Cabinet entitled 'Military Aspects of the Continental Problem'. He was already at odds with naval traditionalists and his emphasis on the need to concentrate on fighting a war against Germany on land was set to make him more so. It threatened to reduce the navy's role to that of a mere escorter of troopships. The Mediterranean Fleet in particular became in this perspective an actual encumbrance. Churchill argued at Cabinet on 15 June 1912 that

> The Malta squadron can do great good at home, and no good where it is. It would be both wrong and futile to leave the present battle squadron at Malta to keep up appearances. It would be a bluff that would deceive nobody. The influence and authority of the Mediterranean Fleet is going to cease, not because of the withdrawal of the Malta battleships, but because of the [imminent] completion of the Italian and Austrian Dreadnoughts.[97]

That, in effect, sea command in the Mediterranean had already passed from Great Britain became an essential theme in Churchill's strategic appreciations during the coming months. His solution was to take the bulk of the fleet home, and entrust British interests in the Mediterranean to France. This fitted with priorities in French policy, which were to keep their own navy well away from the Channel where it might be smashed early on in any conflict with Germany. Instead the French marine would be concentrated in the western Mediterranean to guarantee the essential protection of troop convoys from Algeria to Europe. From the start of 1912 Royal Navy warships in the Mediterranean began drifting north, while French ships were moving in the opposite direction. In these haphazard and unscripted ways Anglo-French strategic dispositions got muddled up together.

In the light of Churchill's later obsession with the Mediterranean as the optimal place for British warfare, all this is highly ironic. But his views in 1912 did not lack for fierce critics in sections of the navy, the Foreign Office, Parliament and the Conservative press. Churchill might be happy to leave Malta to hold out with three months' supply against some sudden descent by an enemy,[98] or to rely on a torpedo flotilla to protect Alexandria, but others dissented passionately. Defenceless Cyprus, on this basis, would be left to any foreign force who happened to pass by. If to Churchill the Mediterranean offered only the appearance of power, to others appearances were what power was all about. It was pointed out that the very presence of the Royal Navy was at the root of British diplomatic and moral authority in the Mediterranean. Once abandoned, Italy would be thrown completely into the arms of Germany and Austria. Sir Eyre Crowe, Permanent Secretary at the Foreign Office, stated that Great Britain's influence at Constantinople, reduced though it was, 'has always rested on her position as the mistress of the Mediterranean Sea'.[99] Her ability to control internal order in Egypt would also implode if that position was abandoned, since it hinged not on bayonets (there were very few there) but on a naval power and prestige making interference by other outsiders highly improbable.

Beyond these headaches there was a more basic consideration stemming from episodes defining much of Great Britain's historical self-consciousness. Having spent decades struggling to maintain British interests in the Mediterranean against Parisian jealousy, what possible merit was there in putting these interests into French hands now? 'What terms', the Home Secretary, Reginald McKenna, pointedly asked, 'will France ultimately ask from us as a condition of protecting us in the Mediterranean?'[100] And while the French were stripping Brest and Cherbourg of warships, what moral obligation would compel Great Britain to assist France by going to war with Germany if and when some final break between Paris and Berlin occurred? This last query went to the heart of what was to be the essential British dilemma in August 1914.

It was a mark of the centrality of these issues that a meeting of the Committee of Imperial Defence was, unusually, convened overseas to discuss them. This took place in Valletta in July 1912. Prime Minister Asquith and Churchill travelled there in the Admiralty yacht *Enchantress*, and Kitchener was invited from Cairo. '[L]ooking quite splendid', Mrs Asquith, also a guest on *Enchantress*, commented on Kitchener's appearance: '(*treble* life size) but alas dressed as a civilian in a Homburg hat'.[101] A compromise resulted in which any wholesale naval evacuation of the Mediterranean was rejected, and several cruiser squadrons were ordered to remain in these waters during hostilities. The general principle of concentrating battleships in the North Sea was nevertheless agreed (leading to the effective marooning of the main British battle fleet for the best part of 1914–18). The maintenance of the Malta dockyard was confirmed, to the relief of the Maltese themselves since so many of their livelihoods were at stake. The fortifications of Alexandria were also to be improved – the first hint of an expansion of the British military presence in Egypt, though its future scale could not have been predicted. On the way home, Asquith and Churchill stopped at Gibraltar and provided similar assurances to those for Malta. 'We cannot recede from our position as a great Mediterranean naval power,' was how Churchill somewhat reluctantly summed up the outcome of these debates.[102]

If Great Britain was to remain active in the Mediterranean, however, it would need collaborators and proxies. France would provide this need in the west. But who would do so in the east? Churchill and Lloyd George, increasingly working together on military issues, sketched out such a role for Greece. That country had long since ceased to be a 'model state' in the Palmerstonian sense of providing an exemplar of British good governance, moderation and stability. But the two young stars in British political life now saw it as a model of another kind: an expansionary regional power supplying the troops and naval flotillas that Britain could not. Indeed, the Greek navy had for some years come under the tutorship of a British Naval Mission, even if relations were not always smooth.[103] This was where British interests and those of Eleutherios Venizelos (Prime Minister of Greece after 1910 but whose English orientation had been forged during his years as a politician in Crete) started to interlock. After years in which philhellenism had ebbed in British intellectual and political life, the phenomenon revived, though its trajectory was to be erratic and would eventually end in disaster.

Lord Grey, still labouring on as Foreign Secretary despite near-blindness, by no means shared such enthusiasm for the Greeks, least of all if it meant spurning Turkey once and for all. Grey belonged to a generation for which Constantinople never really lost its allure, and compared to which Athens was a mere appendage. He struggled to bring an end to the continuing ructions of Italo-Turkish belligerency, and at last in October 1912 these countries signed an accord. But Grey did not have long to take satisfaction. Two days later Greece, Bulgaria and Serbia declared war on Turkey, intending to feed on its carcass. 'You may consider Crete as yours,' Lloyd George said encouragingly to one of Venizelos's go-betweens in London: 'The only power that could prevent you from having it is England, and England will not fire a shot or move a single ship to prevent . . . it.'[104] Grey would have liked to do just that, but it was too late. In early February 1913 the Captain of HMS *Yarmouth* presided over the dignified lowering of the Turkish flag, symbol of the Sultan's residual sovereignty, at Suda Bay for transfer back to the Ottoman capital; and Crete became fully part of Greece at last.[105] This sad little flag ceremony constituted the last echo of an Anglo-Turkish interaction going back to Stratford Canning's work as a young diplomat in Constantinople during 1809. Meanwhile during the Balkan Wars of 1912–13 one striking feature was the rapid movement of suspicious European navies, nervously shadowing each other's tracks. This hyperactive navalism indicated the collapse of a Great Power 'concert' in the east that had, in its muddling way, survived many pressures in recent decades, but was about to be overwhelmed by events.

One of these criss-crossing navies was that of Germany. It was the first time that a German battleship squadron had appeared in the Mediterranean. In its ranks were the battle-cruiser *Goeben* and a light cruiser, *Breslau*. The former, 23,000 tons with ten sixteen-inch gun-turrets, was easily the most powerful warship in Mediterranean waters, with only Royal Navy vessels in the region capable of a speed to match those of the German squadron. When the Balkan fighting eased, it was thought that the German sailors would head for home.

They did not, remaining instead in Adriatic waters, and the resulting anxiety helped to encourage sporadic Anglo-French naval discussions through the spring of 1913. Yet these exchanges still retained a purely informal and even illicit character, pitted with potential misunderstanding in the early phases of any conflict.[106] Amid these uncertainties the Royal Navy instinctively kept to the western end of the Mediterranean in case vital French army transports from Algeria needed protecting, but so that it was equally well placed to dash home if circumstances so required. This western tilt was to carry an unexpected penalty in the first days of war.

In fact the *Goeben* and the *Breslau*, under the command of Rear-Admiral Wilhelm Souchon, were in the Adriatic when war broke out between Austria-Hungary and Serbia on 28 July 1914 following the assassination of Archduke Franz Ferdinand in Sarajevo. Souchon promptly moved his ships out into the Mediterranean to avoid being trapped in narrow waters. Only on 2 August did the British Government at last provide France with the long-awaited assurance that they would protect her coasts and shipping in the Channel and North Sea, and so allow the French to complete their matching concentration in the Mediterranean. This was the point at the heart of Lord Grey's clinching speech to the House of Commons on Britain's moral obligation to France, delivered on the following afternoon. He fatefully told the House:

> But I want to look at the thing without sentiment from the point of view of British interests . . . If we are to say nothing at this moment, what is France to do with her Fleet in the Mediterranean? If she leaves it there with no statement from us on what we will do, she leaves her northern and western coasts absolutely undefended at the mercy of a German fleet coming down from the Channel . . . I say that from the point of view of British interests we felt strongly that France was entitled to know and to know at once [cheers] . . . she could depend on British support.[107]

This argument has led to claims that the essential motive for the Liberal government's decision to go to the aid of France and Belgium was the naval situation in the Mediterranean, and the requirement to provide a quid pro quo for the protection of the British stake in that region. As such, the Mediterranean was a millstone around Britain's neck, a contention some naval theorists such as W. L. Clowes had been making ever since the 1890s.[108] By implication, without being so burdened, Liberal ministers might have retained the flexibility to keep the country out of the nightmare that followed. It is certainly fair to say that in taking one of the biggest decisions ever to face any British Government, the Mediterranean necessarily loomed large. Had it not done so, had British interests in the region been left to the mercy of events, much of the symbolism and identity of nationhood and its most essential interests since Nelson's victories at the Nile and Trafalgar would have had to be put to the sword. This was scarcely likely amid the pressures of August 1914.

Meanwhile at dawn on 4 August, with German troops flooding into Belgium, the *Goeben* and *Breslau* bombarded the Algerian ports of Philippeville and Bône. These were the first shots fired in the Mediterranean during the war. As the hours and minutes to the expiration of Great Britain's ultimatum to Germany ticked by, the British and French naval leaderships were huddled in the Admiralty in London clinching their arrangements for the Channel and the Mediterranean. Central to their plans was that, following the anticipated swift elimination of the *Goeben* and *Breslau*, the British fleet in the Mediterranean should be reduced to a combination of light armoured cruisers and destroyers under the overall authority of a French Commander-in-Chief. Churchill recalled in *The World Crisis* (1923) how at that tense moment Fisher, now back once again as First Sea Lord, accompanied by the Chief of Admiralty Staff, came into his office with the French admirals in tow, having completed their operational decisions. Churchill recalled:

> They were fine figures in uniform, and very grave. One felt in actual contact with these French officers how truly the crisis was life and death for France. They spoke of basing the French fleet on Malta – that same Malta for which we had fought Napoleon for so many years, which was indeed the very pretext of the renewal of war in 1803. *'Malte ou la guerre'*. Little did the Napoleon of St. Helena dream that in her most desperate need France would have at her disposal the great Mediterranean base which his strategic instinct had deemed vital. I said to the Admirals, 'Use Malta as your own as if it were Toulon.[109]

The reference to Malta in this classic Churchillian conceit framed in historical terms was suggestive in relation to the strategic pantheon of British Mediterranean possessions. Churchill could never have invited the French to use Gibraltar as their own in such a manner, not only because of its indispensability, but because the symbolism of the Rock in the English public mind prevented it being shared with anyone. Nor would Churchill have thought of inviting the French admirals to use Cyprus as their own since it could have offered them nothing of note. In fact the French navy was to find the welcome it received in Valletta much more qualified than Churchill suggested, and it became even more so as the war went on. But this lay in the future. On 12 August the French fleet duly entered Grand Harbour at Valletta. It did so early in the morning, welcomed by many spectators on the surrounding bastions, civic bands playing and a throng of Allied flags held aloft.[110] But these French warships did not arrive, as many had in the Crimean conflict, merely on British sufferance. They did so as constituent parts of overall French command in the Mediterranean. A vivid recollection of what this meant, at least in theory, is borne out in the National Museum of Fine Arts, once British naval headquarters in Valletta's South Street. The gleaming white marble staircase remains, and at its top are two engraved boards providing a complete list of 'Commanders-in-Chief, Mediterranean Fleet'. This recalls the resounding names of Hood, Vincent, Keith, Nelson and Collingwood, but at one point the sequence is intriguingly interrupted: 'August 1914–July 1917 post suspended'.

# 5

# 'Indifferent Fruits in the South', 1914–1918

At the outset of war in August 1914, the Anglo-French allies had two main preoccupations in the Mediterranean. The first was to ensure that the troop convoys from Algeria safely reached France. The second was not to be drawn into a major fleet engagement unless certain of victory. This latter necessity shaped the Admiralty's instructions to Admiral Sir Archibald Berkeley Milne as Commander-in-Chief to avoid any battle with a superior force. These instructions were the root cause of a disappointing start to hostilities casting a long shadow over the unfolding conflict: the escape of the *Goeben* and the *Breslau* from British clutches.

The British public was acutely aware of the threat these powerful ships posed. One prominent British official in Egypt, Ronald Storrs, setting off back to Cairo from Portsmouth, was typical in expecting that they would be reduced to 'so much slag' before his arrival.[1] This did not happen. Rear-Admiral Souchon was ordered by Berlin not to punch a way through the Strait of Gibraltar, as Milne himself expected, but to head for Constantinople. The enemy force was intercepted south of Corfu by a flotilla led by Admiral Ernest Troubridge in HMS *Gloucester*. Troubridge's first instinct was to ignore his orders and fight despite Souchon's bigger guns. 'I cannot', he explained to his flag officer regarding a failure to engage, 'have the name of the whole Mediterranean Squadron stink.'[2] But on second thoughts he reluctantly allowed the enemy ships to press eastwards; and on 14 August, after tense negotiations with the Turks, Souchon's two cruisers glided through the Straits to anchor off the Golden Horn. Shortly converted (as a nod to international law in these waters) to Turkish ownership,[3] Souchon's ships could, frustratingly, be seen by the British Ambassador from his summer villa cruising the Bosporus, its sailors sporting the fez as a thin token of their assumed nationality. By that time British warships were reduced to loitering off the Dardanelles in case Souchon ventured back into the Mediterranean. This was something he had no intention of doing. Instead the *Goeben*'s assault against Odessa in the Black Sea on 28 October finally pitched neutral Turkey into war with Russia and her *entente* partners, so triggering a wider war in the east.

The escape of the *Goeben* and the *Breslau* symbolized how far British command of Mediterranean waters had eroded. Much blame was distributed. Lord Fisher, recalled to the Admiralty as First Sea Lord, said he would have liked to see Milne shot like Admiral Byng, executed in 1756 for losing Minorca to the French.[4] Troubridge (a descendant of one of Nelson's captains) was court-martialled, and although acquitted and posted to a desk job, was never given an operational command again. On this episode was blamed not only Turkey's adherence on 5 November 1914 to Berlin and Vienna (now the 'Central Powers'), but also Russia's subsequent military travails and eventually, by stretching a lot of points along the way, even a share of responsibility for the Revolution of 1917. No two ships ever had such a load of historic causation laid on them as these German cruisers. All this was highly exaggerated. Germany's leverage over Turkey in August 1914 was already too far advanced to be contained. Nor was the escape of Souchon's squadron an unmitigated disaster for the *entente*. With the *Breslau* and *Goeben* bottled up behind the Dardanelles, Germany disappeared as a naval factor in the Mediterranean proper, with the exception before long of submarine activity (a very big exception, as we shall see). With Italy too intimidated by Anglo-French naval assault to do anything other than cling to neutrality, the *entente* had only to deal with the Austrians – and they were too circumspect to send their ships outside the Adriatic, much to the Kaiser's irritation. To that degree the start of the war in the Mediterranean proved an anticlimax. No big naval battle occurred and the Algerian garrisons were successfully taken to Europe in time for many to die on the Marne.[5]

The first few months of war witnessed significant Allied troop movements through the Mediterranean. British forces from the Far East,

India and Egypt passed on their way back to Britain; meanwhile Territorial battalions moved in the opposite direction to relieve the regular garrisons in Gibraltar, Malta and the eastern Mediterranean. Had enemy submarines been active – they did not arrive in the region till April 1915 – these toings and froings would have been far more hazardous. For the moment news blackouts and censorship meant that a thick fog surrounded what was going on; 'a blankness enveloped us . . . that leaves near objects clear and blots out the rest with baffling completeness', was how it seemed to a long-time English resident in Alexandria.[6] The Mediterranean was to have a distinctive flavour as a theatre. When Vera Brittain, whose life as a volunteer nurse in wartime Malta is described in *Testament of Youth*, returned to Britain in 1917, she was struck by how London seemed a besieged city compared to an existence amid Malta's 'golden-stoned buildings, of turquoise and sapphire seas, of topaz and amethyst skies'.[7] This reflected a rather rosy afterglow in retrospect, yet there certainly was a difference of intensity in the experience of war in northern and southern Europe after 1914, albeit with notable exceptions. It was widely felt that war service in the Mediterranean was an easy billet compared to elsewhere, and this continued to be so throughout the conflict.

War in the Mediterranean brought with it important political changes. These included matters of constitutional status. Once Great Britain and Turkey were at war with each other in early November, the residual Ottoman ties of Cyprus and Egypt could not remain the same. Cyprus was annexed by Britain forthwith. The official, Harry Luke, who had the task of informing the assembled Muslim notables that they were no longer subjects of the Caliph found that the news was taken with dignified resignation.[8] It was, after all, better than being handed over to Greece. Similarly in Egypt there was a strong temptation to make Egypt a fully fledged British possession. When the British Agency found out that a declaration in London making Egypt into a colony had already been drafted and was supposedly on its way to the printer, they pleaded against a 'death sentence' so far as any hope of retaining good relations with most Egyptians was concerned, asking for it to be commuted instead into a suitably fuzzy 'Protection' (shades of old Corfu).[9] Their wish was granted, but because even a Protectorate needed a reliable Egyptian figurehead, the subsidiary role of the

Khedivate was abolished and Prince Hussein – the son of the long-dead Ismail – reluctantly persuaded to accept the position of 'Sultan'. This did little good in urban Egypt, where Hussein was widely despised as an English stooge. Ronald Storrs, who had helped twist Hussein's arm, recalled:

> The students of the Law School appeared wearing black ties and lugubrious expressions; many girls in the Government Secondary Schools sported black rosettes. When in his inaugural drive to the Palace the [new] Sultan passed the grandstand . . . in Abdin Square they clapped half-heartedly, each one looking sideways to see what his neighbour was doing. The truth was that many were unable to believe that the Germans could be defeated, and were still expecting a victorious Turkish advance upon Egypt.[10]

Many local populations in the Mediterranean at this stage responded a bit like these Egyptian students, looking sideways to see how others were reacting to events, hedging bets wherever possible, and wondering if the English could hold their own in a straight fight with powerful Germany.

The imposition of closer control by Great Britain over Egypt made her liable to accusations of exploiting the present crisis to her own advantage. Britain's allies wanted matching gains for themselves. The Russians pushed their traditional claim to Constantinople more keenly than ever. Desperate to keep Russia in the war following her bloody losses in the Masurian Lakes and on the Carpathian front, in March 1915 the British and French promised the Tsarist government that in any peace settlement Constantinople would fall within their sphere (these were the 'secret treaties' later contemptuously repudiated by the Bolsheviks). But if the prize of Constantinople was allotted in this way, virtually everything else in the Ottoman Levant could be considered as potential spoils as well. The British and French soon began to run a measuring tape over which bits they could grab for themselves, if and when an opportunity arrived. At first this was done in a spirit of mutual co-operation, the peak of the process coming with the so-called Sykes–Picot Agreement (after the names of the negotiators) during May 1916. This provisionally carved up Syria, Lebanon, Palestine and Iraq. In parallel, the British stimulated a revolt by local Hashemite tribal leaders against Ottoman rule in the Arab lands. Vague promises were ladled out to the latter. Who had promised what to whom at this time was to be the cause of much later argument.

Yet all this remained hypothetical. Not only were the Turks far from defeated, but the possibility of their seizing the Suez Canal appeared all too real. It was a considerable Ottoman achievement in late 1914 to move a substantial force under General Djemal Pasha to Palestine's southernmost border. The British community in Alexandria worried about internal as well as external threats, particularly when the local barracks emptied of regular British troops, now urgently called home.[11] Reassurance gradually returned with the arrival of an Indian army contingent, followed by more familiar Lancashire Territorials (since their home county spun so much Egyptian cotton, Kitchener had quipped, it was good that Lancashire lads should see Egypt itself).[12] In January 1915 Australians and New Zealanders en route to Europe were disembarked in Port Said for training; many were to stay for the duration. These troops, however, were kept on the western bank of the Canal, so that it was not entirely clear whether the army was protecting the Canal, or the Canal was protecting the army.

When the Turkish assault finally came in late January 1915 it was successfully repulsed. Yet still the British did not push across the Canal in any force, and Djemal Pasha was able to withdraw in good order. Thereafter the Turks settled down under the skilled leadership of Djemal's adept German Chief of Staff, Kress von Kressenstein, to construct their own encampments in the desert, from which they sporadically harassed the British along the great waterway. Yet occasional skirmishes in the sand scarcely impinged on towns in the fertile Delta to the west, and a certain comfortable semi-normality arose. 'Egypt settled down to wartime conditions with unexpected good humour,' another long-time British Alexandrian remarked. 'The general feeling of uncertainty and of insecurity . . . vanished like a bad dream, to give place to a growing sense of well-being and satisfaction.'[13] For the British, and even for some Egyptians, the country was not a bad place to spend the war in. Certainly many cynics alleged that officers, not least the most senior, showed no urgency to leave.

The first adjustment towards a more aggressive Allied stance in the Mediterranean came in January 1915 and focused on the Dardanelles.

That this was owed to Winston Churchill at the Admiralty is paradoxical. Having once been all for stripping British ships and arms from the Mediterranean, he now became the advocate of doing the opposite. This arose from an insatiable temperamental opportunism. But it also represents a recurring theme: the Mediterranean as Great Britain's instinctive default position in successive modern conflicts. The war in northern France had ground to a bloody halt in a matter of months, and the main British and German fleets were stalemated in the North Sea. For Churchill, as a believer above all in movement, it was essential to do something somewhere. The naval victory at the Battle of the Falklands in the south Atlantic during early December meant that outside the North Sea, the oceans had been cleared of a German threat. This released a surplus of smaller and older ships, including light cruisers. These could not have stood up to a potential German battering in the North Sea but against the Turks – that is, in forcing the Dardanelles as the gateway to Constantinople – they might do the trick. Yet such suggestions attracted harsh criticisms. Fisher recalled that old canard, the failed naval attack at the Bosporus in 1807. More fundamental was the view, from which Churchill had strayed but which others stringently maintained, that the Mediterranean was a fatal diversion. 'We have the game in our hands,' Captain Herbert Richmond, the Assistant Director of Operations at the Admiralty and a leading naval theorist in his own right, asserted. 'It is no business of ours to go trying to pluck . . . indifferent fruits in the south.'[14]

Gradually, however, Churchill got his way, albeit in a qualified and grudging spirit. Kitchener, always 'Egyptian' first and last, and now Minister for War, thought that a demonstration, as he cautiously termed it, at the Straits might at least relieve pressure on the Nile. Grey and the Foreign Office, for their part, were eager to make some 'splash' to maintain Great Britain's wobbling prestige in the east. But nothing could be done without the concurrence of the 'man on the spot'. When Churchill asked Admiral Sir Sackville Carden, commanding the Royal Navy in the Aegean, the plain question of whether the Dardanelles could be forced by ships alone, Carden replied that the Straits could not be rushed in one go, but that they 'might be forced by extended operations with a large number of ships'.[15] This opinion was not universally shared even in the squadron, but people got carried along by the momentum. Nor could the French let the British go ahead alone, lest they hog the benefits of any victory.[16] Finally the War Council in London gave the go-ahead after having been being assured that a purely naval attack could always be broken off if things did not look promising.

When the initial attack was launched at the Dardanelles on 19 February 1915 some modest progress was made against the Outer Forts. But as Allied warships pressed into the Narrows, losses mounted. Mutual backbiting started up. Slurs were made about the tenacity of the trawlers with their fishermen-recruits from Grimsby and Hull, ordered to go in at night under close fire to clear the deadly mines; subsequent comments that the trawlers were asked to do the navy's job 'and had enjoyed no more success than if the Navy had been sent to catch fish off Iceland' were sadly apt.[17] A big frontal assault was attempted on 18 March, resulting in the disabling of HMS *Agamemnon* and HMS *Inflexible*, as well as the sinking of their French counterpart, *Bouvet*, the latter with 639 fatalities – she had 'just slithered down as a saucer slithers down the side of a bath'.[18] Subsequently Carden was sent back to a desk job in Malta, and his successor, Admiral John de Robeck, came down firmly against any further unsupported naval action. Instead of breaking it off altogether, however, the decision was now made to launch a combined land and sea operation. In agreeing to this General Sir Ian Hamilton at the head of a Mediterranean Expeditionary Force was determined that the army should take the principal role. On 25 April 1915 a mixed British, Australian and New Zealand force was landed on the tip of the Gallipoli peninsula. They were immediately confined to a narrow stretch of beach and pounded by Turkish gunfire from the cliffs above. 'Dig, dig, dig until you are safe,' was Hamilton's order to his soldiers.[19] The Gallipoli trauma had begun.

The biggest problem at the Dardanelles, apart from the Turks themselves, was supply.[20] Resources sent to the Mediterranean theatre remained carefully rationed, and much had to be obtained locally.[21] General Hamilton established his initial headquarters at the Metropole Hotel in Alexandria, then emerging as a major base for the first time since its occupation in 1882. The city's bazaars were scoured for oilskins, oildrums, kerosene, anything edible, all at highly inflated prices, while tugs and lighters bustled around the gas-lit harbour night and day. All this activity meant that for many businessmen the war 'glided tranquilly . . . into the making and spending of fortunes'.[22] On 10 April Hamilton transferred his command from Alexandria to Mudros on the island of Lemnos (appropriated pro tem from Greece). Henceforth Mudros was famous for having one of the biggest concentrations of 'brass hats' (senior officers with comfortable staff jobs) in the war.[23] One officer acquainted with the region was not impressed by Lemnos – 'the bleakest, ugliest, most un-Mediterranean island . . . seen or imagined', rather reminiscent of Shetland or the Falklands.[24] Most visitors remarked on the vast heaving mass of vessels (British, French, Greek) littering the seascape, from great dreadnoughts to dredgers and little local caiques. Before long more than 150 vessels were in and out of the harbour daily. Large-scale construction work was required ashore. Much of this was carried out by an Egyptian Labour Corps, paid a pittance. The British military authorities in Egypt had promised that the burdens of war would be kept off Egyptian shoulders.[25] The use of sweated labour in Mudros was among the first signs that this promise would not be kept.[26]

One person came to epitomize Britain's national loss at Gallipoli without actually getting there himself: Rupert Brooke, a young but already noted poet. He had enlisted at home, his imagination fired by the so-called 'Constantinople Expedition' put out by the recruiting machine.[27] In Alexandria, General Hamilton personally offered him a desk job, which he turned down. Being moved closer to the action, he fell sick at sea and was taken onto a French hospital ship on Skyros. He died of septicaemia on 23 April 1915. Faced with the problem of what to do with the body, and with the hospital vessel ordered immediately to Asia Minor, his colleagues decided to bury him swiftly on the island. His coffin was decked with French colours as well as an English flag. It was carried, a witness wrote home, to

> one of the loveliest places on this earth, with grey-green olives round him . . . the ground covered with flowering sage, bluish-grey and smelling more delicious than any other flower I knew . . . Think of it under a clouded moon, with the three mountains around and behind us and those divine scents everywhere. We lined his grave with all the flowers we could find . . .[28]

Brooke became a symbol of young wasted life in the war; it was also often remarked that he was the first leading British poet to die fighting for his country since Sir Philip Sidney in 1586. It was striking that the British public consciousness showed a strong inclination to take its Great War heroes and paragons (as with T. E. Lawrence shortly afterwards) from the Mediterranean rather than from the Western Front, perhaps because an echo of chivalry still seemed attached to the former. It helped in this case that Brooke's wartime poems had nothing of the empty disillusion reflected in Siegfried Sassoon's work. He was buried amid the grey-green olives too early in the war for that.

Getting soldiers to Gallipoli had been messy and often highly inefficient because of shipping shortages, many shuttled between various ports before being dumped on the peninsula. Moving the wounded out was even more complicated. Many lay for days on the beaches with dirty dressings. But a massive hospitalization effort was launched across the British Mediterranean. In the first few months of the war there had been no reason in Malta to anticipate such an emergency. On 4 May 1915, however, the first convoy of the distressed arrived, driven in horse-drawn ambulances through the Strada Reale.[29] By the end of that month there were 4,000 patients accommodated following an improvised expansion of eight hospitals. This rose to 10,000 by January 1916. The badly wounded were taken from the white hospital ships in barges to the dockside, and lowered by cranes to the nurses waiting with fresh swabs and clean linen. Malta reverted to its historic Hospitaller role – the 'Nurse of the Mediterranean', as it was dubbed – and the old Sacra Infermeria of the Knights provided the biggest ward on the island.[30] Before long, accommodation for patients – afflicted not least by dysentery and enteritis – overflowed into tents.[31] During the war some 1,500 British servicemen were buried on the island, along with those of many other nationalities (in 1921 Crown Prince Hirohito visited Malta to honour the Japanese sailors who died when serving with their nation's cruisers under British command after 1916). Alexandria, too, became 'half-camp and half-hospital', with a steady relay of hospital liners arriving in the port.[32] By the spring of 1915, an observer noted, British nurses could be seen everywhere in Alexandria, 'in the cafés, the oriental shops . . . on the esplanade, on the outlying pleasure-roads of Ramleh, the golf-links, the race course;

the *Rue Cherif Pacha* teems with her'.[33] In the wartime Mediterranean, British middle-class women often found a freedom for themselves not so easily available at home.[34]

The Dardanelles stalemate spread poison in many directions. The commanding British and French admirals (de Robeck and Émile Guepratté) were soon 'like a couple of dogs with their hackles up' whenever they met.[35] Fisher, a fierce opponent of the Dardanelles engagement, and Churchill at the Admiralty were at even greater odds. Finally Churchill's decision to bypass the First Sea Lord in sending two submarine reinforcements to the eastern Mediterranean precipitated Fisher's resignation in May 1915. It was the impact of this departure in the House of Commons – testifying to the force that specifically naval emotions still had in British politics – which brought down the long-standing Liberal government and its replacement by a coalition, still, however, led by an increasingly languid Herbert Asquith.[36] To the relief of Admiralty staff, Churchill was moved from that department, though the stain of the Dardanelles on his reputation and indeed on his own psychology never entirely went away.[37]

The formation of a new government, however, was the prelude, not to the liquidation of the Dardanelles commitment, but to its intensification. More troops were landed at Suvla Bay in early August 1915. These reinforcements only heightened what General Hamilton now described as 'the helpless, hopeless fix we are left in'.[38] The fix got still worse when Bulgaria, having swung in the balance, finally mobilized on behalf of the Central Powers in late September. This opened up rail communication between Germany and Constantinople. But the most immediate anxiety lay in another direction: the looming destruction of the *entente* ally Serbia. For the Bulgarians, an opportunity had arrived to crush a dangerous rival. How to save Serbia became for the *entente* the issue of the moment as Mediterranean and Balkan considerations merged into one.

Since the easiest thing was to get somebody else to go to Serbia's rescue, the idea surfaced of persuading Greece to do so in return for the acquisition of Cyprus. British philhellenes rallied in support, and the idea crystallized that the island's Archbishop should be taken to Athens by the Royal Navy to clinch the deal.[39] But when the offer of cession was formally made in mid-October, the government of

Constantine I (who had succeeded to the throne of Greece during October 1912 after the assassination of his father, King George) refused. For Greece, even the gain of Cyprus was not worth the dangers of being, as Constantine saw it, 'wiped off the map'.[40] To the new King and his supporters, protecting gains made in the fighting of 1912–13 rather than adding to them was the real interest of Greece. To some other Greeks, such as Venizelos, to miss the opportunity of teaming up with the British and French, with all the promise this held out of grabbing extra bits of territory, was madness. Here was the basis of a schism in Greek political life which the British and the French were to play a part in wedging open. Meanwhile, to Greek-Cypriots, this rejection brought a certain bemused disappointment. It contained, however, one compensation. Having offered to cede the island to Athens once, the British could not insist henceforth that it was an eventuality that could never be discussed.[41] In this expectation Cypriots were to be frequently disappointed.

The *entente* was left with the question of leaving Serbia to its fate, or intervening directly themselves. The French Government pressed for landing an army as quickly as possible at Salonica, from where troops might be moved northwards to the Serbian frontier. Although reluctant, the British joined this French-led enterprise for the same reason that the French had participated at Gallipoli: they did not trust their ally to go it alone lest they monopolize whatever prizes might eventually be thrown up. By November 1915 more than 15,000 British troops had been disembarked at Salonica under the overall command of General Maurice Sarrail at the head of his 'Army of the Orient', a force formed out of the scrapings of army depots throughout France. British impressions of Salonica on arrival were generally pejorative; 'like a second-rate Port Said, with Alexandrine undertones, neither in Europe, nor in Asia, but both',[42] typified an ambivalence that was always the counterpoint to the Byronic tradition in British life. Meanwhile *entente* troops camped on Greek soil without an invitation only underlined what the British Ambassador in Athens, Sir Francis Elliot, described as the 'deep suspicion of us which has now become ingrained in all classes of the [Greek] population'.[43]

Allied discomfort in Salonica, and in up-country Macedonia, became pronounced as the campaign dragged on. Complaints multiplied about the local authorities. Municipal buildings were not made available for military purposes. Railway officials were accused of hampering troop movements northwards. Prices for almost everything soared, including coffee and drinks at Floca's Café on the famous Esplanade, one of the social landmarks of Allied occupation. Money matters led to increasing grumbles, usually focused on local Jews, a prominent element in the Salonica population (a community overwhelmingly of Spanish Sephardic background). Relations in general were brittle, though modestly alleviated by the prosperity that the military presence brought. British troops called most locals 'Johnnies' as if they were colonials;[44] what the Greeks called the Allied soldiers the latter rarely understood. The occupation certainly left an indelible mark on the city. Much of it was burned down in a fire on 18 August 1917, leaving 72,000 homeless, though how the conflagration arose was never clarified.

Meanwhile Serbia was anyway lost. Its army could not stave off a combined Austro-German and Bulgarian onslaught in October–November 1915, and in December there began a heroic Serbian retreat over the mountains towards Albania. Thereafter the Austro-German Commander, Marshal Erich von Falkenhayn, could quite easily have thrown the *entente* out of the Aegean altogether had he chosen to do so. Instead he stopped at the Greek frontier. The Anglo-French forces in the area retreated to the region around Salonica itself and proceeded to dig themselves in, Gallipoli-fashion, except not under murderous fire (a good deal of the digging was again done by Egyptian labour). The Allied presence in the city became dependent for its supply on the Royal Navy, so that Sarrail grumbled about the city resembling 'an English colony'.[45] The French commander's desire to go on the offensive never came to fruition before he was relieved of his command in December 1917.

Marshal Falkenhayn coined his own description of the Allied presence in Greek Macedonia: he called it 'Germany's largest concentration camp', conveniently run and financed by the *entente* itself. The army of Salonica became the butt of many jibes. A standard joke in wartime music halls in London was: 'If you want a holiday, why not go to Salonica?' The army gained an additional tag as 'The Gardeners of Salonica' because of the order to soldiers to grow their own vegetables, if only because it gave them something to do.[46] After the war no medal was struck in honour of what was often perceived as a mostly forlorn campaign. All this was not entirely fair, since the Salonica front was to play a key role in the climax of 1918. Meanwhile one advantage of the commitment was that it diverted attention from the final evacuation of troops from Gallipoli in January 1916. If the arrival of Allied troops in that location had been a fearful experience, at least their departure was executed with very few losses, though by then some 46,000 Allied troops had been killed on that bleak spit of land.

The longer *entente* troops remained penned up in and around Salonica, the more fragile relations became with King Constantine in Athens. This rising bitterness was a measure of Allied frustration at immobility in the Mediterranean theatre as a whole. 'This [Greek] regime is hell,' remarked the Chief of the Imperial General Staff in London, and the Allies set about bringing it to heel through 1916 by a succession of naval demonstrations and threats of bombardment.[47] Allied machinations were involved in the 'revolution' in Salonica on 30 August. If Sarrail hoped to put a distinctively French imprint on this development, however, he was disappointed. The movement drew what strength it had from Eleutherios Venizelos, and in Venizelos's world-view, shaped by his Cretan experience, the key to the future was to be tied in with the British, not the French, fleet. Suggestively, he first went back to Crete to assure himself of support from his native province, before going to Salonica to establish a provisional government there.[48]

After that there were to be two Greeces, one ('New Greece') under *entente* protection based in Salonica, and the other ('Old' and Constantinist Greece) principally in Athens and the Peloponnese. Partial blockade and spreading malnutrition as grain supplies ran out was not enough to bludgeon the latter into submission. On 1 December 1916 the Allies finally landed more than 3,000 troops in Salamis Bay. In early morning darkness they advanced the short distance to central Athens. Fighting broke out with regular Greek troops. The King and his family sought shelter in the cellar of the palace. One hundred and ninety-four Allied troops were killed or wounded in exchanges in the public gardens.[49] Lord Grey, doubtful about the worth of the entire enterprise, ruled against any shelling of the Acropolis that might turn local feelings even more bitterly against the *entente*.[50] Athens was nevertheless coerced and the Greek army was made to march past and dip its national colours before the Allied flags. In June 1917 the politically beleaguered King finally abdicated, though the ultimatum that brought this about was thought to be unwise by Ambassador Elliot, and thoroughly disliked by King George V because of his family connection.[51] Now there was one Venizelist Greece under the supervision of an Allied High Commissioner in the form of Charles Jonnart, an ex-Governor-General of Algeria (another genuflection to French command in the Mediterranean).[52] These events shaped a fundamental divide in Greek politics, and were still generating acrimonious recriminations among British circles long after the war ended.

The fate of Greece had one particularly colourful facet: a war of espionage, captured in Compton Mackenzie's *Greek Memories* (1932). Mackenzie had been at Gallipoli, but was sent to Athens by General Hamilton, himself something of an aesthete, on the grounds that the loss of one budding literary star in Rupert Brooke was quite enough.[53] Mackenzie combated the German spy network set up by Baron Schenk, working with his French counterpart Commander de Roquefeuil. Schenk's own methods were pedestrian enough, exploiting Court circles and bribing newspapers. Mackenzie and de Roquefeuil, however, went further by employing a variety of thugs,[54] and building up vast amounts of personal information, mostly composed (as Mackenzie himself admitted) of lies and gossip.[55] The British legation complained strongly to London about Mackenzie, whose work it considered counter-productive among the Greeks themselves.[56] A characteristic escapade came after the *entente* incursion into Athens in December 1916, when Mackenzie landed on Syra and commandeered one of King Constantine's own yachts. Donning the elegant white uniform of a marine officer, and armed with a swordstick given to him by 'C' (Head of MI6), Mackenzie 'steamed in palatial style' through the Cyclades, and later to Samos and the Dodecanese, promoting local officials he considered sound, and deposing anybody he took a dislike to.[57] But, comic opera though this was, it was part of a returning British ascendancy in the Aegean.

The Greek imbroglio was related to another question coming gradually to the forefront: the future of Asia Minor. Already in early 1915 the British had held out vague hints to Greece that it might be compensated with a slice of territory there.[58] The encouragement of British agents also helped to stimulate Armenian unrest. A general unsettledness provided the context for the ensuing mass slaughter of the Armenian population by the Ottoman state.[59] In early 1916 the British began to make use of Greek 'irregulars' – often a 'ruffianly crew', as a senior British naval officer admitted – to make fresh raids along the Anatolian coastline.[60] A prominent British figure in these forays was John Myers, a distinguished Oxford classicist, and early cataloguer of the Cyprus Museum's antiquities, but who in wartime changed character to 'the Blackbeard of the Aegean', assisted by a close knowledge of the topography.[61] Influential Greeks in London complained to the Foreign Office that such incursions into Asia Minor simply encouraged further reprisals against exposed Christian villagers.[62] The Armenian Patriarch had for some time been uttering similar fears.[63] Whatever the complex and varied forces at work, the early phases of the war helped to make Asia Minor into an ethnic powder keg.

Meanwhile Italy, joined to Austria and Germany in the peacetime Triple Alliance, might logically have followed them into war as well. In fact she opted for neutrality for the same reason as Greece: fear of Anglo-French naval bombardment.[64] Rome's neutrality was a considerable relief in London, because it met any remaining fear that a combination of Italian and Austrian dreadnoughts would overwhelm the Mediterranean. It was in the nature of Italy's 'balancing' role in southern European diplomacy that she was now able to bargain with both sides to see who might pay the highest price for her assistance (something Greece was never powerful enough to do). In subsequent bargaining the *entente* had the advantage over the Central Powers. The latter sought to tempt the Italians with the lure of Malta and Tunis once victory was achieved, but for Italy this could not match the *entente*'s bait of belatedly completing her northern frontiers with territory currently held by Austria. Afterwards the biddable character of Italian belligerency was held against her as a moral taint, though it arose quite naturally from her ambiguous place in pre-1914 diplomacy.[65] Nevertheless, by the secret Treaty of London in May 1915, Lord Grey played the central role in bringing Italy into the war against Austria (though not against Germany till August 1916). The fact that – submarines, as usual, apart – the central Mediterranean ceased to be such a danger point was a crucial prerequisite for British expansion in the eastern part of the basin that shortly began to take shape.

For some time the only British 'uniformed' presence in Italy was that of the British Red Cross. The historian and admiring biographer of Garibaldi, G. M. Trevelyan, was sent to organize the first ambulance unit. Trevelyan saw Italy's eventual adherence to the *entente* as reconfirmation of her liberal statehood, albeit recently pockmarked by less progressive influences. Writing in a vein influenced by the part Italy had played in his own intellectual and moral development, he captured in a memoir of his wartime experience in the country the nostalgic swell of Risorgimento-type feelings among the urban population, including a strong dose of anti-Austrian and pro-English sentiment. The pro-Englishness had characteristically naval connotations, illustrated by a theatrical event Trevelyan witnessed in Rome with a special tableau featuring a Royal Navy officer keenly applauded by the audience.[66] But his account emphasized that although pro-*entente* demonstrations in the cities brought Italy into the war, it was the peasantry who bore the real burden. Across the country, therefore, views about Italy's part in the war ranged hugely according to the risks and privations endured, and – because dislike of the French was a constant factor – assessments of the British offered a fluctuating and sensitive vector of mass feeling. Trevelyan wrote:

> Both in Rome that summer [of 1915], and in all Italy inside and outside the war zone from 1915 to 1918, the touchstone of enthusiasm for the war had been friendliness to England and the touchstone of indifference or aversion to the war has been Anglophobia. England, more or less unconscious of the matter herself, has been a party for or against [the war] in Italy for the last four years.[67]

Trevelyan typified this vein of Anglophobia by a conversation he had at an Italian sentry-post high up on frozen Monte Sabbottino facing the Austrian positions. 'You English', he was firmly told, were seeking to prolong the war as long as possible because it meant that from the Strait of Gibraltar to the Dardanelles, Great Britain could increasingly sweep the Mediterranean of everybody else and grab their trade and territory. In such allegations could be heard an echo of much European feeling in the latter years of the war against Napoleon. In trying hard to counter this view Trevelyan got nowhere.

Although Italy entered the war later than Britain, she (like Greece) ended up with higher losses proportional to population. This underlay an Italian sense of being abandoned by her allies that neither the few British Ambulance Units, nor the ten British mountain artillery batteries dispatched from the spring of 1917, could allay.[68] The real test came with the large losses sustained by Italy at the Battle of Caporetto in October–November 1917. Five British infantry divisions – led by the Northumberland Fusiliers – were urgently rushed to the main front, and along with a larger French force played a marginal if helpful role in stemming the Austro-German advance on the Piave river (the so-called *Arrestamento*). By the end of 1917 the British casualties on this front amounted to 179 killed and wounded, as opposed to Italian losses of 11,000 killed and 20,000 wounded at Caporetto alone. It was a measure of unstable relations with Italy that by 1918, and even more afterwards, there was a tendency by the British and French to claim that they had been instrumental in stemming the Caporetto disaster, while Italian accounts wholly discounted their contribution.[69]

In fact, from an *entente* perspective, the entry of Italy into the war in May 1915 turned out to be of limited benefit. One reason was that it coincided with the early phases of the 'submarine war' in the Mediterranean. The sinking of the Cunard passenger liner *Lusitania* off Ireland on 7 May with many American fatalities was a propaganda and diplomatic disaster for Germany, and led Berlin to shift more U-boats to the Mediterranean, where fewer Americans were likely to be victims. Getting the boats into the Mediterranean presented challenges. One way was by train to the Adriatic, where they were assembled at what became the main Austro-German submarine base at Cattaro (in today's Croatia). The first, U-boat 21, arrived on 15 May 1915. The other way was for the submarines to sail mostly on the surface to the Strait of Gibraltar, evading interception, and then pass through submerged. This was a long and dangerous haul for such cramped and vulnerable craft, although once in the Mediterranean they were pretty secure. Anti-submarine devices, such as prototype 'directional finders', were still primitive and techniques of containment only evolved very slowly.

The main Allied priority in this branch of the war was to 'bottle up' the U-boat squadrons inside the Adriatic, a task made difficult because the Strait of Otranto was deeper than the English Channel. The 'Otranto Barrage' was established but the term was misleading, since it was all too easily evaded. Its operation required lots of small craft, 'indicator' nets, booms, and shallow-draught monitors, all in desperately short supply. In September 1915 the British sent sixty trawlers, although soon after arrival in November these were diverted to the dramatic evacuation of the Serbian army from the Albanian coast after their epic march from the interior. Most of these emaciated troops were taken to Corfu, now once more full of British and French soldiers, and for some time a vigorous community revolved around the Serbian Government in exile; a Serbian Mausoleum from that time remains on the isle of Vido. Thereafter there was a British anti-submarine flotilla based at Taranto on Italy's southern heel, though Lord Balfour at the Admiralty lamented that 'we cut a poor figure' in this theatre of war.[70] There was still some advantage to be gained, however, from acting as a buffer between the French and Italians. The French Commander-in-Chief in the Mediterranean, Vice-Admiral Augustin de Lapeyrère, allegedly only felt comfortable meeting senior Italian naval officers if the British were present too.[71]

Although tensions in the Anglo-French naval relationship in the wartime Mediterranean remained muted for some time, there was a natural tendency for them to reappear as time went by. One problem was that the command structure was confusing and apt to lead to mutual misunderstanding. Apart from nominal supreme command in the Mediterranean, based at Malta, the French had control of waters between France and Algeria, around Toulon, south and west of Greece, and the eastern Mediterranean around Cyprus and off the Syrian coast; while the British controlled zones around Gibraltar, between Malta and Egypt, and in the Aegean. Not only did French overall command in the region become increasingly vestigial, the British zones showed a natural tendency to expand. This was partly because of the nature of the maritime war. In August 1914 it seemed that capital warships would be the key to victory, and, so far as the Mediterranean was concerned, France had most vessels in that category. But no big naval action ever took place (the handful of major Habsburg units never daring to leave the Adriatic), and in anti-submarine work, and keeping military and commercial traffic on the move, the real key lay in the possession of smaller and more flexible ships. The British had far more of these, and the gap widened after 1916. As a result, a feeling grew among the British that they were carrying out the 'business part' of the war in the Mediterranean, and this fuelled a desire to regain the independence of action, even primacy, that had been enjoyed before 1914.

The position of the French Commander-in-Chief in the Mediterranean was not enviable. Admiral Lapeyrère, occupying that post after August 1914, soon started spending more time in Bizerta, indisputably French, and as little as possible in Malta. His successor after late 1915, Admiral Dartige du Fournet, was forced to remain largely in Valletta, because it was here that information was coming in from the Adriatic and Balkans. The trouble was that, whatever Churchill may once have said to French Admirals about treating it as their own, Malta remained very British indeed. There were more than fifty Royal Navy ships in and out of Grand Harbour every day. Soon du Fournet felt that his supreme Allied title had become 'only a word'.[72] It was a relief when he was able to move his command to Corfu in early 1916. After that the British and French began to go their separate ways, within the exigencies of alliance. British control over the routing of traffic to avoid the threat from submarines, a task necessarily centralized in Malta, accentuated the divergence. Here was the background to the reinstatement of the post of 'British Commander-in-Chief, Mediterranean', abolished at the outbreak of war, but renewed during August 1917 in the person of Admiral Sir Somerset Gough-Calthorpe. Technically the latter still reported to du Fournet's successor, Vice-Admiral Dominique-Marie Gauchet in Corfu Town, but this was merely nominal.

Gough-Calthorpe's main task to start with was to preside over the introduction of a system of convoys, belatedly introduced as anti-submarine protection. This method generally worked much better in the Atlantic than in the Mediterranean, because there the combination of co-ordination, timing and the greater space available was in its favour. Nevertheless, in the Mediterranean, too, a reduction of losses to U-boat attacks was effected, though they were never eliminated (the greatest number of sinkings came in spring 1917). Thereafter the British appointed shipping control officers in many Mediterranean ports, again stirring memories of the blockade and supervision of Napoleonic times and their petty annoyances. Most of the spokes in this wheel went back to naval headquarters in Valletta. It was another way that British power in the region enjoyed a reinvigoration, though detailed oversight from Valletta was not always welcome even to British naval commanders elsewhere in the Mediterranean who in many cases had actually enjoyed having a French supreme commander who could be blithely ignored whenever it suited them.

Malta's own war was defined, as this account has already implied, by hospitals and the comings and goings of navies. Vera Brittain's letters home from the island were 'full of wrecks and drownings', recalling, for example, how the loss in the Aegean of the hospital ship *Britannic* – a vessel that had been a frequent visitor to Grand Harbour – in late November 1916 'galvanized the island like an electric shock'.[73] Internal political tensions died down. At its outbreak there was a loyalist demonstration in front of the Governor's Palace, the usual festive bands and all.[74] Italian neutrality at the outset also avoided a painful clash of identities for some Maltese. The King's Own Malta Regiment and the Royal Malta Artillery helped to replace the regular British garrison called home in September 1914, and one commentator remarked that this innovation led 'politically [to] a valuable link between the garrison and the civil population'.[75] One test of the reconsolidation of Anglo-Maltese ties under war conditions was whether local volunteers would be accepted for combatant service in the war. A sticking point was the refusal of the War Office to pay Maltese recruits the 'British' rate for the job. This refusal was naturally a disincentive to join up, as was the awful state in which casualties arrived from Gallipoli, understandably raising the query of whether Maltese would qualify for a British 'rate' of care. Even in the spring of 1918, when military manpower was at breaking point, the War Office would not budge on the matter of pay for the Maltese, by which time the issue had become highly charged. Nonetheless, around 15,000 Maltese served under one or other of the British armies during the war,[76] including the Royal Naval Air Service. Maltese aviation history, indeed, commenced when a Short Seaplane took off from Grand Harbour on 13 February 1915.[77] There were four navies using the harbour in these years (British, French, Italian and Japanese), and in 1917 the Admiralty reckoned that the dockyard was working at a higher pressure than any other outside the United Kingdom itself.[78] Malta's contribution to the war of 1914–18 was not so obviously heroic as it was to be between 1940 and 1943, but it was certainly substantial in shipping and logistical terms.

Political questions also remained largely under wraps so long as the war lasted. The colonial administration left sensitive language matters severely alone. The 'abstentionist' politicians did not alter their critical stance towards government, but the edge came off their attacks, and there was even some disarray in their ranks.[79] Enrico Mizzi, whose deceased father had been so prominent in opposing anything smacking of Anglicization, was tried for sedition in 1917 and sentenced to a period of hard labour, shortly commuted. Notably, this did not cause much of a stir. The real danger was of industrial action triggered by such grievances as the increase in taxes and persistent inflation. During 1917 there was a strike in the dockyard, but this was soon solved with the mediation of Archbishop Caruana.[80] The Maltese Catholic hierarchy showed no signs of wishing to make life difficult for the civil authorities. Caruana himself had spent most of his life in Scotland before elevation, and struck up a close working relationship with Field-Marshal Lord Methuen once the latter became Governor in 1915. Between 1914 and 1918 the island did not enjoy the booming prosperity of the Napoleonic and Crimean conflicts, and worries set in as to what would happen when peace came. But for the duration food and jobs, especially for workers associated with the British services, were plentiful, while the economy modestly diversified along the lines recommended by the 1912 Royal Commission.[81]

Like Malta, Gibraltar's strategic and imperial role was to a considerable degree validated during these years. It was even more prominent in British public awareness than Malta because it was not only a port of call for traffic en route to the Mediterranean, but was also a collecting centre for convoys across the Atlantic. Troopships and hospital liners were constantly in and out. It was at this stage that Gibraltar was said to have come 'into the first rank among the great ports of the world';[82] 350 warships and 80 merchant vessels received major repairs there. The old garrison identity of the colony was reinforced. Not only was British control over the Neutral Ground strictly maintained, but a runway for airplanes was built across the isthmus, though as yet little used. Control over entry by 'aliens' was further tightened up. Incoming Spanish labour, however, remained vital to the dockyards, and most of the births over this period were to Spanish mothers resident on the Rock. In other words, the distinctive traits and contradictions of Gibraltar's situation and society were underscored, not undermined, by war.

The large sums of money spent over the previous twenty years on strengthening Gibraltar's landward defences were essentially a kind of insurance policy, because what really enabled the colony to play the role it did was not the protection afforded by big guns pointing towards the interior but the simple fact that Spain remained neutral. King Alfonso continued to incline towards an Anglo-French connection (in 1912 he had sent his heir, Don Carlos, to pay respects to King George V when the latter visited Gibraltar, the first time a Spanish royal had set foot on the Rock for more than two hundred years).[83] The Spanish army was too preoccupied with a messy, low-level war in its Moroccan enclave to have any opportunistic thoughts about seizing back the Rock while attention was diverted elsewhere. Germany did try to tempt Spain over to active support of the Central Powers, using the future prize of Gibraltar as bait, and Berlin's spies – often infiltrated through Spanish Morocco – made Spain, like Greece, a principal theatre of the espionage war. U-boat sinkings of Spanish merchant shipping, however, hardly assisted the German cause in Madrid.

Spain may not have been a belligerent, but the war brought some drastic effects.[84] Northern regions boomed, but the south stagnated, especially Andalusia, where there were food riots during 1917. Under these circumstances, Gibraltar's role as a buffer for Andalusian poverty was also reinforced. There was some danger that labour tensions in Spain might seep into the colony, and a strike of Spanish coal-heavers caused temporary problems in the dockyard at one point. The fall of the pro-*entente* Prime Minister, Count Romanones, in April 1917 was a sign that all might not go smoothly in the future. Indeed, the Military Governor of Cadiz, General Miguel de Rivero, gave a speech on 'the Recovery of Gibraltar', albeit suitably vague as to how this might actually be done.[85] The General was promptly sacked, but King Alfonso's neutrality became 'correct' rather than positively friendly towards the *entente*. Court circles became increasingly pro-German, leaving the English Queen Eugenie yet more isolated and unhappy.[86] Meanwhile there was another token of change the implications of which could hardly yet be appreciated. In the early years of the previous century American warships had made their presence felt in the western Mediterranean, not least against Barbary pirates. After early 1917, now 'associated' if not actually allied with Britain and France, the United States navy was back, with Gibraltar providing base facilities for a patrol force of the US Atlantic Fleet.[87] The presence of the USS *Birmingham* in the Gibraltar dock presaged a modern American fleet presence in the Mediterranean.

Cyprus, ambivalent as always in its connection with Britain, had a very different relationship to the war. We have seen that in an attempt to save Serbia the British were even prepared to barter the island.[88] 'It would be very satisfactory if we could say that Cyprus was indissolubly united to the British Empire,' one Colonial Office official remarked in November 1915 just after this episode. 'But I am afraid that we cannot say that.'[89] It was probably true, as Sir George Hill, author of a massive history of Cyprus, observed, that subsequently even a 'little thing might have turned the scale' in favour of a fresh offer to Greece. Such a thing might have been the need to bribe Venizelos into co-operation; though in truth Venizelos was too much in the *entente* pocket after late 1916 to need bribing. But although the attachment of Cyprus to Britain was not yet quite 'indissoluble', the enlargement of a British presence in the eastern Mediterranean from this stage in the war implicitly put a greater value on its retention, even if the British still held back from spending the money needed to convert it into a genuine base. Lord Curzon, the experienced imperial statesman serving in the coalition Cabinet, and who took a close interest in all colonial matters, sought to rule out any abandonment of the island when he said that he regarded it 'as a most valuable possession not to be parted with in any circumstances now above the horizon',[90] although even this still left a possibility that things might change.

Although Cyprus was of little direct military use in the war, it played a not inconsiderable role as a source of provisions. The island was poor, but, unlike tiny Gibraltar and confined Malta, it did have an agriculture generating an exportable surplus. Such a surplus needed a market, and the presence of British armies in the eastern Mediterranean after 1915–16 provided just that. Troops in Egypt, Macedonia and later Palestine absorbed 20,000 tons of Cypriot grain, 38,000 tons of potatoes, 40,000 goats and 800,000 eggs.[91] While Famagusta was not a great naval port, as a commercial harbour it could facilitate a growing trade. Animal transport also played a vital role. Mules were an indispensable part of all eastern campaigns. During the Crimea conflict the British War Office had had to scour Spain and North Africa for these useful animals, and then ship them to the point of need. From the occupation of Cyprus in 1878 onwards British needs in this regard were eased by the availability to them of the hardy Cypriot mule. After 1916 in particular the British army maintained large purchasing commissions in Cyprus, and one of their functions was to oversee extensive mule farms close to Famagusta. 'Not only did Cyprus not suffer through the war,' remarked Harry Luke, who served as District Commissioner in Paphos at this time; 'it did well out of it.'[92] The annual report of the Cyprus Government for 1916–17 went so far as to claim 'that at no time for many hundreds of years has there been so great a demand as at present . . . for the various products of Cyprus'.[93] This brought with it a new prosperity, and one that was more soundly based than that of Malta and Gibraltar, always liable to dissipate as soon as wartime shipping activity fell away.

But prosperity also had pitfalls for expatriate rule. It usually meant more, not less, politics; and in Cyprus – with its assertive Greek population – politics was something the British found peculiarly hard to handle. In the early phases of the war Cypriot affairs were placid enough. After the annexation of November 1914, the loyalty of local Muslims towards the British became still more pronounced.[94] This connection between the colonial administration and the Turkish minority was important for the future. Nor were the Greek-Cypriot politicians as troublesome for the government as they had been between 1912 and 1914. As elsewhere in the Mediterranean, war had at first a deadening effect on politics. The election in 1916 of Archbishop Kyrillos III was welcomed, and indeed facilitated, by the British. Luke called him a 'religious pope',[95] meaning an Archbishop not interested in getting involved in political controversy, always very desirable for the authorities. Kyrillos promised, for example, to keep Hellenic flags off Church buildings. Furthermore, Greek-Cypriots became intensely divided among themselves, some lining up behind the adherents of King Constantine in Greece, and some supporting Venizelos. But what might have tactical advantages for the British also implied future danger, since it indicated that Greek-Cypriots were now not only thinking of themselves as Greeks, but defining themselves in Greek political terms. Sporadic incidents began to occur, especially as more troops in the island sometimes led to friction. When the Archbishop went to Famagusta in 1917 and was welcomed by schoolboys waving the Greek colours, the latter were quickly confiscated by the police for fear that a violent reaction might be triggered among the British soldiers in the town.[96] During the war relations between administrators and Greek-Cypriots remained wary, while the latter's aspirations to join Greece did not decline. When at the end of the war an officer who had been based in Cyprus wrote a study of the island he noted that the gap between the British and the educated Greek-speaking class was widening rather than narrowing.[97] This was a disturbing sign.

It was in Egypt that the effects of Britain's wartime effort in the Mediterranean were to be most powerfully felt. This logic, however, came about only gradually. After the failure of the Turkish attack in February 1915, General Sir John Maxwell, as Commander-in-Chief in Egypt, settled down to a passive defence of the line of the Canal. The limited pressure this entailed on supplies and expenditure meant that the original British promise to carry the burden of the war themselves could at first be kept. But before long Maxwell's passivity attracted criticism. After the evacuation of the Dardanelles in January 1916, the number of British troops swelled. These were transformed into an 'Egyptian Expeditionary Force' (EEF). At one time it was said, no doubt apocryphally, that there were 200 generals staying at Shepheard's

Hotel.[98] Maxwell was shortly called home for urgent duties in Ireland – having kept Egyptians reasonably quiet, it was hoped he could do the same in Dublin after the bloody Easter Rising. He was replaced by General Archibald Murray. At first Murray was as cautious as his predecessor. His scope was limited in two ways. The first was that the EEF was designated a 'strategic reserve' for the Western Front, so that troops were siphoned off whenever necessary to Europe, as at the time of the Somme offensive during the summer of 1916. The second arose from the Cabinet's instruction to do nothing to prejudice the security of Egypt. This meant doing little more than keeping order and fending off the harassments of General von Kressenstein along the Canal, who managed to tie down the equivalent of three British army corps.[99]

From the spring of 1916, however, conscious of the sniping at the EEF's performance at home, Murray sought to move Egypt's line of defence forward into the desert. To do this required the laying down of railways, greatly expanded animal transport, the provision of water, and much else. Inevitably, this required calling on Egyptian resources, most notably labour. So long as this could be rationalized as a defence of Egypt it met with some tolerance by the local population. Egyptians had no particular liking for the British but nor did they love the Turks. Ottoman attempts, for example, to play on shared religious loyalties with Egyptians usually fell on stony ground.[100] In July–August 1916 von Kressenstein launched a fresh attack on the EEF front line now punched into the Sinai, but his forces were repulsed with significant losses. This was the last Turkish movement towards the Canal during the war. By January 1917 the EEF had cleared the Turks from Rafah on the border with southern Palestine. Subsequently the great escalation of the British army requirements – by mid-1917 there were 135,000 forced labourers normally described in reports as 'teams of cheerful Egyptians' – was all the more resented because it had become quite glaringly a 'foreign war' beyond Egyptian boundaries. The requisitioning of 35,000 camels was an especial grievance. 'It is a matter of opinion', an astute British observer wrote 'whether in the end the *fellah* [Egyptian peasant] was more suspicious of the Army than the Army was of him.'[101] Although patchy prosperity in the towns of the Delta meant that discontent there was less overt, rising prices and food shortages hit the poorer classes.

Meanwhile the terms of Britain's Mediterranean warfare were transformed by the political crisis replacing Asquith by Lloyd George at the head of a new coalition government during December 1916. Lloyd George won power by a commitment to continue the war, but he wanted a less punishing conflict than the one being fought on the Western Front, where the failure of the Nivelle offensive and mutinies in the French army the following spring underlined disillusionment.[102] Lloyd George's growing inclination towards the eastern Mediterranean was a facet of this. Murray was promptly ordered to go on the offensive, and when two attacks faltered against the wired entrenchments of the Turkish defences at Gaza, he was himself replaced by General Edmund Allenby. Allenby's reputation on the Western Front had suffered a setback at the Battle of Arras (April 1917), but he more than recovered it in Palestine. He arrived in June 1917, at which point the essentially static British forces in the area totalled approximately 100,000 distributed along the Suez Canal, the lines of communications across the Sinai peninsula and in forward positions stretching from the coast to the Negev desert.[103] Before being willing to make an advance, Allenby demanded and received an extra 20,000 troops, raising the EEF to seven infantry and three cavalry divisions, the latter including an Imperial Camel Corps Brigade. In providing such forces Lloyd George set his own demands: he insisted on Jerusalem as 'a Christmas present for the British nation'.[104] This was not because of Jerusalem's military importance, set on low hills and without resources, but because its symbolic power was so great.[105] In late October 1917 the EEF was thrown against the Gaza–Beersheba line again, this time with overwhelming superiority; the artillery bombardment was the biggest of the war outside Europe.[106] When Ronald Storrs got there he found the main hill overlooking Gaza had been 'almost shelled away'.[107] Even before the bombardment began the Turks had evicted many of the frightened Arab population so they did not get in the way of the defenders.[108]

Afterwards Allenby pushed on towards Jerusalem, though the early onset of winter caused a good deal of privation among the wind-lashed hills of Judaea; the army's clothing was still summer drill brought from Egypt. The Holy City was subsequently vacated without a fight by the Turks, who drew up fresh defences a bit to the north, from which they were not to be moved until the end of the war. When the Arab Mayor of famished Jerusalem ventured out on the morning of 9 December he could only find two bashful sergeants of the 2/29 Lancashire Regiment, cooks sent foraging for some eggs, unwilling to accept the keys of the town offered to them.[109] It took some while before the perplexed Mayor came across General Shea of the 60th London Division, who was more receptive (according to legend Jerusalem had to be surrendered seven times before it became a fact).[110] After that the British occupation of Jerusalem was stage-managed as Lloyd George intended. Allenby dismounted outside the walls, and entered through the Jaffa Gate on foot, in stark contrast to the Kaiser's appearance on a white horse in 1898. He then read a proclamation announcing martial law, and left for his headquarters, set up at a discreet distance away. The Jerusalemites appear to have been entirely welcoming. For them it was an end to privation and relentless Turkification.[111] Once the news reached London the bells of Westminster Abbey were rung, and *Punch*'s leading cartoon on 19 December featured Allenby as a modern-day Richard the Lion-Heart. Biblical Crusader imagery had permeated British coverage of the campaign and gave it the air of a Christian *reconquista*.[112]

The protracted, sometimes halting advance of the EEF up the Mediterranean coast from southern Palestine was in some ways curious. Superficially it would have seemed more sensible to have carried out an amphibious operation, landing an army on the Syrian coast nearer to what proved to be the ultimate destination of Aleppo. Kitchener had originally favoured just that before going down with HMS *Hampshire* – appropriately, a ship the past life of which had also been in warm Mediterranean waters – off freezing Orkney in April 1916. Yet this supposes that the British Cabinet had a thought-out objective in the Levant, whereas the whole operation was highly improvised. Nor was recent experience of amphibious operations in the Mediterranean encouraging. A Syrian operation had also been ruled out because it would have required equal French participation. Such participation under Allenby's command (Détachement Français de Palestine et Syrie) was subsequently kept to a minimum precisely because London feared it would be used to pursue a claim to an enlarged Syria (broadly what we know today as Syria, Lebanon and

Israel combined).[113] The French Government's delegate to the EEF, François Picot himself, strove to counter the growing British tendency to push French interests aside. At a dinner to celebrate the Allied arrival in Jerusalem, the Frenchman announced that he would himself take over civil government in the city. Allenby's staff suddenly stopped eating while they watched their famously explosive chief for a reaction. Allenby, one present remembered, grew red, swallowed hard, stuck his chin forward belligerently, and declared firmly: 'In the military zone the only authority is that of the Commander-in-Chief – myself.' He added that a civilian administration would be established only when he judged it appropriate, though clearly there was to be no hurry on that point at all.

There were others alongside the French who played a supplementary role in the conquest of Palestine. The Royal Navy provided reinsurance along the coastal flank, as well as landing stores at various points, though its contribution did not go much further. The land, or eastern, flank of the EEF was in part covered by a very different force, that of the Sharifian Arab 'irregulars' in revolt against the Turks since June 1916. They were led by an ex-archaeologist and veteran of the Arab Bureau intelligence agency in Cairo, Colonel T. E. Lawrence. 'Lawrence of Arabia' before long provided an image of success and derring-do in the Great War inscribed in popular consciousness by his own classic *The Revolt in the Desert* (1927). In more recent times it has become the norm to condescend to Lawrence and his Arab levies as having provided some good cinematography, epitomized by David Lean's epic film of 1962, but not a great deal else.[114] Whatever their military worth at the time, however, the Arab presence alongside Allenby's army offered a valuable political instrument to sabotage the Sykes–Picot deal and roll back the claims of the French as well as an indication of the shape of things to come.

But there was another group now brought into play to assist British efforts in Palestine: the Zionists. On 2 November 1917 the British Cabinet had issued a Declaration, devised by Arthur Balfour, denoting Palestine as the site of a Jewish homeland, while also stating as a kind of afterthought that this should not be detrimental to the interests of the indigenous Arab population. The motives for this announcement have been intensely disputed.[115] It was not done out of philosemitism.

Many prominent British Jews considered territorial Zionism to be a profoundly misplaced idea,[116] while, to complete the irony, many of its British gentile supporters had a track record of mild anti-Semitism.[117] Many of the latter were rather drawn to the idea of giving Jews a ghetto somewhere far away and out of sight. The biblicism of Lloyd George's Welsh Nonconformity also had a part to play; when writing his memoirs years later he still self-consciously called the country 'Canaan'.

Nevertheless, in Lloyd George's calculations, as for others in the Cabinet, the real motivation in Palestine was entirely hard-headed. Once Palestine was conquered, it had to be kept, and in the latter endeavour the British were bound to need as much help as they could glean from other quarters.[118] In the spring of 1918 a Zionist Commission led by a Manchester-based chemistry professor, Chaim Weizmann, was sent to Palestine to encourage fresh Jewish settlement to add to the number of those already there, and to liaise with the military authorities. The establishment of what was designated Occupied Enemy Territory Administration (OETA) soon took on a Zionist colour. 'Department and public notices were in Hebrew . . .,' Storrs, who set his sights on being made Civil Governor of Jerusalem, stated. 'We had Jewish officers on our staffs, Jewish clerks and interpreters in our offices.'[119] Furthermore, once in Palestine the Zionist Commission acted as if it were a kind of government-in-waiting, going about, one English observer remarked, 'dressed in khaki and wearing Sam Brown belts . . .'[120] Much of this was resented in the army, where anti-Jewish feeling became transparent.[121] Certainly Allenby never allowed the Balfour Declaration to be published in the occupied area so long as war lasted, if only because it would have prejudiced the co-operation of his Arab allies and most local opinion.[122]

Meanwhile hopes of pressing the EEF's advance rapidly onwards after the capture of Jerusalem were disappointed. The Jordan was crossed, but first an approach on Amman was repulsed, and then suddenly troops had to be shifted back to Europe to contain the great German spring offensive of 1918. In September, however, Allenby was able to order a forward movement culminating in the Battle of Megiddo, the last major engagement in which a cavalry charge proved decisive. On 3 October 1918 came the capture of Damascus, so contrived by

Allenby that it seemed to consist of a surrender to Arab arms, boosting Sharifian ambitions as a counter to French claims in northern Palestine (though French marines were allowed to land in Beirut). Finally, the EEF arrived at its northernmost point of advance in Aleppo. By then the Turks had virtually given up in the Levant. The fate of the Ottoman Empire was really decided elsewhere.[123] It was the surrender of Bulgaria on 26 September, and the long delayed break-out from the Salonica salient led by Sarrail's replacement as Commander-in-Chief, General Franchet d'Esperey, or 'Desperate Frankie' as English troops called him, which dealt the fatal blow to the Ottoman-German army.[124]

In tense negotiations at an Allied conference in Paris, Lloyd George now persuaded his French counterpart, Georges Clemenceau, to agree that a British army under General Sir George Milne should be responsible for the push towards Constantinople, provided that Milne himself remained under the titular command, not of Allenby in Palestine-Syria, but of d'Esperey and his Army of the Orient.[125] The latter concentrated on striking as far up the Danube as it could. In the end it got deep into Hungary (from this in part came the French sway in eastern Europe, operating through the so-called 'Little Entente' that was to be a feature of the post-war period). The Lloyd George–Clemenceau compromise marked a momentous decision. The dispatch of such a large British force to the centre of Ottoman power foreshadowed the heightened commitment of Great Britain in and indeed beyond the eastern Mediterranean in the post-war world.[126] Above all, this implied a leading part in the shaping of Turkey's own future. By the end of October Milne's army was within 10 miles of the Turkish frontier and could see the grey and poignant outlines of Gallipoli on the horizon. Lloyd George might deny that 'the British had no desire to exercise a dominating or preponderant influence at Constantinople',[127] but few, especially in the rest of Europe, believed him.

The start of Britain's war in the Mediterranean had been defined in naval terms, not least by the escape of the *Goeben* and *Breslau* to Constantinople, and it was appropriate that its climax concerned the latter. The two ex-German cruisers had, in fact, broken defiantly once more into the Mediterranean during January 1918, sinking two British ships, before the *Breslau* was herself sunk, leaving the *Goeben* to retreat into the safety of the Straits. With Milne now camped on Ottoman soil, the British Cabinet and Admiralty were determined that when Allied ships passed through the Dardanelles after all that had gone before, it should be under British leadership.[128] Admiral Sir Somerset Gough-Calthorpe, as Commander-in-Chief, Mediterranean, was ordered from Malta to Mudros on 8 October 1918. Mudros had by then lost all the bustle associated with its part in the Gallipoli fighting – for Harry Luke, its only redeeming feature left was a restaurant managed by Lord Cromer's old chef in Cairo, who had lost none of his skills.[129] For a brief period, however, the harbour was again packed with vessels of the British Aegean Squadron, including elements of the Greek navy now firmly under British orders.[130]

On 14 October the Turks formally sued for an armistice, and sent their most senior British prisoner of war, General Charles Townshend,[131] to Mudros to assist in making contact with Admiral Calthorpe. When negotiations started aboard HMS *Agamemnon*, Calthorpe's French counterpart, Rear-Admiral Jean-François-Charles Amet, was reduced to 'almost battering on the door of the conference room' to get in.[132] Nor were the Italians, now with ambitions of their own in Asia Minor, happy at their exclusion. Still, both Clemenceau and the Italian premier, Baron Sidney Sonnino, were too preoccupied with other matters to attend very closely to what was happening on Mudros. On 30 October Calthorpe and an Ottoman emissary signed an armistice under which all Ottoman garrisons outside Anatolia surrendered and the Allies secured the right to control the Straits and the Bosporus. Three days after HMS *Britannia* was sunk by a U-boat off Cape Trafalgar (the last British warship to be lost during hostilities), on 13 November Calthorpe led a preponderantly British fleet through the Dardanelles. It anchored off Constantinople. For days some ordinary Turkish inhabitants had been spending hours looking anxiously towards Seraglio Point to witness the fleet's appearance. By the beginning of December the city was full of *entente* officers and men, and Germans and Austrians were being pushed out to the Asiatic shore.[133] The naval war in the Mediterranean had ended. As it did so, one million British and British-Indian troops were spread across the region. The exits and entrances of the Sea were more firmly under British control than ever, and some new haunts such as Haifa had been acquired.

How sustainable this might prove, however, was problematical. Finally, the significance of the *Goeben* in these events had been such that her own post-war fate can conveniently be noted here. Her wartime damage repaired, she returned to service in the Turkish navy, and had the honour of conveying the coffin of Turkey's great leader, Kemal Atatürk, from Istanbul to İzmir in 1938. She was eventually sold to the West German Government in 1973, so returning 'home', as it were, before being broken up. Pictures of the *Goeben* can still be seen in the older sorts of coffee shop in many parts of Turkey.

# 6

# Between Mastery and Abandonment, 1918–1939

Speaking in Milan during 1936 Benito Mussolini, always an obsessive student of the British Mediterranean, declared that for Great Britain that sea was simply a *via*, a passageway, whereas for Italy it was *vita*, or life itself.[1] Although in some ways self-serving as a means of asserting the prior claims of Italy, his declaration also echoed what had sometimes been said in Britain itself. Captain Basil Liddell Hart, the outstanding British military theorist during the inter-war years, predicted that, in a future war, one marked by competition for aerial supremacy, the British would have to abandon the region.[2] In fact Anthony Eden, then Foreign Secretary, whose long diplomatic career carried a deep Mediterranean imprint, was quick to rebut Mussolini's depreciation of what the region meant to Great Britain.[3] This difference indicated a highly complex variable in the making of British overseas policy during a period of systemic crisis. The outstanding feature was to be the sharply alternating pattern of British revivals and retreats, in which what was strength at one moment slid into weakness at another, and then sometimes back again. The effects on Britain's relationships with Mediterranean populations were complicated and lasting.

The opening drama of this gyrating experience was played out in the classic context of Constantinople and the Straits. The first British detachments entered the Ottoman capital in late November 1918. British Military Headquarters was installed in the Pera Palace Hotel, and many well-to-do Turkish families had their homes requisitioned for officers' billets. Harry Luke, who occupied a series of senior posts in the inter-war Mediterranean (nicely evoked in his memoirs) and who at this point served on the staff of the British High Commission in Constantinople, recalled that life in that exotically cosmopolitan but disordered world was 'as interesting as life can be'.[4] At this stage the occupation of the city was only partial, though the Bosporus itself was 'black with battleships'.[5] Because that occupation always remained principally naval the British were determined to take the lead role,[6] though neither the French nor Italians were prepared to accept this easily. As the historian A. J. Toynbee stated, the Allies proved far more concerned with manoeuvring against each other than with actually making terms stick with the Turks.[7] Had those terms been swiftly imposed, events might have turned out differently. But after the Peace Conference convened in Paris during January 1919 it was the German, not the Turkish, question, which hogged the limelight. In so far as eastern questions were raised the British and French showed an immediate disposition to squabble petulantly over interpretations of the Sykes–Picot Agreement of 1916.

The occupation of Constantinople was from the start regarded by Turkish opinion as illegal because it had not been authorized by the Mudros armistice. The Turkish Government's failure to protest indicated an abject desire to win Allied favour. It did them little good. 'They must be reduced,' Curzon, now Foreign Secretary, said of Turkey, 'not only in her own eyes but in the eyes of the Islamic world from her former status as a great imperial power.'[8] It was assumed that the Turks, pliable in Constantinople, would be so in Asia Minor too. The Italians prepared to seize Smyrna on Turkey's west Mediterranean coast under a pretext of a secret Allied wartime agreement. But Lloyd George had no intention whatsoever of permitting such an outcome. He was already germinating the thought of establishing what he described as 'a new Greek empire . . . friendly to Britain' in the eastern Mediterranean.[9] Such a projection of Mediterranean rivalries into Anatolia proved one of the cardinal errors of post-war Allied policy-making.[10]

Smyrna itself had become highly unstable. In November 1918 the visit of HMS *Monitor* had been the occasion of celebrations by local Greeks sensing that their day of domination had come.[11] 'Of course the whole thing is mad,' one of the leading British commanders in Constantinople remarked on hearing that the Greek army was to be encouraged into Asia Minor, but amid the hubris of victory such caution was rare.[12] On 15 May 1919 a Greek force, accompanied by British and French vessels, descended on Smyrna. The landing immediately led to a massacre of hundreds of Muslims, including the town's civil governor. Since the fervent advocates in London of Greek expansion, including such a notable figure as Rudyard Kipling, had argued that Hellenism would introduce a higher level of 'civilization' in a benighted region, these atrocities were an acute embarrassment. The subsequent Allied inquiry took place in secret and its report was never published.

The Greek invasion of western Anatolia fuelled a Turkish patriotism deeper than anything experienced during the preceding war. What is startling is that such a powerful movement was missed by the Allies, and especially by the British, until it was too late. But their view of Turkish affairs was through the prism of Constantinople, and especially of the deferential Sultan's court. British army officers were ordered not to fraternize with any ordinary Turkish families,[13] and over time this meant that sources of information dried up. The first British High Commissioner of occupied Constantinople, Admiral Sir John de Robeck, had some contact with local people as Allied naval commander. His successor, Sir Horace Rumbold, by contrast, proudly proclaimed that he had not had a Turk in his house for two years, and felt disgust that his French and Italian colleagues did not do the same.[14] The most basic fact was a hungry city full of 'wretchedness and impotence'.[15] The extraordinary narrative now so well known was little noticed until it was too late: of how a leading Ottoman army officer, Kemal Atatürk, was dispatched by Sultan Mehmed VI to Samsun on the Black Sea to bring the malcontents to order;[16] of how Atatürk instead put himself at the head of a growing rebellion against the western powers and the Sultan who was their pawn; and of how an alternative 'national' government was organized first at Erzerum and then at Ankara. Some, however, were more alert than others, so that Curzon warned his Cabinet colleagues that 'once out of range of Allied guns, the Turks would become a more dangerous and unpredictable enemy'.[17]

Before long, raids by irregular Turkish militia – 'brigands' as they were termed – began to press on the eastern flank of Constantinople, so that the authority of the Sultan scarcely extended beyond the outer limits of his capital. The Ottoman rump had to be propped up with foreign bayonets, but the steady penetration of Kemalist agents continued. It was because the British, with 8,000 troops already in the city, felt the ground slipping beneath them that on the night of 16 March 1920 an additional force of 3,600 from the ships of the Mediterranean Fleet was landed to take tighter control of the city.[18] Harry Luke drafted the order under which government departments were taken over, including the War Ministry, where several Turkish officers were killed as they offered token resistance; the 'obstructive' Ottoman Parliament was disbanded; and hostile politicians were arrested and sent to Malta for incarceration. All this was messily improvised, but at bottom the British felt convinced that the same process was being played out in Turkey as had unfolded in Egypt after 1882. All that was needed was the toughness and conviction to see things through until a new Protectorate, or something like it, was slotted into place.

Clamping down in Constantinople provided the backdrop to clinching a harsh peace settlement with Turkey enshrined in the Treaty of Sèvres (August 1920), according to which the Straits themselves were to pass under an international authority. But how could these terms be executed? The British could not do it all on their own as pressures mounted on them elsewhere – full-scale rebellions were under way in southern Ireland and Mesopotamia. It also became increasingly apparent that their allies would not do much to help, conscious that they were increasingly reduced to mere camp followers of the British. This was not a role they cherished, and the French and Italians began to explore covert arrangements with the Kemalists. Lloyd George's only credible hope of 'Egyptianizing' Turkey, or more realistically some fragment around Constantinople, was to ensure that a 'Greek shield' was driven remorselessly across Anatolia.[19] In its bloody war with the Kemalist armies in Asia Minor, Greece therefore became Britain's proxy, just as the Sultan in Constantinople had become her puppet.

As Winston Churchill acidly remarked in his history of these events, the trouble with wars fought in this way is that they are very dangerous – above all for the proxy.[20] Ordinary Greeks, exhausted by conflicts that had been going on in their case since 1912, at the elections of November 1920 voted overwhelmingly against the restless Venizelos, who promptly left Athens in a British warship. King

Constantine, that old antagonist of the Allies, returned to power. The French would have nothing to do with him, and eventually (October 1921) unveiled an agreement with Ankara by which they gave up their own territorial claims in Anatolia and the Turks recognized France's mandate in Syria. But Lloyd George had too much staked on the Greeks to liquidate his bet. Instead he got caught between his philhellenic urge and a lingering distaste for the Constantinist regime in Athens.[21] In practice this meant less material support than had been afforded Venizelos, but enough to keep the Greek offensive beyond Smyrna going. As the fighting spread in 1921, vicious revenge was taken on isolated Greek-speaking communities in the interior of Anatolia and the Black Sea hinterland; but though there was reliable evidence of what was happening, the responsible Foreign Office desk advised – and Curzon accepted – that 'there is nothing to be done about it . . . we are in no position to permit ourselves luxuries like justice and reparation'.[22]

What the British feared most was a collapse of the Greek army in Anatolia since it would allow the Kemalists to advance on the Straits themselves. The British army commander in Constantinople, General Sir Charles Harington, exhorted the Greeks to 'show your determination and you will have England's support'.[23] But if Greece was to brace itself for one last effort, it needed fresh assurances from a higher source. This was seemingly provided on 4 August 1922 by Lloyd George in a speech to the House of Commons which in its strident anti-Turkishness was interpreted by the Greek leadership as 'an encouragement to . . . seek a decision by force' in Anatolia.[24] Extracts from the speech were incorporated into the battle orders circulated to the Greek army.[25] The result was a military disaster with irreversible consequences for the region.

Kemal Atatürk had been planning his own counter-offensive in Asia Minor for some time. On 22 August, with the Greek lines precariously extended, a massive Turkish bombardment commenced. The Greek lines broke and a complete rout took place. Some Greeks cut their way towards Smyrna, often burning villages as they went. The British Consul-General in that town had been warning for some time that unless the Allies intervened, a bloody climax was certain.[26] It was already too late. Instead, the flagship of the Mediterranean Fleet, the

*Iron Duke*, together with the *George V*, hurried to the city to protect British nationals. The local Orthodox Bishop, Chrysostom, pleaded for the protection of his co-religionists, only to receive the guarded assurance from Admiral Sir Osmond Brock that he 'did not expect a disorderly occupation by the Turks, but [he] would give protection to those who needed it if disorder ensued'.[27] The Bishop was unimpressed. Although on the morning of 9 September a British marine detachment briefly formed a screen between the last remnant of exhausted Greek troops and advancing Turkish cavalry, it was largely token.[28] Regular Turkish troops appear to have remained disciplined, but widespread killing of ordinary Christians occurred in the chaos. Chrysostom himself (the only Greek personage in Smyrna who did not seek to escape) was horribly butchered. Finally, a disastrous fire broke out, with many forced into the water. The Allied warships out at sea played their lights on the desperate crowds along the harbour-front to afford some protection. Admiral Brock, by this point concerned with mutiny among his own crew, finally ordered cutters to be lowered to save as many people as possible. Of the 200,000 taken off, British vessels were responsible for around 60,000 people (one of them was Alec Issigonis, later the designer of the Austin Mini motor car, and his family).[29] So ended the Graeco-Turkish war in Asia Minor in which Lloyd George's diplomacy was deeply implicated.

Yet even as one war ended, another one loomed. Kemalist forces swung northwards and converged on the British position staked out with flags: the so-called 'Chanak Lines' along the Asian shore. Allied authority buckled. The British High Commissioner's wife remarked on a 'reign of terror' in Constantinople, those connected with the ailing regime sometimes mysteriously disappearing.[30] The French and Italians withdrew their contingents. In Churchill's estimation this was the worst moment in Anglo-French relations since the *entente cordiale* in 1904.[31] British military and naval stations in the Mediterranean were denuded of troops to shore up Harington's puny force at Chanak,[32] and the Governor of Malta, Field-Marshal Lord Plumer, the one general on the Western Front whose professional reputation had remained intact, rushed across.[33] The British Cabinet wanted Harington to fall back into Constantinople itself, but retreating into a city with barely enough food to feed itself was not an attractive proposition. He preferred to hang on at Chanak and play political roulette with Atatürk's powerful lieutenant, Ismet Inonu, who unexpectedly invited him to a conference at Mudania on 3 October. In his memoirs Harington remembered how this negotiation seemed to come unstuck over the matter of British troops remaining *in situ* during the inevitable transition to a new Turkish regime in the area:

> Ismet Pasha said he could not agree, and there was a deadlock . . . The scene is before me now – that awful room – only an oil lamp . . . I paced up one side of the room saying I must have that [neutral] Area and nothing less. Ismet paced up the other side saying he would not agree. Then quite suddenly he said 'J'accepte!' I was never so surprised in my life.[34]

But it was not so surprising. The Kemalists held the whip-hand on land at Chanak. But they did not want war with the British, and, the closer they got to the Bosporus, the more they had to recalibrate the costs of a confrontation, not so much with Harington, but with the Mediterranean Fleet, reinforced with three first-line battleships and numerous destroyers and cruisers.[35] After last-minute ruptures, the Mudania Agreement (11 October 1922) finally laid down that the British Army of the Black Sea should be allowed to remain temporarily in control of the city and surrounding 'neutral' zone, until a real peace settlement replaced the empty farce of Sèvres. Negotiations to this end began in Lausanne on 20 November (this was Mussolini's first appearance on a wider European stage as Italy's ruler – 'most impressive and Napoleonic', according to one British observer'[36]). Three days before, a historic scene had been played out in Constantinople. Mehmed VI, the last of the Ottoman Sultans, departed on HMS *Malaya* for Malta. But it was not only the Sultanate that was liquidated. So also was the effective authority of the High Commissioners. The city was now Kemalist to all intents and purposes, and in the following months the occasional killing of a British soldier patrolling the street evoked only a forlorn protest.[37]

At Lausanne, Lord Curzon presided as chairman, and tried to make the most of it. Ismet complained it was 'always the English voice, and the English fist banging on the table'.[38] But as Ismet knew, this was – like Mussolini's strutting – mostly for effect. For some time it had been clear that there was dirt to be eaten at Turkish behest, and Curzon swallowed his share (the Greeks had a much bigger portion). The security of the Straits, however, was the one matter on which the British might still fight if they had to – and everybody knew it.[39] When the treaty was concluded in July 1923, Curzon ensured free access through those waters in peace and war, while both the European and Asian shores were demilitarized. The way had been cleared for the Allied occupation of Constantinople to end.

Harington was determined that it should do so 'with the British flag flying high'.[40] On the morning of 2 October 1923 he stood to salute as the Guards regiments paraded before embarkation, the Coldstream marching band playing the British national anthem and a few Turkish melodies. The following day a crowd broke into the British Crimean War Cemetery and vandalized a number of graves. Nevertheless, the British occupation of Constantinople between 1919 and 1923, hated though it was by most Turks, could perhaps be said to have screened the city from the much more bloody experiences of surrounding regions. Thereafter the very name of Constantinople passed into history, while the city was relegated from the centre of Turkish political life. When Atatürk travelled down the Bosporus in 1924 he did not even visit Istanbul. It was, in Philip Mansel's words, the 'Death of a Capital'.[41] It was not a death the British embassy readily concurred in, since it would have meant leaving its fabulous building constructed by Sir Charles Barry in 1834 in the European suburb of Pera, with delightful saloons and gardens overlooking the Horn. British Ambassadors still insisted on living there right up to the Second World War, only visiting the dull and remote capital of Ankara as and when necessary, on which occasions they preferred to stay in a carriage at the railway station.[42]

These events have been told in some detail because they constituted the defining crisis in the Mediterranean during the 1920s. It marked the low ebb of an inflated war-driven imperialism lapping around its shores. Lloyd George had ignored a lesson his predecessor, Lord Salisbury, had painfully learned in the 1890s: that in the Near East British leverage was defined by her fleet, and the fact was that British warships could not climb mountains and traverse plains. In the uproar surrounding the crisis at Chanak, Lloyd George's hold on power cracked apart. He was replaced as Prime Minister by Bonar Law at the head of a Conservative government. Bonar Law summed up the change in announcing that Britain could no longer be 'the policeman of the world'.[43] Here were the roots of what later became the doctrine of appeasement. But Lausanne also underlined that Britain must still protect essential points of vantage. It was to prove important that British appeasement – with its deep yearning for stability and tranquillity – was grounded in Mediterranean experience.

In Egypt, the elusiveness of tranquillity was also shown early on. An ex-minister, Saad Zaghloul, who had drifted steadily apart from the British Residency, began a campaign for an Egyptian delegation, or *wafd*, to represent the nation at the Peace Conference in Paris (Wafd became the name of the Zaghloulist party). The background was one of accelerating prices and food shortages, and general fears that the British were contemplating changes to make Egypt into a straightforward colony following the demise of the Ottoman Empire; any link with the Sultan had disappeared in November 1914.[44] Such concerns were not ill-founded. The leading British legal official in Cairo was pressing for the law courts to be Anglicized while an opportunity presented itself.[45] The Residency failed to detect an underswell of popular feeling. A senior official even assured Balfour in London on 24 February 1919 that the agitation was quiescent.[46] Just getting Zaghloul out of the country was judged sufficient. On 9 March he was arrested and sent to Malta. What was to become a classic pattern then unfolded: a rowdy protest of students got out of control in Cairo, their professors joined in, the trouble spread from street to street, and then town to town, claiming lives, including foreigners'. It reached Upper Egypt, where a group of British soldiers and the country's Inspector of Prisons were taken off a train and brutally killed. Since Allenby himself was in Paris, the commanding officer in Syria, General Edward Bulfin, rushed to Egypt to restore order. Armoured cars, aircraft and mounted troops were used to disperse the crowds.[47] By the end of March quiet descended. The pasha-politicians had no desire for a social revolution, nor were the British in any danger of being driven into the sea. But during the outbreak, and the spluttering violence over the summer, 75 Europeans were killed or seriously wounded. Egyptian fatalities were about 1,000, and 57 were executed.

These events were a serious shock. The British Government dispatched

Allenby to Cairo as 'Special High Commissioner' in the hope that his great name would have a calming effect.[48] He immediately recommended the release of Zaghloul. This was not something London wanted to hear. To set Zaghloul free from Malta was to admit that Egypt had become uncontrollable without local co-operation; in effect, that the Protectorate in its current form was dead. This was exactly what Allenby did think. He certainly had no intention of sacrificing essential British interests. His most fundamental conviction regarding the latter, however, was 'that seapower and our garrison were pledges enough, and that these, and not any so-called Protectorate, were the basis of our position in Egypt'.[49] This was not as easy as it sounded. For such pledges to have their effect they needed to be plainly visible to ordinary Egyptians. Both the number and the distribution of British troops – whether they should remain in Cairo and Alexandria, or be restricted to the Canal Zone, and with what freedom of movement in a crisis – were to remain highly contentious questions for years to come.

Lloyd George and his colleagues reluctantly yielded to Allenby over releasing Zaghloul, but giving up the Protectorate itself was another matter. They prevaricated by establishing a mission led by Lord Milner. If it had gone immediately to Egypt perhaps things might have gone more smoothly. But the mission deliberated in London, hoping that Egypt would sink into customary lethargy, and only arrived in Cairo in December. Once they were there, no Egyptians of consequence would talk to them. With lots of time on his hands, Milner tried to breathe life into 'British' institutions.[50] He helped a funding appeal for Victoria College in Alexandria, which operated on English public school lines and catered for expatriate children and those of wealthy Egyptians. But Egyptian realities could not fail to concentrate the mind. 'It is quite possible', he hinted as his principal conclusion, 'that what we mean by "Protectorate" is not really incompatible with what they [the Egyptians] mean by independence.'[51] In short, an independent Egypt might be as effectively 'veiled' as the British occupation had largely been since 1882. The casuistry of this was plain. But then casuistry in Egyptian affairs was endemic at every level. Somewhere in the murky zone between Protection and independence it was logical to think that some new Anglo-Egyptian balance might be struck.

Milner and his colleagues returned to London in March 1920. They mulled over their report, and even met with Zaghloul himself, though the 'Agreement' they came to was really nothing of the kind. The Mission's findings subsequently disappeared into the black hole of Cabinet discussion. Meanwhile the Sultan Fuad – who had succeeded Hussein in 1917 – warned that if Zaghloul was allowed back to Egypt, trouble would erupt. This is what happened in March 1921. Alexandria again sank into chaos. On 23 May, at its nadir, fourteen Europeans and thirty Egyptians were killed in disturbances.

The foreign communities were now gripped by insecurity, and retreated more than ever into themselves – just as the writer, E. M. Forster, who disliked Egypt, 'withdrew . . . into a vision of ancient Alexandria' when composing his guide to the city at this time.[52] Expatriates were issued with instructions for personal safety, and assembly-points designated in case of complete breakdown.[53] Sharp differences arose. The British community in Alexandria, generally more sophisticated, and with deeper if very partial roots in the country, kept its counterparts in Cairo at arm's length since the latter's starkly imperialist attitudes were thought to be provocative.[54] Expatriates criticized Allenby for not cracking down harder against disorder through the summer of 1921. He had his reasons. The British garrison was down to 20,000 troops (though this was still significantly above pre-war levels). Above all, he hoped that Zaghloul, or some Egyptian 'moderate', would strike a deal with the Residency. In the end he despaired and in December 1921 Zaghloul was arrested and deported once more, this time to the Seychelles, suitably more remote than Malta.

Zaghloul himself came to be criticized later for failing to come to terms with the British in ways that might have stabilized Egyptian political development. Like Arabi Pasha of old, Zaghloul did not spring from the old Turkish or Albanian elite. He was 'of Nile blood'; T. E. Lawrence called him *echt* Egyptian.[55] Zaghloul wanted the British out of his country – not a quarter out, not half out, but *out*. That was why he became the *za'im al-umma* ('uncompromising hero') to the masses. It was also why to the British he remained an enigma, or even a 'monster of unreason'.[56] Had he become party to any deal affording the British new reasons for staying on, his magic would have evaporated – he would not have been Zaghloul. He defined an implacability that was to confront the British in a range of Mediterranean settings as the twentieth century unfolded.

If, in deporting Zaghloul for a second time, Allenby had despaired of getting Egyptian politicians to 'settle' with him directly, he concluded that it was all the more urgent for the British Government to announce a new dispensation unilaterally. By issuing a definitive proclamation of Egyptian independence, the British Government could establish a framework around which reasonable Egyptian opinion might rally. He therefore went to London in January 1922 and pressed his case. He met with stiff resistance in the Cabinet. But Lloyd George and Curzon occupied a very weak position. Their own recent intelligence on the situation in Egypt was that 'we do not possess a sincere friend in the country'.[57] They caved in, and on 28 February 1922 the Allenby Declaration recognized Egyptian independence. Essential British interests were carefully protected in a number of reserved points, including the presence of British troops in Cairo and Alexandria. The most fundamental guarantee was of Britain's status as the 'paramount foreign power', since what London most feared – more even than Zaghloul's nationalism – was that another power might replace them.[58] In that sense nothing much had changed since 1882, or even since 1841.

In crucial respects, however, Egypt after 1922 was a changed place. The civil service was no longer directly under British surveillance. Expatriates enjoying senior posts in the bureaucracy found that their prospects dived.[59] The same applied to the considerable numbers of British schoolteachers, though not those in the elite Victoria College. A drain began as individuals left, taking what compensation they could negotiate. At this time there were approximately 5,000 British civilians in the country (besides 20,000 troops). But these cadres were the expendable chaff of 'British' Egypt. The real question was whether the Allenby Declaration marked the limits of British retreat, or a process that once in motion would be irreversible. If the latter, any vestiges of paramountcy would sooner or later disintegrate.

But there was a still more pressing issue. What sort of polity would Egypt now be? After 1922 the Sultan was designated a King, and Fuad was bent on making the country a royal absolutism. Had he got his way, Egypt would have ended up like Iraq and Persia as a feudalistic monarchy, and the British role would have been to provide the bayonets – or the tanks – that kept the throne intact. Allenby blocked this, and insisted on a constitutional and parliamentary regime. One reason was that the British had never placed much trust in the Khedivial house. Fuad himself was said to be exclusively Italian in his taste for art, investment and mistresses,[60] and his politics might follow in their wake. The King grudgingly approved the new constitution inaugurated in April 1923. A kaleidoscope of rival factions and parties emerged, defined by clashing personalities rather than ideas or principles, in classic Mediterranean style. But behind the chaos there was a battle for succession to the pre-1922 system, in which the British were now only one among a galaxy of competitors.

Once such a competitive and constitutional race got under way the British could not easily guide its direction or pace. A paradigm took shape whereby all the other players used them as an Aunt Sally, or punchbag, so that whenever one party or faction seemed on the verge of striking a deal recognizing the legitimacy of Britain's position, another one would scream betrayal and reap the popular and electoral benefits. Worst of all, the spectre of violence did not go away, and Zaghloul as usual provided its touchstone. He had been moved to Gibraltar, where fear for his deteriorating health meant that the medical authorities were kept on alert.[61] Since his death in detention would have been a disaster, he was reluctantly released, and once back in Egypt there was nothing to stop him becoming Prime Minister in January 1924. For months he tried to hold a delicate balance.[62] On 19 November, however, the car of Sir Lee Stack, *Sirdar* or Commander-in-Chief of the Egyptian army, was blocked on a busy corner of the main road on the Midhan Ismail Pasha in central Cairo. Stack was shot several times. In panic, the Egyptian driver sped towards the Residency, and the bleeding body was taken into the main lounge where Allenby was hosting a lunch (Stack died the next day). Allenby went straight from this upsetting scene with a cavalry detachment to Zaghloul's office and personally delivered a set of severe demands. George V said he regretted that Allenby did so dressed as a civilian, rather than waiting to put on his Field-Marshal's uniform.[63] Allenby was critically weakened, and in July 1925 he left Egypt for good.

There followed under his successor, Lord Lloyd, a reaction extending beyond the conviction and execution of Stack's assassins. Lloyd had previously been Governor of Bombay. The Prince of Wales once joked that it was only when he stayed with Lloyd in that city during 1921 that he came to understand what the word *regal* truly meant.[64] Lloyd took his taste for ceremony with him to Cairo, so that when he travelled around the city he did so accompanied by lancers and blaring horns, with any Egyptian traffic swept onto the side roads. Politicians did not fare much better. One senior Residency official recalled how as soon as any Prime Minister seemed to be getting into the job, Lloyd decided that it was time to 'cut him down to size', which could be easily done through some manipulation of the Palace, or through promoting a rival faction.[65] For Lloyd, the 1922 settlement – never a true settlement, because no Egyptian had ever signed it – had to be defended with 'meticulous rigidity',[66] not least by the summoning of British warships to Alexandria whenever an opportunity occurred. Such circumstances usually arose in spring, when Egyptian politics enjoyed a seasonal vigour. Lloyd remarked that he had only to see jacarandas in blossom to feel that it was time to send a request to the Commander-in-Chief in Malta for a warship.[67] In the end he was as much an irritant to the Admiralty as he was to the Foreign Office.

A caricature though this could easily seem, there was method in Lloyd's proconsularism. As he told Admiral Sir Roger Keyes, Commander-in-Chief of the Mediterranean Fleet, the Allenby Declaration of 1922 was 'a pure fraud . . . To tell a country she is independent while you keep an army of occupation is not only a contradiction but a fraud.'[68] Lloyd's searing critique reflected a desire to see that experiment founder, just as he wanted to see the constitution of 1923 fall apart.[69] In the Foreign Office he was accused of being under a 'very serious misapprehension' as to the direction of British policy,[70] and Lloyd was eventually sacked after a new Labour government was formed in April 1929. But Lloyd's style of High Commissionership had fitted with a mounting nervousness throughout the British Mediterranean. Nor was Lloyd's successor, Sir Percy Loraine, any more successful at getting to grips with Egyptian political life. Instead, the Residency became wrapped up with the Palace. As the constitution wilted, both Loraine and King Fuad sought safety in the strong-arm ministry of Sidky Pasha, with its imprisonments, kickbacks and police spies.[71] This brought some relief. The direct Anglo-Egyptian confrontation of earlier days was now partially hidden behind localized struggles. That was Allenby's real achievement.[72] But it also carried the danger that one day a popular explosion might erupt, and when it did so the British were not likely to escape the blast. By the early 1930s, then, many of the old uncertainties and dilemmas of 'British' Egypt remained unchanged.

In 1919 Malta, like Egypt, had been rocked by disorder. The background was not wholly dissimilar: rising prices, student discontent, resentment of new taxes and fear of the future. In Valletta dockyard the great increase in wartime employment made lay-offs certain. Pent-up anxiety fed into a desire for a real constitution rather than what the Colonial Secretary, Leopold Amery, admitted was the existing 'camouflage system'.[73] In February 1919 a National Assembly was organized by the Comitato Patriottica, with its pro-Italian ideals. When Plumer had set out to take up the post of Governor of Malta, he carried instructions to consider a constitutional advance to encourage moderates to come forward, a recognition that the war had changed things substantially. It proved, however, too late to avoid trouble. He was held up at Gibraltar as news came on 7 June that Valletta was gripped by an open riot.[74]

On that day a large crowd gathered at an *italianità* club, and proceeded to the Strada Reale in the city centre. Shops promptly closed. A few Union Jacks were pulled down; soldiers were insulted at the Main Guard in Palace Square; and the offices of the pro-government *Malta Daily Chronicle* wrecked. Because the police could not be fully relied upon, military reinforcements were rushed from the Floriana barracks. Drawn up in front of protesters, the soldiers had strict instructions not to shoot. But when a shot was fired from a window, a volley resulted, causing several fatalities. Six Maltese were killed during the disturbance. Afterwards it was felt in the War Office that the affair 'was an excellent example of how not to deal with a riot', on the grounds that complete control should have been taken immediately.[75] This was typical of the way that Whitehall shovelled blame onto those handling trouble on the ground. Suggestively, most violence during what became known as the *Sette Giugno* was not directed at British emblems, but at other unpopular elements, such as millers responsible for bread prices. The *Sette Giugno* became a notable event in Maltese history through the contingent circumstance that British soldiers opened fire on a Maltese crowd when a riot was already under way.[76]

Order was restored within days, and British rule would never face another similar upset. Yet the event revealed subtle inflections. The Church had kept a discreet distance. When Plumer arrived a few days later he immediately reduced the number of bluejackets around his own Residence as a sign of unbecoming nervousness.[77] Thereafter his approach as Governor was to reform the 'rotten' police, improve wages for the King's Own Malta Regiment, minimize job losses in the dockyard, not upset the Church, and spend as much money as possible ('Plumer's deficit' as the Treasury complained). But such things on their own were no longer enough. When settling into his post, Plumer found that senior British officials in Valletta were mostly convinced that the time had come to risk a move towards real responsible government.[78] The new Governor described the goal of an advanced constitution as 'in mid-Mediterranean an active loyal community', rather than a sullen discontented one.[79] Leopold Amery in London expressed it even more tellingly: 'We must give up thinking of Malta as a curious little old-world dependency, living on the outskirts of a British fortress and providing cheap labour for a British dockyard. We must regard it rather as an outlier of the British islands . . . its people in a very direct and intimate sense our fellow citizens and fellow countrymen.'[80]

The outbreak of 1919 in Malta, like the more violent troubles in Egypt, was a sharp setback, but its effects were not similarly lasting. While Plumer was sceptical of Amery's desire to see the Maltese become British in a cultural sense, he subsequently put a lot of effort into encouraging such institutions as the Boy Scouts and Girl Guides, with their 'imperial' connotations.[81] In the same vein Maltese students were made eligible for Rhodes Scholarships at Oxford University, with their focus on the English-speaking world (one beneficiary was to be Dom Mintoff, later to loom large in Anglo-Maltese controversy). Of all the Mediterranean populations the British ruled over, the one that came closest to being regarded as 'our fellow citizens' were indeed the Maltese (the civilian inhabitants of Gibraltar being too polyglot for that, however much loyalty they professed). How far such fellow feeling might go, however, was to become a central question.

It followed that if the British were ever going to experiment with genuine self-government in the Mediterranean, Malta provided the most favourable conditions. Under the resulting arrangement, known as a 'diarchy', there was to be a Maltese Government, responsible for internal administration, and a Malta Imperial Government looking after 'imperial' business. From London's vantage point, the beauty of this lay in two characteristics. The first was that, since Maltese politicians would now exercise real power, with real spoils attached, none of them would refuse to join in. The old abstentionism would be killed at a stroke. Secondly, although public squabbles would be as intense as ever, they would be between the Maltese themselves, leaving the British free to get on with their own affairs uninterrupted. The trick was to keep the two parts of the government from tripping each other up, and to remain above the political fray. On 1 November 1921 the Prince of Wales proclaimed the new Parliament in Valletta.

There were some encouraging signs of a new and stable politics in the next few years. The language question, source of so much ill feeling, lost its edge. With the spread of the Maltese vernacular the best defence of Italian-usage now lay in the existing *pari passu* system whereby English and Italian were taught alongside each other in schools; the two 'foreign' languages were no longer pitted directly against each other. In fact, beneath the surface of island life, it was not a British Malta or an Italian Malta that was imposing itself, but a Maltese Malta. Political reconfigurations were partly a response to this. The forces of *italianità*, long split between secular nationalists and a very conservative clericalism, merged into a Partito Nazionale. On the other side was a loose combination between a new Labour Party with its core support in the naval dockyards and the overtly 'imperial' Constitutional Party of Lord Strickland (now succeeded to a family baronetcy in England, and married to an American heiress whose money helped to oil the wheels of Strickland's ambitions). Yet the real powers in the island remained the British authorities and the Catholic Church. As long as Governor and Archbishop remained in tandem, all seemed likely to go well. When Plumer left the island in

1925 to take up a more taxing job in Palestine, the Colonial Office felt things had panned out rather well.

If there was one thing likely to upset this equilibrium, it was not so much 'nationalism', always so qualified in Maltese circumstances, but rather an over-heated imperialism. Strickland had always stood for an assertive Englishness, but this now became more pronounced. Beyond that, his wider political views, like his views on Maltese constitutional development, were very difficult to pin down,[82] fraught with paradoxes which could never survive for the long term. But they also reflected the ambivalences inherent in the island's situation. These ambiguities were accentuated during the first half of the 1920s. The Admiralty, for example, concentrated the repair work of the Mediterranean Fleet in the island, much to the disadvantage of Gibraltar. The striking argument for this was that Malta possessed a bigger pool of 'British' labour.[83] In this way Malta was cushioned against the worst of the post-war slump. As much as ever, the index of the island's prosperity was dictated by the presence or absence of the Fleet, the summer cruises of which in the Mediterranean became such a feature of the 1920s. Grand Harbour was sometimes filled with more than fifty warships. If time ultimately proved to be against the 'Anglo' politics of Strickland, it did not seem like it then. Nor did he care if his views were seen as unnecessarily bombastic in the Colonial Office or Governor's Palace. This became clear when he squeezed into office as Chief Minister in 1927. The Malta he governed internally was one where *italianità*, to use the words of a Maltese historian, still moved by its values at the end of the twentieth century, 'hung like a veil: in the names of streets, of shops, of institutions; in primary and secondary schools and their curricula; in notarial and other archives; in the courts of . . . law . . . [and] the curia'.[84] It was a veil Strickland and his supporters wished to tear away in the name of English modernity and prerogative. To achieve his goal he set out on a campaign of de-Italianization, rationalized as a response to an alleged 'conspiracy' between a purblind Whitehall, 'disloyal' elements in the island and irredentist ambitions in Italy. Since the more heated the political climate the better for his purposes, incidents arose, as when two Italians were harassed on Senglea promenade. The shadow of petty violence came to lie over Maltese politics and never dissipated thereafter.[85]

In fact, as Plumer's successor, General Sir Walter Congreve, admitted, it would have been hard to find twenty-five Maltese who actually wanted the Italian flag to fly over Valletta.[86] An *italianità* newspaper pointed out that Maltese people knew very well that if it did, their island would lose what importance it had.[87] Being ruled over by Mussolini had no appeal, least of all for the Church, whose distaste for English Protestantism was nothing compared to its hatred for Fascist irreligion. As for Mussolini himself, there was absolutely no chance in the 1920s of a grab at the island. Fascist propaganda in the Italian press sporadically took up Strickland's oppression of 'Italianism' in Malta, but this was merely rhetorical.

What brought down the Maltese constitution was not outside intervention but the fact that the internal contest between Strickland and his opponents got out of control. Strickland, a Catholic himself, had always tried to keep on terms with the Church. But he could not restrain his anti-clerical supporters. A dividing line came when a crowd gathered outside Archbishop Caruana's palace during July 1928, shouting anti-papal abuse. This was too much even for the ageing Caruana.[88] A series of confrontations ensued, all of which came to be lumped together as 'the Strickland Affair'.[89] Everybody got carried away by partisan feeling, including the Vatican, encouraged to express itself more forcefully after the Concordat with the Italian state. A mission to Malta by a respected monsignor did not have the expected moderating effect. Cardinal Gasparri, the Vatican Secretary of State, spoke of a 'reign of terror and despotism' in Malta, and the Foreign Office in London responded with a prickly sensitivity to interference in the affairs of a British colony.[90] These antagonisms came to a head in the Maltese elections due to be held in July 1930.

In effect, the 1921 Malta constitution had functioned in such a way as to further internalize and deepen what had always really been local struggles, not dilute them. After all, although at the top of the governing structure there sat a British Governor and a few senior expatriates, for decades Malta had actually been administered mostly by the Maltese themselves, with the splits and rivalries this brought with it.[91] The resulting impasse impinged on the 'imperial' as well as domestic government of the island. Neither the Church nor the British were happy with their respective would-be champions in bringing this about, but they could not let them go down to crushing defeat.[92] The Church sought to settle the matter with a pastoral letter read out on 3 May in all Catholic churches in Malta stating that anybody who voted for the Constitutional Party would commit a mortal sin. Any election in the wake of such an announcement would have wiped out Strickland's candidates. A botched attempt to shoot Strickland as he entered the law courts on 23 May afforded a pretext for the British Government to suspend the constitution and to move against what the Governor, General Sir John Du Cane, called 'a nasty little set of pro-Italians' in the form of Enrico Mizzi, still resolutely opposing the colonial administration, as well as the Chief Justice, the Director of Fine Arts at the Museum and an ex-Italian Consul.[93] Constitutional suspension brought some relief, and the authorities hoped to hold an election when things calmed down; but when an election was held in 1932 the Nationalists won again. The constitution was duly re-suspended. By this stage Plumer's liberal post-war vision of an active and loyal community in mid-Mediterranean had taken a very hard knock.[94]

Even in Gibraltar after 1919 there had been a desire for some sort of change. The Rock's Governor, General Sir Horace Smith-Dorrien, was favourable to a fresh course.[95] The old Sanitary Commission was transformed into an elected City Council, though it was still one with a guaranteed official majority, and in which the Governor nominated most of the unofficial members. City elections turned out to be lively occasions, with seats tending to be won by representatives of trade unions. By the time Smith-Dorrien left in mid-1923, however, there was already a feeling that things had gone far enough. The new Governor, Sir Charles Munro, advised the Colonial Office that it was time to settle once and for all whether Gibraltar was a fortress or a colony, and he left no doubt that to his mind it would always be the former.[96] In the garrison, a tendency to resist any further erosion of military prerogative became marked. Even the Calpe Hunt, that old staple of garrison life, was felt to have become 'too Spanish and too civilian an affair'.[97]

Trade unions in Gibraltar were themselves changing, and becoming less Spanish and more British. The old anarcho-syndicalist tendency with its roots in the *campo* was fading. In 1919 a representative from the Transport and General Workers Union (TGWU) in the United

Kingdom visited Gibraltar and set about establishing an organizational culture in which union leaders delivered on contracts made with employers and threats of violence played no part. Removing the Spanish elements in Gibraltar trade unionism and replacing them with distinctively British norms offered a means by which the working class could display its political maturity and gain entry into the institutional structures of the colony.[98] This tendency was also driven by a desire to ensure that incoming Spanish labour did not bring wage-rates down. Gibraltar trade unionists accordingly began to take their place in the conventional order of precedence on such occasions as royal visits, albeit inevitably at the tail-end. At the top was the Governor, followed by the Anglican Archbishop, and then his Roman Catholic counterpart. Most people living on the Rock remained staunchly Catholic, but if there was one thing separating Gibraltar Catholicism from the Spanish Church it was its warm relationship with the English episcopacy.

The Gibraltar economy was more hard hit than most in the post-war Mediterranean. In the years before 1914 the port had increasingly dominated its economy, and the war intensified this dependence. The sharp fall in shipping after 1919 hit prosperity. The Gibraltar garrison was roughly halved in line with falling British defence spending, amounting with their families to 3,478 in 1921 (16 per cent of the total population on the Rock). These developments coincided with the crackdown on the smuggling trade from Gibraltar by the dictator Primo di Rivera after his coup in Spain during 1923, involving a closer customs check on the La Linea border and more active coast-guard patrols. But from the mid-1920s there was a gradual revival in Gibraltar's fortunes. In the port a new cruiser market began to appear. Here were the beginnings of a tourist economy marketing 'British Heritage', a striking indicator being the construction of a first-class, art-deco-style hotel, The Rock, though its completion was delayed by a strike of Spanish construction workers.[99]

The biggest threat to British Gibraltar, as ever, lay beyond, rather than on, the Rock. With all the bartering of territories that went on at the Paris Peace Conference it was hardly surprising that the idea of Gibraltar reverting to Spain was raised by Madrid. But after 1919 there was even less chance of Gibraltar becoming Spanish than of

Cyprus becoming Greek. Lord Curzon remarked: 'Even now the Rock of Gibraltar was regarded by a great number of [British] people as a pivot and symbol of Britain's naval strength in the Mediterranean, and any suggestion to give it up would . . . create such a commotion throughout the Empire as had not been known for a century.'[100] Primo de Rivera was himself no more likely to risk a break with Britain over Gibraltar than his fellow dictator, Mussolini, was over Malta. He was too preoccupied with such issues as the bloody Rif war in Morocco – 'like a cancer in the life of the country', commented Sir Horace Rumbold, who, as Ambassador in Madrid after 1924, found little to trouble Anglo-Spanish relations generally.[101] All the usual touches of accommodation over Gibraltar continued. The Governor sent messages of congratulation to his military counterpart in Algeciras whenever news came of a Spanish military success in Morocco, while a Spanish detachment came to Gibraltar to participate in celebrations for George V's birthday. The security of colonial Gibraltar still lay in Spanish weakness, but it was important that Spain should not be too weak and certainly not unstable. In this sense the fall of Primo di Rivera and the proclamation of a new Spanish Republic in April 1931 was therefore a source of anxiety. Right-wing refugees flooded into Gibraltar, where they often stayed with their rich Gibraltarian business friends or put up in comfort at The Rock. Here was the harbinger of a destabilization of Gibraltar's hinterland eventually to prove more serious than anything since the approach of Napoleon's troops in 1808.

In Cyprus – misconceived as Britain's 'Gibraltar in the east' – the post-war decade crucially shaped the island's history, and Britain's place in it. Venizelos, then still premier of Greece and one of the outstanding Allied figures at the Paris Conference, fended off Greek-Cypriot attempts to get him to promote their Hellenic aspirations with scarcely veiled irritation. It was still the case, however, that a vein of uncertainty ran through the British community in the island. The Anglican Church in Nicosia could not recruit an expatriate chaplain because it was not clear how long the job might last.[102] But this was about to change. The Asia Minor disaster and the Lausanne settlement shortly recast much of the region, involving a huge exchange of Greek and Turkish minority populations. Crucially, Cyprus was not included in this reconfiguration – as ever, it was the odd one out. Turkey now formally recognized Britain's annexation of the island. Muslim Cypriots had to choose between remaining as colonial British citizens, or going to the Turkish Republic; only 2,400 left. In July 1925 a formal ceremony in Nicosia inaugurated the island as a fully fledged British colony. This marked a clear watershed, even if it simply regularized the existing order. The Orthodox Archbishop, Kyrillos III, as befitted an *ethnarch* of the Greek majority population, issued a formal protest, but neither Kyrillos (whose relations with the British were still cordial) nor anybody else expected it to matter a jot.

If ever there was to be a chance of making Cyprus authentically British, this was it.[103] Common sense dictated the limits of such a conception. It did not mean British like the Gibraltar garrison or even the Malta dockyards, but rather the encouragement of an atmosphere in which Cypriots openly acknowledged at least a passive loyalty to membership of the British Empire. More visible tokens of the benefits of the British presence were necessary. Imposing new architecture helped here, such as a modern post office and public library in the capital, both still today notable features of central Nicosia. When Admiral Sir John de Robeck visited Cyprus as Commander-in-Chief of the Mediterranean Fleet in 1921 he had been shocked that Union Jacks were as rare as ever on the island.[104] After 1925 they became more common, though always far outnumbered by Greek flags. The biggest challenge was for British administration to extend its reach into those areas of island life from which it had hitherto been largely excluded, especially in education, where from the mid-1920s legislation was passed giving the government more control over the appointment and salaries of teachers. This met stiff resistance from school committees, though many teachers were by no means unhappy at seeing their profession released from the deadening hand of petty politicians. There was also a 'public weariness and . . . sense of disillusion' flowing from Greece's shattering defeat in Asia Minor,[105] and if some Greek-Cypriots stuck rigidly by the old line of '*Enosis* and only *Enosis*', others argued that it was time to make the best of a bad job and seek the kind of advanced colonial-type constitution that Malta now possessed. More active British intervention in Cypriot affairs extended to the Turkish minority. The affairs of the *Evkaf*, the body charged to look after Muslim religious edifices and charities, was put under closer surveillance by the administration.

The outlook for British rule when Sir Ronald Storrs arrived in Nicosia as Governor during 1926 was therefore broadly encouraging. T. E. Lawrence described Storrs as the most brilliant Englishman in the Near East.[106] Cypriot circumstances appeared tailor-made for that brilliance. His classical learning meant he was able to make neat quotations from the ancient Athenians when addressing Greek audiences. On the other hand, his experiences in Egypt and as Governor of Jerusalem meant that he was adept at the intercourse required by the old-fashioned, Ottoman-type Muslims whom the British used as their interlocutors with the Turkish minority (the Mufti, Munir Bey, had 'the mentality of the old Turkish Pasha').[107] Storrs acknowledged the special status of the Orthodox Archbishop, upgrading his precedence at public functions, and going to see Kyrillos at his palace, rather than the other way round. A Greek-Cypriot was appointed Solicitor-General. But the most significant concession to Greek-Cypriot feelings was the abolition of the old Ottoman Tribute, symbol of what the British themselves (apart from the Treasury) admitted was their niggardly treatment of Cyprus.[108] Although Churchill, now Chancellor of the Exchequer, initially tried to block Storrs's request, he backed down when reminded that he had made one of the most eloquent attacks on the Cypriot Tribute himself when visiting there in 1907. The abolition of this blatant pilfering of the Cypriot purse was announced in mid-1927.

But despite this, the 'honeymoon' of Storrs's governorship all too soon came to an end, and the inherent limitations in making a real British colony out of Cyprus kicked in once more. It was probably a mistake, for example, to hold a celebration of the fiftieth anniversary of Disraeli's occupation. In fact the fate of Storrs's governorship bears suggestively on some key British Mediterranean themes. Greek-Cypriot leaders became keenly aware that what Storrs said to them was one thing, and what he said to others quite another. A tendency towards mutual sarcasm crept in, indicating a marked psychological deterioration in relations.[109] There was in this process a similar dynamic to the one characterizing Storrs's equally important – and even more prolonged – interaction with Zionism. What seemed even-handed to him when navigating between contending ethnic and cultural groups, or in his attitude to other people's ideals – be it a Jewish national home in Palestine or Cypriot *Enosis* – appeared offensive to those on the other side of an apparent condescension. Zionists said they preferred plain and honest opposition to Storrs's roundabout methods in Jerusalem,[110] and Greek-Cypriots felt something similar. It was his subtle indirectness – what a Cypriot historian sums up as 'oriental methods of administrative tactics'[111] – which made it difficult to say whether he was Zionist or not in Jerusalem, and he took this sort of flexibility to Nicosia.[112] Storrs himself, and probably anybody facing the same challenges, would have said this stance was entirely appropriate and necessary. The degree to which his 'sympathy', entirely sincere, nevertheless infuriated some recipients exemplifies the psychological pitfalls of British colonialism in the Mediterranean.

Had the British introduced a constitution like that of Malta at this time, they would probably have been better placed to exploit the fissures that undoubtedly existed in the Greek-Cypriot majority. But there was no chance of that. British officialdom was convinced it would make Cyprus ungovernable as a colony, and in that they were probably justified. In fact the British were on the look-out for a convenient moment to scrap the existing constitution (essentially still that of 1882). A Greek-Cypriot delegation, led by the ever-patient Archbishop, went to the Colonial Office to lodge various requests, but got nowhere.[113] By then some already saw trouble coming. The British Ambassador in Greece told the Foreign Office that matters were drifting into the sort of crisis Gladstone had failed to solve in the Ionian Islands in 1859.[114] But the embassy in Athens was often seen from Whitehall as being too Hellenic in its tendencies. More representative was the analysis of A. J. Dawe, the chief Mediterranean expert in the Colonial Office. He pointed out that in the past decade Cyprus 'had been the only place in the troubled region of the Eastern Mediterranean to maintain continued ordered government without serious commotion'. It followed that the *Enosis* dream – what Dawe called 'the dying embers of the pro-Greek movement' – was as doomed to extinction in Cyprus as *italianità* was in Malta, and for the same reason: it belonged to a stale past, not the future.[115]

What then happened took most people completely by surprise. The catalyst, suggestively, was not a demand for *Enosis*, or even a constitution, but annual budget estimates involving a need for extra taxes. When Storrs imposed the Cypriot budget in the spring of 1931 by an official majority, feelings ran high and became unmanageable over the summer. The Bishop of Kition, head of a Church faction dissatisfied with the passivity of the aged Kyrillos, became the spokesman. On 17 October he led a walk-out from the Legislative Council, denouncing 'this abomination which is called English occupation'. A heated meeting took place four days later at the Commercial Club in Nicosia, and the crowd proceeded to Government House – still the improvised wooden structure put up in 1878.[116] After the protesters had milled around for some hours the demonstration got out of control. Some legislative councillors discreetly left as they realized what might happen. Fires were lit, and then somebody threw a torch into the porch of Government House. The building was burned to the ground. Storrs managed to escape from the back, but his magnificent collection of *objets d'art* – the fruit of a lifetime's dabbling in eastern bazaars, sometimes accompanied in the old days by Kitchener – was destroyed. During the following days unrest spread through much of the island. The District Commissioner's house in Limassol was incinerated and British women and children were evacuated in a Khedivial Line steamer from Famagusta.

With the help of reinforcements brought by warships from Valletta and Alexandria, order was soon restored (seven Greek-Cypriots were killed by British troops). The alleged ringleaders, including the Bishop of Kition, were deported to Malta, and a fine of £34,115 was imposed on the population. More revealing than these punishments was the programme of repression introduced, not so much by Storrs (widely held responsible in British circles for 'weakness', he was soon demoted to Governor of Northern Rhodesia) as by his successors. The constitution was suspended, the ringing of church bells subjected to police supervision, and the flying of Greek flags limited to specified occasions. The events of 1931 were to provide a basic reference point for both the British and the Greek-Cypriots for many years ahead, though given widely contrasting interpretations.

British rule may have had problems in Cyprus, Egypt, Malta and even surrounding Gibraltar but these were nothing compared with Palestine. There an Occupied Enemy Territory Administration held responsibility after the war. Among British army officers there was little of the optimism that Jews and Arabs would lie down 'like lions and lambs' as some enthusiasts had predicted following the Balfour Declaration on a Jewish national home.[117] Army sentiment in post-war Palestine was not favourable to Zionists at all. In this there was a good deal of anti-Semitism. The mess talk was of 'Jew boys', 'Jew villages', 'Jew government'.[118] But the main determinant was an acute awareness that, with Arabs constituting 90 per cent of the population, Balfour's vision would lead straight to a second Ireland – 'namely', as a leading British army figure predicted, 'two peoples living in a small country hating each other like hell'.[119] Allenby himself thought that Lloyd George's decision to appoint a British Jew, Herbert Samuel, as the first High Commissioner was a mistake. Samuel's Zionism was a very mild blend of Gladstonian liberalism and English Judaism.[120] He never thought that a Jewish national home was something that could be driven through. Its evolution would depend on conditions, and meanwhile the priority was to get on and govern the country as best one could. Samuel stepped off the British warship that brought him to Haifa in June 1920 in the sartorial get-up of a British colonial Governor. General anxiety about his safety meant that he was closely protected throughout the journey to Jerusalem – where his Residence was the old German hospice on Mount Scopus inaugurated by the Kaiser.

The first serious watershed was the riot in May 1921 during Nabi Musa (a Muslim pilgrimage in Palestine on the eve of Good Friday). As so often with such violence, it was sparked by trouble within one group – in this case, a clash between left- and right-wing Zionists – before spreading to the main ethnic divide. An Arab crowd attacked a Jewish migrants' hostel in Jaffa, killing many of the occupants, and it took a week before the army restored order; forty-seven Jews and forty-eight Arabs lost their lives.[121] A subsequent inquiry chaired by an English judge from Cyprus put the onus of responsibility for the killings on the Arabs, but at the same time highlighted the essential background of Muslim fears of Jewish immigration – at the outset of the Mandate there were around 60,000 Jews in the territory compared to 650,000 Arabs, so less than 10 per cent of the whole. Most

Jews blamed Storrs as Governor of Jerusalem for not having acted quickly enough to defend their community (the bad blood towards Storrs never lifted). From this arose a strong Jewish presentiment that in seeking protection it was no good looking to the British; here were the origins of a defensive militia (and finally of the Israeli Defence Force), Haganah. It remained true for a long period that the Jewish presence in Palestine, and above all the national-home ideal itself, was 'utterly dependent' on continuing British rule.[122] But the Anglo-Zionist tie had a kink in it from the start.

In many ways it would have been much the best if the British had wriggled out of the Balfour Declaration's obligations there and then. But this was never really possible. Curzon remarked that there was no way of doing so without throwing up the Mandate (recently conferred by the League of Nations) itself and leaving.[123] This was not something the British wanted. The reason did not lie in the strategic value of Palestine, about which there was always a lot of scepticism.[124] The British were tied to the territory for the same reason they were tied to Cyprus. If they went, it was feared another power would probably find a way of getting in. But one thing they did do was to make Palestine smaller and more manageable, so that the east bank of the Jordan was detached and made into the separate Kingdom of Transjordan. This was to be a very important decision in the history of the Middle East.

In line with his liberal beliefs, Samuel would have liked to introduce a constitution as a signal of good intentions. But this proved a dead end straight away. The Arabs refused to participate unless their large numerical majority was recognized, and, since it was not, scarcely any Arabs voted in the elections during 1921. 'An impossible set of people,' Samuel commented after one meeting with Arab leaders.[125] Thereafter Mandatory Palestine was governed through Orders-in-Council under the High Commissioner's direct authority, just like the most dependent colony. The British might complain in Malta and Cyprus about the workings of constitutions. But if there was one thing worse for colonial administration than having a constitution, it was not having one at all. Palestine was to be an outstanding illustration of this truth. There was no effective institution to draw people together, if only to argue with each other. Jews and Arabs subsequently came under their discrete agencies during the Mandate, with their own schools, hospitals and even labour markets.[126] It was said that the only places where they cohabited were the prisons and mental asylums.[127] To this could have been added the domestic residences of senior British officials. Storrs's successor was typical in having a Jewish cook, a Muslim butler and a Christian Arab houseboy.[128] There was a pervasive air of impermanence summed up in government buildings. Lord Plumer, who followed Samuel as High Commissioner, lost his Government House not to arson, like Storrs in Nicosia, but to an earthquake, so that he and his wife had to put up for some time in a Jewish girls' school. Permanent government offices for the Mandatory regime were never built, being accommodated in a rented wing of the King David Hotel. The latter was ultimately to provide a defining scene of the Mandate's debacle.

The era of Plumer's High Commissionership, indeed, was as good as it got for the British Mandate in Palestine. Not being Jewish himself was an advantage for Plumer, as was the fact that there was a net outflow of Jewish migrants during the later 1920s. Arab opinion remained generally passive. Plumer also arrived with a ready-made Maltese recipe for damping down trouble that had some relevance in his new job. This meant spending money on public works, including a new harbour at Haifa, soon to emerge as a vital point of exit for supplies from the British-owned oilfields in Iraq,[129] and encouraging agriculture and some light industry where feasible. Two things were to be left very well alone: religion and politics. 'Crosland, there is no political situation,' Plumer replied when one official remarked that at the Executive Council nothing had been said of political affairs, 'and don't you create one.'[130] It was said of Plumer that he 'erred on the side of optimism' in Palestine, exemplified by his reduction of expenditure on troops and police in order to release cash for more productive uses.[131] It was, perhaps, the only way of going on.

Tranquillity in Palestine may in part, as one of his aides once claimed, have been 'maintained largely through the force of Lord Plumer's personality', though luck and circumstance probably had more to do with it.[132] But he left in July 1928 when a severe tremor was about to spread across the Mediterranean from Spain to the Levant. One example was the tension surrounding the Wailing Wall in

Jerusalem, where a traditional modus vivendi between Jews and Muslims had so far held up. An incident over a Jewish screen at Yom Kippur in 1928 – interpreted by Arabs as an attempt to convert the Wall into a synagogue – was contained, but it led to a growth of Arab protest and petitioning. Then on 23 August 1929 violence broke out in Jerusalem, quickly spreading to Hebron, where some particularly brutal killings occurred (though, as in 1921, there were stories of Jews and Arabs hiding each other in their homes).[133] In total, 133 Jews and 116 Arabs died. 'We have built for ten years,' one British official remarked with reference to the policing of the territory, 'and it has crumbled to pieces in ten days.'[134] Harry Luke, then responsible for Jerusalem, and well known for his pro-Muslim sympathies, bore the same sort of attacks from the Zionists for not providing protection as Storrs had suffered years earlier.

In the wake of the bloodshed in Jerusalem and Hebron, a local Commission of Inquiry was followed by a White Paper in London further redefining the Balfour Declaration to emphasize obligations to Arabs as well as Jews, not least with regard to immigration. This new policy was soon overturned, however, once Zionist lobbyists got to work on Labour ministers. It was no accident that around the same time signs of disturbances in Arab villages escalated, though these were passed off for some time as mere 'banditry'. The truth was that nobody trusted anybody else in Palestine by the early 1930s. Herbert Samuel might once have dreamed of constitutionalizing the territory, and Plumer at least of administering it firmly and fairly. All Plumer's successor, Sir John Chancellor, could do was to cling to the appearance of authority and hope people did not notice that real authority was slipping away. Palestine was not yet a nightmare, but the possibility emerged that it might become one.

Each of Britain's varied engagements in the Mediterranean had distinctive complications. Some were more intractable than others, but all could be coped with for the moment providing that the region itself remained tranquil. But strategic conditions worsened progressively after 1930. Some of the reasons for this were at a distance. Japan's attack on Manchuria in September 1931 began the long slide of the League of Nations into decrepitude. This was to have substantial effects in southern Europe. The British role was deeply affected, since the guiding principle in her naval and military policy from the mid-1920s was put into shorthand as 'Main Fleet to the East'. In other words the Mediterranean would be virtually cleared of warships in a crisis so as to protect the Empire in the Pacific, though it remained absolutely essential somehow to maintain a clear passage. Here was the emerging global dilemma of British foreign policy, in which the Mediterranean – in theory at least subordinated to Home and Far Eastern priorities – became a crucial index of the policy of appeasement.

Italy was central to Britain's emerging conundrum. One reason why during the early 1930s London fended off French pressure to collaborate in a Mediterranean Locarno – that is, a collective guarantee system of the sort that successfully stabilized continental Europe after 1925 – was so as not to offend Mussolini. This might be regarded as a lost opportunity, except that there were to be so many of these that it is fruitless to speculate on any particular case. There was to some degree nothing preordained about Anglo-Italian hostility, and preventing it was always one of Neville Chamberlain's principal goals. During his first decade in power Mussolini had concentrated on consolidating the Italian stake in North Africa and the Aegean, redolent with the Fascist ideology of *Mare Nostrum* (Our Sea). But this was not particularly aimed at Britain. The Italians built a smart new highway – nicknamed the Balbia after the Libyan Viceroy Italo Balbo[135] – right up to the Egyptian border, putting to shame the pathetic dirt tracks on the other side; but although officers who manned the Italian frontier posts could not resist a certain feeling of superiority, they were under strict instructions not to clash with their Anglo-Egyptian counterparts.[136] In the Aegean, Anglo-Italian relations were positively warm. British officials in Cyprus envied the dynamism of Italian colonial rule so near by. They also had more than a sneaking admiration for the fact that in the entire Dodecanese archipelago the only Greek flag allowed to fly was the one over the consulate of Greece. They felt that had this been emulated many of the problems of Cyprus would have faded away. Storrs even exchanged fraternal visits with his Italian counterpart in Rhodes, Mario Lago, with whom he shared a deep immersion in Mediterranean cultures.

But one basic fact made confrontation between London and Rome very hard to avoid, given the nature of Mussolini's ambitions. As the

First Lord of the Admiralty remarked, the British had too much valuable property in the Mediterranean waiting to be attacked.[137] Mussolini developed a theory and rhetoric of Italy's 'imprisonment' at the hands of her various oppressors, with the British always coming to the forefront: 'The bars of this prison are Corsica, Tunisia, Malta, Cyprus. The guards of this prison are Gibraltar and Suez. Corsica is a pistol pointed at the heart of Italy; Tunisia at Sicily. Malta and Cyprus constitute a threat to all our positions in the central and western Mediterranean.'[138] That Mussolini might try and smash through one or other of these bars became part of Anglo-French risk-planning. Mussolini, however, chose a softer target. This was Ethiopia, and after simmering tension for a year, on 3 October 1935 Mussolini unleashed an attack from Italian Eritrea. The ensuing crisis served to reinforce the continuing necessity of keeping up a strong Mediterranean Fleet; but it also raised the issue of where such a squadron should be kept, since Malta was only 60 miles from Italy's main airbases. Although the Commander-in-Chief, Admiral William Fisher, was reluctant to be seen leaving Valletta under such pressure, the Admiralty insisted as soon as the crisis erupted that the British warships proceed to Alexandria and so out of immediate harm's way.[139] 'Magnificent sight. Stuffed with British warships,' Loraine's successor as High Commissioner in Egypt, Sir Miles Lampson, wrote in his diary after flying over Alexandria harbour.[140] But this instinctive British flinching from Malta – the first of four such episodes before September 1939 – was a sign of mounting nervousness and a distinct loss of prestige.

The Abyssinian crisis – in its strategic essence, a Mediterranean crisis – had Egyptian repercussions. It interrupted what Lampson called a 'long stagnation' in local politics.[141] During November 1935 riots broke out in Cairo, and soon spread to Alexandria; their Zaghloulist spirit inevitably meant they were anti-British. These troubles might have ebbed away like many before them. But Egyptians were as quick as Italians to grasp that England's weakness might be their opportunity. Politicians and parties put aside their intense rivalries to join in a 'United Front' to demand negotiations on a treaty with Great Britain that would regularize relations at last. Still undecided among themselves as to what their real needs in the country were, the British preferred to meet the 'United Front' with a blank refusal. The threat of spreading violence, 1919-style, at a time of grave international uncertainty, however, left their representatives little choice but to sit down with the Egyptian delegation at the Zaafaran Palace in Cairo on 2 March 1936.

Lampson still thought the chances of anything emerging from this were '100 to one' against.[142] But certain factors were coming into play with unanticipated effects. Italian troopships had passed through the Suez Canal on their way to the Horn of Africa, sometimes in chauvinist mood, and if this was not cheering for the British, it was distinctly perturbing for the Egyptians. The British were not often popular but they were less unpopular than the Italians, except with some members of the Egyptian royal house. For one thing, there were many more Italian nationals than Britons in Egypt, with all the usual frictions this led to with local people. Mussolini liked to project himself as a 'Defender of Islam', but the ferocity of Italian repression in Libya was well known; even the nerve centre of Egyptian Islam, the leadership at al-Azhar mosque and university, on occasions now adopted a slightly more favourable attitude to Britain. As it dawned on Lampson and the local military commanders that the Egyptian negotiators were sincere about coming to an agreement, they were forced to clarify their own requirements.[143]

This took some time, as the talks unwound. The British presence in Cairo and Alexandria was ever the sticking point. The Ground Officer Commanding in Egypt already thought such a presence to be redundant.[144] So far as Cairo was concerned, the real argument for retention was political. Once British troops were evacuated, they could not easily go back to protect foreign nationals if riots erupted (the centrality of this issue ran from the original occupation in 1882 through to its very end). Alexandria was a bit different in so far as the use of its harbour, at a time when there was a question mark hovering over Malta, was clearly important.[145] The opening of a new social club for British naval officers was the surest sign of an intention to stay (one of the naval wives residing there in these years was Daphne du Maurier, who began writing her novel *Rebecca* in Alexandria).[146] As these issues were thrashed out, it looked as if proceedings in the rich surroundings of Zaafaran Palace would collapse. But then the Egyptian delegation led by Nahas Pasha dangled something original before the British: a 'perpetual alliance' binding together British and Egyptian military necessities. On this basis the British at last agreed to a staggered withdrawal of their forces to the Canal Zone, with a limit of 10,000 troops and 400 Royal Air Force pilots; a right of unrestricted re-entry to the rest of the country in time of war was also specified. These terms were to be subject to review after twenty years, which explains why 1956 was to be a lurking ghost in Anglo-Egyptian calculations long before that fateful year arrived.

An Anglo-Egyptian treaty on this basis was concluded on 2 August 1936. The formal British 'occupation' of Egypt stretching back to 1882 came to an end (though not of course the presence of British troops on Egyptian soil). In retrospect, the making of this treaty was a lucky stroke for Britain. Without it her position later on would have been much more problematical.[147] Some Egyptians still thought that the new reality – symbolized by Egypt's entry to the League of Nations – was the old system under another name;[148] and both Lampson and Anthony Eden felt in the back of their minds that in the end 'the only fundamental solution was the inclusion of Egypt in the British Empire'.[149] But external pressures had brought about a substantial Anglo-Egyptian convergence. Far from calling on the British to get their troops out of the country, leading public figures now called for more to be brought in to protect against invasion by a potentially voracious predator; 'more troops and still more troops', Lampson was exhorted by one Egyptian interlocutor, reminding him that in the last war the British had stationed 100,000 men in the country.[150] Here was an essential paradox in Britain's Mediterranean situation from 1936 onwards. Escalating tension made her weak and vulnerable, but it made others more so. In that relativity were the seeds of a new if necessarily precarious strength, though it was to take dramatic events to bring the process more into the open.

As Alexandria was gradually elevated in the pecking-order of Britain's Mediterranean defences, especially by upgrading its anti-aircraft defences, Malta was relegated again. The feeling was deeply uncomfortable for everybody there, British and Maltese alike. The island had not been at ease ever since political deadlock emerged after 1930. Regional uncertainty accentuated this and made the British authorities even less disposed to authorize an election. But how long they could continue not to do so was questionable. In February 1936 Sir Charles Bonham-Carter was appointed Governor. From a family well known in British society, he was further illustration that Malta generally received a better class of Governor than, say, relatively neglected Cyprus. Against the international background, however, worrisome rumours accumulated about espionage within the island. Whitehall gave the green light for a further crackdown against persisting traces of Italian culture. Italian was replaced by English and Maltese as the medium of teaching at the university, and such institutions as the Instituta di Cultura Italiano and the Umberto I primary schools were closed down, despite the fact that the education provided by the last of these was so good that even British parents liked to send their children there.[151]

The assumption that *italianità* was on its last legs at this stage had some validity. Fear of the Regia Aeronautica waiting to pounce from Sicily and Naples did not do much for pro-Italian feeling in Maltese towns and villages (rumours spread that Italian bombers could devastate the dockyards and their communities in one hour).[152] For his part, Bonham-Carter enjoyed a modest popularity. He visited all parts of the island, and made a special point in his relations with the Church of making contact with parish priests and not, like previous governors, only with bishops. It was easy to make fun of a government programme based on the pasteurization of milk, the immunization of goats and a new hospital, but at least this showed a concern with practical issues.[153] There was not much, after all, that Bonham-Carter could do about Mussolini. Apart from keeping the divisive Lord Strickland – now 'off his rocker' according to that old Mediterranean hand Sir Harry Luke, comfortably ensconced as Malta's Lieutenant-Governor[154] – at arm's length, Bonham-Carter sought to win Maltese goodwill by pressing London for a new constitution, albeit by no means resembling the one that had been lost. This was finally proclaimed in Valletta on 25 March 1939. The Governor could not help noticing on that occasion when passing through the Porta de Reale surrounded by mounted troops that very few male passers-by bothered to take off their hats.[155] But by then everybody's thoughts were very much in other directions, and one more pallid British constitution hardly mattered one way or the other.

From 1935 onwards it became axiomatic in London that in any war involving Italy, Malta would incur 'unquestionably heavy damage'.[156] Influential circles in the Admiralty came to assume that both Malta and Cyprus would have to be abandoned at the outset of a conflict – meaning that they would be left essentially defenceless, potentially seized by whichever enemy could be bothered to do so.[157] It followed that there was little point in sending scarce guns and aeroplanes to places that would probably be overrun. Some were not happy about this. Eden in particular rejected an appeasement policy geared to winning Mussolini's friendship. Italophobia, or rather the question 'Who shall rule the Mediterranean?' and not ideological anti-Fascism, one historian concludes, shaped Eden's preferences up to his resignation in February 1938.[158] Duff Cooper, appointed First Lord of the Admiralty in early 1937, shared Eden's assumptions. That summer, accompanied by a wife whose fame as an actress and noted beauty easily outshone his, Duff Cooper toured the Mediterranean in the yacht *Enchantress* to lift sagging British spirits (something Diana Cooper was incomparable at doing). In Valletta, the First Lord assured Bonham-Carter that he would press the Cabinet at home 'to make ... Malta a truly impregnable fortress', and asked him to confer with service staffs as to what the island's needs were.[159] But even when the lists of requirements were duly provided, the 'stuff' never seemed to arrive.

For Malta, the Munich crisis over the future of Czechoslovakia in September 1938 – when Duff Cooper himself resigned from the Admiralty – marked a turning point. The British Fleet made another nervous dash to Alexandria. Nobody in the island needed telling that they were much less safe as a result. Bonham-Carter tried to keep everybody's spirits up by insisting that there was still time, as he put it in his diary, 'to get our house in order', and that even if war broke out with Germany, every Italian interest lay in keeping out of the conflict.[160] But a tangible loss of confidence was confirmed in October by the 'alarming impression' created when many gunnery officers in Malta were ordered to follow in the Fleet's wake to Egypt.[161] This was when evacuation planning for a devastating attack on Valletta and the surrounding Three Cities started.

Awkward questions then posed themselves. Were there enough gas masks to go round? What would happen if a mass panic led to a collective rush through the cramped exits from the Three Cities? Would the Church (ultimately indispensable) help to keep order? At least ordinary Maltese had the comfort of their own extended families. For British families whose menfolk had left for Egypt reassurance was often lacking, and the pressure told. In the new scare surrounding Italy's invasion of Albania in April 1939, and with the Fleet gone, some British women allegedly lost control and fled into the open countryside, taking bedding and other necessities with them.[162] Bonham-Carter was told that some Maltese regarded this so-called White Feather Brigade with disdain. Another interpretation was possible. In the island, ordinary Britons and Maltese were increasingly equal in one vital respect: their common vulnerability. This was forerunner of a shared and to some extent unifying – even if artificial – solidarity.

In Spain, conflict of another sort had been in progress for some time. The Second Republic established in early 1931 set the scene for an acute and fluctuating social struggle. The right-wing refugees who had begun to flow into Gibraltar were now followed by left-wing refugees following the bloody repression of a rising in Asturias in 1934. These became a flood once civil war proper erupted in July 1936. Financed by a business tycoon, Juan March, whose wealth was partly based on the Gibraltar smuggling industry, Nationalist rebel forces under General Franco invaded the Andalusian mainland from Spanish Morocco. Algeciras quickly fell, but Republican forces held on for short while in working-class La Linea. Gibraltar therefore had a 'grandstand view' of the opening phases of the Spanish Civil War, with the sound of firing in the *campo* resounding on the Rock.[163] A semblance of calm came only when the fighting veered off towards Malaga, leaving the *campo* in the hands of rebel Nationalists. But normality was gone, and, as we shall see, nothing in Gibraltar was to be really normal for a long time.

The refugee presence in Gibraltar helped ensure that the fierce ideological divisions of the Civil War came to be superimposed onto the colony's own subtle fissures. The Bishop of Gibraltar, for example, was a staunch Francoist. Nothing spoke so much to the degree of Spanishness within Gibraltar as the fact that rival supporters had their own establishments – the Café Imperial was Republican, the Café Universal Nationalist, and demonstrations sometimes took over

Main Street. Maps in public places plotted the moving positions of the contending forces, while Spanish-language newspapers such as *El Calpense* continued to outsell the *Gibraltar Chronicle* (since the colony was accessible to both Nationalist- and Republican-held Spain by sea, it was a unique collecting house for news of the struggle). An American writer caught up in Malaga recalled what appeared to be 'an erotic lust for atrocities' among the inhabitants of Gibraltar, adding that it was 'a most unpleasant place during the civil war'.[164] This was harsh. If there was any voyeurism in Gibraltar, it arose naturally from the ambivalence of its relationship to the Spanish tragedy, so near and yet so much apart.

The Spanish Civil War consequently had an important impact on Gibraltar's evolving identity, including its 'Britishness'. Some have seen these years as finally separating out the consciousness and orientation of the British colonial town from its Spanish hinterland, clinching a 'Gibraltarian' loyalty the elements of which went back a long time. Others contest that the real break between the Rock and its neighbour only came after Franco's victory, and not really till after the Second World War. Nevertheless, the very proximity of the Spanish trauma after 1936 led Gibraltar's resident population to define themselves more distinctly by their very absence from it. Such a differentiation was deepened by the interventionist role played by Italy and Germany on the Nationalist side, so clearly in opposition to the democratic powers of Britain and France (some 75,000 Italian troops were sent to help the Nationalists, and 12,000 Germans). Franco's forces eventually entered Madrid in April 1939, and within days a build-up of regular Spanish troops in the *campo* adjoining Gibraltar was visible.

The Governor on the Rock who had to steer a delicate path through much of this period was Sir Charles Harington, whose political and military skills had helped to keep Britain out of a war with Turkey in 1922.[165] Harington, like most garrison officers, lumped Spanish Republicans together with Communist 'Reds' and harboured a scarcely veiled preference for Franco and the Nationalists. This bias came out early on in the revolt when the fleet of the legitimate Republican government tried to put into Gibraltar port to take on oil, and was turned away (Republican crews had hanged some of their officers, not something which recommended itself in Gibraltar mess-rooms). But more powerful than any ideological or emotional leaning was the necessity to keep on working terms with the rebels who were de facto masters immediately across the border. The Nationalist complaint that Gibraltar was a haven for their enemies could not be ignored. Harington beefed up the guards around the Rock to ensure that the inward flow of refugees was curtailed. The camp at North Front was closed down once an initial flood had been contained, and most of its inmates returned to either Nationalist- or Republican-held Spain. Gibraltar's administration, however, was punctilious in not compelling the return of any refugee liable to be shot. The basic goal was to maintain a pretence of business as usual, including goods and workers moving back and forth across the border. Apart from occasional closures of the frontier, this is broadly what happened.

Pragmatism tinged with bias reflected the approach of foreign policy in London to Spanish events.[166] There the underlying principles were that the Civil War should not be allowed to spread (above all, to Britain's ally, Portugal), that whatever regime emerged in Spain it should be stable, and not unduly beholden to hostile powers. These principles lay at the heart of Britain's 'Non-Intervention' policy, epitomized by the Nyon Agreement (September 1937) under which maritime nations jointly patrolled the Spanish coastline against so-called 'pirates'. The latter were in fact Italian submarines, which had clandestinely started to sink British and French shipping (the fact that Italian warships were included in the Nyon patrols added a touch of farce). The burden of international patrolling fell largely upon the Royal Navy and the obligations imposed by the Spanish troubles were strongly resented as a tiresome diversion.[167] British warships were in and out of Spanish ports, rescuing expatriate nationals, and taking off distressed refugees. The family of Primo de Rivera, for example, were removed from Valencia in HMS *Shamrock* after a touchy negotiation with the Republicans, quite probably saving their lives.

In all this, Gibraltar was by no means the centre of Whitehall's attention. The value put on the Rock was not subject to the same gyrations as Malta, but nonetheless it felt diminished. Harington's successor as Governor, Sir Edmund Ironside – the most senior general in the British army – wrote privately after a briefing in the Colonial Office that he had been told that Gibraltar was 'only a "garage" ...

I dread to think what the Gilbraltarians would say if they knew'.[168] There were certain improvements, so that an airfield was for the first time laid out on the old racecourse, though when war with Germany broke out only three Swordfish seaplanes were to be found there.[169] After the Nationalists' triumphant entry into Madrid, Franco's Foreign Minister soon started talking ominously of 'solving' the historical problem of Gibraltar. The British Ambassador in Madrid took the sanguine view, however, that Spain was simply too exhausted and materially bereft to do any such thing. Hoping for the best conjured up much of the psychology, not only of exposed Gibraltar, but of the wider British Mediterranean by the later 1930s.

Gibraltar's proximity to Spanish upheavals, and Malta's proximity to Italy, meant that they could hardly avoid being caught up in the maelstrom of the times. The remarkable thing about Cyprus was the degree to which it lived within a cocoon of its own. This feature was attributable perhaps to a long history as an out-of-the way Ottoman province, subsequently mirrored in its peripheral status within the hierarchy of Britain's regional possessions. Cyprus after 1935 might well have been brought into the strategic limelight, since on two occasions (mid-1936 and again in late 1938) the British briefly gave thought to building a new base on the island as an alternative to Malta. After all, it was further away from Italy, and had an advantage over Alexandria that as a British colony, pure and simple, the British could do what they liked there. But this would have required time and money, both of which were in short supply; and in any case the navy always preferred insalubrious, rowdy but diverting Alexandria to the dull prospect of Famagusta. Arguably in this outcome Cyprus was fortunate. It meant that when war came there were no new facilities to attract the attention of likely occupiers. But it also meant that by the end of the 1930s all British officialdom in Cyprus could do was issue periodic reassurances that if necessary the great British Mediterranean Fleet would reach out its mighty arm in protection.

In this distinctive, even surreal, atmosphere the British colonial administration and its Greek-Cypriot critics played and replayed the small-scale drama of the 1931 troubles and their aftermath. Sir Richmond Palmer, Governor after January 1933, was a plain colonial service officer with stereotypical Victorian views, which was indeed why, with Storrs's failure in the island so fresh, he had been appointed in the first place. 'I know of no community', Palmer laid down as his bedrock principle, 'which is so utterly unfit to take any responsible part in the Government of its native country as is that of Cyprus.'[170] Even municipal elections were now put on ice. For the first time, a small detachment of British troops was kept on hand in Nicosia itself to snuff out any trouble; one disadvantage of this was that the personnel fell victim to urban temptations, and consequently to venereal diseases, so long characteristic of the garrisons in Cairo and Alexandria (there had been no such temptations up in the Cypriot hills, dotted as they were with monasteries). In Greek-Cypriot political folklore this period remains known as the *Palmerkratia*, or Palmer's Dictatorship. Palmer's Arcadian ideal was characterized by an attempt at eliciting co-operation through a wholly unelected Advisory Council of Notables, the handing out of medals and the odd knighthood, an elaborate protocol for arranging social precedence at public functions and similar ploys.[171] Legislation was passed to hamper the election of a new archbishop after Kyrillos's death, and the younger and far more dissident Bishop of Paphos had his movements restricted.[172] This was not so much an authentic dictatorship as a renewed and somewhat bathetic attempt to make a model British colony out of Cypriot raw material.

The trouble was that, once the shock of 1931 passed away, all this seemed to outsiders, even in the Colonial Office, as increasingly old-fashioned and impractical. From the mid-1930s the island's government administration was producing a minor version of the embarrassment that the Ionian Protectorate caused Britain in the 1850s. In May 1939 an acerbic official in Whitehall remarked that the Cyprus administration 'is becoming imbued with the political philosophy of Mussolini, and . . . thoroughly afraid of criticism in any form'; the first part of this description was no longer a compliment as it would have been a few years before.[173] When Palmer was at last eased into retirement, his successor was Sir William Battershill, who before going to Palestine had been a rather disillusioned member of Palmer's staff in Nicosia. His job was to put things onto a different tack. The Secretary of State for the Colonies, Malcolm MacDonald, even spoke in Parliament during July 1939 of an intention to reintroduce a form of representative politics into Cyprus. But intentions were one thing and carrying them out very much another under Cypriot conditions. The foundations for a carefully controlled experiment in the reintroduction of representative government were highly uncertain; and an uncontrolled experiment of any kind in the contemporary Mediterranean was not something that could lightly be risked. Battershill was therefore pleased by the warm welcome he got as Governor from the usually polite Cypriots, but had little confidence this would last. 'The newspapers continue to say what a fine fellow I am . . . they feel sure I shall give self-government to Cypriots,' he wrote home to his mother, but added more darkly: 'When they know what I am going to recommend – I have not made up my mind yet but it certainly won't be self-government or anything like it – they will be furious . . .'[174] But then such misunderstanding had surrounded the British in Cyprus for many years.

In fact Battershill had been over the moon when given the job in Nicosia, because it meant leaving Jerusalem, where, like all Mandatory officials, it had become necessary for him to carry a pistol. Cyprus was still a long way from that.[175] Sir Hugh Foot – whose distinguished career was bound up with both that island and Palestine – recalled the Mandate during the 1930s as 'direct, authoritarian, bureaucratic, straightforward administration at its best – and its worst'.[176] Its abiding weakness, Foot added, was that 'No one could say what the eventual aim was'. What made this weakness fatal was that Jews and Arabs both suspected that whatever the aim might be, it ran directly counter to their own interests and even survival. Perhaps if Palestinian society could have been frozen demographically somewhere around 1932, and if the British had devised a policy shunting the rival communities into co-operation, a different future might have been charted. The increase in Jewish immigration from Europe, accelerating with Nazi persecution of German Jewry after Adolf Hitler's arrival in power in January 1933, tilted the odds against co-existence under beneficent British government. During the 1930s more than a quarter of a million Jews arrived, twice as many as in the 1920s.[177] Many came under the continuing quota scheme that General Sir Arthur Wauchope, as High Commissioner after 1931, insisted should be expanded to take account of what was happening in Germany. It was in this, and his great encouragement of agricultural *kibbutzim*, that

Wauchope's reputation for Zionism lay. But many Jews arrived illegally. Chaim Weizmann warned Wauchope they would swim over if necessary, and certainly the Royal Navy was not very successful at intercepting vessels entering Palestinian waters clandestinely. As in their Spanish patrolling, it is doubtful that they tried all that hard. It was the kind of task British naval officers hated more than any other.

In Palestine, land, immigration and politics were locked together so that they could not be prised apart, least of all by anything so feeble as Mandatory power. The Arabs continued to reject any constitutional innovation that did not recognize their majority status, but Balfour's legacy – the principle of a national home for Jews – always barred the way to this. Simultaneously the sale of land by Arabs to Jews shifted the balance of social power. Certain controls were implemented but they amounted to little. The British pretended that they were protecting the Arab peasant from dispossession, while the Arabs pretended that the sales were not taking place at all, especially after the Mufti of Jerusalem's ritual *fatwa* against such transactions in 1935.[178] Amid these pretences, rural society in Arab Palestine started to be consumed by mutual suspicion between clan and family networks. Some British administrators in rural districts managed to maintain good relations with Arab village authorities throughout this period, but they were the exception that proved the rule. In April 1936, overlapping with the formation of an Arab Higher Committee, a popular general strike erupted, which then gradually slid into a physical rebellion, including attacks on Jewish settlements and – mimicking Egyptian methods in 1919 – the disruption of communications. The ultimate disaster for any colonial occupier was to be caught between warring and irreconcilable parties. In the eastern Mediterranean, with the implacability of its religious and cultural differences, such a fate was even worse. This was the Palestinian reality the British faced by mid-1936.

Could they escape from it? An opportunity loomed when the intervention of Arab leaderships in Egypt, Iraq and Transjordan led to the suspension of the general strike in October 1936; this mediation signified that, if it succeeded in nothing else, Arab Palestinian resistance was regionalizing the problem. In the interval gained the British Government sent out a Royal Commission under Lord Peel. The views of its members reflected the alienation from all things Palestinian now characterizing opinion in Britain. The Commissioners' discussions revealed a scathing contempt for the ineffectiveness of the Mandatory authorities[179] – though such impotence really derived from the evasion of decisions in London itself. They took umbrage at the Arabs' refusal to budge an inch. 'My own dislike of the Palestinian Arabs', Sir Horace Rumbold remarked, echoing the feelings he once had for Turks in Constantinople, 'increases daily.'[180] Their criticisms of the Jews were almost as sharp. The Commission Report in July 1937 recommended that the only solution was to divide Palestine and quit – or virtually quit, since the British would retain Jerusalem, Haifa and a narrow corridor between the two. Jerusalem was to be retained simply because there was no safe way of cutting it up between Jews and Arabs, Haifa because its harbour might prove handy in future,[181] and a linking corridor was necessary just in case a quick exit was needed at some point. This recipe for partition acknowledged that Palestine had ceased to be worth fighting for.

In retrospect we can see that here was the last chance for the British to cut themselves loose from Balfour's burden and to do so from a position of relative strength. But even in 1937 such a policy would have meant transparent retreat, exactly the sort of impression that the British were with difficulty trying to counter elsewhere in the Mediterranean. Having agreed on the Peel formula, British ministers began to backtrack. This was the worst of all possible worlds: to have raised the spectre of partition, while drawing back from implementation. Everybody's rhetoric went up a notch. Chaim Weizmann, visiting Cairo, told Lampson that 'unless the Jews get what they want they might turn nasty'.[182] Lampson did not think they would dare, but the intimation that Palestinian Jews actually might become aggressive themselves had to enter the realm of calculation. In the ensuing hiatus of Palestine policy, however, the danger that Arabs outside the territory might turn even more nasty dominated British thinking. 'If we must offend one side,' Neville Chamberlain summed up, 'let us offend the Jews rather than the Arabs.'[183] After all, the Jews did not have many friends to replace the British in the world of the 1930s, whereas the Italians and the Germans were already courting the Arabs, however ineptly.

Meanwhile the most immediate fact from the summer of 1937 was the renewal and intensification of Arab rebellion within Palestine. The murder during September of the District Commissioner of Galilee, and ex-veteran of the Australian Light Horse, Lewis Andrews – visiting a church in Nazareth on his birthday – marked a turning point; whether he was selected as a target because of the land sales he had recently facilitated or because he was known to possess intelligence on Arab political leadership was never clarified. The vital feature of the revolt was that, although the Arabs knew that the Jews were ultimately their most deadly enemy, they concentrated their violence against the British, so that in the southern desert a senior official stated that they 'destroyed every form of British rule; police, ports, wireless communications and dispensaries alike'.[184] This made sense. The Jews wanted the power to decide things, but did not have it yet. The British did, therefore they were the ones to intimidate and kill. All the little compensations of life for less-than-lavishly paid Mandatory officials – picnics in the countryside, leisurely strolls in the evening warmth of the eastern Mediterranean – disappeared. British employees had to remain constantly alert in case of attack (at this time the British presence fluctuated at around 18,000 troops and 2,000 civilians). For a few days in October 1938 the British lost all control within the Old City of Jerusalem. We have seen that wherever they exercised significant influence in the Mediterranean, the British faced considerable pressure of one kind or another. But nowhere else were nerves as taut as in Palestine.

To stay in the saddle, the British developed counter-insurgent tactics or 'Emergency Regulations' largely derived from experience in Bengal.[185] This was something less than martial rule, but tantamount to it. These methods included destruction of individual property, collective punishment of villages, brusque house searches, and large-scale screening of suspects in which men were led off with their heads covered in hoods. The British built a fence along the northern border to prevent infiltration – walls always being the mark of a regime in serious trouble. Just over 100 Arabs were hanged for capital offences. Some British military officers carried out their anti-insurgent tasks with as much discretion and sensitivity as conditions allowed; but others less so. The Anglican Bishop of Jerusalem described one soldier sent to Palestine to get a grip, General Bernard Montgomery, as 'blood mad'.[186] The most vicious excesses were those committed by the Special Night Squads organized by the unbalanced Orde Wingate, working in tandem with the new phenomenon of Jewish 'terror' against Arabs.[187] A paradox, indeed, of the later phases of the rebellion was that, just as externally the British were trying to dilute the Zionist project and ingratiate themselves with Arab opinion, in Palestine the British army felt pressed into co-operation with Jewish military organizations, especially Haganah. All in all, though British methods under these conditions were often harsh, the brutality employed was not of a systematic, and certainly not a systemic, character.[188]

Palestinian troubles considerably complicated British strategic planning in the Mediterranean. More than 20,000 troops were deployed there, and during the Munich crisis of September 1938 this commitment meant that there was no reserve available for an expedition to Europe in case of war.[189] The petering out of the rebellion from early 1939 was therefore a considerable relief, although both Lampson and General Archibald Wavell as newly appointed Commander-in-Chief Middle East constantly worried about its renewal. The essential goal of the British Government's new Palestine policy, partition having been dumped, was enshrined in a White Paper of April 1939. This was intended to keep the country quiet for the duration. An independent and possibly federal state was contemplated ten years hence, and in the meantime an annual maximum of 75,000 was placed on immigration – not so much a policy, in truth, as a prevarication. At bottom, British policy reflected a basic feeling that that they were at a dead end, and could only await what further events had in store.[190]

We have seen that from the early 1930s the Mediterranean was defined in London as a lesser priority than the Far East. Yet this assumption was always more theoretical, and therefore unlikely to become operational, than it seemed. It had arisen partly from the necessity to provide reassurance to Australia and New Zealand, who were perilously exposed to assault by Japan. The principle was therefore reaffirmed at the Imperial Conference of 1937 to curb their fears. Behind this apparent ordering of priorities also lay the assumption that British possessions in the Mediterranean, if forfeited during the early stages of a conflict, were inherently recoverable later; this was not true in the Far East, so that losses there had to be avoided in the first place.[191] By the time of Munich it had become central to British thinking that their forces in Malta and, even more importantly, Egypt should be sufficiently strong and stocked up to hold out for three months entirely on their own. Cyprus, as so often in British strategic planning, slipped away once more to the margins.

Nevertheless, although Munich by no means exhausted Chamberlain's commitment to appeasement, subtle shifts occurred for which the Mediterranean was the touchstone. The more war loomed, the less palatable the prospect of losing the Mediterranean became. A reversal of priorities began, so that by the end of 1938 the Admiralty was already beginning to be of the view that it was the Far East that was most dispensable; on the outbreak of war the Home Fleet should therefore have some of its resources diverted to Gibraltar – a shift away from the 'Main Fleet to the East' principle.[192] A conviction took hold in military circles that Britain could not win a future war just by defending itself.[193] There would be a need to go on the offensive somewhere, and the obvious place was the Mediterranean. Whenever officers from other Royal Navy squadrons visited their Mediterranean counterparts, they noticed how the atmosphere there was more confident and geared for action.[194] During the early months of 1939 this aggressive spirit filtered back into Whitehall. 'If we lose the Mediterranean, we will lose the war,' one prominent member of the Admiralty planning staff was already warning,[195] while Winston Churchill – still on the sidelines, but with his ear firmly clamped to the ground – told the House of Commons during April that the Mediterranean was destined to be 'England's First Battlefield'.[196]

Yet such rhetoric was still for a while hemmed in by countervailing realities. Fighting in the Mediterranean was automatically assumed to mean fighting alongside France, and this was something that the British remained deeply unsure about. Anglo-French staff talks started in January 1939, but they were desultory and remained so as long as peace lasted. The French suspected, with some justification, that sooner or later the British might try to simply buy off Mussolini by offering him, not any of their own territories in the Mediterranean, but French territories instead. The British also struggled to build up a Balkan barrier by giving qualified guarantees to Greece and Turkey. At one point the British considered making a new naval base ('Port

X', as it was called) at Navarino Bay in western Greece. The fact that this involved no apparent consultation with the Greek authorities highlighted a traditional British attitude to the sovereignty of that country. The proposition was abandoned, and a tendency to gloss over where Greece fitted into British priorities was to exact a considerable cost later on. Meanwhile keeping Mussolini on side remained at the heart of the British Government's foreign policy with Hitler's 'liquidation' of Prague in March and mounting pressure on Poland. In late August, with the denouement of peace being played out around the fate of little Danzig, the Admiralty ordered an increased state of readiness for all its forces, and the concentration of the Mediterranean Fleet in Alexandria.[197]

When the British and the French finally went to war with Germany on 3 September 1939 all Allied merchant shipping in the Mediterranean was instantly stopped. But whatever was going on elsewhere, nothing happened here – an eerie silence prevailed. Within hours it became clear that Mussolini would, after all, stay out, as did Franco's Spain, and tension relaxed.[198] Governor Bonham-Carter in Valletta expressed widespread relief when he wrote in his diary on 6 October that henceforth Italy would enter the war only if it was forced to do so.[199] War had come at last, but far from the Mediterranean being dominated by an enemy, its shorelines remained overwhelmingly neutral or subject to Anglo-French control; and equally swiftly commercial traffic began flowing unescorted once more, as it had in August 1914. There was even an agreement between the British and Italian navies on submarine movements, so that the British did not sink any Italian vessels by mistaking them for German U-boats. The 'phoney' war that broke out in September 1939 was to be at its phoniest in the Mediterranean, though who this interlude favoured most – and how long it could possibly last – was a matter for debate.[200]

For two decades after 1919 the British in the Mediterranean had see-sawed between competing visions of mastery and acute vulnerability. The pattern was repeated from Gibraltar to Alexandria, though the local configuration of affairs was always subtly different. What made the Mediterranean so dangerous by 1939 was not so much the growth of Italian power, but rather the fact that it was in clear decline, making some 'wild dog' action on Mussolini's part seemingly more likely. For some local populations British rule or nagging supervision by the end of the 1930s was something they very much wanted to see the back of. But the world people faced was not one of hope and optimism, but of mounting fear, and in these circumstances everybody's options became boxed in. As time had gone on, Britain's leading position in the Mediterranean had been buttressed, not so much by its own intrinsic leverage or 'mastery', but by the fact that on balance a connection with Great Britain represented for many the best option available. The crisis of the 1930s gave an even sharper edge to this variable. An intuitive understanding of these dynamics infused Eden's assessment of the realities in the Mediterranean as war got under way that 'we shall not be faced with serious trouble . . . during [the] war unless things go very badly against us; but this will not necessarily be true in [the] period immediately following hostilities'.[201] The politics of the wartime Mediterranean, as elsewhere, was to be crucially shaped from the start by its various populations calculating what would come after, and the opportunities this might bring if present dangers could be survived. But, as Eden's caveat implied, in the immediate conflict it was possible that things might go very badly wrong in ways not easily conceivable at the outset. The puzzle remained as to whether the British in the Mediterranean were strong or weak, still firmly in the saddle or on the slide, reliable protectors or scuttlers and betrayers.

# 7
# Britain's First Battlefield, 1939–1945

Ultimately the Mediterranean did prove to be Britain's preferred battlefield in the new war – after, that is, the aerial Battle of Britain during the summer of 1940 had secured the survival of the homeland itself. Early on in the struggle, Winston Churchill, installed for the second time as First Lord of the Admiralty, foresaw that the Mediterranean could provide 'the sort of war which would suit the English people once they got used to it'.[1] One very important way it suited them was by not involving loss of life on an industrial scale. This was one reason for the southern inflection in Churchill's war policy. Even more than between 1914 and 1918, it was the series of Mediterranean fronts on land and sea – alongside the Blitz at home – that came to shape British popular remembrance, epitomized by a stream of memoirs which for twenty years after the war explored every aspect of the fighting there, with greater or lesser realism. The image of Britain and 'Britishness' moulded by the experience and stereotypes of 1939–45 retain an indelible Mediterranean imprint.

For the Mediterranean societies themselves, the second great war of the twentieth century was both more intensive and extensive in impact than the first. In the First World War there was no major fighting at sea, while operations on land were limited to the Levant and northern Greece. In the Second World War wide tracts of the Mediterranean were fought over and often re-fought over with the result that countries experienced hunger, occupation and resistance, though – with the exception of Greece – not for the most part on the devastating scale of northern and east-central Europe. The British and the relationships they had with Mediterranean populations got caught up in this intensity. The effects could be binding one moment and disintegrative the next, so that successive layers of loyalty, solidarity, suspicion and betrayal were laid down.

Yet the prominence of the Mediterranean theatre was scarcely predictable at first. The shores fronting its waters remained either neutral or under Anglo-French control after September 1939, though neutrality had subtle variations, including the friendly (Greece), the sullen (Italy and Spain) and the ambivalent (Turkey). According to a prior understanding, the French navy assumed prime responsibility for the western, and the British for the eastern, Mediterranean. With a British naval destroyer force guarding Gibraltar, and the bulk of the Mediterranean Fleet concentrated in Alexandria, both ends of the Sea were sealed while the initial panic lasted. They were promptly unsealed when it became clear that neither Italy nor Spain was going to take the opportunity to grab spoils for themselves. When maritime business resumed, British and French warships began a 'visit and search' campaign to stifle contraband trade with Germany. Cargoes seized were taken to Port Said, Haifa and Malta for inspection.

According to a later Admiralty account, on the face of it this situation seemed 'pretty good'.[2] Sharp anxiety was followed by relief that actually nothing much had changed. The overall prospect was that the Mediterranean would remain on the sidelines. The Anglo-French alliance could gradually harness its resources, strangle German overseas imports, and block the advance of Hitler's armies into western Europe until it was realized in Berlin that a negotiation was the only sensible outcome for all concerned. The fact that British preparations for war in the Mediterranean remained sketchy, therefore, did not seem unduly worrisome. In Malta – where priests had been equipped with gas masks so they could attend to the dead and dying in the streets following a feared attack from the air[3] – there was an overwhelming sense of relief. Reflecting on this at the New Year of 1940, the Governor, Sir Charles Bonham-Carter, noted that 'Here in Malta we have much to be grateful for; we have . . . indeed been most fortunate'.[4]

For Admiral Sir Andrew Cunningham, Commander-in-Chief of the Mediterranean Fleet since the previous June, there were mixed feelings about such a start. The trademark belligerency of the Fleet meant that its personnel chafed at the lack of action,[5] and the possibility of having to remain largely passive was irksome. Worse for Cunningham, within a month of the outbreak the Fleet itself, having been brought up to a strength of two powerful battle squadrons including the aircraft carrier HMS *Eagle*, started gradually to melt away as warships – first cruisers, then the battleships – were withdrawn to the Atlantic and Home stations.[6] By the end of 1939 the Mediterranean force was almost entirely composed of destroyers, and some of those were Australian. One question requiring resolution was where Cunningham should maintain his own 'flag'. He would have preferred Alexandria because that was where most of his remaining ships were stationed, and also where he could co-ordinate efficiently with General Wavell's Middle East command. He was instructed from London, however, to remain at Malta, though this meant that the Commander-in-Chief's ensign had to be kept ashore rather than afloat, never an encouraging sign.[7] Suggestively, Churchill at the Admiralty did not put Grand Harbour under the responsibility of the French as he had in 1914, and although after September 1939 British and French naval staffs met regularly at their respective headquarters in Valletta and Bizerta, this time the Royal Navy had absolutely no intention of allowing France to gain any sort of primacy, however titular.[8] This feeling towards France was to prove very important, as was a British determination to hang on to Malta itself. 'Fretful and impatient' summed up Cunningham's mood, fearful of replicating the marooned role of the British Grand Fleet after 1914.

Another thing that did not change when war with Germany first came was the British hold over Egypt. The garrison had been reinforced to 20,000 troops. Anti-aircraft defences in the Delta towns and Alexandria admittedly remained weak. The Italian army in Libya, however, was unlikely to make a surprise assault when its own western flank was vulnerable from French-ruled Tunisia. This had been a factor in Mussolini's neutrality. British concerns in Egypt under these conditions involved politics and internal security. Under the 1936 treaty, Egyptian resources were meant to be available to Britain on the outbreak of war with Germany. It had been assumed that this meant that Egypt would become a formal belligerent. But when the High Commissioner, Sir Miles Lampson, tried to synchronize a joint declaration, he found that the Egyptian Prime Minister, Ali Maher, was evasive.[9] Although British troops began to move outside the zones designated by the 1936 treaty, they had to be routed through Cairo at night – visibility, as usual, was a sensitive matter.

Several factors governed the reactions of Ali Maher's ministry.[10] It reflected the feeling of most Egyptians (keenly aware of sufferings during the last war), who were opposed to involvement. Neutrality held out some hope of limiting exposure to British demands. But one practical matter especially militated in favour of non-belligerency: the expectation that if Italy decided after a short interval to enter the war, one of her first acts would be a devastating bombardment of Alexandria and Cairo, where the elite classes mostly lived.[11] Reinsurance with Mussolini's regime was therefore a critical motivation. During the autumn of 1939 the Mediterranean witnessed no outright conflict, but fear, trepidation and manoeuvring for safety became endemic.

The Egyptian Government nevertheless proved punctilious from the start in their co-operation with British military requirements. They broke off diplomatic relations with Germany and declared a 'state of siege'. Germans were interned under the watchful eye of the long-time British head of the Egyptian police, Russell Pasha. Ports, including Alexandria, were put under British control. If the British army demanded that a new road be constructed, it was. True, neutrality meant that the Egyptian army was not at Britain's disposal, but Wavell and his senior commanders had no great confidence in that body in any case. For war purposes, the resulting compromises proved workable and durable on both sides. There remained an underlying sense that the Egyptian leadership was 'not entirely with the British',[12] and this was never to go away. But Wavell and Cunningham did not care what Egyptians thought so long as they acted in the full spirit of the 1936 treaty and otherwise kept quiet.

But for Lampson at the Residency things were not quite so straightforward. His own position as the centre of British authority in Cairo was immediately reduced once the war machinery shifted authority towards soldiers and sailors. Army and navy commanders regarded Lampson with disdain, and he responded by disliking them.[13] Above all, from the point of view of the High Commission it was the local politics which mattered, since sooner or later the war would end. Somehow the longer-term basis of Britain's position must be preserved. Lampson was therefore constantly on the lookout for ways to reassert Britain's fluctuating prestige. He was determined that eventually Ali Maher would have to go, while his habitually contemptuous attitude to the youthful King Farouk (who had succeeded to the throne in 1936) was reinforced. The entertainer Noel Coward once remarked when visiting wartime Egypt that nobody knew how to make an entrance like the intimidating Lampson. But this often fell into swagger and did not make a good impression on Egyptians. In this there was scope for alienation and, perhaps for the first time, a latent enmity in Anglo-Egyptian affairs. Still, by the start of 1940 the situation in Egypt had stabilized.[14]

A similarly complex and uncertain flux prevailed in Palestine. The polarization revolving around the British Government's recent White Paper, with its diluted commitment to a national home for Jews, was not interrupted by war. 'We shall fight the war as if there was no White Paper,' the rising Zionist leader David Ben-Gurion stated, 'and the White Paper as if there was no war.'[15] Already some on the British side feared that the two struggles might actually merge, and were anything but enthusiastic about allowing eager Jewish volunteers to join the British army lest guns get into the wrong hands. Suggestions for a separate Jewish army were anathema, and when Haganah operatives, including a young activist called Moshe Dayan,[16] were found in possession of weapons they were controversially imprisoned.

The most that British military and civilian authorities on the spot were prepared to authorize was the formation of a Palestinian battalion (in practice, mostly Jewish) attached to the East Kent Regiment.[17] The air of tension inside the Mandate was undiminished. The implementation of new Land Regulations in February 1940, ostensibly cracking down on sales by Arabs, led to bitter Jewish protests. Even though the Arab rebellion was in abeyance, soldiers in Jerusalem could only go about in pairs; by this stage, however, the danger was quite as likely to be from the Zionist side.[18] So far as most British personnel were concerned, Palestine was more unpleasant and uncomfortable than ever. 'It seems to me sometimes', one of the High Commissioner's staff was later to note in her diary, 'that there is a curse on Jerusalem. I so seldom meet anyone who is happy here.'[19] Had the war ever come directly to Palestine, the British and the Jews, sharing a common anti-Nazi stance, would almost certainly have been pressed together by circumstances. The traditional leader of Arab Palestine, the Grand Mufti Amin al-Husseni, for example, spent much of the war in Berlin as Hitler's guest. There were indeed renewed hints of solidarity between the British and the Zionists at moments of crisis but basically the things that drove them apart never really diminished.

Whatever the problems the British had in nearby Cyprus, at this stage it seemed they could never reach an impasse quite so bad. On the outbreak of war the stream of Greek-Cypriot complaints about the colonial regime abruptly halted. In mid-October a Cypriot section of the Royal Army Service Corps left for Egypt, while in January 1940 Neville Chamberlain publicly acknowledged that the first colonials to join the British Expeditionary Force in France were from Cyprus. The Governor, Sir William Battershill, felt it important that credit should be given where it was due. He informed the Colonial Office that 'the Cypriot is a volatile subject. His allegiances, when inspired by deep feeling, are generously given.'[20] It was felt that some mark of appreciation was needed. One of the leading Greek-Cypriots exiled after the 1931 troubles was allowed to return home; and in February 1940 a Cyprus Regiment was authorized, consisting of combat troops and transport pioneers (some 8,000 volunteered, both Greeks and Turks). But like Lampson in Egypt, Battershill and his colleagues soon began to worry where all this might lead. It was telling that when the Governor spoke of generous Cypriot allegiances, he had used the plural. To whom were these allegiances really due: to Britain, Greece or (for the island's main minority) to Turkey? A suspicion quickly took hold that Cypriots might play their part in the war but, unless everyone was very careful, at a price of their own choosing. Fending off political dangers for the future became a key preoccupation of British officialdom in Nicosia. In March 1940, against a background of strikes by public workers generated by rising prices, the Governor asserted that the island was 'riddled with politics at the moment ... The so called ... truce is a farce'.[21] Cyprus was to share one general trait with Palestine. Because it was never actually fought over, deeply ingrained rivalries were not erased or markedly reduced, and even penetrated more deeply.

By early 1940 the likelihood of the Mediterranean staying clear of the European conflict was ebbing fast. The Anglo-French aim of forcing

Hitler into a new negotiation was Mussolini's nightmare. One thing the French, British and Germans would then probably all agree on was to keep the feeble Italians well away from the conference table. At some point or other Mussolini had to get into the 'picture' of the war, even at the cost of soaking up some damage. Damage was occurring in any case. The British navy made sure that no confrontations took place with the Regina Marina, but Italian commercial shipping was caught up in Allied inspection procedures. Mussolini stormed against the reduction of Italy to a 'de facto British colony' and was contemptuous of compatriots who felt that an Italy no more than 'a Malta multiplied a million times' was a price worth paying to keep at peace.[22] By the end of March rumours that the Italian dictator was gearing himself up for action led the Admiralty in London to order the reinforcement of the Mediterranean Fleet. Returning ships were once more concentrated in Alexandria, since any stationed in Gibraltar and Malta might present Franco as well as Mussolini with an irresistible temptation to strike without warning.

As tension rose, the desire in the Mediterranean Fleet to make a 'show of force' increased.[23] These tentative plans focused on the eastern Mediterranean. Both the Dodecanese and Crete emerged as potential acquisitions, each affording control over the entry to the eastern Aegean. Mussolini was already making overt threats to Athens, further evidence that Greece was unlikely to emerge unscathed. Meanwhile protagonists also began to look to Turkey, whose reactions would clearly be very important in affecting strategic outcomes. Here Cunningham misjudged British leverage when insisting that in any joint action the Turkish fleet should come directly under his authority. Turkey was playing for time, but in doing so her leaders were determined to be judges of their own fate, and not be told what to do by Cunningham or indeed any German counterpart.[24] Ankara's fierce commitment to neutrality bore the essential hallmark of the Kemalist state, and screened the Levant from any invasion by Germany. The region, in contrast to 1917–18, and except for a brief Syrian interlude in 1941, was not to be the scene of large-scale or sustained fighting. Turkish and Spanish neutrality between them operated massively in favour of Britain and protected the southern Mediterranean at both ends far more than the continued possession of Gibraltar and Cyprus.

Cunningham and Churchill were never quite to see eye to eye on strategic matters, and this was so from the outbreak of the Mediterranean war proper. Cunningham, for all his enthusiasm for operations, was cautious about sending British warships from Alexandria post-haste into the central Mediterranean, where they might be picked off in some sudden attack. When Churchill sent a message to Cunningham on 5 June 1940 that was critical of a lack of activity, Cunningham felt it to be 'hasty and ungracious'.[25] There was indeed to be a habitual tension between Churchill and British military commanders in the Mediterranean on such grounds. The difference was that, although Churchill later sacked successive army heads, ostensibly for not taking enough risks, he had always to watch his step with Cunningham. Churchill never forgot that it was a breakdown with Lord John Fisher that had cost him his job at the Admiralty in May 1915 and frozen him out of the rest of the war. In Britain, the navy could always unleash more powerful political emotions than the army, and Churchill was not going to make the same mistake again.

By the time of Churchill's passing brush with Cunningham he had already become Prime Minister. Ironically, this arose from the catastrophe of the botched intervention in Norway, for which Churchill himself was largely responsible. But the mud stuck to Neville Chamberlain, and on 9 May 1940 Churchill had succeeded him. This transition was immediately overtaken by Hitler's assault, first on the Low Countries and then on France, whose resistance quickly crumbled. Mussolini's need to be in at the death became compelling, and on 11 June Italy finally joined Germany's side. On 25 June France formally signed a preliminary armistice. Immediately on the outbreak of hostilities with Italy, Cunningham sent a naval force on a cautious 'sweep' into the central Mediterranean to test out enemy dispositions. Notably, the remaining warships still at Malta were withdrawn to Alexandria. Under these circumstances, shores unequivocally 'friendly' to Britain in the Mediterranean had shrunk drastically to the immediate vicinity of Egypt, Palestine, Cyprus, Gibraltar and Malta. How long the last of these could hold out was doubted, and over Gibraltar, too, Spain's attitude remained unclear. With France gone there was no partner-guardian in the western Mediterranean. The war came to the

Mediterranean haphazardly and in such a way as to maximize Britain's potential weakness.[26]

Nowhere was more vulnerable than Malta. There was no Fleet there and no Commander-in-Chief (though Cunningham's wife and daughter, like many service families, had remained). There were also no up-to-date fighter aircraft, and only a few rugged old Gladiators. Three of the latter, named Faith, Hope and Charity by locals, were to achieve legendary fame for resistance against crushing odds in the air during the early days of the siege. The War Office was reluctant to send any men or equipment to the island, though 145 bicycles (cars disappeared off the roads as soon as hostilities started, owing to a petrol shortage), 450 tons of sandbags, and a Middle East Pigeon Section composed of 15 soldiers, 200 pigeons and 8 rabbits had been sent.[27] There was also a new Governor in Sir William Dobbie. Sending a staunch member of the Plymouth Brethren to rule over a Catholic population was odd, but the job hardly seemed a plum posting. In a curious way, it worked, partly because Dobbie was unusually humble, and also because his religiosity – in the dark days ahead he would be apt to turn up in the most unlikely places and drop to his knees to seek God's blessing where a bomb had landed – struck a chord with a devout population.[28]

The first Italian air raid, early in the morning on 11 June 1940, targeted Grand Harbour. A mother and two sons were killed in the dockyard, and a direct hit on Fort St Elmo caused six fatalities in the Royal Malta Artillery. Since the government had not put into place an evacuation plan, for fear of exacerbating anxieties, a spontaneous exodus began: around 70,000 people, taking what possessions they could, flowed out of the Three Cities and Valletta towards the villages. There had always remained a doubt among ordinary Maltese whether the Italians would drop bombs on them. When they did, Maltese opinion turned solidly against Italy.[29] The measure of this was that when Dobbie ordered the internment of leading Nationalists suspected of pro-Italian leanings, including the respected Chief Justice, his action met with near universal acquiescence. In truth those interned were not seditious in any way, and one assessment is that the outbreak of war was simply 'too good an opportunity' not to deal the proponents of *italianità* a final blow.[30] Yet there was a real possibility that events might present future quislings with opportunities, and getting a decisive blow in first was prudent in the circumstances.

The strategic implications of the fall of France, however, were so forbidding that at first it was doubtful whether the British would remain in the Mediterranean at all. With so much at stake in Home and Atlantic waters, the Admiralty veered towards abandonment – in effect, falling back on Gibraltar and Alexandria, but yielding everything in between. To Churchill, such action was unacceptable. In his first speech to the House of Commons as Prime Minister he had staked out Britain's aim as 'victory at all costs . . . however long and hard the road may be'. But for victory to be credible, defeats in the wake of Dunkirk could not be unending. There had to be one place where British gains, even modest ones, could maintain the national spirit; and it had become an assumption that the only front where British forces could conceivably go on the offensive was in the Mediterranean. The decision against abandonment was of vital significance. Without it the 'Mediterranean Strategy', that hinge of the British war effort as the conflict unfolded, could never have emerged.

It has often been suggested that Mussolini's failure to invade Malta very soon after June 1940 was a grave error. But this could only have been done by sea, and Cunningham's counterpart, Admiral Domenico Cavagnari, feared that the British Mediterranean Fleet at Alexandria would rush out to intercept his ships and smash them to bits with their bigger guns. Here again was what was to prove a persistent trait: a fragile Mediterranean equilibrium created by the combined sum of Anglo-Italian fears. Apart from a few skirmishes, the most notable of which was off Cape Matapan on 28–9 March 1941 when the Italians broke off the engagement before losing their flagship, the *Vittoria Veneto*, the two fleets never hurled themselves at each other. As in 1915–18, so after June 1940 Italy clung to a 'fleet in being' – one that could justify the country's presence at a future peace conference, and that could not therefore be lost prematurely. This was an implicit British 'victory', although not one that was immediately obvious. The Royal Navy was able to provision Malta through the autumn, and deliver a small number of Hurricane fighter planes and extra troops. Maltese who had fled Valletta even began to trickle back. In December 1940

Cunningham and his squadron at last returned to Grand Harbour with 20,000 Maltese crowding the shore.

Although Gibraltar was never to suffer the same degree of misfortune as Malta later, it remained very precarious. One of the first maritime actions of the war in the Mediterranean was the scuttling of Italian shipping in Gibraltar harbour. There was one very distinctive feature of the wartime Rock: there was hardly any civilian population left. In Gibraltar, evacuation of what were inelegantly called 'useless mouths' began before actual hostilities. The Governor, Sir Edmund Ironside, had opposed this efflux as a sign of weakness,[31] but the military wanted unnecessary civilians out of the way, and an official announcement was made on 21 May 1940. Since evacuation to the United Kingdom was regarded only as a last resort, the first evacuees were shipped out three days later, bound for Casablanca in French Morocco, with some emotional scenes as the steamer left the wharf.[32] By 20 June more than 11,000 had left for the same destination. Since by that time France was in the throes of defeat, for the evacuees this was merely going from the frying pan into the fire. The intense frigidity of Anglo- French relations meant that the local authorities in Morocco were hardly pleased to take responsibility for feeding and sheltering British itinerants. Equally, Ironside was adamant that they could not go back to Gibraltar. Reluctantly, the British Government redirected these anxious families, mainly women and children, to the United Kingdom, though some were diverted to Jamaica and Portuguese Madeira, where they remained for the duration.

This evacuation was a seminal event in the history of Gibraltar, and has become a building-block in the construction of a Gibraltarian identity; as one writer remarks, the evacuation 'drove home to many Gibraltarians that they had no real control over their own affairs'.[33] Certainly the fact that such a large part of the colony's population was physically removed, and subsequently exposed directly to a British education and social system, whether in Earls Court, Cardiff or Kingston, Jamaica, confirmed the triumph of Anglicized norms. To this there was one counterweight in Gibraltar after mid-1940: a continuing demand for female labour in shops, restaurants and medical facilities meant that Spanish women daily flowed in (and out) across the border in even bigger numbers. Intercourse and intermarriage among those who remained continued. But with the evacuation the Rock became 'a ghostly gloomy place', especially in the evenings.[34] The fact that the frontier with Spain closed every night at 11.30 p.m. throughout the war, and that the Victoria Gardens and various sports pitches were destroyed to permit the expansion of what was previously only an emergency landing area into a real airfeld, compounded the grey effect.

After June 1940, however, Gibraltar's future seemed to hinge on one major question. Would Franco, like Mussolini, enter the conflict? And if he did, was not Gibraltar the obvious place to make a spectacular start? There was a new British Ambassador in Madrid, who was tasked with stopping that eventuality. On becoming Prime Minister, Churchill was determined to get rid of the arch-Chamberlainite Samuel Hoare from his Cabinet, and promptly exiled him to the Madrid embassy. This was partly Churchill's acid political wit at work; it was often said at the time that Hoare's weakness for dictators suggested him as an eminently suitable emissary to Franco. His predecessor had been convinced that Spain was simply too weak to take advantage of anybody, let alone Britain with its naval power. But this was felt to be complacent in the circumstances, and Hoare's job was to do everything possible to make absolutely sure Spain stayed out of the war. The demonstrations outside the embassy on his arrival calling for the return of Gibraltar, although not a good sign, could be taken with a pinch of salt. But Franco was not like Primo de Rivera in the 1920s, whose autocracy had been instinctively moderate. He was a military adventurer, with a deep obligation to the Axis powers. His regime needed to summon up a newly grandiloquent Spain. Crucially, within days of the Franco-German armistice a German army turned up on the Spain's Pyrenean frontier. Its presence was enough to make it all too conceivable that Spain would before long do Hitler's bidding, whatever that might be.

'Spain had much to give,' Churchill once remarked on that country in relation to the war, 'and even more to take away.'[35] Franco's potential belligerency was a constant object of concern throughout 1940 and 1941. Hoare and Lord Halifax (Foreign Secretary till January 1941) strove to stabilize the neutrality of Spain and thereby that of Portugal, bound to follow in Spain's wake. There were various possible ways to ensure this. These did not include giving Gibraltar away to Franco immediately. It was far too vital, not only in Mediterranean terms, but also in policing Atlantic and Cape shipping routes. But Spain could be given a promise, or the hint of a promise, of Gibraltar's cession once the war was over. Later on Franco's regime claimed that this is exactly what the British did do in the panic of June 1940.[36] Churchill, however, opposed any such formal commitment, arguing that it would mean little: the Spanish were not so foolish as to be unaware that if Britain were defeated they would get Gibraltar anyway, and that if Britain won the Union Jack would remain over the Rock regardless.[37] However, there is some evidence that Hoare was authorized to float the hypothesis of a post-war cession.

But it was the future of French Morocco as much as Gibraltar which governed Anglo-Spanish relations.[38] Franco was above all 'a man of Africa' – his rebellion in 1936 had after all started there – and the prospect of preying on French possessions held more exotic possibilities than acquiring a mere rock opposite Algeciras. Hitler's own wish to keep Pétain on side made it impossible for him to promise any French African territory to Franco. The latter had always therefore to calculate that to bring his dream of expansion to fruition he would probably need British acquiescence. In addition to such Moroccan factors, there was the option of giving Spain a warning punch of some sort, most feasibly by seizing some of her islands, probably the Canaries. Churchill's natural pugnacity made this highly appealing. But this might in fact have precipitated a final Spanish rush into Hitler's arms, and Hoare and Lord Halifax fought a sustained and successful campaign against such a course.[39]

There was another, even more basic method of exerting British influence over Spain. The Royal Navy dictated how hungry Spaniards became, and the degree to which their ruined economy kept operating. Continental Europe was hardly in a condition to meet Spanish needs, while the British Mediterranean Fleet regulated shipping in and out of Iberian ports. Controls over imports under the Anglo-Spanish agreement of September 1940 were fine-tuned for political ends. In London the Churchill government was a coalition, and there were Labour ministers who loathed Franco for ideological reasons. Hugh Dalton, as Minister of Economic Warfare, felt that the starvation of

Spain was a price worth paying to smash his regime.[40] Economic pressure was never pushed that far, but it was consistently brought to bear to influence any perceived leaning towards Berlin. The long-standing flow of goods between Gibraltar and the adjoining *campo*, far from being stopped in its tracks by war, actually grew, and helped cement an unwritten Anglo-Spanish understanding. Almost the whole of Spain became a black market after 1940; and 'British' Gibraltar was what made that market tick along and kept Spaniards from the extreme want that many other European populations endured. We can therefore see why Hitler found Franco impossible to pin down to any firm agreement to co-operate. The Führer met him in the French Basque town of Hendaye in October 1940 and afterwards said he would rather have a tooth pulled than meet him again.[41]

Preserving a complicated Anglo-Spanish equilibrium was all the more vital after the shocking collapse of Britain's main ally in June 1940. The fate of the French navy was the most immediately pressing question. In the chaos of defeat, some French warships made for Portsmouth, some for the French West Indies, and those in eastern Mediterranean waters for Alexandria. But the biggest concentration was in the Algerian port of Mers-el-Kebir. During armistice negotiations with Germany the French leaders under Marshal Pétain bargained hard to keep control of these warships. An emergency Royal Navy contingent (Force H) under Admiral James Somerville had been dispatched to Gibraltar as France tottered. Early on the morning of 3 July one of Somerville's destroyers arrived at Mers-el-Kebir to negotiate. The French commander, Admiral Marcel-Bruno Gensoul, was presented with various options to take his ships peacefully out of the war.[42] All of these, however, would have confirmed the humiliation of France. Somerville instinctively sympathized with the plight of Gensoul's fleet, and would have given him the benefit of the doubt. The British and French navies had often been rivals, yet even their rivalry had usually been respectful and even chivalrous. But to Churchill Somerville's hesitation showed that 'he did not have the root of the matter in him'.[43] For the Prime Minister, the only cast-iron guarantee of British naval superiority, even survival, in the Mediterranean lay in destroying as many French ships as possible before they fell into enemy hands.

That same evening at 5.56 p.m., after the expiry of an ultimatum, Force H opened fire. It ceased after twenty minutes. In between, some 1,500 French sailors died, and eleven French warships were sunk. A similar denouement would have been played out with the French vessels at Alexandria had Cunningham not fended off Churchill. The substantial French community in Alexandria was in a highly febrile mood and Cunningham sought to head off trouble.[44] Although Admiral René Émile Godfroy refused to abandon loyalty to what he saw as the legitimate Pétainist authorities, Cunningham brought sufficient pressure to bear to make him agree to the engines in his ships in Alexandria harbour being disabled. Afterwards Churchill never lost an opportunity to make the situation of Godfroy's marooned squadron uncomfortable by suggesting that its supplies and the pay for its crews – chargeable to Britain – be interrupted.[45] Meanwhile at the funeral service for the fatalities at Mers-el-Kebir, Gensoul said scathingly that 'If there is a stain on the flag it is certainly not ours'.[46] To his wife, Somerville admitted feeling 'thoroughly dirty and ashamed'.[47] Hitler thought the British had 'gone mad', and for the first time his thoughts turned seriously to the Mediterranean as a seat of possible action (though they never fixed there for very long).[48] Most profoundly, the action at Mers-el-Kebir demonstrated beyond doubt that the British were in the war for the long haul, and in parliamentary terms it confirmed Churchill's now unchallenged authority. Once again Mediterranean events had shown their capacity for crucially shaping the British domestic scene.

Arguably, just as important a consequence of this sequence was to root into French minds that in a crisis Britain was ready to desert them.[49] The Vichy regime was thereafter defined by Anglophobia. Its warplanes landed a number of bombs on Gibraltar, and later Vichy troops were to fight bitterly against the British in Syria and Morocco. The possibility that France's remaining fleet might help tip the Mediterranean balance continued to be a concern. Barring these vessels was something Churchill remained deeply concerned about. When Admiral Sir Dudley North, whose 'flag' commanded at Gibraltar, allowed six Vichy ships to pass through the Strait unmolested in September 1940 he was immediately dismissed for lack of bellicosity. Although British and French warships never fought at close quarters over the next two years, there were frequent skirmishes. Because a deep gulf fell between Britain and Vichy, Churchill had to find a potential French leader seemingly friendly to Britain and settled on General Charles de Gaulle. Precisely because the British played a primary role in making de Gaulle he was more or less bound to advertise that he was anything but a British stooge. The contorted psychological sparring which followed was to be played out in a variety of venues but above all in the Mediterranean.

Admiral Godfroy's crippled squadron in Alexandria provided an extra touch to the many paradoxes of wartime Egypt: a country that was part of a British war effort, yet also self-consciously neutral and with large pockets of anti-British feeling (when HMS *Ark Royal* was sunk in November 1941 it was said King Farouk broke open a bottle of champagne).[50] In June 1940 Egypt did not declare war against Italy, repeating her stance of September 1939, and the government took a laxer attitude towards the internment of Italians than to the previous rounding up of Germans. Nor did Italian bombing of Alexandria, with its extensive British military installations, alter this. Egyptian opinion was full of inevitable contradictions under such circumstances. The inflow of British troops was for some while still welcomed as offering 'protection', yet at the same time it led to all the usual frictions and sense of subjugation.[51] Off-duty British soldiers sometimes played the 'tarbush-game' (how much headgear could be snatched from local pedestrians in twenty minutes).[52] Had High Commissioner Lampson been prepared to permit elections to take place, it is possible that a ministry with some claim to popularity might have provided a stable partner. But Lampson dared not take the risk, and so wartime relations had to be mediated through a series of weak ministries. Meanwhile the delicate equilibrium between tolerance of and active hostility towards the British themselves fluctuated with the war, with its endless rumours of triumphs and disasters out in the distant haze of the desert.

That war really began for Egypt in September 1940 when an Italian army crossed the Egyptian frontier. One of the most effective defences for the country was that there were hardly any roads on the Egyptian side of the border, and after advancing 50 miles the Italians stopped at Sidi Barrani. General Wavell's plan was to lure the enemy on with light screening forces, and then knock them hard. This is what happened in early December, when General Sir Richard O'Connor counter-attacked with only 31,000 men and destroyed five Italian divisions in two days, taking 25,000 prisoners of war. He swept into Cyrenaica and captured Tobruk, destined to be one of the emblematic strongpoints of the war; simultaneously the Royal Navy bombarded the Libyan ports. O'Connor wanted to drive on to Tripoli, and it was often suggested that had he been allowed to do so the war in North Africa would have been terminated once and for all. But he was instructed to halt, just when German air forces (Fliegerkorps X) moved to new bases in southern Italy, including Sicily, during late December. Churchill ominously noted 'this may be the beginning of evil developments in the Central Mediterranean'.[53] Two Panzer divisions under General Erwin Rommel arrived in North Africa during January 1941. Shortly named the Afrika Korps, Rommel's army was only nominally under Italian command. By April 1941 his counter-offensive retook Benghazi and Derna, though not the 'pocket' of Tobruk, and finally recrossed into Egypt itself.

The fighting was characterized by erratic surges back and forth thereafter of the Afrika Korps and various British armies, epitomized by the 7th Armoured Division (the 'Desert Rats'). Much of the fighting was utterly chaotic, tanks of both sides crazily intermingled, 'friendly fire' so endemic that the British Eighth Army often fought itself, and operations constantly stopping and starting again according to both sides' vulnerable supply routes. It was partly because Churchill never grasped these circumstances that he was so hard on commanders like Wavell when they failed to deliver the advances he wanted.[54] Field surgeries on both sides paid no attention whatsoever to nationality. It was perhaps the chaos that allowed human decency to prevail in ways that often got ground down in other theatres.

The reason behind Rommel's sudden intrusion into Mediterranean Africa was contingent and almost accidental. Mussolini always had doubts about Italy's ability to boot the British out of Egypt. As an easier proposition, he invaded Greece instead in late October 1940. The Greeks, however, not only resisted, but drove the Italians back over the Albanian frontier. They did so alone, although a British military mission arrived in November, and a small Royal Air Force contingent lent modest assistance. Hitler himself had little interest in Greece, and was generally 'bored and exasperated' by the Mediterranean.[55] He was a land animal, and had little regard for the view of some of his advisers that the Mediterranean was the pivot of the British Empire, and therefore the place to strike first. He despised Mussolini's puny Greek adventure, especially as it gave the British a window of opportunity to insert herself back into continental Europe. Yet equally Hitler could not let Italy collapse. Just as Admiral Cunningham returned on his flagship to Valletta in December, therefore, in Berlin plans were in train for exerting German power in the region for the first time. If Hitler chose to do this seriously nothing much could save 'British' Malta, Egypt or probably anywhere else. In the first instance Rommel had been dispatched not to destroy British power but to get the Italians off the hook. In addition, as brutal diplomatic pressure built up on Bulgaria and Yugoslavia, Operation Marita swiftly took shape to bring the Balkans under the Reich's sway.

The choice confronting the British from early February 1941 was either to concentrate on securing Egypt or to 'save' Greece. Some on the British side, Wavell included, thought that Egypt was far too important to risk diverting troops elsewhere. Many practical considerations pointed to this conclusion. But moral arguments and considerations of 'honour' told powerfully in the opposite direction. What was meant by morality and honour was admittedly unclear. British prestige in the Mediterranean hinged on protecting small countries from aggressors. If Greece – a country with a strong, if volatile, British connection – went the way of France, a tipping point might come. It was true, as the Chief of the Imperial General Staff, Sir John Dill, initially contended, that Turkey was more important strategically to Britain than Greece.[56] But if Greece was lost, Turkey (and therefore the Straits) would probably follow. Whether the British were able to find enough troops to intervene effectively in Greece was another matter. In the Foreign Office it was felt that 'it must, in the end, be a failure'.[57] Cunningham was against the operation purely on naval grounds.[58] But opposed to this was the view that it was important to make the attempt, or, as Churchill put it, to 'share their [the Greeks'] ordeal'.[59] Unless one did so, Britain's standing when it came in due course to fight its way back into the Balkans later on would be wretched.

Whether the Greeks wanted to be 'saved' by Britain was itself not entirely clear. They had been able to fend off the Italians. But the Germans were another matter, and if by letting a small British expedition into their territory the Germans were to come down all the harder, the risk was hardly worth taking. These issues – wrapped up with joint military dispositions to oppose a German invasion – were the subject of tense Anglo-Greek talks in Athens during February and March 1941. The change of Greek political leadership following General Metaxas' sudden death, and the extra weight this gave to the influence of the Anglophile King George II, affected the outcome. In the end a compromise was agreed, its tentativeness suggested by the fact that when the British expeditionary commander, General Maitland Wilson, arrived in the country he did so wearing civilian clothes.[60] What the British called Operation Lustre was thus 'born out of a welter of uncertainty', and afterwards held to have been doomed by it.[61]

Inevitably, there was more than one version of responsibility for what occurred. The British thought that the Greeks ensured defeat by failing to concentrate along the Aliakmon Line, as allegedly they had agreed. The Greeks, especially General Alexander Papagos at the head of the army, having seen how small the British forces were, wondered even more whether being saved was a good idea at all (the British expedition consisted of a New Zealand Division, the 6th and 7th Divisions of the 1st Australian Corps, and seven RAF squadrons). Consequently the Greeks kept many of their troops fighting the Italians on the Albanian front, where they could win, instead of diverting them against the Germans, where they could only lose. From a British perspective, sending a force of approximately 58,000 was enough to constitute a major commitment, but it had no real chance of success against the vastly superior numbers of enemy troops now heading south. What followed was a disaster. Under crushing German assault after 6 April, the flight of British civilians – conjured up in Olivia Manning's novel *Friends and Heroes* – was soon followed by that of the expeditionary force itself. British officers expected to make a stand in the Peloponnese, but the order to do so never came.[62] In effective control after the Greek premier Alexandros Koryzis committed suicide, General Papagos wanted the British out as soon as possible to avoid the devastation of the entire country.[63] The legend that villagers cheered the retreating British troops (including many Australians and New Zealanders) on their way, throwing flowers and calling out 'Come back soon' was often to be repeated in British accounts.[64]

Because the Wehrmacht already controlled the ports and possessed complete air mastery, fleeing British Commonwealth troops could only make it to the more isolated beaches, and hope that the Royal Navy could get them off. Not all were lucky. Those left at Kalamata, including Cypriot and Jewish Palestinian volunteer units, ended up as prisoners of war. Still, of the 58,000 who went in, by the end of April 1941 43,000 had escaped, courtesy of Admiral Cunningham's ships rushing from Alexandria. The ensuing voyages, pursued by German dive-bombers, were often the worst part of the whole experience. The Greek ordeal had been shared; but one unintended effect was that while Greek belief in British promises received a strong check, so did British estimates of the value of a Greek alliance.[65] Whereas, therefore, in the 1914–18 war the Anglo-Greek tie, after a wobbly start, had become closer as the war proceeded, after 1941 the opposite was to be true, even though the Government of Greece was given shelter in London and Cairo.

Since the British and the Germans shared the view that Crete – straddling the eastern Mediterranean passage – was more strategically valuable than the Greek mainland itself, that island was never likely to escape. Frustrated at any diversion from his looming attack on Russia, Hitler decided to conquer Crete quickly from the air with crack parachute formations. Churchill's decision to hold the island at all costs was to be controversial. It indicated a continuing inability to grasp the limits of sea power without control of the air.[66] Even if the parachutists of General Kurt Student had been repelled, as they nearly were, the British would probably not have been able to keep Crete supplied (unless they sacrificed Malta first). Convinced of their invincibility, Student's elite troops were shocked by the resistance they met, many pinioned on olive trees on landing or killed as they tried to wriggle out of their harnesses.[67] Only the error of General Cyril Freyburg, the New Zealander commanding the British garrison, in failing to secure Maleme airfield, allowed Hitler to flood in urgently needed reinforcements. After bitter fighting in which Greek troops fought well, and partisan resistance by the Cretans instantly erupted, a British retreat to the southern coast began. On three nights from 28 May 1941, 12,000 troops were lifted by the navy from the port of Sphakia. The novelist Evelyn Waugh, whose caustic appreciation of military experience had already been shaped by his participation in the failed expedition against Dakar in West Africa in September 1940, served in a commando platoon during the tail-end of the loss of Crete. He later used the experience as an allegory for the implosion of the British Empire itself, so that a sense of moral disintegration, a biographer writes, 'seeps like a stain through [Waugh's trilogy] *Officers and Gentlemen*'.[68]

Significantly, the reputation of the Royal Navy was to emerge unscathed from the battle for Crete, epitomized by the 1942 film *In Which We Serve*. In Cunningham's view, the original instruction from the Chiefs of Staff in London to accept any loss of ships to save Crete 'failed most lamentably to appreciate the realities of the situation'.[69] But when it came to getting the army off, Cunningham and his men paid the price. 'It takes the Navy three years to build a new ship,' he famously said when some thought that the operation had to be cut short. 'It will take three hundred years to build a new tradition. The evacuation will continue.'[70] It did so under such unremitting attack from the air that mutiny at one point seemed a real possibility.[71] When the operation ended, 18,000 troops had been got away in total, but at the cost in ships of three cruisers and six destroyers sunk and others (including two battleships) severely disabled. There were 1,283 navy fatalities and many wounded.

The Mediterranean Fleet was decimated and Cunningham was in tears when the surviving vessels limped back into Alexandria.[72] The Fleet's control now became pressed into the south-eastern corner of the Mediterranean and never fully recovered. All British-held territory, including Alexandria, was less safe thereafter.[73] We know now that after Hitler's invasion of Russia (Operation Barbarossa) began on 22 June 1941 the pressure was to ease for a time, and indeed that Crete convinced Hitler that airborne troops could never be risked again as an invading force. In retrospect, the loss of Crete is paradoxically seen to have saved Malta from a similar fate.[74] Yet at the time only the immediate defeat was obvious. This was the nadir of the wartime British Mediterranean.

Greek-Cypriots had naturally been emotionally caught up after

Greece's entry into the war in October 1940. Governor Battershill reported that 'the spirit of excitement reached the bounds of hysteria'.[75] Donations on the island to the Greek Red Cross outstripped those to its British equivalent. Feelings of attachment to Greece received an enormous boost, and long-standing legislation outlawing expressions of support for *Enosis* was simply ignored. The Axis occupation of Greece after May 1941 inevitably dampened some of these Greek-Cypriot spirits. Fear that Cyprus was next on Hitler's list concentrated everybody's mind. The dependants of British personnel were evacuated, including the Governor's own family. Defence works were speeded up, especially around the aerodromes. The temporary deployment of the 50th Northumbrian Infantry Division (approximately 18,000 troops) from July helped to give some assurance after the biggest Italian air raid on the island during the war (though the thirty bombs dropped were a mere pinprick by Maltese standards). Churchill impressed on Cypriots that the subsequent British conquest of Vichy Syria – despite the unexpected ferocity of its defence – meant that Cyprus was finally secure. The continuing reliance on 'deception', including the invention of non-existent brigades in signals traffic, was an indication, however, that should the enemy ever show up in force, Cyprus was likely to be left pretty much on its own.

The fragile hold that the British had on the island was matched by their uncertain grip on local politics. This uncertainty intensified when AKEL, a radical progressive party of Communist leanings, was set up in April 1941. The new party became warmly pro-war with the entry of its Soviet mentor and by early 1942 it was clear to the recently arrived Governor, Sir Charles Woolley, that AKEL was 'a new power in the land'.[76] As such it was sure to be a danger to the conservative Church. Any weakening of the latter was not necessarily a bad thing. But then AKEL was also likely to be no friend to the British regime either, as continuing strikes showed. The administration began to fear that it was losing the local initiative, and an acute nervousness set in that was to prove permanent.

The Greek Government argued in February 1941 that Britain should cede Cyprus to it immediately as a way of heightening enthusiasm for the fight against Hitler. Some in the British Foreign Office, no doubt recalling the 'offer' to Greece of 1915 and seeing possession of the island as more than ever a nuisance, favoured this. But among politicians in London there was a hardening of tone. Prime Minister Koryzis, when he raised the issue personally with Anthony Eden, only days before committing suicide, wrote that Eden 'replied with a smile that the final victory has yet to come and already we ask to annex lands'.[77] Here were the roots of a tendency on Eden's part to retreat into sarcasm whenever Cyprus cropped up. Henceforth the British Cabinet sought to stifle the question behind the contention that all territorial issues were to be settled after the war was over. Nevertheless, the Greek Government, homeless and dependent though it was, continued to maintain a claim to the island.[78] It became a means of validating its own Hellenic credentials as genuinely 'national'. For the British it meant, however, that the old Cypriot sore did not go away, though for the moment it could be largely ignored.

Malta's war proved far tougher than that of Cyprus. The island's luck ran out as soon as the Luftwaffe settled in Sicily at the end of 1940. During January 1941 Grand Harbour was subjected to an assault of a new and savage kind. The principal target was HMS *Illustrious*, which had limped badly damaged into French Creek, scarcely visible as massive plumes of smoke and water erupted around it. It provided a blistering and lifelong memory for those who witnessed the scene,[79] not least of the courage of the German pilots who dived so low that the anti-aircraft batteries on Upper Barracca heights had to point their guns downwards at the targets.[80] Amazingly, *Illustrious* survived and after emergency repairs made a night-run to Alexandria, since to remain in Grand Harbour meant certain destruction. Thereafter more bombs were dropped on Malta during its siege than on either London or Coventry at the height of the Blitz.[81] Much of Valletta was destroyed, and only the fact that so many of its buildings were of stone kept the outer structures standing, even when the fronts were blown in.

Some of the civilian population escaped to the villages, marking a major watershed in social life and attitudes towards a more urban and (in some quarters at least) less overtly religious society. Even if the enemy did not invade, there was the disturbing prospect of food shortages. By the early summer of 1941 the risk to convoys from Gibraltar was simply too great for them to be attempted. When one convoy tried to make it from Alexandria it was decimated, and for a while after that reliance had to be placed on what could be got in on submarines. It is possible to be critical of the British authorities in dealing with this situation, for concentrating at first on possible gas attacks that never came, not preparing adequate evacuation plans, being slow to build the public shelters into which ordinary Maltese might crowd for safety in the appalling conditions, and for not introducing rationing earlier.[82] But the colonial government was by its nature an under-resourced and even feeble entity. The surprising thing is that the administrative machine kept going at all.

The key to the siege was in large part Maltese co-operation. The civil tasks of government could not have gone on without indigenous leadership at virtually every level. Church support for the civil power was never in doubt. Given the previous significance of language and educational issues in the island's affairs, it is notable that the teaching profession responded to the Governor's calls for help. 'We're counting on you and your teachers to run things,' Dobbie told the Maltese Director of Education;[83] even Oxford and Cambridge Examinations continued during the war, and teachers played a multitude of roles outside school. In the years before 1939 there had been some resistance in the British garrison to the King's Own Malta Regiment taking full responsibility for gun batteries. Such reservations disappeared after January 1941, if not earlier. Work in the harbour, often under fearful conditions, would have come to a halt without ordinary Maltese grit and determination. Similarly it was Maltese as well as British personnel who desperately cleared the runways with little more than wheelbarrows and bare hands between enemy air raids, so that the Royal Air Force Gladiators – whose own armament was almost obsolete, but who retained their speed – could be urgently got up in the air.[84] There was some grumbling when conscription was introduced, but in other places, such as Cyprus, conscription was impossible even to contemplate. Considering the sheer density of enemy bombing, casualties were surprisingly limited. But everything is relative. In a small island, with close-knit familial structures, scores of dead a month (as at the peak in 1942) might well have been paralysing. Under all this pressure, the Maltese, inevitably motivated by a variety of factors, set aside differences among themselves as well as with the British; the deprivations of the latter were no less.

In the history of the war Malta came to be lauded as Britain's unsinkable aircraft carrier in the Mediterranean, crucially allowing deadly air attacks on enemy supply lines to their North African garrisons. A contrary argument has nevertheless persisted that its defence by Britain 'was so much wasted effort', since although the Axis never succeeded in taking Malta, the island was effectively neutralized.[85] Hitler was continually warned, above all by his naval commanders, that the island had to be definitively annihilated,[86] but he withheld the resources required. This was partly because he thought that the seizure of the island was the proper responsibility of the Italian navy. But even more important was his suspicion that behind such advice lay opposition to his commitment to conquering *Lebensraum* in east-central Europe.[87] The military historiography of 1939–40 is littered with might-have-beens, of which this Axis failure to deal a final blow to Malta is one. What we do know for certain is that although there were periods when the passage of British ships through the Mediterranean virtually ceased, as in the spring of 1941, invariably after a while movement started up again. Without Malta these recurrent revivals would not have been possible; and despite the desperateness of the island's situation, its offensive capacity was never entirely lost, though it necessarily hinged on aeroplanes and submarines rather than surface ships. The submarine force (Flotilla X) had a base dug deep into Manoel Island, and except for a brief interval it operated throughout the war. Between 1940 and 1943 just over one-third of Italian commercial shipping losses in the Mediterranean were victims of submarines, mostly coming out from Malta. Italian traffic through the Sicilian narrows, past Malta and on to Libyan ports, passed through what became known as 'the death route'. 'I have a name for my disease,' Mussolini once said of his nervous condition. 'It is called convoys.'[88]

In understanding the survival of Malta the nature of the naval equilibrium in the Mediterranean is vital. We have seen that the Mediterranean Fleet suffered grievous losses in Cretan waters in April 1941. The nadir of the British war at sea, however, came the following December, and ironically at the hands of not the Luftwaffe but rather the much-derided Italian navy. The latter's human torpedoes (one-man explosive motor boats) had previously made several attempts to penetrate British ports in the Mediterranean, including Gibraltar. They failed, but now they managed to infiltrate Alexandria's inner harbour and sank the two great battleships, *Queen Elizabeth* and *Valiant*. That Cunningham still kept his Commander-in-Chief's flag on board the former – resting on the harbour bottom, its decks were, nonetheless, above water – provides an appropriately ironic image to encapsulate the state of British naval power in the region.[89] Practically, not only was the Fleet deprived of any large-scale fire-power, but Malta was now left completely exposed.[90] Yet so long as the British held on to airfields in Cyrenaica, sufficient shore-based air cover existed for British ships to occasionally rush through to the island from the east past an Italian fleet preoccupied with protecting traffic to Libya. The British could therefore just about keep a grip in eastern Mediterranean waters, while the Italians could dominate the centre, but neither could exert an exclusive domination over the linking passages and so prevent the other getting through to their respective destinations. The crucial point is that the Britain Mediterranean Fleet may have lost its traditional, if never unqualified, mastery, but this by no means meant that control slipped into the hands of anybody else. In the end this was to be sufficient for victory in Mediterranean waters.

After late 1941, however, it seemed that this fragile equilibrium might be ended in favour of the Axis. The Luftwaffe was reinforced in Sicily, the British Fleet had been gravely reduced and Rommel now began a new offensive towards the Egyptian frontier. One sign that the British position might be slipping was the panicky action that was taken against King Farouk in Cairo in February 1942. Against the advice of senior military commanders, Lampson insisted that the King appoint an unambiguously co-operative Prime Minister.[91] When he refused, the High Commissioner surrounded the Abdin Palace with tanks, stormed into the King's apartment and told him to change his premier or sign a document of abdication. According to legend, Farouk considered using the gun kept in the drawer of his desk, but decided against. Lampson had his way over the minister, but at the cost of fatally damaging that delicate triangle of negotiation between the monarchy, the political parties and the British presence that had broadly held together since the early 1930s. A social boycott of the embassy by notables was immediately noticeable, and one of the features of Egyptian developments for the rest of the war was a more tangible anti-Britishness on the part of the educated classes.[92]

Meanwhile, although Rommel paused for some months to gather his strength, he renewed his advance after the Battle of Gazala in May 1942, while the resistance of Tobruk to his rear was finally overwhelmed a few weeks later. This was arguably Churchill's grimmest moment during the war (worse than the loss of Singapore).[93] By this stage it was nervously joked that Rommel had already booked a suite of rooms in Shepheard's Hotel in Cairo.[94] The embassy began burning files, the sure sign of a regime on the brink.[95] With the enemy advance-guard only 160 miles away, the Fleet at last began to leave Alexandria – a measure of disintegration the Germans had long looked for. British personnel drifted off to the security of Suez and Port Tewfik, leaving the Cecil Hotel on the Alexandrian seafront, usually packed for early evening drinks, eerily empty.[96] At no point since 1882 had the British hold on Mediterranean Egypt been so at risk.

These months, too, were Malta's worst nightmare, as the German air presence in Sicily was beefed up, and the mainland of Cyrenaica opposite ceased to be in British possession. At this point Malta's political detainees were transferred to Uganda. There is evidence that Governor Dobbie acted under pressure from the old anti-*italianità* faction who 'simply did not want these people around any more'[97] – just in case they might soon be able to make a grab at power. Although this action met with public acceptance, the effects (as with Lampson's harassment of Farouk) were to prove harmful. The death of one of the two Nationalists on the Council of Government, Sir Ugo Mifsud, while giving a passionate speech against the deportations still stirred feelings decades later.[98] But the nervousness of the authorities was understandable. From late March 1942 there were five straight weeks of constant bombardment of Malta; government offices moved out of Valletta altogether; supplies failed to get through, and when a vessel from Gibraltar finally sneaked into Grand Harbour, most of the goods were destroyed before they could even be could be got off the quayside. Even in the Governor's Palace the diet was down to dried bread and raisins.[99] To keep up spirits, King George VI awarded the George

Cross to the island collectively on 24 April. The unusual honour was announced in Valletta's shattered Palace Square, and the medal afterwards paraded from village to village.

Nobody's spirits were flagging more than those of Governor Dobbie, who knew that no medal could atone for what Malta was suffering unless relief came very soon. On 7 May he finally resigned without any prior announcement and immediately left with his family, a small group of officials seeing him off at the airfield. Though this episode is shrouded in obscurity, the Governor had been under immense stress, and seems to have begun to entertain the notion that surrendering the island might indeed be the most sensible thing for all concerned.[100] As other leading British figures in the Mediterranean discovered, too much caution, let alone the contemplation of surrender, was enough for Churchill to deliver the *coup de grâce*. Wavell himself had been dismissed as Commander-in-Chief Middle East during December 1941 for his assumed passivity, and replaced by General Claude Auchinleck. But at least Wavell, as Churchill scathingly decreed, was sent to 'sit on a pagoda tree' as Viceroy of India. Dobbie disappeared into the obscurity of rural retirement in England.

Dobbie's successor, General Sir John Gort, the commander who had overseen Dunkirk, was sworn in in a dilapidated shed overlooking Grand Harbour as Dobbie's plane disappeared over the horizon. Gort had just come from governing Gibraltar, where he had been busy deepening the cavernous defences in the Rock and extending the airfield; these works would soon prove very important. He arrived in Malta just when British commitment to it was being reasserted in one vital respect. The Chiefs of Staff decided to send scarce Spitfire fighters to the island. The first batch had already been 'flicked off' the decks of a United States supercarrier (USS *Wasp*) in early April. This co-operative gesture was the first sign of a nascent American engagement in the Mediterranean after the United States had entered the war the previous December following Japan's attack on Pearl Harbor. The fact, however, that these invaluable Spitfires were blown to bits by the Luftwaffe before they could even be got off the airfield in Malta was a bad blow to Dobbie's reputation. After Gort's appointment, it was ensured that future consignments of Spitfires were airborne within fifteen minutes of arrival, and not left as sitting ducks on the runway.

Gradually through the summer of 1942 the potency of these Malta-based fighters was augmented. But this did not alleviate the food situation. By high summer starvation loomed again. Gort himself was soon said to be depressed, and feeling 'shoved away in a corner out of the real war'.[101]

It was to prevent Gort coming to the same conclusion as his predecessor that the Chief of the Imperial General Staff, General Alan Brooke, came to Malta and told the Governor confidentially that a 'big move' was in the offing to clear North Africa by the end of 1942. Gort scarcely needed telling that such an offensive must involve the Americans. A necessary precursor, however, was Operation Pedestal. This was the most heavily escorted Allied convoy of the war, and its goal was to ensure the survival of Malta.[102] Planning for it had begun in July, and the ships were assembled in Glasgow, Liverpool and Bristol. But Malta's most urgent need, apart from food, was fuel oil. The British Fleet no longer had any tankers left of sufficient speed or size, and to fill this gap Roosevelt offered an old Texaco oil company vessel, the *Ohio*. The convoy, with two components designated Force Z and Force X and fourteen merchantmen including the *Ohio* with its largely British crew, set out from the Clyde on 2 August. The First Lord of the Admiralty sent a personal message: 'Malta looks to us for help. We shall not fail them.'[103]

Overnight on 9/10 August the convoy passed through the Strait of Gibraltar, the destroyers taking in some last fuel in the port (afterwards refuelling had to be accomplished under hazardous conditions at sea, since none was to be had at Malta). Although it was hoped to evade enemy detection, the Axis naval command in Rome was fully aware of the movements of Pedestal. The first attack on the early afternoon of 11 August was devastating. The aircraft carrier HMS *Eagle* was sunk by a U-boat. Most of the crew were saved, but its Sea Hurricanes were lost, severely depleting the convoy's fighter protection. The dangers increased as Pedestal moved eastwards towards enemy bases in Sicily and Sardinia. An almost continuous fight developed between British naval guns and the twisting and turning Italian and German aircraft.[104] As intended, Force Z, including the two remaining aircraft carriers, duly turned back to Gibraltar. The convoy, with its reduced warship escort, and beyond the range of fighter protection, continued at the greatest risk. On 12 August the *Empire Hope* was bombed and sunk, and the following day four other merchant vessels, the largest such loss ever suffered in the Mediterranean from a single attack.[105] 'I am left', one of the senior naval commanders recalled, 'with one main impression. Those merchantmen . . . going steadily on and on, surrounded by "near misses".'[106] Amid mounting chaos, the convoy kept its formation and steamed ahead in the right direction.

The German Stuka bombers, however, were now concentrating on the *Ohio*. It was eventually hit, its boilers ruptured, and the tanker virtually left dead in the water. As it limped on, its list became increasingly pronounced. At last on 14 August the first of the convoy, the *Brisbane Star*, entered Grand Harbour and discharged its cargo. The *Ohio*, its decks awash, was surrounded by what remained of the escort, and nursed with the help of tugs into the great anchorage early on the morning of 15 August under continuing attack. The battlements, with a naval band playing 'Rule, Britannia', were crowded with people who knew that their future hinged on these ships getting through. The relief at their safe, if battered, arrival was intense. When the oil of the *Ohio* was pumped out, her hull finally settled on the bottom.

To the Maltese this was the 'Miracle of Santa Maria', whose feast day it was on 15 August, and the scene also became etched into British memory of the war. The 1953 film *Malta Story* re-created Operation Pedestal and included contemporary film of the *Ohio*. In some ways the outcome of the operation was tactically mixed, given the loss of nine merchantmen, one aircraft carrier, two cruisers and a destroyer. These ships were precious. But Pedestal was a strategic success because it saved Malta. Another convoy arrived in November, this time from Alexandria, testifying that the Mediterranean passage was unsealed at both ends. Although fear of invasion continued into 1943, and some effects, like the prevalence of scabies, took months to ease,[107] the siege of the island was effectively over, especially after Germany lost its airbases in southern Italy. Life on Malta slowly returned to at least a semblance of normality. Band clubs reopened, religious processions around village squares were renewed, and some of the old Maltese preoccupations, such as highly partisan politics, could come back into the reckoning.[108]

The turnaround in the military situation in North Africa had clinched Malta's salvation. With Tobruk no longer an irritant, Rommel had pressed on towards Egypt, but when only a mere 60 miles west of Alexandria supply problems and General Auchinleck's decision to concentrate his defences pulled the Germans and Italians up short. That did not save Auchinleck's job. In August he was sacked by Churchill as Commander-in-Chief Middle East and replaced by General Harold Alexander, with General Bernard Montgomery commanding the Eighth Army. Rommel tried to break through the British lines at Alam Halfa in September, but was thrown back. This was the decisive moment in the western desert. Meanwhile the forces under Montgomery were heavily reinforced with tanks and men, and after 23 October these launched an offensive from the village of El Alamein. By early November 1942 Rommel had been thrust back deep into Libya. Montgomery took 30,000 prisoners. British and imperial casualties were 13,560. The Afrika Korps was never to cross the Egyptian frontier again.

Churchill's eagerness to accomplish victory against Rommel in the east arose in part from the fact that the Americans were about to enter the scene from the west. During late summer large Anglo-American forces had been built up in Gibraltar under General Dwight D. Eisenhower as Commander-in-Chief, Allied Expeditionary Force. Accepting an American in this position was the price Churchill paid for persuading President Roosevelt to commit troops on the ground in the Mediterranean. It was not clear to the Germans that this was their destination. One other possibility from Gibraltar was a strike into Spain itself, and one anxiety was that Franco might try to pre-empt any such threat by launching an attack on the Rock while it was so congested with men and equipment. Having Allied headquarters dug deep into the interior of the Rock itself gave Eisenhower's staff some protection against a sudden attack. Working and living conditions were hardly ideal, though the Supreme Commander himself lodged more comfortably in the Governor's residence of The Convent on Main Street.

The aim of Operation Torch was to clear North Africa completely of Axis armies, something Roosevelt and the United States Chiefs of Staff reluctantly accepted as a necessary prelude to an invasion of

Europe and the continental defeat of Hitler. It may be the case that the sheer weight of Torch coming down from the west would have sucked Rommel's Panzer divisions out of Egypt sooner or later. Strategic factors, however, never operate in a vacuum, which is why conclusions drawn from them are usually so problematical. The overriding necessity was to bring about Rommel's military destruction. But a subsidiary effect was that his defeat would ensure the safety of Britain's own position in Egypt, and to both these ends it was important that Montgomery's army should enjoy a victory of its own, even if the pursuit of Rommel was bound to be just as laborious as it would have been under the more cautious approach displayed by Wavell and Auchinleck in earlier phases of the war in the western desert.

The Torch landings in North Africa – involving 65,000 troops – unfolded on 8 November 1942. They did so at three locations: Casablanca, Oran, and Algiers, where the same beach was used as in the French invasion of 1830. This pattern represented the sort of muddled Anglo-American compromise that was to become such a feature in the period ahead. The British wanted the invasion's centre of gravity to be as far east as possible. By making a daring strike right into the Mediterranean, the British hoped to ensure a continued focus on the theatre.[109] By contrast, the American command was keen to ensure that their own troops were not thrown too quickly into combat situations for which they were not yet fully prepared. Various contacts had been made to ensure that the French forces in Morocco and Algeria deserted Vichy. The lasting French resentment of the British over Mers-el-Kebir was one reason why the Americans were given the lead in the first place, and also why de Gaulle and his anti-Vichy elements were rigidly excluded from the operation by Roosevelt – a decision from which the Gaullist–American relationship never really recovered. Nothing worked at all smoothly. To the strongly Vichy French community in North Africa, any British presence was enough to tar the Americans. French troops fought bitterly, and nowhere more so than against the Americans wading ashore at Casablanca. In all, 1,400 American and 700 French soldiers were killed. As always, the fate of the French fleet was the prime British concern. The Vichy regime had always said it would never let French warships be taken over by Hitler and Mussolini. Nor did they; as Germany responded to the North African landings by taking over Vichy administration in southern France, the French marine proceeded to scuttle its main fleet in Toulon harbour. The final liquidation of this force was a significant step towards confirming the revival of British superiority in Mediterranean waters.

Eisenhower set up his new headquarters at the palm-fringed, somewhat peeling, Hôtel Saint-George overlooking Algiers, a welcome change to the dankness inside the Rock. The key operational issue was to integrate thousands of British and American staff. Meanwhile the local French settler population were generally pushed aside and humiliated by the sudden intrusion of such a vast Anglo-Saxon presence. The sullenness of the *colons* was scarcely surprising. The civilian authorities in Algiers, however, had little choice but to co-operate with the invaders. But equally, the Allied commanders could not afford to become responsible for governing the place themselves since they had a war to fight. A deal was therefore struck between the Vichy representative, Admiral François Darlan, and Eisenhower's deputy, General Mark Clark, that undoubtedly saved lives by terminating resistance, and which was to survive Darlan's assassination on 24 December 1942 by a French monarchist (Darlan was succeeded by General Henri Giraud). This understanding crucially shaped the basis of the relationship between the Anglo-Americans and local French authorities, leaving the British to coax along the excluded and morose de Gaulle as best they could. Although over time de Gaulle was gradually to overtake the ineffectual Giraud in gaining French loyalties in the Mediterranean, the Darlan–Clark agreement was the founding source for de Gaulle's attitude towards Britain and the United States. Nor was it only Gaullists who did not like the smell. It was regarded by increasingly 'liberal' opinion in Britain as well as in the United States as a tawdry caving-in to all that was worst in the pre-war colonial order. This was just the start of an unhappy mixing up of an Allied war effort and the political realities of Mediterranean societies.

Confronted with Torch, Hitler might have decided to abandon North Africa altogether, but far from it. Large new forces were airlifted into Tunis with remarkable efficiency, while the Italians seized Corsica. Hitler, as we have seen, had never been prepared to commit the resources to acquire Mediterranean primacy himself. But he was determined to commit enough now to keep the Allies bogged down there for as long as possible. The key objective was to prevent a meeting of the combined Allied forces advancing from Algeria and the British Eighth Army painfully grinding its way across Libya. The early months of 1943 witnessed muddled and bitter fighting, most notably at the Kasserine Pass, in which the German forces under General Giovanni Messe (Rommel had himself left for good during March) succeeded in holding their ground, and even in pushing forward. Because of the severity of the fighting, the relatively inexperienced Americans inevitably made slow progress. Churchill was able to inform King George VI's Private Secretary that in practice control of the campaign was falling into the hands of British generals on the ground and Admiral Cunningham at sea.[110] The garrotte that the Royal Navy slowly but effectively applied to Axis shipping along the North African coast made the German-Italian position untenable.

In January 1943 Churchill dispatched Harold Macmillan, a rising young Tory politician, to be Minister Resident attached to Allied Forces Headquarters (AFHQ) in the Mediterranean. He had a roving commission to ensure that British interests did not get lost in the higher Allied machinery in the region. For some time much of his energy was taken up with negotiating a delicate compromise between de Gaulle, Giraud and Eisenhower. Macmillan understood early on that the British could best secure their essential interests by playing Greeks to the Americans' Romans. 'We must run AFHQ', a junior British official later recalled Macmillan musing, 'as the Greek slaves ran the operations of the Emperor Claudius.'[111] Macmillan's grasp of how to play off the strengths and weaknesses of others, his very obliqueness as a personality, and his decision to stick resolutely to civilian appearances and not compete with the soldiers – a game he could not win – suited the circumstances.[112] Macmillan's chief aide, John Wyndham, noted how he eventually became 'Britain's Viceroy in the Mediterranean by stealth'.[113] The stealth was a critical component in line with the long-standing truth that the British presence in the region was at its most effective when it was subtle and least imposing.

Macmillan arrived in North Africa just when the decisive elements in Anglo-American strategy were laid out at the Casablanca Conference (14–24 January 1943), presided over by Roosevelt and Churchill.[114]

The essential point was that the British succeeded in putting off for the rest of the coming year any strike into France once North Africa was cleared of the enemy, and instead substituted for it a lateral movement into Sicily. Beyond that no further operations in the Mediterranean were specified. Churchill had had his eye fixed on Sicily for some time; now the addition of American resources brought it within the realm of possibility. The leverage provided by Britain still having more troops on the ground than the United States allowed Churchill to get his way. One result, however, was that American suspicions grew that the British were trying to avoid confronting Hitler in Europe proper, and were bent on exploiting American help to secure their distinctive Mediterranean interests. Henry Stimson, Secretary of State for War, echoed a common view in Washington when stating that the British 'were straining every nerve to lay a foundation throughout the Mediterranean area for their own empire after the war is over'. This was exaggerated but it was undoubtedly clear to Churchill that, whoever came out on top in the main European struggle, it was not going to be Britain. At best, the British could reap gains at the margins, and that meant overwhelmingly in the Mediterranean. This was therefore where Churchill wanted the war to be fought, always deeply conscious of the historical associations involved. The consequent tensions within the Anglo-American relationship were to become acute.

Meanwhile the Axis forces under General Messe were pressed into a pocket around Tunis. General Alexander launched a full-scale offensive (Vulcan) on 22 April 1943, and on 7 May British troops reached that city as German officers enjoyed their final cognacs on hotel terraces.[115] The closeness of Cunningham's naval blockade ensured there were no evacuations. After the formal surrender on 13 May, 230,000 prisoners of war were taken. This climax constituted the most unqualified success that British land forces enjoyed during the war. On 12 June 1943 King George VI arrived in Algiers to cap the triumph, shortly proceeding to Tripoli. This was his first trip outside Britain since December 1940. Like many in Britain, the King had never quite relished having let the United States into the Mediterranean, and he querulously made it clear in private that in going there he had 'come to see his own armies, not the American'.[116] But neither Algiers nor Tripoli was a 'British' city, or was ever likely to become so. There was one place in particular that he was determined to visit: Malta. It was undoubtedly risky to go there. He could have been smuggled in and out by air, but Cunningham was persuaded at the last minute that the monarch should go in the most visible and symbolic manner. That was by sea. On 22 June George VI – standing in white naval uniform on a specially built platform – entered Grand Harbour aboard HMS *Aurora*, accompanied by four destroyers, a fighter escort above, and several minesweepers. The battlements were crowded. Cunningham said it was the greatest spectacle he ever saw.[117] On the island the King awarded General Gort a field-marshal's baton, and was then driven from town to town before leaving next day. The Mediterranean, the British were now able to claim, 'had been cleared for our King'.[118] Beyond such British hubris, convoys from this point onwards were indeed able to pass right through the Mediterranean from Gibraltar to Alexandria. One consequence was that the warships stationed at Gibraltar (Force H) began to drift back to Portsmouth. 'By the summer of 1944,' Simon Ball writes, 'well over 800 convoys, comprising 12,000 ships, were to pass through the Mediterranean.'[119]

North African ports were now being made assembly-points for the invasion of Sicily (Operation Husky). American doubts about the value of this enterprise continued almost to the last minute.[120] The largely unopposed landings – the second biggest of the war after Normandy – took place on 10 July 1943, headed by Montgomery's Eighth Army and General Patton's US Seventh Army. But the ensuing operation did not go according to plan. One reason was the patchy co-ordination, even outright rivalry, between Montgomery and Patton epitomized by a desire of each man to beat the other to Messina.[121] Besides personalities there was something more fundamental: a semi-veiled divergence of interest that in the later phases of the war in the Mediterranean created the impression of separate British and American formations operating with very different agendas.[122] When the German Commander-in-Chief, General Albert Kesselring, after presiding over effective resistance, finally ordered a complete evacuation from Sicily on 11–12 August, it was meticulously planned and executed. Whereas Cunningham as Supreme Allied Naval Commander had been able to ensure that there were no enemy evacuations from North Africa, here the attempt was half-hearted. For this Cunningham has been criticized, but the two cases were different. In North African waters the Royal Navy could operate at will along the coast, whereas in getting his troops across the Strait of Messina Kesselring could call on the support of the shore-based Luftwaffe. Cunningham knew painfully from Cretan experience what that could mean, and he was not going to sacrifice the Mediterranean Fleet (now gradually being resuscitated) twice. Around 60,000 Axis troops were therefore evacuated by Kesselring, many of them on the scheduled Messina–Naples ferry service.[123] An Allied physical victory, and a German moral victory, has been a judicious summary of the outcome in Sicily.[124]

Sicily's significance at this stage of the Mediterranean war was far from just military. It marked the spot of Allied re-entry into Europe proper. That the island was also a location with long-standing British connections was not without significance. Some American observers suggested that Britain aimed to take the island under its wing again.[125] This was scarcely the case, but General Harold Alexander (in operational command of Allied armies) and Macmillan together managed to insist that Lord Rennell was nominated Chief Civil Affairs Officer under the first Allied Military Government of Occupied Territory (AMGOT). Here too, however, the precedent proved less than glowing, since Rennell admitted, 'we are in the process of making a first class mess of the first European country we have partially occupied.'[126] There was also a high level of looting and drunkenness among the troops.[127] This situation proved deeply embarrassing, and the postwar travails of Sicilian governance had something to do with these circumstances. Still, in the island the Allies were generally well received, helped by lots of chocolate and tobacco to hand out, and the experience of occupation there was not for the most part characterized by the lamentable conditions that followed on much of the peninsula.

While Operation Husky had been in gestation, surrender terms for Italy had been debated in London and Washington. Suggestively, the British – and especially Eden, his Italophobia coming to the fore – stuck rigidly on 'long' (that is, harsh) armistice terms. A punished and weak Italy after the war could prove as big a plus for Britain's Mediterranean position as a weak Spain had always been. Events moved very rapidly indeed after the fall of Sicily, since Mussolini was displaced by a coup among his own intimates on 25 July, and Italy surrendered on 8 September 1943. As with France in 1940, so with Italy the immediate contingency for Britain was the fate of the Italian main fleet. If the Italian navy passed into German hands, the whole Mediterranean balance could be reversed once again. By the same token, these warships were the prime bargaining chip in the hands of Italian negotiators, and they needed to make the most of what they had.[128]

On 8 September Cunningham broadcast the instruction that the Italian warships should go to Malta. They did so only with intense reluctance. The Italian navy had been ideologically the least Fascist of all national institutions. It did not therefore simply collapse with the regime. The bulk of the fleet went first to Sardinia, and then diverted to the Algerian coast, before finally heading for Malta, where it arrived on the evening of 10 September and put itself under British control. The courtesies of the occasion were scrupulously observed (the Greek navy was accorded a supporting place in the receiving line). Though the Italian navy insisted then and later that they were not surrendering as such, seeing themselves as joining the Allies rather than having collapsed into defeat, Cunningham did nothing to hide the realities as he saw them. 'Be pleased to inform Their Lordships', he signalled to the Admiralty with a Nelsonian flourish, 'that the Italian battle fleet now lies at anchor beneath the guns of the fortress of Malta.'[129] This was the climax of the British war at sea in the Mediterranean.

'In September 1943 Italy withdrew from the war,' one writer summarizes the ensuing paradox, 'but the war came to Italy.'[130] Anglo-American forces waded ashore at Reggio di Calabria and Salerno on Italy's heel the day after the formal surrender. In Sicily the landings had been at first unopposed, and it was hoped that the same would happen here with the Germans getting out of Italy as fast as they could. But the Germans decided to fight. The Allies were almost forced back into the sea by German resistance, and they only managed to establish a bridgehead with the utmost difficulty.[131] It had been hoped that Rome would be taken by October 1943, but it was a measure of the grinding, attritional nature of the campaign that that did not happen until 4 June 1944. The strategic theory of the Italian campaign was that it tied down German armies that might otherwise have been available in northern Europe. In reality this theory worked just as well in the opposite sense, in that much needed Allied troops were themselves diverted from the main front against Hitler. The resulting tensions were only mitigated by reluctant British acquiescence in the American insistence that Allied troop levels in the peninsula be subordinated to operations in Normandy. In the end German soldiers were still on Italian soil even when the war in Europe was ending in May 1945.

Whatever personal, institutional or national inclinations were at work in all of this, the larger point was that from the Salerno landings in September 1943 any Allied strategy in the Mediterranean progressively lost coherence. The Mediterranean was never a single strategic region, even if there had to be a pretence that it was, and the seeming abundance of options made decisions difficult. The real dynamic at work was mostly political. This was especially true for Churchill. After the Italian surrender, the weight of the alliance in the Mediterranean shifted to the western part of the basin, as the Americans looked to get back into France. This was necessarily reflected in command arrangements, so the Royal Navy's Levant Fleet in eastern waters became secondary to the squadrons in the western and central Mediterranean.[132] Cunningham kept his Fleet headquarters in Algiers for the same reason. Churchill, however, was to spend much of the rest of the war seeking to counter this bias. After Sicily, his mind was to drift constantly eastwards, and the long bitter slog up the Apennines intensified, not eroded, this preference on his part. For Churchill, as Roosevelt suspected, Italy was significant essentially as a jumping-off point back into the Balkans, not as a prelude to leaping directly over the Alps.[133] Churchill's most senior military adviser, General Brooke, later remarked that 'There lay . . . at the back of his mind the desire to form a purely British theatre . . . where the laurels would be all his own'.[134]

Churchill's thoughts were illustrated by the venture into the Italian-ruled Dodecanese immediately after the Italian surrender.[135] On the day of signature a single British officer had parachuted into Rhodes to persuade the Italian garrison to round up the German troops in that island. But instead it was the Germans who took control, backed by complete local mastery in the air. Churchill's determination, however, was intense, not least because he saw the Dodecanese as potentially instrumental in triggering Turkish entry into the war. If that could be brought about, opportunities for a regional reconfiguration of a sort exploited by Lloyd George in 1917–18 might beckon. That Churchill should look back to such parallels was natural. 'It is clear that the key to the strategic situation in the Mediterranean', he stated, 'is expressed in two words: Storm Rhodes.'[136] Some of his closest military advisers, and especially the Americans, thought this was going off at a complete tangent, but they invariably lacked Churchill's historical consciousness.[137] A British infantry brigade was duly dispatched to the area, and a variety of special forces, having been gathered together on the island of Samos, were transported among the islands in caiques operated by the Levant Schooner Flotilla. By early October nearly 30,000 British troops had been diverted to the eastern Aegean.

But the intervention in the Dodecanese proved disastrous. German reinforcements overwhelmed their opponents, and the few fighters scrambled from the nearest British airbase at Nicosia were helpless against the much larger Luftwaffe. It was a bit like Crete all over again. Churchill had been especially adamant on seizing the island of Leros, if only because it became plain even to him that Rhodes was now unattainable.[138] The forces rushed to that small island, however, soon had to surrender ignominiously. 'Leros lost last night,' the head of the Foreign Office in London moaned on 17 November 1943. 'First German success for a year.'[139] In the event, the British were only able to start 'nibbling away' at the Dodecanese, taking one island after another, from the summer of 1944 when the Germans simply started leaving, and Rhodes was liberated (but not 'stormed') by British and Indian troops in May 1945. The 4,800 British army fatalities and six Royal Navy destroyers lost in the Dodecanese during late 1943 had been expended to no profit. Turkey did finally enter the war in February 1945, but by then her belligerence did not trigger the sort of regional upheavals and associated opportunities which had started to form in Churchill's always vivid imagination.

Turkey's rigid insistence – consistent with the Kemalist legacy – on playing its own game and nobody else's reduced the range of possibilities by which Britain might have ended the war on a high, not only on water in the eastern Mediterranean, but also on land. In this dilemma lay the causes of Churchill's (and indeed Eden's) near obsession with getting back into Greece. The country had fallen into a kind of limbo – under mixed German, Italian and Bulgarian occupation – following the disastrous campaign of 1941.[140] Internal but very patchy resistance to the Axis had got under way spontaneously by early 1942 without significant British instigation. The few British agents on the ground were mainly concerned with arranging the escape of Commonwealth soldiers still on the run from the earlier disastrous campaign. When the Special Operations Executive, first formed after Dunkirk to 'set Europe ablaze' by encouraging local insurrection, finally turned to southern Europe it looked first to Yugoslavia rather than Greece. Still, the successful blowing-up of the Gorgopotamos railway viaduct in November 1942 by British parachutists and Greek guerrillas showed for the first time in occupied Europe that a resistance movement, with the support of Allied officers, could carry out tactical operations in co-ordination with wider strategic plans.[141] Even more importantly, it meant that the Greek Communists, in the form of ELAS (National Popular Liberation Army), did not thereafter have a complete monopoly of the resistance movement in Greece. Nevertheless, it was true that resistance and ELAS were almost synonymous in Greece, though this, and the danger that went with it, was something that the British themselves only grasped from early 1943.

After the Italian armistice in September 1943 activation of resistance groups in the Balkans by parachuting in agents from Egypt was stepped up by the Allies. There was a vital difference here between the Yugoslav and Greek situations. In the former the Partisans, principally under Tito (Josip Broz), developed autonomously, and mostly kept British liaison officers at arm's length. The British finally swung behind Tito in his struggle for control over Yugoslavia's future, but in this case they merely recognized an outcome already in the making.[142] In Greece, British leadership, backed by arms supplies and gold coins, came much more to the fore. ELAS also craved approval and patronage from London. The assumption, so central in modern Greek history, that the British were bound in the end to remain the dominant power in the Mediterranean was still firmly entrenched. Whatever was true elsewhere,[143] 'In the name of the British' remained a curiously beguiling mantra in mountainous Greek villages.[144] This was testimony to the degree to which the resistance there was cut off from the outside world.

Through the rest of 1943 and into 1944 the authorities in London and Cairo were still more interested in fluctuations among Greek opinion outside Greece than what was happening inside that country, where the aim was simply 'a loose confederation of independent guerrillas whose operation they could control through British Liaison Officers'.[145] Maintaining leverage over the resistance was itself more important than military operations against the Axis presence as such, especially if that meant, as it did, creeping ELAS domination. Proof that things were running out of control came unexpectedly with the mutiny among the Royal Hellenic Forces in Egypt in April 1944. This disaffection was suppressed by British units and 'loyal' elements in the Greek navy. Some 8,000 Greeks were incarcerated in Egypt, Sudan, Libya and South Africa. The outbreak sprang from deeply republican feelings in Greek military circles and suspicion that when liberation came the monarchy would be reimposed on Greece by foreign bayonets. But to the British the mutinies generated panic that Communist influences from Greece itself were managing to subvert what was in any case an unstable and by no means wholly reliable ally.

This was where British aims in the Mediterranean and the balance of Greek feelings made an awkward fit. Among most Greeks, Communist or non-Communist, King George II was detested for his association with dictatorship in the 1930s, and in a lingering way for the very 'foreignness' of the Glücksberg dynasty. For this reason the Foreign Office in London also saw him as a liability. To Churchill and Eden, however, he seemed indispensable. There were personal factors at work here, including Churchill's innate royalism and his sense of obligation to George II for sharing British ordeals in 1941. But the real reasons were more hard-headed. Returning to Greece in some way or another now offered the only means by which Britain could retain an influence in the southern Balkans. For the British, the latter was not a region of choice but of necessity.[146] As had always been the case, Greece was an integral part of Britain's traditional sphere of influence along Europe's southern rim. In using Greece as a conduit back into the southern Balkans, however, Churchill and Eden needed some instrument on which they could rely with the utmost confidence. Given all that had happened, George II offered one of the few tools, and really the only tool, of this sort. From this came Churchill's fierce commitment to putting George II back on his throne.

Had the British, with American help, launched a large-scale invasion of the Balkans, they could still pretty much have dictated the terms of Greek 'liberation' with little regard to others. But there was no possibility of persuading the Americans to co-operate in such a venture. The quagmire in Italy was too dire, and anyway the Mediterranean was becoming peripheral to the struggle against Hitler. The watershed here was the invasion of southern France in August 1944 (Operation Dragoon, said by some cynics to be so named because Churchill had to be dragooned into it). The implications of this choice were profound. Any possibility that the Soviets could be stopped from overrunning most of the Balkans disappeared. The assumption that ELAS would meekly follow a British lead also weakened as it began to liquidate local rivals. By the late summer it had become vital that the British get back into Greece quickly, not to defeat the Germans, who by early September were already leaving, but to get a grip on ELAS. Under a fragile agreement in September 1944 at the Palace of Caserta in Italy (where Allied Forces Headquarters was now located) the various resistance groups accepted the authority of General Sir Ronald Scobie as British Commander in Greece. Just how much authority was ceded became a matter of dispute almost at once. On 17 October 1944 two reconnaissance units and a Special Boat Section landed at Patras and a parachute battalion was dropped at Megara. The swift concentration of this modest force to the south of the Corinth canal was because it was felt a warmer welcome would be likely there. A strong Royal Navy squadron was present in case things went wrong. Key members of the exiled Greek political leadership, anxious as to the adequacy of the British forces involved, had to be prodded into joining an uncertain enterprise.[147] Meanwhile King George II agreed to stay away so as not to stir up further discontent among the Greeks themselves.

There was one essential preliminary to this operation: a deal between Churchill and Stalin whereby the former traded away any say in the future of Romania and Bulgaria in return for primacy in Greece. This was laid down by the notorious 'percentages agreement' at the Moscow Conference (9 October 1944). As Churchill emphasized to Eden, having paid the price elsewhere in the Balkans, there was no point in Britain hesitating to use force to ensure British control over Athens.[148] That meant the subordination, if not liquidation, of ELAS. The ensuing 'days of December' (*Dekemvriana*) scarred Greek political history. ELAS, whose forces in the Athens–Piraeus area numbered around 10,500 and were markedly superior to their right-wing opponents, tried hard to avoid giving the British any excuse to crack down against them. Its aim was still to gain not complete power, since that was probably beyond its reach, but a prominent place in a coalition government.[149] An ELAS proclamation welcomed back to the Greek capital 'the brave children of Great Britain, our freedom-loving ally', though the British decision to move into the old German headquarters in the Hôtel Grand Bretagne aroused wry comment.[150] On 4 December a massive column of ELAS demonstrators descended on Constitution (*Syndagma*) Square and approached the police line. The police opened fire, killing sixteen people. It was not until three days later, however, that the ELAS leadership authorized attacks on British troops, who had already occupied key points in the centre of the city, including the Acropolis.[151] What followed was known as the Battle of Athens, in which the British used tanks, artillery and aircraft while Royal Navy warships gathered in the Bay of Salamis. Reinforcements from Italy were rushed to secure the centre of Athens and Piraeus, bringing the force at that point to two divisions, a brigade and some battalions. These events, apart from definitively turning right and left against each other in Greek politics, thereafter posed the central query surrounding Britain's position in Greece: how much manpower was she prepared to commit to sustain her influence in the country?

It was in this setting that on Christmas Eve 1944 Churchill undertook the most personally dramatic mission of his wartime premiership. He flew to strife-torn Athens and was driven in a tank through the streets to the British embassy, its outer wall already pockmarked by rifle-fire, where the Foreign Secretary and General Alexander, as Supreme Allied Commander Middle East, were holed up. It had become imperative to distance the British from any immediate restoration of the Crown since otherwise even Greek anti-Communists might line up with ELAS as the lesser evil. Churchill therefore presided over a conference during which the strongly anti-Communist Archbishop of Athens, Damaskinos, was appointed Regent, sidelining for now the explosive question of the monarchy. By early 1945 there were around

80,000 British troops in Greece, but full control did not at first extend much beyond the capital. In the fighting ELAS had lost around 2,000–3,000 killed (the numbers were inevitably unclear), the right-wing combatants 3,480 and the British 210 killed as well as 55 whose bodies were never found.[152] Having deflected what they saw as a certain ELAS takeover, and negotiated a shaky truce under the Varkiza Agreement of 12 February 1945, the British hoped now to encourage a stable, broad-based and moderate government, rather than one that descended into any embarrassing 'white terror'. The British search for moderation (as they understood it) in the Mediterranean, however, had never been entirely successful, and was not to be any more fortunate here.

Churchill's intervention in Greece in December 1944 was intensely controversial. In Britain it even overshadowed for a while debates about post-war social policy, and helped to trigger a process in which unity drained out of the wartime coalition at home, where feelings in Labour circles on Greece ran very high.[153] Although Greek issues did not bring Churchill down as the debacle in Asia Minor had destroyed Lloyd George politically in 1922, they played a part in undermining his authority before the general election of July 1945. Perhaps more importantly, what had been done in Greece met with intense criticism in the United States. The head of the US navy, Admiral Ernest King, ruled that no American ships or landing-craft should assist the British intervention in Greece in any way, while the leaking through an American newspaper of Churchill's instruction to General Scobie to 'treat Athens as if it was a conquered city in revolt' stoked an American public reaction against British 'colonialism'.[154] Harold Macmillan, before giving up his roving post as Britain's 'Viceroy' in the region, and concerned at what he saw as a dangerous tendency of British policy to stray outside Allied guidelines, had already put the question to the Prime Minister: 'Is it our desire to attract and keep American interest to the Mediterranean? Or is it our policy to keep it in respect of some parts and not in respect of other parts?'[155] Wrapped up in this were dilemmas that continued into the post-war period and were to lead to the political destruction of Anthony Eden's own premiership and the elevation of Macmillan himself.

As always, the fate of Greece held much significance for Cyprus.

After the Axis had secured Crete an invasion of Cyprus could not be ruled out as a next step, and at the height of Rommel's North African successes during mid-1942 the possibility of a military evacuation from the island was seriously considered. Plans included the destruction of airfields and harbour facilities to deny them to the enemy and Special Operations laid the groundwork for underground resistance. In stark contrast to Crete and mainland Greece, suggestively, this did not involve providing weapons for local groups, since in Cyprus there was no guarantee that they might not be used against the British themselves.[156] This was a powerful reflection of the tenuousness always felt by the colonial power. The security situation eased once Italy was knocked out of the war, and in any case it became clear that the Germans showed no sign of being interested in the island. It was also clear that the vast majority of Cypriots continued to support the British war effort both in civilian employment and in the fighting services (one future President of independent Cyprus, Glafkos Clerides, won the Distinguished Flying Cross serving with the RAF during bombing raids over Germany). When Churchill spent a day in Cyprus, on his way back from a visit to Turkey in January 1943, he declared outside Government House that 'after this war is over, the name of Cyprus will be included in the name of those who have deserved well . . .';[157] and it was in part as a political reward that municipal elections, on hold since 1931, were at long last allowed to go ahead.

As the island itself was no longer under threat, however, manoeuvring for position at the end of the war became the essence of Cypriot affairs. Such manoeuvring could not be separated from the future of Greece itself. From the British perspective, a profound paradox resulted. Some kind of unity among factions inside Greece was much to be desired. But if such unity came about, in Cyprus it was all too likely to find expression in a common Greek-Cypriot front against continuing British rule. Already the colonial government was worried about the military experience some Cypriots had recently acquired, and although the new Governor, Sir Charles Woolley, did not think that a clash would occur in the immediately foreseeable period, he did not feel able to rule it out.[158] Thefts from military armouries in Nicosia underlined anxiety that sooner or later the British would be faced with some kind of outbreak. There was always the hope that knowledge of material deprivation in Greece would persuade Cypriots that they were actually much better off under British oversight. But such practical logic rarely worked in Cyprus. Towards the end of the war the writer Laurie Lee was sent to the island to make a documentary highlighting the advantages flowing from British colonial status. In his memoir *We Made a Film in Cyprus*, Lee recalled a conversation with a village priest impervious to all the arguments put to him, but whose eyes glittered with tears at any mention of Greece.

As always, increasingly problematic though conditions were in Cyprus, they remained vastly worse in Mandatory Palestine. British suspicions that Zionist organizations were bent on building up a physical supremacy of their own had become sharper as the war proceeded. The decision to keep out Jewish refugees fleeing Europe in crowded and unseaworthy vessels, and their detention mostly in Cypriot camps, played a key role in tearing through the thin tissue binding the British authorities and 'moderate' Zionism. The sinking of the *Struma* in February 1942 in the Black Sea, after it had been held up by endless bureaucratic delays with the port authorities in the Bosporus, with many children among those drowned, marked a psychological dividing line. Still, so long as Rommel threw his shadow from North Africa, there remained a possibility that the British and the Jews might after all need each other in a crisis. Some members of Haganah were trained by the Special Operations Executive at its school in Haifa for undercover work in occupied Europe, and, as troops were increasingly scoured for service from every source, a Jewish Brigade was belatedly recruited in Palestine, serving in Libya, Italy and later the Netherlands. Furthermore, economic conditions in Palestine during the war were better than anywhere in the region. British military expenditure expanded the economy by over 10 per cent per annum. Nor did the territory suffer extensive damage by bombing, though both Haifa and Tel Aviv had periodic air raids.[159] Indeed one way, really the only way, out of the wider political impasse lay in a vision of development for all in Palestine once the war was over. This was the spirit – 'Let us hitch our wagon to a star', the start of a prosperity for everybody as individuals and communities – in which High Commissioner Harold MacMichael introduced a plan for post-war economic reconstruction in March 1943.

But harmonious sharing between communities was not what the brutal politics of the Mandate was all about. It was about the monopoly of power. To the Zionist leader David Ben-Gurion, now shunting the Anglophile Chaim Weizmann to one side, ideas of reconstruction were simply a ruse devised by 'English clerks with Jewish money, to benefit Arabs'.[160] Without the support of Jewish organizations, such ideas could never get off the ground. In any case, by the end of 1943 the spectre of a German presence in North Africa had been dispelled. The effect was to encourage Palestinian animosities to flow more freely down their accustomed channels. Rivals of Haganah, such as the Lehi and Stern paramilitary organizations, with an openly violent and anti-British agenda, stepped up their activities in 1944. At first they tended to target the British administration and police, as well as Arabs, rather than the army. Firearms and explosives began to leak from the Jewish Brigade to illegal militias.[161] So far as British policy was concerned, the old White Paper of 1939 – in theory still operational – offered some kind of framework, but it was increasingly irrelevant and deeply resented by Jews. The Cabinet itself was split between the fervent Zionism of Churchill and colleagues with different prejudices and priorities. Their only common 'policy' – barely meriting the term – over Palestine was to get to the end of the war and then see the lie of the political land, though the balance was clearly shifting once more towards partition as offering the only feasible exit. Meanwhile the administration was left to muddle on as best it could. The frustration was acute. MacMichael, shortly before being replaced by General Gort, told Ben-Gurion on one occasion that he did not know what anybody really wanted of him, not even his own bosses in London.[162]

On 6 November 1944, however, an event occurred raising the Palestinian stakes to a new height. Lord Moyne, the British Minister Resident in the Middle East and a close friend of Churchill, was assassinated as he got out of his car in front of his house in Cairo. His driver was also fatally shot. The echo of Sir Lee Stack's killing in 1924 could not be missed. The murderers were two Lehi operatives. Since it was most unlikely that they would get away – they were indeed captured close to the scene – this was really a suicide mission.[163] An important result was the sudden curtailment of Churchill's sympathy for Zionist aims.[164] The Prime Minister told Parliament on 17 November 1944: 'If our dream of Zionism should be dissolved in the smoke of the revolvers of assassins . . . many persons like myself will have to reconsider the position that we have maintained so firmly for [such] a long time.'[165] The aim of Lehi by such a desperate gambit was to drive a final wedge between the Mandatory regime and the mainstream Zionism represented by the Jewish Agency. The latter, responsible for so much of Jewish life in the territory, feared that even now an open break with the British could prove a trapdoor for Zionism, and sought to fend this off by declaring a 'hunting season' on the Jewish perpetrators of violence. The Agency had the intelligence the British lacked as to the whereabouts of terrorist cells in their own community. But this 'hunt' was not conducted with much intensity, nor did it last long. In truth, the elements of a sustainable Anglo-Zionist accommodation had drained away.

Some have argued that Moyne's murder had a fatal political effect in heading off a scenario that was otherwise in the making: that at the end of the war the British might cut themselves loose from Palestine quickly and cleanly through partition, using their own troops to establish successor states in a way that the Jews and at least some Arabs might have accepted.[166] The resulting Zionist polity would, this argument goes, have been smaller than the one that eventually emerged in 1948–9, but it would have been born in circumstances that endowed lasting legitimacy. It was, however, probably too late for such a relatively smooth trajectory into a post-Mandate future. Partition was bound to be a defeat for the British, and the latter were still some way from accepting this. Meanwhile the deadlock continued, only with more venom all round. As for the assassins of Moyne, they were put on trial in Cairo, where the accused allegedly met with sympathy among Egyptian opinion, if only because Moyne, like Stack in 1924, so clearly represented the British Empire.[167] After the accused had been found guilty and sentenced but had yet to be hanged, Churchill intervened to ensure that they went to the gallows with 'all proper despatch' on 22 March 1945 (the two men were eventually reburied with full military honours in the presence of Israeli ministers on Mount Herzl outside Jerusalem during 1975).[168]

If the British footing in Palestine was slipping once again as the war drew to a close, so it was in Egypt. Assassination was again a telltale sign. The Egyptian Prime Minister was shot dead emerging from Parliament, having at last declared formal belligerency against Germany in February 1945. For the first time in many years Egyptian politicians started to call for a complete British military evacuation after hostilities. Admittedly the growing Islamist movement, Ikwhan, seemed to adopt a softer approach for a while, but it made tactical sense for some Egyptian dissidents (as it did for Greek Communists, and even, briefly, for a dwindling band of Zionist moderates in Palestine) to avoid an outright confrontation with the British.[169] Peering dimly into Egypt's post-war future, Lampson (now raised to the peerage as Lord Killearn) reckoned that at some point there would have to be a return to pre-war conditions, with a reduction of British troops to levels prescribed under the 1936 treaty, and, crucially, a complete evacuation from the cities of Cairo and Alexandria to the Canal Zone. 'We shall be in a stronger position to resist Egyptian claims,' Killearn wrote, 'if on our side we are careful to execute strictly and punctually the terms of the Treaty which impose obligations on us.'[170] But getting back to pre-war normalcy in Egypt, as in other places, was to pose enormous difficulties.

Soon after the coming of peace a senior German naval officer who had served on the Axis naval co-ordination staff in Rome, Vice-Admiral Eberhard Weichold, was commissioned by the Ministry of Defence in London to write an overall appreciation of the war in the Mediterranean. Weichold's analysis merits attention. He pointed out that Italy's entry into the war had greatly expanded the possibilities of waging war against Britain. 'The geographical strategical position of Italy', he stated, 'provided an Axis war with jumping-off bases for an attack on vital outposts of the British Empire. It was therefore an ideal situation . . .' This did not mean that pressure should not have continued to be brought to bear against Britain at other maritime points. But Weichold maintained that German sea and air attacks on British shipping routes in the north should have been calibrated with a sustained offensive in the Mediterranean. Instead, Germany committed forces to the Mediterranean only when the defensive position of Italy was seriously at risk. Had it not committed this grave error,

(*top*) HMS *Agamemnon* steams into Malta's Grand Harbour, 1920.

(*bottom*) The King's Birthday Parade at District Commissioner's House, Nicosia, on 3 June 1930.

(*top*) The burnt-out car of Governor Sir Ronald Storrs outside the ruins of Government House, Nicosia, on 21 October 1931.

(*bottom*) Palestine Police face Arab demonstrators in Clock House Square, Jaffa, 27 October 1933.

(*top*) A British naval escort enters Valletta's Grand Harbour, September 1941.

(*bottom*) Empire Day, Cairo, 27 May 1942.

(*above*) Maltese women and children cheer the arrival of the 'Pedestal' convoy, 14 August 1942.

(*left*) Anthony Eden and Harold Macmillan, Britain's 'Viceroy in the Mediterranean', in Algiers, 28 May 1943.

(*above*) Churchill addresses the British Army and Royal Air Force at Carthage, Tunisia, 9 June 1943.

(*left*) George VI, accompanied by the parish priest, views the ruins of Senglea in Malta, 22 June 1943.

The aircraft carrier HMS *Formidable* exercising with destroyers in the Strait of Gibraltar, December 1943.

(*above*) A Spanish worker crosses the frontier into Gibraltar, 1943.

(*left*) Workers in Gibraltar collect their rations from a NAAFI store.

(*top*) The Victory Parade for British Forces in Alexandria, July 1945.

(*bottom*) The gutted shell of the old Navy House in Port Said after the British assault on 6 November 1956.

(*above*) Michael Karaolis, the first of nine Greek-Cypriots to be executed during the Emergency, leaving Nicosia court-house, December 1955.

(*left*) Anti-British signs in Kingway, Valletta, during 1960.

Britain, with its Mediterranean position unsecured, would have enjoyed no freedom of movement to its rear, and later would have been incapacitated from assisting an invasion of Europe. 'The loss of the Mediterranean', Weichold summed up the position for the Axis, 'was therefore the turning point of the war.'[171]

He attributed this outcome to an obsession with purely continental ambitions and an underestimation of power at sea. This mistaken bias, Weichold concluded, was not just the fault of Hitler but one that ran through the German High Command, and emerged from the pattern of German history since unification.[172] These views in part reflected the prejudices of a defeated German navy. Nevertheless, the reasons for the military failure of the Axis between 1940 and 1945 were the mirror-image of those explaining British success in the Mediterranean, with its dogged commitment to naval and amphibious operations and a refusal to be diverted from attainable goals. Both the Americans and the Russians as allies may often have found these British preferences frustratingly peripheral and marginal, but what was peripheral to them was central to the British view of themselves and their capacity to affect outcomes elsewhere. Britain, then, did indeed find a war that 'suited' her, as Churchill had anticipated, and above all one that went with the grain of her own historical experience with a deep Mediterranean imprint.

Anthony Eden, too, had been proved right in his prediction that, bad though things had at one time appeared, the British would be able to come through the war in the Mediterranean with their interests intact. Their achievements in that theatre – enshrined in such legends as the 'Desert Rats' of North Africa and the heroic resistance of Malta – emerged as prime symbols of the general experience of war after 1940. The emerging geopolitics of the region by mid-1945, furthermore, appeared relatively favourable from a British perspective. Germany was crushed. France was seemingly a bit-part player in the wider Mediterranean, epitomized by the brusqueness with which the British foreclosed de Gaulle's attempt to reassert French predominance in Syria in May 1945. Italy and Spain needed to work their passage back to respectability. Their weakness could only be an advantage. The United States showed every sign of accepting, as an American diplomat with experience of the region stated, that the Mediterranean was a 'purely

British baby', to the extent that the US navy was preparing to leave those waters once peace was firmly established.[173] The prospect was opening up of a good old-fashioned, nineteenth-century type of controlled quasi-imperial rivalry between the British and the Russians.[174] This was a game that Churchill, so immersed in Mediterranean affairs, could eagerly look forward to playing opposite his natural jousting-partner, Joseph Stalin. At the general election of 5 July 1945, however, Churchill and the Conservative Party went down to a crushing defeat. It was his successor as Prime Minister, the Labour leader Clement Attlee, with a far more cursory engagement with the Mediterranean, who was left to be confronted with the gloomier part of Eden's prediction: that the real trouble would come when the war was over. The conflict after 1940, indeed, had not only brought violence but the spirit of violence, not to mention more guns, into quite a few Mediterranean societies. Such ominous effects might not disappear as quickly as some hoped.

# 8

# The Passing of the British Mediterranean, 1945–1979

The place of the Mediterranean in British overseas power emerged from the Second World War as more important than ever. Investigations by Mass Opinion, the first British polling organization, showed that anything east of Suez had scarcely featured in the thoughts of most ordinary Britons during the war; by contrast, the dramas of Malta, North Africa, Sicily, the mainland of Italy and Greece had been seared into British imaginations. The Mediterranean was where the United Kingdom had, within the limitations of a grand alliance, been able to fight her own war according to her own lights. In doing so she had suffered defeats but also won victories elusive in other theatres. It was completely logical that when the Chiefs of Staff in Whitehall drew up their 'Principles of Defence' for the post-war world the region ranked in significance alongside the homeland itself and routes across the Atlantic.[1]

One way or another, however, expectations in the Mediterranean were to be confounded. A region that was malleable in war and a theatre for climactic British successes frequently proved obdurate in peacetime, a zone of political anxiety and occasional humiliations. This final breaking up of the British Mediterranean world was inevitable. Since its origins during the war against Napoleon it had always been vulnerable to internal and external challenges, but had also been resilient and expansive under pressure. Not surprisingly, the process was not a consistent or steady one. Much of its fascination, however, lay in the contrast between Britain's various exits, since their complicated pathologies varied enormously and left traces that are still visible in the Mediterranean today.

The sequence of renewed British commitment, agonizing reappraisal and improvised withdrawal under post-war conditions was first played out in Greece. In February 1945 British forces had presided over a fragile truce between the bitterly divided right and left in Greek political life. In the next few months British Military and Police Missions were set up to resuscitate the Greek army and gendarmerie; the Royal Hellenic Navy, for its part, had long been under British patronage. Law and order, such as they were, hinged on a continued British presence. So did having something to eat. Only supplies of the United Nations Relief and Rehabilitation Administration (UNRRA) stood between much of the population and starvation. If these vital goods came overwhelmingly from the United States, in Greece they could only be effectively distributed under British supervision (Oxfam as a leading United Kingdom charity began in Greece at this time).[2] In September 1946, 31,000 British troops were engaged in carrying out such tasks. The authority wielded over Greece could easily seem colonial, so that the country could be described as 'an Egypt without a Cromer';[3] that is, under de facto British supremacy, even if it lacked a viceregal figure on the spot. British 'experts' shaped policy in finance, economics, diplomacy and security. This was so much taken for granted on all sides that subsequently the leader of the Greek Communists, Nikos Zachariades, was to blame the fatal delay in his side's decision to unleash a new offensive on a misplaced belief in the need to win British approval first.[4]

The British role in the unfolding Greek struggle was skewed in various ways. It was true that British representatives consistently sought to ensure that moderation prevailed among local contenders. Harold Macmillan in his final days as Minister Resident in the Mediterranean, repeatedly stressed to British subordinates that 'we were *not*, repeat *not*, prepared to become the tool of a right-wing reaction'.[5] Yet if the British were not a mere tool, they did prove complacent about, and to some degree complicit in, a 'white terror' carried out by a mixture of local conservatives, monarchists and liberals frightened by the growth of Communist power elsewhere in the Balkans.

Various factors brought about this polarization. Extreme rightists, in such units as the Greek Sacred Legion, had served under British command in the Middle East, and the British Military Mission (BMM) simply advanced the people they knew.[6] But just as important was timing. Already by the spring of 1946 demobilization pressures in Britain made it clear that a significant troop presence could not be maintained for long. March 1947 was set as a provisional date for getting the soldiers out. The need to speed everything up meant that increasingly the British skimped on the 'training' given by their Missions, and looked the other way as violence between Greeks spread. British bayonets thus held the ring while a blatantly rigged general election in April 1946 confirmed the right in power, and an even more obviously rigged plebiscite the following September restored the Glücksberg dynasty, with all its Anglophiliac connections.

There was in this situation another aspect redolent of the wider British Mediterranean experience. Whereas to local people the British often appeared to be in charge, in reality their power was often precarious. The gap between image and reality generated many misunderstandings. Furthermore, even if the British leant more in one direction than another, they still attracted suspicion from all sides in the internal struggle by trying to maintain a central and mediating position. There gradually dawned on Greeks, too, the first inkling of something that had hitherto been opaque. The British were no longer the leading power in the Mediterranean. In early February 1946 the United States Navy Department stopped referring to 'North African Waters' and stated that it now had an admiral commanding 'in the Mediterranean';[7] and the USS *Missouri*, fresh from having provided the platform for the signature of Japan's surrender, was dispatched to its new Mediterranean station. When the *Missouri* visited Piraeus, it was welcomed by excited crowds, as was the USS *Roosevelt* that September. In grasping a new configuration of authority, the Greeks were driven by their own necessities, since by the final months of 1946 the country was close to material collapse and civil war. The Greek Government needed help, and the more it feared the British might be in no position to provide assistance, the more it looked instead to other, less familiar but apparently even richer states.

The Foreign Secretary in Britain's Labour government, Ernest Bevin, had supported this Greek commitment once he assumed his post in July 1945. It was part of a broader engagement with the Mediterranean and Middle East that was to be a key feature of his tenure.[8] But with the United Kingdom itself in the grip of a severe winter and acute fuel and manpower shortages, Bevin was constrained by the shifting priorities of his Cabinet colleagues, and especially by Prime Minister Attlee's scepticism towards overseas commitments, including those in the Mediterranean. In New York for a session of the United Nations in early December 1946, Bevin was informed by the Foreign Office that Cabinet discussion in London had suddenly put policy towards Greece 'in the melting pot'.[9] In the following weeks British troops left in Greece were concentrated in the north around Salonica, leaving the Peloponnese undefended. Finally, in a decision intimately connected to related dilemmas in India and Palestine, on 24 February 1947 the British Government informed Washington that the imminent deadline of 31 March for terminating its current level of support for Greece would be adhered to.

This was the background to the promulgation on 12 March 1947 by President Harry S Truman of a Doctrine under which America would henceforth assume the principal burden for defending Greece and Turkey. For some months the Americans had become alarmed over a persistent Soviet claim to a predominant role over the Turkish Straits;[10] and for the Truman administration, propping up Greece was concomitant to ensuring that this challenge was met. It was entirely logical that such a transformation of United States policy pivoted on the Straits that had for so long loomed large in British naval thought. More narrowly, the handover to the Americans of primary responsibility for 'saving' Greece represented Britain's first major retraction in the Mediterranean.

However, such retreats were often only partial and prolonged in execution. The British Military Mission in Greece was by no means fully liquidated in early 1947. American military personnel did not begin arriving till the end of that year, and once they were there the Greeks sometimes found that the Americans were even less easy to deal with than the remaining British.[11] The worsening situation meant that the stationing of British officers with Greek army units at divisional and brigade level continued to be a feature of a bloody civil war. Suggestively, the Labour government, conscious that intervention on behalf of conservative forces in Greece remained controversial at home, always maintained a 'black-out policy' regarding publicity of the Military Mission's activities in that country.[12] As late as October

1948 the British Ambassador in Athens warned that without continued intervention a Communist takeover was 'a racing certainty'.[13] Within a few months, however, the Communists had been defeated. The fact that this came as a surprise to both the British and the Americans suggests that it was really an achievement of the Greek army itself.[14]

By then the British Military Mission had become only a token presence around Salonica, from which city it finally left on 5 February 1950 when the 1st Battalion Bedfordshire and Hertfordshire Regiment embarked on HMS *Empire Windrush*.[15] On the eve of this departure a large reception was held by British officers in their mess for Greek army colleagues and local dignitaries. The Anglo-Hellenic League of Salonica took possession of the flag that had hung over the British barracks. The climax was a military parade held in Thessalonika's Aristotle Square. Despite the intense cold a large crowd turned out, and the British Consul-General recorded that several Greek women were so overcome with emotion that they wept as the Bedfordshire and Hertfordshire ranks marched past the saluting base.[16] The Consul-General had no doubt that this and other expressions of regret at the British disappearance were wholly sincere.[17] As late as 1950 there still remained a distinctive Anglo-Greek phenomenon, reaching back to a Byronic past, in which those involved felt it authentic to enact such visibly emotional responses. Paradoxically, however, as we shall see, this was also the point at which that phenomenon was subject to rapid disintegration.

The British decision during February 1947 to reduce their responsibilities in Greece was matched by a similar turning point in Palestine. An uneasy lull had prevailed in the Mandate during the months following the end of the war. Because the British Labour Party was traditionally susceptible to Zionist ideas, the Jewish Agency in Palestine entertained hopes that the new Attlee administration would chart a course in their favour. When it did not, the Agency threw in their lot, and that of the Haganah militia, with the extremist Irgun and Stern organizations. The first clash between Haganah and British forces took place in early October 1945. In November four British soldiers were killed in a joint Irgun/Stern attack on a police headquarters in Jerusalem. Such assaults intensified in early 1946, and in June Haganah blew up a series of bridges on the frontiers of Palestine to demonstrate that they could seal the country off if they wished. Up to this point Zionist moderates had conceived of the use of force as a method of 'persuading' the British to do what they wanted. The persuasion in question was to make the British understand that all they had to do was to help stifle the Arabs and hand the country over to the Zionists. But when this did not happen, the 'persuasion' of Haganah and the Agency was fused with the virulent anti-Britishness and calculated terrorism of more militant elements.

The high point of this process, and a symbolic moment in the entire struggle, came with the blowing up of the King David Hotel, the headquarters of British Mandatory administration. Concerns had been expressed that the building might be the target of a major assault, but none were heeded. Despite haphazard terrorism, there was a conviction that the Jews in Palestine remained too dependent on the British in shaping a political endgame to risk a real 'spectacular' claiming numerous victims. On 22 July 1946, however, following a British army raid on Jewish Agency offices, Irgun operatives on the instructions of their leader, Menachem Begin, gained access to the King David Hotel through a section still functioning commercially and placed 770 pounds of explosive under its southern wing. There was much controversy later over whether any meaningful warnings had been given. The devastating explosion at 12.37 p.m. killed 91 people, 41 Britons, 17 Jews, 28 Arabs and 5 others. This event drove a final wedge between the British and Jews in Palestine, immediately characterized by the 'non-fraternization' order issued by the British Commander-in-Chief, General Evelyn Barker. But the bombing also caused bitter disputes between Zionist organizations, since Haganah quickly tried to distance themselves. Nor has the controversy ever entirely gone away. In July 2006, on the fiftieth anniversary of the bombing, the Menachem Begin Centre in Jerusalem organized a celebration controversially attended by the Prime Minister of Israel, Binyamin Netanyahu.

By this stage the approach of the Labour government in London was already in disarray. Bevin often came to be accused of an anti-Semitic bias, driven by his determination not to fall out with Arab states in the region. In truth it was not his prejudices but the practical imperatives he worked under that necessarily curtailed sympathy for the Zionist case. A risk developed that he and Attlee would be seriously at odds with the Truman administration. There had been an attempt in the early months of peace to explore a settlement of Palestine on the basis of an understanding between London and Washington. A joint approach was the Labour government's ideal solution. An Anglo-American Committee had been set up to visit Palestine and make recommendations. Its report proposed semi-autonomous Jewish and Arab regions, with the British left in control of certain central functions and control over Jerusalem. But it also recommended the immediate entry of 100,000 Jewish refugees, the implementation of which was bound to alter radically the balance of Jewish and Arab power within Palestine. The report was swiftly rejected by the British Government. Nevertheless, the symbolic gesture of 100,000 Jewish immigrants was subsequently taken up by the Americans as a sop to be thrown to Zionist lobbies in the United States. It featured prominently in President Truman's statement on 4 October 1946 (Yom Kippur) and resulted in something rare in post-war affairs: a direct rebuke from a British Prime Minister to a United States President.[18] Attlee wrote to Truman: 'I have received with great regret your letter refusing even a few hours grace to the Prime Minister of the country which has the actual responsibility for the government of Palestine in order that he might acquaint you with the actual situation and the probable results of your action.' Tart though Attlee's words were, a striking aspect of the Palestine issue was how it was managed in both London and Washington so as not to destabilize fundamentally their relations. Both governments shared a basic supposition: that although it was hoped a major breakdown between Arabs and Jews in Palestine might be avoided, it was above all important that in such an event the struggle should be localized, contained and cordoned off. In the same vein Bevin was insistent that discussion about Palestine among his own officials was carried out with minimal reference to regional strategic issues. Palestinian matters were complex and intractable enough without piling on such variables. Here the Zionists themselves made a miscalculation. They thought that the territory was so important as a base to the United Kingdom that by prejudicing its operation they could lever the British into meeting their demands. They failed to appreciate that by the end of 1946 the British Government had already decided that Palestine was a liability rather than an asset. Separated out from Anglo-American diplomatic relations, as well as British strategic calculations, the denouement of the Palestine Mandate unfolded in a curious bubble of its own.

Coping with the 'illegal' immigration of refugees displaced by the Holocaust in Europe constituted an especially sensitive challenge for the British authorities after 1945. A high proportion of women and children were among the refugee passengers, crammed into boats that were bigger and even more unseaworthy than those used in the later 1930s. The Royal Navy hated such work, entailing the use of coercion against civilians. From four to six destroyers and a minesweeper were regularly based in Haifa. It was very unusual for a refugee ship to make it to the shore without being identified. When the *Susanna* did so in March 1947, it was the first since April 1946. On that occasion 135 Jews were unable to beach the ship through the surf. They were rescued by a British warship and taken to the camps for Displaced Persons set up in Cyprus. In total, 52,221 illegal refugees were detained in the latter, arousing a good deal of Cypriot criticism, where it was feared that the population balance might be affected. The last releases from Cyprus were not made till December 1949, by which time the state of Israel was fully in being.[19]

The interception of refugee ships within the narrow 3-mile zone posed considerable difficulty. The bigger ships had to be brought to a complete standstill to allow boarding by naval personnel. Capsizing was a constant hazard. Sometimes boarding took place under a hail of objects being thrown, but just as often the passengers were passive but resentful. The work of the Palestine Patrol was regulated with scrupulous attention to legality, not least because of its political delicacy, the use of force being carefully regulated.[20] There was no firing into ships, and any use of firearms was restricted to the most acute circumstances. Fire hoses were used to clear decks when necessary. This is not to say that methods were gentle. A 2-foot cosh was specially designed for use. A training course was also established in Malta tailored for the Palestine Patrol's 'stop and search' tasks. The navy perhaps inevitably became 'Public Enemy No. 1' to militant Zionists, and the naval base at Haifa required close protection. As one person recalled, a 'night at Haifa was always an arduous experience', with frequent security alarms, though significantly not even Irgun or Stern risked a major attack.[21] But despite the circumstances, loss of life or injury afloat among both sailors and refugees was surprisingly rare.[22]

In seeking to keep control in Palestine the British army kept around 100,000 troops, some 10 per cent of its entire strength, tied down in a country the size of Wales (though only about 20,000 of these troops were in a combat role). Units, however, were rotated frequently, causing considerable inefficiency. A still more basic weakness was lack of intelligence, compounded by the fact that few in the army or police spoke Hebrew.[23] What information became available tended to focus on the Jewish Agency and Haganah, not on the more dangerous extremists. There was a strong feeling that the army was fighting Zionist militants with its hands tied behind its back, especially compared to the methods used against the Arab rebellion in the 1930s. Then the homes of many ordinary Arabs had been bulldozed, and Arabs found guilty of capital crimes had often been hanged. Especially galling were the large number of reprieves given to Jews convicted of the murders of British military and civilians from early 1946. Field-Marshal Montgomery, as Chief of the Imperial General Staff, after visiting Palestine later that year, was adamant (with his own experience of the Arab revolt) that the army needed more leeway if it was to act forcibly.[24]

But the adoption of such methods in the urban setting of Jewish insurgency in the 1940s, as opposed to the rural context of its earlier Arab counterpart, was not so easy. The High Commissioner, Sir Alan Cunningham, was against reprisals, and so for the most part were senior army commanders on the spot. The alternative, however, was increasingly to fall back into barbed-wire compounds ('Bevingrads'), which gave the troops little freedom of movement. Morale plumbed new depths in July 1947 with the murder by Irgun of two British sergeants in the Intelligence Corps. The pair were abducted and held hostage for the reprieve of three convicted Zionist terrorists. When the latter hangings went ahead, the two sergeants were killed and their booby-trapped bodies stuck on trees in a grove near Netanya. During the army crackdown in Tel Aviv that followed several Jews died. What most people, British and Jews, considered a vile episode, was perhaps the last straw that finally broke the back of the Mandate.[25] Certainly soon afterwards Cunningham warned ministers in London that the security situation in Palestine was now threatening to become uncontrollable.[26]

What made the army's task so impossible was the lack of clear policy direction from London, or what today would be called an exit strategy. Partition had faded as an option towards the end of the war, but it remained the preference of the Colonial Office in London. It alone offered, in theory, clarity and finality as a solution. But partition met strong opposition in the Foreign Office, sensitive to insistence from diplomats in Arab capitals that any such move would permanently impair British influence. Partition was lambasted as 'a counsel of despair'.[27] The Labour government consequently went back one more time to the hoary old ideal of a bi-national, one-state solution embracing Jewish and Arab zones. A conference was even convened in London to this end, though no Palestinians from either side took part directly. Indistinctly, but inevitably, by early 1947 the British, including Bevin, had wobbled yet again towards the concept of partition.

The real problem with partition, however, was entirely practical: how would it actually be executed, and by whom? Where would the physical lines be drawn, and in whose favour? These issues had become even more difficult to resolve than in 1937, when partition had first been officially mooted. It was hardly feasible to impose such a formula against Jewish *and* Arab resistance. A choice of evils had to be made, so that one either teamed up with the Jews against the Arabs, or vice versa. The truth was that though Bevin might gravitate towards partition in principle, in practice there was not the slightest prospect that the British Government would be prepared to lift such a poisoned chalice to its lips. It could only undertake partition, with all the collateral damage involved, if the exercise carried some collective international sanction and responsibility; that is, unless there was somebody to do it with. In announcing during February 1947 that it would take the Palestine matter to the United Nations, the Labour government tacitly admitted that the United Kingdom was no longer able or willing to carry the burden of shaping the territory's future. Whether anybody else had the slightest inclination to come and share the task remained highly doubtful.

Amid these shifts, British Mandatory officials in Palestine sat, increasingly hopeless, on the sidelines. They carried on their duties, but what they administered went on shrinking. They felt ignored by London, and High Commissioner Cunningham's depression merely reflected that of his subordinates. His chief adviser, Chief Secretary Henry Gurney, conjured up the flavour when privately telling a colleague in the Colonial Office:

> now . . . [that] the remaining British are all behind barbed wire we are beginning to wonder how long it will be possible to carry on civilian administration here at all . . . [H]ow utterly incongruous . . . a spectacle is that of a lorry convoy of British officials being transported to their offices in Jerusalem through streets in which the rest of the population move freely.[28]

Gurney spoke of his own struggle, typical of his colleagues, to suppress an anti-Semitism stoked up by events.[29] Inevitably, British officials came to look more sympathetically on Arab grievances, and even to advise Arabs on how best to present their case. Gurney, for example, sought to impress on such contacts that their interests would be best served by stressing the specifically racial aspect of Jewish discrimination, since that gelled with contemporary opinion in the world at large. He pointed out that 'the Jewish plans for their constitution and minorities make no provision at all for the rights of . . . nearly half a million Arabs'.[30] As the Mandate entered a final tailspin the Anglo-Zionism which thirty years before had underpinned the Balfour Declaration on a Jewish national home was dead, and a pro-Arab bias more often that not – though there were always exceptions – took its place.

Following the British referral to the Assembly in New York, a United Nations Special Committee on Palestine (UNSCOP) was set up during May. This Committee visited Palestine and made recommendations in early September 1947, including the termination of the Mandate on the basis of independence. There was a resounding silence, however, as to who might undertake the task. The British Government was quick to make clear it would not be the British, announcing its intention to evacuate Palestine regardless of whether a successor authority was appointed, or of the absence of any agreement between

Jews and Arabs. This pushed the ball firmly back into the UN's court, and in November 1947 the General Assembly passed a resolution on a territorial basis broadly favourable to the Jews, but without suggesting any mechanism to bring it about. The British representative rigidly abstained in the vote. An implacable determination to make an exit with minimal losses to their own personnel characterized what remained of British conduct of the Mandate up to its appointed end on 15 May 1948.

Packing up the Mandate was a dangerous and complicated task. From early February 1948 Operation Polly, the evacuation of all non-essential British personnel and civilians, got under way. They were assembled in batches at Sarafand transit camp, bused to Lydda and put on trains to Alexandria in Egypt, from where they were shipped home. With only some 200 British officials left in Palestine to preside over a rump administration, the task of the army was now to ensure as safe and honourable a departure as conditions allowed. An essential priority was the control of Jerusalem, Haifa (the point of exit) and, crucially, communications between them, just as it had been when partition was planned in 1937. Throughout this process bitter clashes broke out between Arabs and Jews. The British Cabinet's instructions to army commanders were quite plain. From 15 May onwards there would be no obligation to preserve law and order beyond that of 'a military force in occupation of foreign territory'.[31] In practice, this compression of residual responsibility – a responsibility really to the British themselves and nobody else – occurred even before 15 May. As Gurney admitted, 'we have always foreseen that the difficult period would be the last ten days [of the Mandate] with each side jockeying for position and fighting for strategic points.'[32] It was for this reason that Gurney and other colleagues pressed for the terminal date to be foreshortened by ten days to avoid the nightmare of troops and administration being cut off in Jerusalem as Zionist militias approached the Arab-majority capital.[33] The Cabinet in London, however, was adamant: 15 May was the date they had specified to the world at large, and it was the one obligation they were determined on keeping to.[34]

Paradoxically, the fact that, as Cunningham remarked, 'the Jewish military star is in the ascendant' helped to smooth the British path towards withdrawal.[35] Although the British were not able to maintain their grip on Haifa, the local army commander and Haganah came to an informal understanding in the town.[36] This was deeply embarrassing to the Cabinet in London.[37] Fleeing Arabs poured into the British-controlled port area, where under the supervision of troops they scrambled onto boats to get out. It was in such circumstances that Arab claims that the British conspired in the Jewish takeover first began.[38] At 6.45 p.m. on 14 May the Union Jack was lowered over what remained of the King David Hotel and the flag of the International Red Cross raised in its place. Early the following morning Cunningham left Government House and made his way along roads covered by army machine-gun outposts at exposed points. He had to pass through several checkpoints under the control of rival Jewish and Arab militias. The High Commissioner was then flown to Haifa, the nerve centre of the British evacuation, where he was taken to the harbour and piped aboard HMS *Euralyus* to a seventeen-gun salute. The warship left precisely at midnight when the Mandate formally ended. 'A few rockets and searchlights', Norman Rose writes, 'spotlighted the cruiser as it steamed from harbour for home escorted by HMS *Ocean* and three destroyers.'[39] 'Whoever goes there will have a bad time,' somebody had remarked of Palestine way back in 1919. The prediction had proved all too true; but at least now the British were free of a fatal encumbrance, even if they were subject to what they felt to be wholly unjustified criticisms of having left chaos and bloodshed behind them.[40]

Eight thousand of the British troops evacuated from Palestine were shipped to Cyrenaica, where a British military administration was trying to bed down in that ex-Italian colony. They could not easily have gone to Egypt, where post-war tensions were never far below the surface. In Egypt, as elsewhere, the basic problem was that the foreign garrison – 200,000 British troops when war ended – was viewed as a badge of servitude that could no longer be tolerated. Bevin had a policy designed to counter such a feeling: 'non-intervention'.[41] But if this sounded convincing when inscribed in Whitehall memoranda, it seemed bogus to local populations. Lord Killearn's successor as British Ambassador in Cairo, Ronald Campbell, got close to the heart of the matter when he remarked in June 1946 that, even if non-intervention was accepted as a guide for British actions, the fact remained that 'so long as our troops are here, we cannot wholeheartedly practise it, *because* we are here . . . at present we have the worst of both worlds'.[42]

Campbell's insight was triggered by the renewal of the first serious anti-British demonstrations in Egypt since 1936. This included haphazard violence against expatriates, especially in Cairo and Alexandria, 'ranging', Hoda Nasser recounts, 'from stoning British military personnel in the streets [to] throwing bombs at their barracks and at the clubs, hotels and bars they frequented'.[43] For Attlee, the problems posed by the British military presence in Egypt – the occupation of which he regarded as practically useless – became 'the plague of my life'.[44] The total of British troops was whittled down to around 100,000 and gradually they were moved away from the main towns, where they were so visible, to the arid and bare Canal Zone. The Fleet presence at Alexandria was reduced and the flag of 'Commander-in-Chief, Mediterranean' returned to Malta. Attlee persuaded his Cabinet colleagues to announce in May 1946 an intention to leave Egypt altogether. The problem was to negotiate the terms of a deal, including a controversial 'right of return', in the hope that some Egyptian politician could be persuaded to accept responsibility for it even at some personal risk.

Bevin did eventually sign a preliminary document with the Egyptian Prime Minister, Ismail Sidky, in October 1946. One leading commentator suggests that had this been ratified not only would later British diplomatic convulsions have been avoided, but, perhaps more importantly, constitutional and parliamentary rule in Egypt would have evolved differently too.[45] But the Bevin–Sidky protocol was shot down by Egyptian critics. Desperate to identify a fallback position, the Labour government went ahead in evacuating increasingly untenable garrisons in heavily populated areas. On 9 February 1947 British troops left Alexandria altogether, the 2nd Royal Fusiliers handing over the Mustapha barracks to the Egyptians. At the end of March the Life Guards gave up the famous Kasr-el-Nil citadel in Cairo, and moved to the Canal Zone. These military redeployments, however, were only undertaken with very strong reluctance by the army,[46] and were opposed by right-wing politicians in Westminster. In this way the Canal Zone itself came to constitute a dividing line in British political life.

A temporary lull then prevailed as Palestine preoccupied everybody's attention. As the British left that territory, Egyptian troops had invaded Palestine alongside other Arab armies. Their defeat by the Israeli Defence Force was a crushing experience that turned anger to hatred against the West in general, and Great Britain in particular, not least among a younger cadre of Egyptian army officers. The fact that Egyptian forces had to be checked through the British-controlled Suez Canal on the way to Palestine, and then, in humiliating disarray, on the way back, added to the bitterness. It was against this background that 'moderation' – that evanescent phenomenon on which the British presence always depended – finally expired. In January 1950 the Wafd party, with whom the British had successfully if vicariously collaborated during the Second World War, came to power once more. But this was a Wafd for whom any co-operation was now likely to be fatal by damaging their nationalist image. Before long harassment of British troops in the Canal Zone, and occasional murders of soldiers, started up again, but this time with more sustained aggression. These attacks were carried out by bands of *fedeyeen* (or volunteer freedom fighters), seemingly with official connivance. Finally, on 8 October 1951 the Egyptian Government formally abrogated the 1936 treaty with Great Britain. For many years the British military stake in Egypt had been covered by at least a fig-leaf of legality. Now even that was ripped away.

In the wake of abrogation the *fedeyeen* campaign was stepped up still further: British vehicles were attacked as they passed through villages in the Zone, soldiers were at risk of sniping, and military personnel banned from using Egyptian state railways. The refusal of local labourers to turn up for army employment threatened to cripple the British presence altogether. A vital concern was the security of the expatriate communities still living in Cairo and Alexandria, numbering around 15,000. The British occupation of Egypt, after all, had been triggered by a massacre of Europeans in Alexandria in 1882, and the shadow of a repetition was to lie over the new Conservative government in London led by Churchill, in which Eden was Foreign Secretary. Plans had already been drawn up for the evacuation of Europeans in an emergency. The codenames for these operations were Rodeo for Cairo and Flail for Alexandria. Since the appearance of British warships was still considered the surest means of making an effective show of strength in Alexandria, Flail depended on the warships arriving in the nick of time.[47] Since the main European quarters were situated away from the insalubrious port area, however, whether an angry Egyptian mob would notice the Fleet's appearance, or take any notice even if they did, was uncertain.

Amid this insecurity there nonetheless remained a more hopeful British assumption: that in a crisis a display of firmness on their part would quieten things down. This was the memory, not so much of 1882 as of 1942, when Lord Killearn had sent troops to surround the Palace in Cairo and dictate terms.[48] In the dying days of 1951 the British army edged towards a re-enactment. Substantial reinforcements were flown in, including from Cyprus (troop numbers exceeded 80,000 again). Oil deliveries to the Delta were briefly interdicted, despite the considerable penalty this imposed on the Egyptian economy. On 8 December 1951 more than 100 civilian homes were pulled down for security purposes close to an important water plant. Reminiscent of actions taken during the Arab rebellion in the 1930s, in one later British account this is held to have been a 'monumental blunder'.[49] Following a clash with *fedeyeen*, an army patrol crossed over the Sweet Water Canal and so beyond the sensitive limits of the Zone.

The critical point was reached on 25 January 1952 when the British Commander-in-Chief, General Bryan Robertson, ordered the auxiliary Egyptian personnel at the police station in Ismailia to surrender. This was where the current narrative diverged from earlier scripts. The Egyptians, instead of surrendering, fought back when British troops advanced. Forty-two Egyptians were killed and 800 detained; three British soldiers died, and thirteen were wounded. The next day Cairo was torn by riots ('Black Saturday'). Buildings associated with expatriate life were targeted, including offices of BOAC, cinemas, bars, the main department stores and the Turf Club. Shepheard's Hotel was razed to the ground. Several Europeans were killed, including the British Council representative, and a Canadian diplomat also died. General Robertson drew back from a thorough reoccupation of the Delta that he knew was unsustainable, and an uneasy calm was at last imposed by the local authorities. Afterwards Robertson informed London that the Egyptian population

> has undoubtedly been given a severe jolt by the events which have taken place in Ismailia and Cairo, but there is no evidence of national penitence. The crowds of sightseers who flocked into Cairo to see the devastation caused by the riots did not give the impression of being shocked. On the contrary they gazed at the ruins of Shepheard's Hotel with apparent satisfaction at these monuments to a luxury of which they had no share.[50]

Here at least was some kind of subtle glimpse into material conditions beyond the scope of British policy, but that Robertson was surprised at the absence of collective remorse still indicated a gulf of understanding. Yet Black Saturday highlighted the risks being run by everybody. If it happened again there was a chance that the British army would have no choice but to take repressive action itself – like 1919 or 1935 all over again. But the effect of doing so might only be to ignite an inferno nobody could extinguish, leading to a large number of European fatalities in Cairo and Alexandria. This might well bring down the British Government as its own public reacted to such scenes of horror. Eden was therefore determined to take a firmer grip. This meant making sure that the decision to undertake 'rescues' such as Rodeo or Flail lay henceforth exclusively with Whitehall, not with the soldiers on the ground.[51] It also meant restarting negotiations with the Egyptian Government for an agreement on evacuation as soon as possible. The *coup d'état* in Cairo during July 1952 bringing to power a military regime under General Muhammad Naguib and Colonel Abdul Nasser interrupted such a prospect (though the latter gave an immediate assurance that no European lives were at risk). This alteration of regime was not unwelcome in London. The British had long given up on Egyptian politicians, and hoped that a military dictatorship might be easier to deal with.[52]

In truth, the British stake in the Canal Zone had become militarily useless by early 1953.[53] Troops there led what a visiting Conservative MP described as a 'monastic and uncomfortable existence . . . In short, 80,000 troops are neither guarding the base nor the Canal. They are merely guarding each other.'[54] By the end of the year negotiations were at last under way again. But many sticking points remained. For the British, the underlying problem had long been one of accommodation. Assuming that there was no intention of abandoning the entire region, where else in the Mediterranean were the departing troops to be housed? To dilute any unpopularity, the sensible thing was to disperse forces in as many places as possible.[55] But there were not many receptacles left. Apart from Malta, two locations now moved into the foreground. The first was Cyprus, destined to become British Middle East Land Force Headquarters. Cyprus, however, was a quite small island where British troops were apt to stick out like a sore thumb, if only because hitherto there had been relatively few of them there. The second alternative was Cyrenaica, 'conceived', as one writer puts it, 'as the venue where the British tried to repent for their political failures in Egypt and Palestine'.[56] In entrenching themselves in this ex-Italian possession, with its extensive wastelands of sand and general emptiness, the British had several advantages. There were very old-fashioned tribal clans of the sort the British felt they could handle. Idris, too, king of a now united Libya, was a monarch who (unlike the proud and obstinate Farouk in Egypt) was prepared to swallow the fact that without British help he was lost. Once the UN had recognized British Trusteeship in 1949, such relationships were exploited to the full, including looking the other way when ballot boxes were stuffed full of forged signatures.[57] But even in Cyrenaican towns British troops excited resentment among local people. Their barracks were moved into the eastern desert, where there were not even the bare facilities of Egypt's Canal Zone.[58]

Meanwhile the grindingly slow Anglo-Egyptian negotiations, on such issues as to whether technicians left in the base area after an agreement should wear military uniform or not, were interspersed by renewed instability. One such spasm occurred in early 1954, by which time Robertson's successor as Commander-in-Chief, General Charles Keightley, was under no illusion about his ability to maintain order or rescue stranded expatriates should another 'Black Saturday' erupt.[59] As he sought to focus minds in London, Keightley stressed that they were all just 'a slip of a knife' – a knife, that is, into some innocent British civilian – from impending chaos. The response of the Chief of the Imperial General Staff at the War Office, Field-Marshal Sir John Harding, was telling. He divided British subjects in Egypt into three categories. First were British officials, who could be got out at the last moment. Second were businessmen, who normally had an opportunity to escape before major trouble began. Third were those who were not really British at all, but, as he put it, Levantines, Maltese, Cypriots and other minorities, 'who could merge with the population and were unlikely to be singled out for attack'.[60] In fact they would probably be the first to be attacked precisely because they were most in contact with ordinary Egyptians. This was symptomatic of the subterfuges and the casting aside of old connections that were characteristic of a fading British Mediterranean commitment.

In the event, the British and Egyptian governments – the latter now firmly under Nasser's personal control – came to an agreement in October 1954 before any such frightful denouement intervened. Under these terms the new arrangement was to last seven years, during which time the Suez base would be maintained jointly by British and Egyptian civilian staff, freedom of movement through the Canal was guaranteed, and if any war broke out in the region the British would have the right to re-enter with their own military forces. All British troops, however, were to leave Egypt by June 1956. We have already seen that this settlement had never really been about military realities, since the value of the base had long since dissolved. Pride was the true stake, and in this small things told. The Royal Navy argued long and hard to retain ownership of Navy House on the Port Said waterfront as a residual token of palmy days fast slipping away.[61] But the Egyptians were adamant, and Navy House, too, was slated for the handover.

Yet far from this new treaty improving relations between Britain and Egypt, the opposite effect was part of its underlying logic. For the British, and above all for Eden after he succeeded Churchill as Prime Minister in April 1955, inherent in the treaty's logic was to be able to tell the Egyptians henceforth 'to go to blazes'.[62] Egypt, from this perspective, had been an impoverished, irrelevant and misgoverned country before 1882, and it was now to be so again. The new direction in Britain's Middle Eastern diplomacy – building a 'northern tier' of regional defence, based on understandings with Iraq and Turkey known as the 'Baghdad Pact' – was designed to bring this about, as Nasser was all too well aware.[63] The genesis of the Suez crisis was a mix of the corrosive effects of British refusal to provide arms to Egypt, bloody Israeli raids on Egyptian-controlled Gaza,[64] and Nasser's finding of an alternative arms supplier in Communist Czechoslovakia. These interactions were already in full flow when the last British troops on Egyptian soil left from Navy House in Port Said just after midnight on 13 June 1956, so ending seventy-four years of what was meant at the start to be a 'temporary occupation'.[65]

This was a historic occasion in Egyptian history: the first time since the Pharaohs that a foreign army had left without being replaced by another foreign army. The new regime understandably wanted to make the most of it. Arab delegations were invited, along with other international representatives, including the Soviet Foreign Minister. For Eden's government in London an overt display of anti-Britishness might have agitated its own sullen backbenchers (the 'Suez Group'). Ministers were therefore concerned to see that the British exit was as unobtrusive as possible, and to avoid participation in any Egyptian ceremonies.[66] Nasser's invitation to a senior personage in Her Majesty's Government to participate was therefore ignored. When a follow-up invitation was sent to the ex-Commander-in-Chief in Egypt, General Robertson, it was nevertheless felt not possible to reject it.

Having enticed Robertson to Cairo, however, it was too much to ask that the Egyptians would not make the point that henceforth the British could no longer expect special treatment in the country. At a celebratory dinner held at the Officers' Club, the British Ambassador, Humphrey Trevelyan, had to intervene twice to see that Robertson even got access to the buffet table.[67] The pageant on the next day, attended by Nasser, and in which floats recalled significant events in Egypt's past, was also dubious from a British perspective, since among these staged remembrances was the bombardment of Alexandria in 1882, the infamous Denshaiwai incident of 1906,[68] and the uprisings of 1919 and 1935. Trevelyan sought to pacify feelings at home by reporting that there was 'no more applause for the anti-British items than for the rest of the show', though for form's sake, and also to cover his own flank, he lodged a protest with the Egyptians.[69] All told, the Ambassador felt that the whole thing had gone off as well as could have been expected in the circumstances. Had the British military presence ended there, indeed, this judgement might have had a wider application to the ending of Britain's Egyptian bondage.

The British engagements in Greece, Palestine and Egypt were in a sense resolvable because none of them was a formal colonial possession. This was not the case with Gibraltar, Malta and Cyprus. Each was idiosyncratic. In Gibraltar soon after the end of the war only 9,300 of the 16,500 evacuated from the Rock in 1940 had been repatriated. What was more, both the Governor and the military authorities had got so used to running things as they liked that they did not want the pre-war civilian population to be fully reconstituted.[70] They would take up scarce accommodation and lead to the airing of awkward views, epitomized by the Association for the Advancement of Civil Rights, established in 1942, the first 'modern' political organization in Gibraltar. Although the Colonial Office correctly predicted that it would prove impossible to fend off pressure for full repatriation, the evacuees of 1940 were in fact not fully returned from their temporary domiciles in Jamaica, Madeira and Britain until 1951. It was therefore a long time before real 'normality' was restored in post-war Gibraltar.

It was partly because of the distortions created by war that an academic economist, F. A. von Hayek, was sent from London during 1945 to report on conditions in Gibraltar. He was the recent author of *The Road to Serfdom*, a book later to provide the essential template for Margaret's Thatcher's distinctive political economy as leader of the Conservative Party.[71] His remarks provide an interesting perspective on Gibraltar after the war. It is telling that it was still possible for him to state that 'the town of Gibraltar is little more than the commercial centre of an urban agglomeration of nearly 100,000 inhabitants, whose working-class suburbs are still in Spain'.[72] The subtle interweaving of Gibraltar and its hinterland in the adjoining *campo*, though weakened by civil and then world war, had yet to be decisively ruptured. Hayek's most telling recommendation was to end all restrictions on rents and so force Gibraltar's poor over the frontier, from which they might then migrate inwards to work alongside Spanish co-workers. The advantage he saw in this was to align prices throughout the Gibraltar–*campo* world. Hayek rejected the old Admiralty fear that if the Rock itself did not possess a diversity of labour, the dockyard might one day face a grave shortage. Hayek argued that La Linea across the frontier 'is so completely dependent on the livelihood of its people on Gibraltar that the possibility of Spain for any length of time closing the frontier and not allowing labour into Gibraltar need not seriously be taken into account'.[73] Underlying Hayek's analysis was a preoccupation with Gibraltar's cultural identity. He noted that Gibraltar's poorer classes had never been British anyway (indeed, even in 1950 one-third of the population did not speak English). By ensuring that the Rock was overwhelmingly middle class, its Britishness, Hayek contended, would be guaranteed. The submerged agendas in this were clearly formidable and in the Colonial Office Hayek's views were dryly described as 'bloodless'.

Politically, as well as economically, any Spanish threat to British Gibraltar had faded away more or less completely for the first time since the mid-1930s. Spain was ostracized in international relations after the war, excluded from the United Nations in 1945 and even from American Marshall Aid after 1947.[74] In these circumstances, not getting embroiled with the British Government continued to be a very necessary principle in Madrid. The British authorities therefore had an opportunity to carry out certain changes – such as putting up large permanent buildings on the contested area occupied by the airfield – which otherwise might have been forestalled.[75] So long as Franco felt thus corralled by international isolation, the Gibraltar 'question' remained dead. In October 1949 Real Madrid even came to play against a Gibraltar football team and scraped a 2–2 draw.

Under these conditions the existing municipal institutions in Gibraltar were broadened into a more mature conception of constitutional development, though only in a restricted sense. There is little evidence that such development had to be wrenched from the imperial metropole. By November 1945 the Labour government in London had accepted the principle that Gibraltar should have a Legislative Council. 'The plain truth', remarked a Colonial Office expert on the Mediterranean, 'is that Gibraltar is a Victorian museum-piece and it is high time a fresh wind blew through it' (in fact, a bit like the Colonial Office).[76] The details took some time to work out, and the Legislative Council formally established in 1950 still had an official majority buttressed by the reserved powers of the Governor. One of the prime concerns of the elected members was to ensure that better social provisions on the Rock were financed by the Treasury in London, and not through local taxation, as any move towards 'responsible' government proper would necessarily have entailed (though a modest Income Tax was legislated after 1951). With the Association for the Advancement of Civil Rights already shedding any trouble-making tendencies, British officialdom and Gibraltarian representatives co-operated easily during the first half of the 1950s.[77] In late 1954 a Colonial Office official remarked on 'the smooth functioning of Government in Gibraltar in the last few years in relation . . . to conditions elsewhere'.[78] The Rock was bucking more sinister trends in some other Mediterranean locations, and thereby stored up goodwill in London. This was to stand Gibraltarians in good stead later on.

Nineteen fifty-four, however, was to provide an intimation that not everything was looking favourable for the status quo in Gibraltar. The background to this lay in the Mediterranean's relationship to the emergent Cold War. In 1952 Greece and Turkey joined NATO at the eastern end of the region. There was not any prospect of Spain joining at the western end so long as she remained a dictatorship. But that did not stop the Americans wanting to normalize the relationship as much as possible. In 1950 a United States Navy squadron visited the port of Ferrol. Irritated by having to constantly rely on guest facilities in Gibraltar and wanting its own facilities somewhere nearby, the Sixth Fleet began to eye the possibility of a base somewhere near Cadiz.[79] Preliminary negotiations between the United States and Spain began in April 1952, leading to the signature of the Pact of Madrid in September 1953. These were the first steps of the Franco regime out of international quarantine.

The British viewed this development with concern, as did France, whose relations with Spain were even more frosty. Sooner or later the process was likely to touch the Gibraltar nerve. A pretext was provided by the visit of Great Britain's young Queen Elizabeth II to Gibraltar in May 1954, at the end of her prolonged tour of the Commonwealth. Despite a campaign in the period leading up to the visit, focusing on the claim to Gibraltar's return, the British Ambassador in Madrid, John Balfour, still hoped that Spain would not risk pressing the matter.[80] A hint to the contrary, however, came when the Spanish dictator gave a speech at the Pontifical University in Salamanca in which he stated that he 'did not desire to arrive in the after-life with empty hands' – a clear reference to Gibraltar. Balfour subsequently explained why the British royal visitation clashed with the regenerationist ideology of the Spanish dictatorship:

> it has proved peculiarly exacerbating to ... [the Spanish] that a monarch, in the visits of whose predecessors to Gibraltar earlier in this century an enfeebled Spain had no choice but to acquiesce, should have reaffirmed sovereignty over a Rock, the regaining of which they view as the ultimate and crowning achievement of their effort to achieve the national glories of the past. The visit of Her Majesty aroused all the great bitterness in the minds of the *Caudillo* and his henchmen because they had genuinely persuaded themselves that the US–Spanish Agreement would further their aim of regaining Gibraltar from a Britain thought to be in the process of imperial decline.[81]

This perception of British decline as a Mediterranean power was becoming general, but it was only *circa* 1954 that some protagonists began to see a chance to take advantage of it. In this Spain, as we shall see, was by no means alone. On the eve of the Queen's visit the Spanish consulate in Gibraltar was suddenly closed, and when asked by a leading Gibraltar official how long it was likely to be shut, the Consul replied that he 'doubted whether it would be reopened for some time to come' (it never has been).[82] Balfour warned London that henceforth it was likely that Spanish policy towards Gibraltar would move from verbal intemperance towards a progressive economic blockade. As yet this was too gloomy an assessment. The Pact of Madrid had not specified either the number or location of American bases in Spain, and until this agreement was nailed down further Franco could not afford to be more aggressive. Spanish interests had anyway hinged far more on North Africa than the tiny Rock, and before long these were caught up in an intense crisis in Morocco, itself partly a reflection of turmoil in French Algeria. On Gibraltar a marker, then, had been put down, but that was all it was for the time at least.

A bigger cloud hung over Cyprus. The situation there was habitually characterized by a barely suppressed tension. In part, this was driven by the old Greek-Cypriot desire for union with Greece. But it was also stimulated by a new factor in a sharp internal division between right and left. It was the fatal synergy overlapping from these different sorts of fracture which drove Cypriot affairs into a corner. But initially at least there was some cause for optimism. A new Governor, Lord Winster, was sent out in the spring of 1947 hoping to oversee a programme of economic development and progressive reform, since in Whitehall it was obvious that to go on without any kind of constitution was unlikely to be sustainable for long. The boycott of his inauguration by Greek-Cypriot politicians, however, was not a good start. That November he convened a consultative constitutional assembly. Its venue was the English School, that symbol of a plural, multi-ethnic Cyprus under British colonial authority. The assembly was hobbled from the start by the refusal of the right to participate but also by the limitations of what the British felt they could offer. They still fretted about any restored constitution where the whip-hand might be held by uncontrollable Greek-Cypriot politicians. The consultative assembly broke down, and although the Governor felt able in October 1948 to assure Whitehall that widespread violence was not a probability, he felt bound to warn 'it was not out of the question'.[83] His successor in Government House was Sir Andrew Wright, a veteran of the 1931 outbreak in Cyprus and described by an admittedly unsympathetic American observer as 'a fine Victorian type now almost extinct in the British Colonial Service'.[84] His appointment was evidence of a reaction setting in by the end of the 1940s, and of a persisting tendency for colonial Cyprus to slip back into the habits of the past.

Simultaneously, the ideal of union with Greece became more pervasive than ever among Greek-Cypriots, so that leaderships of the left and right competed to be at its head. Greek-Cypriot politicians, casting about for bait to catch British sympathy, made more rhetorical use than ever of the Ionian precedent of 1864. This precedent was reinforced by a more recent act. In 1948 the British handed over their military administration of the Dodecanese to Greece. This was where Anglo-Greek misunderstanding started to set in, and not just in Cyprus. Whereas to Greeks the acquisition of the Dodecanese was seen as merely the first of several just claims for territorial enlargement – another one being Epirus in what is now southern Albania – it was judged in London to be 'ample compensation' for the country's uneven war record, and not to be added to further.[85] Nor was Greece generally perceived as being, or likely to become, the 'model state in the east' which nine decades earlier had been the hope on which the British gift of the Ionian Islands was based. The falling apart of the 'traditional framework of Anglo-Hellenic friendship' still had some way to go by 1950, but its outlines were already visible. Nevertheless, in Cyprus itself not everything was going wrong. By the end of the 1940s the colonial administration won a competition with the provincial government of Sardinia to be the first in the Mediterranean to eliminate malaria.[86] This is often cited as the most lasting achievement of British rule in Cyprus.

These considerations were complicated enough without becoming inextricably bound up with strategic questions, but this is exactly what happened. In 1945 the military attractions of Cyprus remained limited. The war seemed to confirm that. It was one Mediterranean island not fought over by contending armies. When it had been suggested that money might be invested in upgrading post-war facilities for the Royal Navy, the feeling at the Admiralty was that there was no point since before long the island might cease to be British anyway.[87] Strategic calculations began to shift with the departure from Palestine, since Cyprus provided an alternative. Yet the rise in the premium attached to the island was still gradual. As late as July 1948 the British Chiefs of Staff continued to doubt whether it merited building an airfield there capable of handling up-to-date fighters.[88] Thereafter two factors became apparent. The first, already mentioned, was the pressing need to disperse British army garrisons throughout the region. In this regard Cyprus was a convenient barracks – like Cyrenaica, only a bit less arid and remote.

The second reason proved especially significant. During the late 1940s the British came to feel that their position in and around the eastern Mediterranean was precarious wherever it depended on sufferance, either through treaties, leases or some other kind of written agreement. In contrast, the British felt that they owned Cyprus by virtue of its status as a Crown Colony. It followed that they could do what they liked with it. More and more this trait appeared invaluable. Here was the root of a stubborn British refusal to put their sovereignty over Cyprus at risk, even when it was being wound down elsewhere in the British Empire. Its culmination was a statement by a

Colonial Office minister, Henry Hopkinson, in the House of Commons on 28 July 1954, coming just after confirmation that British Middle East Land Force Headquarters was to move from Suez to the island. Hopkinson's statement now floated the possibility that Cyprus might never qualify for self-determination. 'I am not going so far as that this afternoon,' Hopkinson told the House, trying vainly to mitigate a clearly controversial announcement, 'but I have said that the question of the abrogation of British sovereignty cannot arise – that British sovereignty will remain.'[89] Though this bald intervention was not by any means the sole cause of the subsequent breakdown, it symbolized the gulf that existed.

The move of the Middle East Headquarters to Cyprus had in fact been under way for some time. The *Sunday Times* reported 'scores of Army and Air Force officers and their families [from Egypt] are dividing their time between relaxing on golden beaches and anxious surveys of available private accommodation in Cyprus'.[90] The original idea had been for a planning and logistical centre on the island, and as such one with limited infrastructure (the operation of the Anglo-Libyan Treaty presently eased the pressure on the accommodation of troops). But concern grew in Whitehall – where inflated overseas spending was a key preoccupation – that the move to Cyprus was nonetheless getting out of hand. Churchill's Private Secretary referred to it as being 'absurdly exaggerated' in scale.[91] Churchill ordered an inquiry on the matter, and its subsequent report was in fact to be the last document that he read in 10 Downing Street before handing over to Anthony Eden.[92] Sensitivity on this matter would have been less if the attempt to secure from the Pentagon a convenient affirmation of the strategic significance of Cyprus had not been unavailing. According to the Americans, it did not matter which flag flew over the island, provided it was a friendly one – implying that Greek sovereignty would be just as acceptable to them as British.[93] Nagging doubts as to the validity of Britain's arguments as to the indispensability of their Middle East Headquarters for Western defence were to consistently undermine their position in international opinion.

Although British officialdom in Cyprus had for some time feared an outbreak of violence, they still reckoned that the Greek-Cypriots were too law-abiding to go down such a hazardous route. And even if an outbreak occurred, it was assumed it would be short, sharp and localized like that in 1931. What was wholly unexpected was a Cypriot version of terrorism reminiscent of the Stern and Irgun gangs in Palestine. Why did some Greek-Cypriots, with an indeterminate complicity on the part of 'official' Greece itself, go down such a dangerous route? It was true that Greek-Cypriot leaders, now firmly under the control of the young and determined Archbishop Makarios III, exhausted all other possibilities, including, with Greece's help, a reference to the United Nations in 1954. Yet in retrospect it seems madness to have gambled in this way when the British had lots of ways to exact retribution if they wished. The answer lies partly in the fact that the British had been pushed on the defensive in many parts of the region, so why not, it was argued, in Cyprus? Makarios and his supporters felt, as Franco did in Spain, that Great Britain was an imperial power in decline and vulnerable to pressure (though Franco himself was far too astute to push things to extremes). This was the psychological background to the outbreak of rebellion on April Fool's Day, 1955, when a series of explosions rocked government buildings in Nicosia, Limassol and Larnaca. The perpetrator was an organization called EOKA (Organization of Greek-Cypriot Fighters), led by Colonel George Grivas, a Cypriot veteran in the Greek army with boundless determination but limited understanding of the political ramifications set off by his own actions.

From the first there were three ways that the British could avoid any deadlock in Cyprus. One was to frighten the Greeks into submission by making them understand that continued violence would allow Turkey to get its foot back in the Cypriot door. This was to remain the preferred method of Harold Macmillan, Foreign Secretary in Eden's government. His abrasively cynical attitude was shaped by his own long experience with Greek affairs. 'They [the Greeks] are foolish,' he noted in his diary on 31 August 1955, 'because if seven or eight million Greeks come up against 20 million . . . Turks, they will get a bloody nose.'[94] His chief purpose in convening an international conference on Cyprus during early September 1955 was to make this plain. In fact it became too plain in so far as it led to large anti-Greek riots in Istanbul and threatened a war between Greece and Turkey as fellow members of NATO. For the moment at least this high-risk approach had to be abandoned. The other two approaches were to negotiate with Archbishop Makarios and to ratchet up the security campaign to deal EOKA a knock-out blow. These possibilities were interwoven since, before any draconian repression could be attempted, it was important for publicity reasons to seek a reasonable agreement. To oversee this attempt, and in the wake of the burning down of the British Institute in Nicosia, Eden sacked the hapless Governor, Sir Robert Armitage, and appointed as his replacement Field-Marshal Sir John Harding, who arrived in Cyprus in early October 1955.

A British field-marshal on one side, and a highly political Greek archbishop on the other were bound to make an odd couple, including visually. Each in his way tried hard. As the new Governor put it, their discussions went up hill and down dale.[95] Neither was really his own master. Harding's elbow was jogged by Eden from London, and Makarios's by EOKA from its concealed hide-outs. The Governor stressed throughout that failure to agree would lead to much unpleasantness for all concerned. But when it came to the crunch in late February 1956 the two could not agree. Harding could not promise real responsible government, and Makarios could not promise to stuff the genie of violence back into its bottle. On 9 March 1956 the Archbishop, on his way to Athens, was surrounded on the tarmac of Nicosia Airport by British troops and flown to Mombasa. He was then taken aboard HMS *Loch Fada* and on to exile in the Seychelles. There he was due to be detained in a residence which, while perfectly comfortable in itself, happened to be called 'La Bastille'. Fortunately somebody in Whitehall recognized at the last minute a looming public relations disaster. The local Governor, to his dismay, was swiftly evicted from his country mansion, with its innocuous name of 'Sans Souci', to make way instead for the itinerant Archbishop.[96] Meanwhile, Makarios's absence opened the way to a physical surge against EOKA, though the *Spectator* magazine in London predicted that exile would give the Archbishop 'all the advantage of political martyrdom, without the salient disadvantage of being dead'.[97]

From the early spring of 1956 the British army cracked down hard in Cyprus. With 20,000 troops now in the island, extensive sweeps were made in the countryside. Villages were curfewed. Camps were filled up with detainees. The first of nine capital punishments were carried out on two convicted EOKA operatives on 9 May 1956 (two British corporals were shortly afterwards killed in a 'revenge' execution by EOKA reminiscent of the two sergeants killed by the Stern Gang in Palestine in July 1947). It was in the wake of these executions that for expatriates the old colonial life began to be disrupted. Summer villas in the cool Troodos mountains had to be vacated, and the 'Kyrenia colony' with its curious mix of retired officials and louche writers and artists began to drift off to safer climes, an atmosphere captured by Lawrence Durrell in his *Bitter Lemons*.[98] Durrell had unwisely been persuaded to put his writing skills and rather prosy philhellenism at the disposal of the British propaganda machine in the colony. This proved a forlorn enterprise. One of its notable costs was Durrell's friendship with the Greek poet-diplomat George Seferis.[99]

As in Palestine, the weakest link in the British anti-insurgency effort in Cyprus was intelligence. Very few British officers spoke Greek, and as repression intensified, the few lines of communication that led into the majority community that remained dried up. Had the British army enjoyed some stroke of luck and bagged Grivas himself all might have been well. Virtually cornered in a security drive (Operation Alphonse) in the Troodos mountains in mid-June 1956, EOKA's leader escaped at the last moment. This operation ended in the biggest British loss of the Emergency when twenty-one soldiers were killed during a forest fire, a convoy of Bedford trucks stuck on a single-track mountain road caught in the inferno (such accidents were always a bigger threat than EOKA itself). Already the struggle in Cyprus constituted a parody of the island's curious development as a British colony. The British and the Greek-Cypriots could bash each other about but neither could come out on top. All they did was to play into the hands of other people. By the time this was realized it was too late for the protagonists to retrace their steps.

By mid-1956, however, the British had become almost as worried about the political outlook in Malta as they were about Cyprus. After all, Malta was always more important than Cyprus, and any prospect of disorder there was potentially more troubling. How had things on the George Cross Island of the war years taken such a turn for the worse? To some degree this represented a partial recrudescence of the 'ungovernability' of Malta so prominent in the late 1920s and early

1930s. But it was also made more complicated by the legacy of war. The notable loyalty of the Maltese after 1940 meant that they had a clear claim on the generosity of the London exchequer. As in the case of Gibraltar, a professional economist had been dispatched to Malta in 1945 to assess matters. The ensuing report repeated the obvious: that for centuries the economy had been artificially dependent on 'invisible' exports constituted by services rendered to a foreign military presence, first the Knights and then the British Empire. The report's conclusion on post-war prospects was that this situation might be slightly modified but not fundamentally altered.[100] £42.3 million was duly designated by the British Government to help cover the repair of Malta's war damage. Malta also qualified for political as well as financial generosity, since a firm promise had been made to the Maltese that their old self-governing constitution would be restored to them. But here lay the problem, since the key to the dilemma of public affairs in the island had long been that a community so dependent on external in-flows of capital could not authentically govern itself. What followed was a somewhat tawdry postscript to the wartime experience, with the Maltese feeling that the British were reneging on their earlier commitments, and the British resenting the fact that the Maltese politicians were apparently bent on squeezing the last farthing out of an already overstretched Treasury at home.

In 1947 a new constitution was duly introduced into Malta, incorporating the old diarchical principle of internal self-government married to British control of all external matters such as defence and foreign relations. A general election led to a Labour government headed by Paul Boffa. In so far as it kept out the Nationalists, with the shreds of pro-Italian feeling clinging to them, this was generally welcomed in London. But it also broadly coincided with financial constraints operating in Whitehall that began to rewrite the traditional script of Maltese politics. The first discharge of Maltese dockworkers by the Admiralty occurred in March 1946, and thereafter the Treasury tried to claw back as much of the money promised to Malta as possible, not least to limit the expensive social services that the island's politicians held out to their constituencies while banking on the costs being met by British subventions. Particularly sensitive was the withdrawal of aid for food subsidies in 1949, the year of sterling's first post-war devaluation. As a Colonial Office official sourly put it, the Treasury never forgave Malta for the commitments made to it at the end of the recent conflict.[101] The underlying cycle this created was to be endlessly played out over the next twenty years.

The epicentre of this cycle was Prime Minister Boffa's dynamic deputy, Dom Mintoff. Despite or perhaps compounded by his Oxford education facilitated by a Rhodes Scholarship, Mintoff was as abrasive a politician as any Cypriot counterpart (unlike Archbishop Makarios, for example, he never tried to offset his stringency with personal charm). Mintoff and Makarios, however, shared a key insight: that the British were 'squeezable', providing the pressure was kept up long enough. But whereas the Cypriot Archbishop wanted to get away from Britain, Mintoff was willing to get even closer to them if the price was right. But if he could not get the price he wanted – if, less crudely, the British were not willing to provide the money to transform Malta's dependent and unstable economy – then Mintoff was prepared to pursue an anti-British line. He went significantly beyond anything ever contemplated by the gentlemanly *italianità* Nationalists whom he so despised. A vision of a Maltese Malta, with a distinctly leftist colouring, was always to be at the heart of Mintoff's politics, and from which it derived its edgy feel; this was the era, too, when the Maltese vernacular was ceasing to be just the medium of everyday speech and acquired a much wider usage. Meanwhile Mintoff's style and strong inclinations clashed with those of Boffa, and their rivalry culminated in splitting the Malta Labour Party and letting in a Nationalist ministry led first by Enrico Mizzi and then by Borg Olivier.

Before long Maltese politics experienced a familiar 'descent into the abyss', defined by fiscal impasse and political deadlock. Sir John Martin, highly influential on Mediterranean matters in Whitehall, commented that the proper working of the present constitution depended on give-and-take, something absent from Maltese ministers of either party in power, 'whose dealings with HMG are those of a Levantine carpet-seller'.[102] Full self-government Martin considered completely out of the question for wayward Malta. Borg Olivier's relationship with the British always bore the scars of this time. For one thing, he believed that the British retained a sneaking preference for Mintoff, despite the latter's aggressive manners. In the light of later events this is paradoxical, but there was some cause for Borg Olivier's suspicion. Lord Mountbatten, as Commander-in-Chief of the Mediterranean Fleet, still saw Mintoff as being on the right side of the old Anglo-*italianità* divide and, for much the same reason, rather approved of his anti-clericalism.[103] When after a general election Mintoff became Labour Prime Minister of Malta in June 1955 there was therefore uncertainty in London, but by no means complete pessimism.

Mintoff came to power with one central aim that might on the face of it seem entirely comforting in Whitehall: that of integrating Malta with the United Kingdom itself. This was logical if it was believed that in the words of the British politician Richard Crossman, the island 'was as much part of Britain as . . . Portsmouth, Devonport and Pembroke'.[104] Mintoff's urgent advocacy was also propitious in its timing. Regional tensions in 1955 meant that the Chiefs of Staff in London were adamant that Malta was actually becoming more important rather than less. The Maltese could not now simply be left 'to go bust in their own way', as had sometimes been suggested.[105] The rapidly deteriorating situation in Cyprus put a gloss on Mintoff's desire to make Malta one with Britain. 'If we don't accept,' Harold Macmillan noted with his trademark acidity, 'we shall be shooting the Cypriots for wanting to leave us and the Maltese for wanting to join us.'[106] But the most fundamental appeal was intrinsic to Malta itself: to solve those constitutional dilemmas, so intractable ever since the 1880s.[107]

Yet although the British Government approved the principle of integration, and convened an Anglo-Maltese Round Table Conference to discuss its terms, there were problems. Above all, Mintoff's conception involved bringing about an 'equivalence' of United Kingdom and Maltese living standards. The likely cost of this met with an overwhelming lack of enthusiasm in the Treasury. There were also domestic British implications. A Scottish Office minister resigned over the matter, since any union with Malta would reduce the cash available to sustain the older Union of 1707.[108] In the House of Lords, a high Protestant faction raised the problem of unacceptable marriage laws, a traditional Anglo-Maltese stumbling block. Religious sensitivity in England paled before the opposition of the clerical hierarchy in Malta. When a British delegation went to Valletta in October 1955, they sought to assure Archbishop Gonzi that integration would not harm his Church, but this got nowhere. It was clear that any move towards Anglo-Maltese union would split the island down the middle in a replay of the early 1930s, only worse. The result of the Maltese referendum on the matter in March 1956 did not dissipate these concerns, because although – somewhat to Archbishop Gonzi's discomfiture – a majority of those who voted approved integration, this represented significantly less than half of the eligible electorate. As so often in Maltese elections, the outcome was interpreted in wholly contrasting ways by the main protagonists.

Many felt integration was a recipe for heightened Anglo-Maltese disillusionment rather than otherwise. Yet British ministers were aware that if it stalled completely there might be disorder as Mintoff carried out his threat to veer off on a very different course.[109] The Governor's information that the police were 'rotten to the core' helped to emphasize the dangerous situation taking shape.[110] It was against this background, and the far worse events in Cyprus, that during a balmy evening on 26 July 1956 Gamal Abdul Nasser announced to the delight of a huge crowd in Alexandria that the Suez Canal Company had been nationalized. In the crisis conditions that followed, during which the emergency use of Valletta's Grand Harbour for an invasion of Egypt loomed, it was crucial for Britain to keep integration on the table, if only to avoid a complete break with Mintoff.[111] For the latter here was a heaven-sent opportunity to make his influence tell.[112] Keenly aware that the Governor, Sir Robert Laycock, had all the reserved powers he needed in an emergency, at no point did Mintoff try openly to block the military and naval build-up that got under way. But there is some evidence that information was passed to the Egyptian leader, who had sent his own agents to both Malta and Cyprus to assess British readiness for action.[113]

Indeed, the very timing of Nasser's historic speech in Alexandria on the Canal was determined by the arrival of this intelligence from Valletta and Cyprus, symbolizing the close connections between Britain's various Mediterranean embarrassments.[114] Meanwhile the news of the Canal's fate reached London when Eden was hosting a dinner at 10 Downing Street for guests including the Iraqi strong-man premier, Nuri-es-Said. Nuri's advice to Eden was: 'You must hit him [Nasser] hard, and you must hit him now.'[115] As Mountbatten – First Sea Lord at the Admiralty, and soon to be a critic of the invasion of Egypt – advised, the Fleet could be ready to sail from Valletta in eight hours.[116] It has often been argued that had the British struck quickly, perhaps Nasser might have been cowed, or a coup against him precipitated in Cairo. It was the decision to go through the motions of seeking a negotiated solution, and then a laborious and delayed intervention in what proved a fatal tie-up with France and Israel, which brought about such a deeply humiliating outcome. It is clear though that for Britain any solution based on large-scale force was bound to end badly.

Eden was determined from the first to use force, as soon as he could. The assault had to be seaborne as this was the only way of delivering the troops and logistics to seize a sufficient slice of Egyptian soil to hold as a bargaining chip or what Eden called a 'gauge'. But where should the point of entry be? Alexandria was the obvious choice, because it offered the most direct route to press on to Cairo if necessary. The other option, Port Said, had the disadvantage of British troops having to traverse a long causeway cutting inland. But a frontal attack on Egypt's second city was in the end too forbidding. 'There is one thing in this that I simply cannot stomach,' a British minister summed it up, 'and that is the bombardment of the open city of Alexandria.'[117] Wrapped up in moral revulsion was something practical. Any such bombardment might well trigger that recurring nightmare, a massacre of Europeans. Nor was it likely that help for the Europeans could arrive in time. The choice of Port Said, where it would be easier to provide protection for a much smaller European community, arose from these concerns. Significantly, at no point in the ensuing events were any European civilians in fact physically harmed, though physical assets were seized and foreign nationals were interned for the duration. Suez was undoubtedly a serious diplomatic disaster; but it was not a major human tragedy as in some scenarios it might well have become. This explains the irony that the after-effects on British foreign policy were to prove more lasting than on Anglo-Egyptian relations, which recovered remarkably quickly.

Over the late summer and early autumn of 1956 the deployments for an invasion of Egypt (Operation Musketeer) were made. The preliminary aerial attacks were to be launched necessarily from Cyprus, but since there was still no proper airbase there aeroplanes had to be crammed wing-tip to wing-tip on the Nicosia strip. Parachute units currently on duty had to be taken home to Britain for last-minute training, because there were no local facilities. Cyprus' general limitations meant that the main seaborne thrust had to come from Malta, more than 900 miles from Port Said. The Mediterranean Fleet at Valletta was reinforced, including three aircraft carriers. The intention had been also to concentrate an armoured division in Libya on Egypt's border, so adding to Nasser's anxieties. Libyan opinion, however, swung heavily to Egypt's side, and the British Ambassador warned that troop movements would only trigger a wave of protest.[118] A Royal Navy cruiser even had to be readied to take King Idris away if the situation deteriorated.[119] This exposed the strategic hollowness of Britain's Libyan engagement. At last, on the night of Saturday, 28 October notices passed around the pubs and clubs of Valletta and its harbour towns that all naval officers were called to an urgent briefing. The following day truckloads of men and equipment gathered on the parade-ground at Floriana before rumbling down to the harbour, from which the aircraft carriers sailed out of Grand Harbour, as always with a large crowd of Maltese gathered to watch. This spectacle, unknown to anyone present, was the swansong, by now delusive, of a century and a half of British military operations in the Mediterranean. A much larger flotilla followed in their wake.[120] Bitter fighting was already taking place as the Israelis made their pre-arranged attack on Egypt, feinting towards the Canal, before making for their real objective, Sharm-el-Shaikh, controlling the entry to the Gulf of Aqaba. This provided the British and the French – the latter hoping to end Nasser's support for the rebellion against their rule in Algeria – with a patently rigged excuse to invade Egypt.

Early on the morning of 1 November the first wave of British planes from Cyprus arrived over Cairo and dropped their bombs on the international airport (some inevitably missed and landed on civilian areas). The object was to 'take out' the Egyptian air force, most of which anyway had been moved away for safety. At 7.15 a.m. on 5 November the 3rd Parachute Battalion was dropped onto a small spit of land 4 miles from Port Said, with one fatality. The 2nd Régiment Parachutiste Coloniaux followed. Photographic reconnaissance indicating that there would be strong resistance proved correct, and hand-to-hand fighting took place with Egyptian troops. That night British soldiers were holed up near a sewage farm. Meanwhile in Port Said loudspeakers were calling on the population to take up arms and European civilians still at large took refuge in the Italian consulate. Next day Royal Navy gunfire – its calibre kept to a minimum – opened up on the Port Said beachfront to 'soften it up' for landings by marine commandos. After they got ashore light armoured vehicles went up and down the streets of the town with a continued line of fire on all sides.[121] With the importance that symbols always had in Britain's Mediterranean affairs, Navy House – which had been so reluctantly relinquished to the Egyptians two years before – was the chief British goal, and equally the point most strongly held by defenders. The fierce fighting there held up the British advance. Perhaps appropriately, shortly before dark this old symbol of British naval preponderance was completely destroyed.

Already, however, the international storm was making the continuance of the invasion impossible. With Port Said securely held, British units made a dash down the causeway, but they were caught in the middle when the ceasefire cut off the offensive. 'Tactically,' a senior brigadier remarked of the prevailing situation, 'our position could not be worse.'[122] British and French forces had suffered 23 killed and 121 wounded. The 'gauge' held in return for these losses was much smaller than had been intended; but even a bigger one would have made no difference since the diplomatic leverage of the Eden government was broken. No British personnel served in the United Nations Emergency Force shortly sent in to police the affected areas, and British salvage vessels were not permitted to help clear the Canal of blockages. On 23 December 1956 the last British troops left Port Said. This time it was a definitive military departure from Egyptian soil. The troops did so at night – as Lord Cromer, Britain's greatest proconsul in the country, had once done – to avoid incidents. Immediately a large crowd gathered in the harbour area, where the statue of Ferdinand de Lesseps, that French facilitator of British ascendancy in Egypt, was blown off his pedestal. This, too, was appropriate. Since before the days of Napoleon and Nelson, the British and the French had striven to dominate the Mediterranean, sometimes against each other, sometimes yoked against a common enemy. It was logical that at this juncture they went down together. In Philip Mansel's vivid description, this was the end of Alexandria's modern history as a cosmopolitan and Levantine city, in which the British had long been a leading, if not the largest, element in the foreign population.[123]

The United States' key role in ensuring that the gamble at Suez failed highlighted the specifically Mediterranean background of Anglo-American mutual suspicion. British and American differences over Palestine had been contained in the later 1940s but it was as the NATO alliance bedded down after its formation in 1949 that problems emerged over regional command structures, including the nationality of commanders-in-chief. In the Mediterranean, the British were determined to retain supreme Allied command over naval forces, and furthermore that this British-led force should not be subordinated to a higher authority in continental Europe.[124] Before 1945 the Americans backed down whenever the British insisted on their desired prerogatives in this area at least. By the early 1950s they were ceasing to do so, and particularly insistent on retaining control over the Sixth Fleet. This meant keeping that force firmly under an American supremo at Southern European Command based in Naples. This Command's duties were defined within the overall concept of the southern flank of NATO, depriving the Mediterranean, with its Black Sea adjunct, of that coherence long associated with the doctrines of the British Fleet.

Permanently on station after mid-1948, the Sixth Fleet also overshadowed the Royal Navy in terms of sheer power afloat. 'We [British] in the Mediterranean', Mountbatten, then Commander-in-Chief in Valletta, complained during February 1952, 'are being shown up the whole time by the Sixth Fleet who send their colossal ships following largely in our wake, with powerful press propaganda to show how much superior they are to us.'[125] Mountbatten's relations with his Naples-based American counterpart, Admiral Robert Carney, were extremely poor. With Mountbatten's departure to become First Sea Lord, tensions eased. A compromise was cobbled together whereby his successor combined being British Commander-in-Chief with an Allied Forces Mediterranean Command based in Malta, still subordinate, however, to NATO's Commander-in-Chief South at Naples. Inevitably in these conditions the two main navies in the area regarded each other with distrust during the botched invasion of Egypt.[126] Nor did this distrust wholly disappear afterwards, extending well into the 1960s.

Suez also had an impact on developments in Cyprus, not least by presenting EOKA with unforeseen opportunities. The organization's 'kill rate', hitherto averaging ten per month, shot up to twenty-five after October 1956, before falling back again in early 1957. Eden's successor as Prime Minister, Harold Macmillan, was conscious from the first that Cyprus might prove his nemesis as Egypt had been that of Eden. Very early on in his leadership the suggestion came up that what Britain needed was no longer Cyprus as an island, but just bases on Cyprus – a very different proposition altogether. But sensitive Tory emotions at home meant that any transition had to be tentative and ready to be reversed if necessary. A crucial marker was the release from detention of Archbishop Makarios in April 1957, though he was not allowed back into Cyprus and went to Athens instead, where he lingered in helpless impotence. The severity of anti-insurgency operations in the island was reduced, while for its part EOKA called a truce. Harding's recall in October was another important change. He was replaced not by a soldier but by Sir Hugh Foot, who possessed liberal credentials both in his record as a colonial service official and through his family background (he was the elder brother of the radical Labour politician Michael Foot). Before going back to London, Harding nonetheless made clear his opinion that the responsibility for failure to end violence lay not with the British security machinery, nor really with EOKA; it lay, he told British colleagues assembled for his emotional farewell, with the Greek-Cypriot people themselves, who had been given the chance to turn away from murder and had not done so.[127] This was a highly simplified and prejudicial view. A mirror-image version was entertained by most Greek-Cypriots.

The most fundamental division was now not one between the British and Greek-Cypriots, but that between the Greeks and Turks in Cyprus (respectively 80 and 18 per cent of the overall population). Partly because the Turkish-Cypriots played a prominent role within the British security apparatus after 1955, ethnic tensions had been exacerbated. The allegation made against the British is that they divided and ruled between the opposing communities. It may be true that had the British helped to actively suppress Turkish-Cypriot protests,

Cyprus might have been safely passed to Greece without triggering a crisis, not least because Turkey was not yet in a position to do much about it. But the British had no intention of doing this because by 1956 Turkey had acquired a new significance for their interests in the eastern Mediterranean and Middle East. This was why the British Government made it clear that, if self-determination was ever to be applied to Cyprus, it would be offered not to the Cypriots as a single people, but to the two peoples in the island, that is, to the separate Greek and Turkish communities. Just in case Macmillan and Sir Hugh Foot shared any temptation to go back on this promise, the Turkish-Cypriots launched a series of violent riots of their own after early 1958. By this stage Britain seemed to be confronting the same nightmare scenario as in Palestine a decade earlier: caught between two intractable ethnic and 'national' forces with no way out except a humiliating exit.

There was one 'solution', however, from which the British had drawn back in Palestine, but which was still possible in Cyprus. This was to make what a senior British official in Nicosia termed a 'choice of evils', meaning to side more or less openly with one of the protagonists, and to press the resulting logic relentlessly until the weaker (that is, the Greek) party caved in.[128] This was the essence of the so-called Macmillan Plan which unfolded through the summer of 1958, under the terms of which Cyprus would remain British for seven more years, but in the meantime Greece and Turkey would be associated with the administration. In this way Ankara was accorded a formal role in Cypriot affairs for the first time since 1923. It was in a desperate attempt to throw this plan off course that in September 1958 Archbishop Makarios and the Greek Government reluctantly accepted in principle that *Enosis* was impossible, and that some form of 'protected' or guaranteed independence offered the only escape. So began a series of diplomatic moves, culminating under purely Graeco-Turkish auspices at the Zurich Conference in early February 1959, and immediately afterwards at a conference at Lancaster House in London that included the British Government and the various Cypriot parties. From these exchanges emerged an agreement to establish an independent Republic of Cyprus, but one where independence was qualified (or as Greek-Cypriots thought, 'fettered') both by special rights for the Turkish minority and also by the right of intervention given to Britain, Greece and Turkey as guarantors of the settlement. Crucially for Britain, she was to retain base areas under her own sovereignty, as well as various other facilities spread through the island. As Macmillan defined the British requirement at this stage by way of analogy, 'we only need our Gibraltars'.[129]

As with most settlements after similar late-colonial struggles, claims and counterclaims were always to be made as to who won and who lost the struggle over Cyprus in the 1950s. According to the subsequent folk memory of the Greek-Cypriot majority, EOKA won a glorious victory against the British, even if it was one mitigated by devious Great Power politics. In contrast, the British army claimed at the time that EOKA was on the ropes, and would have been completely defeated if the Emergency had continued for much longer (the same kind of claim the French army was to make for itself in Algeria). According to the Commander-in-Chief, General Sir Kenneth Darling, British intelligence even knew where Grivas was hiding during the Lancaster House meeting, and only Macmillan's firm instruction prevented EOKA's leader from being killed in the course of an arrest.[130] Certainly in the wake of agreement the British made sure that Grivas's exit from the island back to Greece provided no opportunity for a public display of Greek triumphalism. The British officer put in charge of overseeing this event on 19 March 1959 was a patrician member of the Coldstream Guards, Colonel Bill Gore-Langton. This officer had two recommendations for the task. The first was that he was six feet five inches tall, and so could look down on the diminutive Grivas as he proceeded to the waiting aircraft, and the second was that he had no right arm, and so had the best possible excuse for not saluting.[131]

Yet the particularity of the British colonial experience in Cyprus by no means ended there. A medley of factors repeatedly delayed the implementation of independence.[132] For one thing, a constitution had to be drawn up, and it is notable that this was one colony where the British themselves did not have any part in drafting the details, if only because to varying degrees they were mistrusted on all sides. Another cause of delay lay in the haggling between Archbishop Makarios and Governor Foot over the precise size and status of the British base areas. It was only when this matter was cleared up to British satisfaction in July 1960 that the way was open for Cypriot independence to take place on the following 16 August. This was, however, far from being an unreservedly enthusiastic event on anybody's part. The Greek-Cypriots were not receiving the gift of *Enosis* they had craved and the Turkish-Cypriots were not gaining the partition they thought had come within their grasp. As for the British, there was, strikingly, no personal representative sent by Queen Elizabeth II to Nicosia to underline good wishes for the future, nor any Cabinet-level representative of the British Government. Cypriots had to make do with Governor Foot presiding over the more formal parts of the handover. The judgement of a junior Whitehall official sent to observe the occasion concluded that Cypriot independence had got off to as good a start as could be expected in all the circumstances. This description was uncannily like that of Ambassador Trevelyan in the wake of the British departure from Egypt in June 1954. British departures from the Mediterranean, indeed, shared a certain pathology, one very different from the pomp and circumstance but also, perhaps, plain fakery that accompanied 'freedoms at midnight' in the contemporary Afro-Caribbean world.

Just as the Suez affair had shifted the foundations of British rule in Cyprus, predictably it shaped developments in Malta as well. A United Kingdom White Paper on defence heralded a greater reliance on the atomic deterrent, and less on conventional forces, including bases and garrisons overseas. The implications were profound. With regard to Malta it offered a useful bludgeon to use against Prime Minister Mintoff's attempts to put a high price on his continuing co-operation, including terms for sealing a deal on integration with the United Kingdom. The British Defence Minister, Duncan Sandys, struck a firm note in Valletta during April 1957 when he told Mintoff and his colleagues that there remained a deep sentiment of goodwill for Malta in Britain, but bluntly warned them that in the strategic circumstances of the post-Suez world the island was of much less importance than heretofore.[133] Sandys seemed little moved when reminded of the moral obligation that the British owed to the Maltese for their wartime sacrifices. But announcing grandiose new defence policies was one thing, and implementing them was quite another. Mintoff was still prepared to gamble that the British were by no means willing to actually leave the island, and until they did that they remained vulnerable to his special brand of blackmail: pay up or face trouble. Hard bargaining continued sporadically through 1957, but amid the ill-feeling the dream of integration had really died. In early March 1958 Mintoff decided to resign as premier. In doing so he posed the issue of whether the British were able to govern Malta without him. In fact he was to remain out of power for over a decade.

Mintoff, however, was right in one thing. The British could not yet govern Malta with Borg Olivier and his Nationalist party, because the latter demanded full independence, and this was no more acceptable in London than Mintoff's expensive integration. But there remained a further option. This was a reversion to direct rule, or, as one British official in Valletta put it, 'closing down Maltese democracy for a while'.[134] In late April this is what happened. With the Emergency still going on in Cyprus, it was a risky enterprise, especially with a question mark over the reliability of the police. But in Malta certain factors lessened the dangers. Much of the island's more affluent classes were happy to see British authority reasserted. Archbishop Gonzi positively opposed independence because it could be used by the Church's enemies on the left. The hesitation of many Maltese was understandable when such a large percentage remained directly or indirectly dependent on employment offered by the British military services. In the event, local personnel in the police and the administration remained at their posts. Although there was some trouble on the streets, it was effectively contained. The island settled down for a further period of rule from the Governor's palace, or as Wellington had liked to think of it, the foredeck of a British man-of-war.

An immediate task for the colonial administration was to stabilize the economy.[135] In the first instance this meant the dockyard, slated for cuts in the new British defence programme. A private company, Baileys, was brought in after 1958 to offset these losses by developing private dock contracts. So began a long and unsatisfactory saga. Ultimately more important was ensuring that new jobs were created outside the docks. A Five Year Development Plan was introduced in 1959. Malta was not without practical advantages. The island had a good education system, a stock of skills (not least in the old Admiralty workshops) transferable to fresh tasks, a central position in the

Mediterranean and proximity to substantial markets. These advantages were often what had made Malta important to the British in the first place. The island also had sunshine and culture, so that tourism offered real possibilities, though the obstacles were initially considerable. There were very few hotels, many of them still catering mostly for Royal Naval business. For some time after the war public entertainment consisted, as the *Times of Malta* observed, only of poor cinemas with hard seats.[136] Nor did Malta's image as a proud fortress reduced to rubble after 1941 help. It did not suggest the sort of place that one wanted to take a holiday. But cruise ships started visiting Grand Harbour again in 1950, and British travel agents experimented with family air packages from the middle of the decade. By the late 1950s there was the basis for a push towards development. This transition to a very different Malta was to face many disappointments, and meanwhile reductions in local British defence spending caused successive spurts of unemployment. Nevertheless, even if this only became clear in retrospect, the 1960s were to prove an era of change. Without it, the political turbulence, in which the British were so much involved, might have spilled out in more dangerous directions than eventually proved to be the case.

But direct British rule could hardly go on for long. It was, as the Colonial Office admitted, like 'a cork in a bottle', liable to fly out at any moment from accumulated pressure.[137] During July 1960 the British Government announced a Constitutional Commission, led by Sir Hilary Blood, to explore a new representative (but still not responsible) constitution for Malta. The result was unveiled in March 1961. Along with the essentially rhetorical flourish of an Anglo-Maltese partnership, it offered a modified version of the old diarchy, with internal self-government plus an innovation in concurrent or shared responsibility in external affairs.[138] Defence, internal security and especially police matters, however, remained a solely British sphere. But this limited form of self-government, though ostensibly inaugurating a new 'State of Malta', was not likely to prove durable, any more than earlier hybrid Maltese constitutions in 1887, 1921 or 1947 had done. The vital question was: could the British persuade enough Maltese politicians to accept office on such a basis? Above all, could they persuade

Borg Olivier to do so, with the temptation that the powers involved might be enough to keep Mintoff out in the cold?

This persuasion took some time, but in March 1962 Borg Olivier agreed to take the plunge and form a ministry on the basis of the Blood formula. In a general election in August 1962 the combined influences of the Church, the old Maltese bourgeoisie and the British managed to fend off the challenge of Mintoff and the Malta Labour Party. By this time Whitehall, and more particularly the armed services, were gradually coming round to the idea that independence combined with a defence agreement was now enough to ensure the scaled-down military presence that was required. As Sir Roy Grantham, the Governor, rather sourly described the message coming from his masters at home, it was clear that Malta 'is no longer to be regarded as of real importance as a Navy, Army and Air Force base'.[139] Since the Church could not allow itself to be seen as the only remaining obstacle in the path of a new Malta, even Archbishop Gonzi had tactfully to qualify his intransigent opposition to independence. Finally, a conference at Marlborough House in London in August 1963 set the goal of Maltese independence for the following May.

Yet in Malta any step forward was always subject to several steps backwards. The Maltese political parties themselves might fall apart on exploring the details of an independence constitution. For one thing, it was clear that independence would not lessen the acute divisiveness in the island's politics. There was also a chance that the British would entertain second thoughts themselves. The old colonial wing of the Conservative Party indeed had second thoughts in the light of the clashes between Greek- and Turkish-Cypriots at the outset of 1964, and the de facto collapse of the 1960 Cyprus settlement. This raised a query over the long-term future of the British bases there, leading to the argument that Malta, after all, was too valuable to be given up.[140] But any retreat from Maltese independence so late in the day meant facing the likelihood of uniting all the island's parties against the British. It would also irreparably damage Borg Olivier's reputation; and by 1964, whatever his perceived deficiencies in London, he had become the only real vehicle for British interests.[141] It was therefore essential to elevate him as 'the architect of Malta's independence'.[142] Independence Day at last arrived slightly later than originally planned, therefore, on 21 September 1964.

If Cypriot independence in 1960 had been a low-key affair, nobody had expected the day itself to end in violence. This, however, was an apprehension in Malta, where there was talk about possible civil war in the run-up to the handover.[143] In the eyes of Mintoff and his supporters, the approach to the impending change had been rigged in favour of their opponents. They believed that the new regime was to be one of form rather than substance, one with Malta continuing to recognize Queen Elizabeth II as sovereign, and Grantham's successor as Governor, Sir Maurice Dorman, staying on in the alternative role of Governor-General. At least in Cyprus the British had been penned into two base areas. In Malta the British service presence was to remain more or less throughout the island. Lack of consensus fuelled concern over internal security surrounding the transfer of power. In particular, anxiety attached to the Duke of Edinburgh as the Queen's representative at the ceremony. It was feared that he might get caught in the cross-fire of an attempt to assassinate Borg Olivier during the main event held in the graceful Valletta suburb of Floriana.[144] Fortunately on 21 September nothing drastic occurred to the Duke or anybody else. Many thousands of Maltese gathered to watch the massed service bands. Naval teams put on an elaborate display, culminating in the formation of the Maltese Cross with its wartime associations. Grand Harbour was illuminated for the occasion, and there was much waving of the Maltese flag and even a few Union Jacks. But there was a darker side. Throughout the celebrations, along the main street of Kingsway and in Palace Square, groups of rowdy Malta Labour Party supporters engaged in scuffles and traded insults.[145] But then politics in Malta had always been a rough trade, and the celebration – with its festa-like mix of bands, navalism, royalty, clerical dignitaries, visitors from the villages and urban fisticuffs – was somehow appropriate.

Had Maltese independence come at a time of growing prosperity and escalating tax revenues, the idiosyncratic compromise it represented – in which British sovereignty had gone, but the British themselves remained much as always – could have worked. Instead, 1964 was the precursor of severe economic difficulties. The treasury in Valletta was almost empty, and the one in London was in no position to top it up. A new British Labour government under Harold Wilson after October 1964 was immediately beset by financial and currency pressures, and set out on a succession of defence cuts. Here was another all too familiar cycle. The Maltese saw the British as still 'trying to buy their way out of Malta on the cheap', while the British thought that the Maltese were not living up to their new responsibilities.[146]

The psychological pitfalls were exemplified when Sir John Martin, Britain's High Commissioner in Valletta, spoke at the most prestigious social club, the Casino Maltese, in November 1966. In defending Britain's record, he energetically listed examples of the tangible evidence of British aid: the new University, the Law Courts, the College of Arts, Science and Technology, the multiplying hotels and the industrial estates. But what grated badly with his hearers was the stark comment that Malta 'could not be a British pensioner for ever'.[147] This seemed a bit rich given the fact that for decades past the Maltese had, as one Governor had once put it, been 'taught to look to Great Britain for all their benefits'[148] (indeed, the politics of Dom Mintoff had always essentially been about holding the British to such rhetoric). One of Martin's staff afterwards commented that although the members of Maltese society that he constantly met at cocktail parties were outwardly well-disposed to Britain, even sending their children to be educated there, he could not help wondering whether beneath such surface cordiality political attitudes were not drifting in other directions.[149]

Yet not everything was bleak in Anglo-Maltese relations. The tourist industry was beginning to boom, and most holidaymakers arrived at Luqa Airport on BOAC flights from Britain. When the Labour government, indeed, put limits on currency transfers outside the sterling area at this time, Malta was an important beneficiary.[150] Whatever their squabbles, one factor in particular still pushed Borg Olivier and the British together, and ensured that a bit more money was squeezed from Whitehall to finance a revised defence agreement: the spectre of a Mintoff victory at the next Maltese general election.[151]

In contrast to Malta, Gibraltar had escaped the worst of the cuts in British defence spending in the Mediterranean from 1957 onwards. A record of 'good behaviour' and overt loyalty helped. But that very loyalty was increasingly a provocation to Madrid as it continued to emerge from post-war ostracism. An important change came with the more or less enforced abandonment of the Spanish Protectorate in Morocco during 1955, though the little enclaves of Ceuta and Melilla were retained. This gave more flexibility to Spanish diplomacy. Three American bases had been built by the end of the 1950s, including what the *New York Times* hailed as 'the mightiest American naval installation in Europe'[152] at Rota, previously a small fishing village near Cadiz. Rota was generally regarded as more important for NATO than British facilities at Gibraltar. In December 1959 President Eisenhower visited Spain – a considerable lift for Franco's standing. Simultaneously a stabilization plan backed by the World Bank offered the prospect of alleviating Spain's considerable economic problems. Spain was still fragile, and still not in NATO, but she was more able to strike poses, and poses were important for a regime increasingly under pressure – above all among its own people – for having outlived its purposes.

Britain's continuing hold over Gibraltar presented the obvious outlet for pent-up Spanish feelings and its constitutional development provided a pretext. As long as the colony's constitutional evolution had kept within certain strict limits the process had been ignored in Madrid. The move to a ministerial system in 1964, however, led to a Spanish complaint that the Treaty of Utrecht had now been fundamentally breached. But what gave force to this protest was the novel tendency to wrap Spain's sense of injustice up in anti-colonial rhetoric, less burdened as she was with her own long-standing North African baggage. Spanish diplomats were able to develop arguments arising from a recent resolution by the United Nations Special Committee that 'all peoples have an inalienable right to complete freedom, the exercise of their sovereignty and the integrity of their national territory', meaning in this case that Spanish integrity would not be complete till Gibraltar was returned. The UN body simply 'noted' the Anglo-Spanish disagreement over Gibraltar and encouraged the two governments to go into negotiations, which they did in a rather stuttering fashion. But the whole balance of debate in New York now favoured Spain as a victim of a bigger imperial power.

Activity at the United Nations was only one tactic on the part of

Spain to prod the British over Gibraltar. Another was an increase in the impediments to movement across the Rock's land frontier. From 1963 Fernando Maria Castiella as Franco's Foreign Minister, with a track record of pressing the Gibraltar issue, introduced a variety of vexatious restrictions. In 1964 vehicle traffic into and out of Gibraltar was down by some 70 per cent, hitting business and tourism.[153] An enhanced nervousness was expressed in the suspicions of Gibraltarians that British ministers might actually welcome a face-saving deal, such as an Anglo-Spanish condominium, if they could get one without causing a political storm in the House of Commons. These suspicions were not without some cause;[154] and if Franco had died, say, in the early 1960s, so removing an ideological obstacle, perhaps something along these lines might indeed have emerged.

But there was little prospect of that after the election in October 1964 of the Labour government which had so many important ideological roots in the Spanish Civil War. Denis Healey, the Minister of Defence in the new Cabinet and as such concerned with Gibraltar, once referred to Franco's rule as 'a dictatorship softened by slovenliness'.[155] When Castiella tightened the screw on Gibraltar further, so that cars were now taking up to six hours to cross the frontier, and with rumours circulating of a complete closure of the frontier gates, the Labour government sought to reinforce its position by announcing a referendum among Gibraltar's inhabitants in September 1967. The result was a foregone conclusion. In the weeks before the referendum whole streets had been painted red, white and blue by residents while the Union Jack flew from the windows and balconies of most dwellings.[156] Of 12,138 electors, only 44 signified a wish for a change from British sovereignty. The process carried further what had become a slow-moving but increasingly assertive affirmation of a specifically Gibraltarian feeling, in which the natural obverse of being pro-British was now to be fiercely anti-Spanish. This dialectical and slightly embarrassing zeal was not something that Whitehall wished to encourage, since it would be difficult to 'manage down' if that ever appeared necessary, but circumstances made it hard to stop.

By this stage there was a possibility that the Spanish authorities would themselves go down the most direct route possible: a military *coup de main* against the fortress itself. Had such a physical attack been launched there was little the British could have done, although a reinforcement of the garrison was made in the wake of the referendum. Yet Spanish diplomats had spent too much effort over the years digging themselves out of isolation to undertake such a damaging exercise. It also had to be considered what the delayed British response to coercion might be, especially by a government already accused of weakness and vacillation over Rhodesia.[157] In the febrile atmosphere of British politics prevailing from the mid-1960s, the final reaction would probably have been severe – the later eruption over the Falklands showed how aggressive Britain could still be over such matters.[158] It was in any case in the tradition of Anglo-Spanish controversy over the Rock that Madrid discreetly chose the next level down in terms of escalation, and eventually closed the frontier to Gibraltar completely on 8 June 1969. Shortly afterwards the ferry link between Algeciras and the Rock was cut – again, never renewed so far.

Because this action had been foreshadowed, contingency plans were already in place. What mattered was not the closure of the frontier as such, apart from hitting tourism, but the loss of the incoming Spanish workforce. This was met in part by the arrangements made for the import of Moroccan labour. In the longer term what occurred was a radical reshaping of Gibraltar's economy away from its traditional if much eroded orientation towards a Spanish hinterland. Its most immediate effect was the deserted air over the bars in La Linea that traditionally catered to customers passing to and from the Rock. Meanwhile the Labour government had now become something of a hostage on the Gibraltar issue. The crucial outcome was the granting of a new constitution in July 1969, the last clause of which resoundingly declared that 'Her Majesty's Government will never enter into arrangements under which the people of Gibraltar will pass under the sovereignty of another state against their freely and democratically expressed wishes'. There was nothing wholly novel about such a declaration. British ministers had said similar things in various settings. But now it was entrenched in a constitutional document under the authority of the Crown. No future Prime Minister or Cabinet was going to get out of that very easily. Arguably this was the single most important statement made on the sovereignty of Gibraltar since the signature of the Treaty of Utrecht.[159]

In order to damp down any Spanish reaction to this constitutional move, the Royal Navy's presence at Gibraltar had been boosted by the presence of an aircraft carrier and two guided missile destroyers. The fact that a British general election loomed was not unrelated.[160] But Gibraltar was always surrounded by shadow-play. Neither the British nor the Spanish government wanted to face a potentially uncontrollable crisis over the Rock. The Spanish were soon much more preoccupied with issues of succession as Franco's health deteriorated, and with the dangers of Basque terrorism. By 1974 the question was very much in abeyance.[161] After Franco's death in November 1975 it was relegated to the margins during the bumpy transition to Spanish democracy. This did not mean that Madrid's claim was abandoned. British royalty and Gibraltar had always been touchy matters for Spanish opinion, and in 1981 King Juan Carlos and Queen Sophia did not attend the wedding of the Prince of Wales and Lady Diana Spencer, because the honeymoon cruise was to begin in Gibraltar.[162] Yet any fear of an attack on the Rock entirely faded from view. In December 1982, with Spain negotiating entry to the European Union, the land frontier with Gibraltar was at last reopened, though the years of closure had consigned the old hyphenated, Anglo-Spanish world of the Rock and its *campo* to a distant memory. What had taken its place was a more cosmopolitan, economically diverse, self-conscious, Anglo-Gibraltarian Rock, one prepared to wave a Union Jack at the slightest sign of any perceived threat to its security or identity. This overseas patriotism might seem distinctly quaint viewed from the United Kingdom of the 1980s and 1990s, but even quaintness could be turned to advantage, so that the Rock somehow came to symbolize values and beliefs from which Britain itself had long strayed.

Meanwhile, in the grand narrative of the British Mediterranean, the later 1960s heralded a basic change. The great Fleet that had brought it into being and sustained its existence was gradually ceasing to exist. British naval strength in the Mediterranean had been the main victim of the pronounced 'East of Suez' shift after 1960 (with its emphasis on protecting British client states in the Persian Gulf). By 1964 the Mediterranean Fleet was down to a small escort squadron and some coastal minesweepers, with larger warships depending on circumstances.[163] There remained an organizational and logistical framework, mainly based on Malta, ready for activation in a Mediterranean emergency. It was on the requirement for such a capacity *in extremis* that Maltese politicians still counted in their financial duels with the British Treasury. But after 1966 the British decided not only to further reduce the facilities on Malta, but to liquidate the Mediterranean naval station itself, so that there would be in future no Royal Navy warships permanently stationed there. On 5 June 1967 a symbolic moment arrived. That office of splendour, 'Commander-in-Chief, Mediterranean', was abolished. Henceforth there was to be a Rear-Admiral as Flag Officer Malta carrying out remaining naval functions. Admiral Sir John Hamilton duly became the last of the ninety Commanders-in-Chief, Mediterranean Fleet, since 1711.[164]

Yet irony had always been a feature of the British Mediterranean. On the very day of this historic change a war of the first importance in the region broke out between Israel and the Arab states (the Six Day War, 5–11 June 1967). A substantial Royal Navy force, including an aircraft carrier, was scrambled to the eastern Mediterranean. Furthermore, in the wake of Arab–Israeli hostilities the Soviet Union began to fill the naval vacuum in the area, though in doing so its motives were clearly also political. This put a somewhat different gloss on British decisions regarding their own run-down. In April 1968 Sir Evelyn Shuckburgh, British Ambassador in Rome, used the imminent departure of the last British frigates stationed in Mediterranean waters to spark such a reaction. In a strongly argued plea to Whitehall, one that was backed up by his counterpart in Athens, Shuckburgh pointed out that key Mediterranean countries such as Italy were deeply unhappy to see the British vacating waters in which they had played such a part for so long.[165] These countries were worried about the Soviets, but they did not fully trust in the Americans either, for all the immense power of the Sixth Fleet. The British, for all their faults, had themselves been a Mediterranean power, and something of this past still clung to them. By contrast, for each of the two superpowers the region was really a sideshow, one in which to flex their muscles and favour the odd protégé, but not much more. The Mediterranean, that old linchpin of Great Power rivalry, was being relegated in the geopolitical stakes, and those who lived there were uneasily aware of the process.[166]

Ambassador Shuckburgh's call from Rome for a modest but identifiably British squadron, one not simply tasked with NATO responsibilities, to continue in the Mediterranean was at first unavailing. He was told by the Foreign Office that the basic decision on the Fleet could not be reversed, though Royal Navy warships would continue to visit Mediterranean ports and show the white ensign.[167] This was in essence a return to the pattern of the eighteenth century. Even so, a number of factors continued at least to mitigate this process. These included the continuing Soviet penetration, but also a consciousness that the French were beginning to see more opportunities for their own wider influence in the Mediterranean. This touched an old British nerve. But added to these was the fact that after 1968 the British Government engaged suddenly in managing a rapid exit from east of Suez, including Aden, and it seemed that the obvious place for redeployment for some of the ships and personnel involved was in the Mediterranean. The Mediterranean therefore regained something of its earlier importance right at the end of the 1960s.[168]

It was this revival, however faint and transitory, in Britain's Mediterranean commitment that provided Dom Mintoff, at last Maltese Prime Minister again after elections in June 1971, with a little renewed leverage over London. By this time Mintoff was a man in a hurry. Having been sidelined for so long by the British and Borg Olivier, he picked up where he had left off when he lost power in 1958. His first act was to replace Sir Maurice Dorman as Governor-General by a Maltese national, and followed that up by kicking out the Italian Admiral who headed the NATO naval presence on the island.[169] He then set about trying to negotiate a more generous defence agreement with the British Government (suggestively, on returning home, Dorman pronounced himself 'four square' behind the justice of Malta's case).[170] By this time, however, Mintoff was becoming a bogeyman for the British press, especially once his threats concerning the harassment of the British military presence became real, with various facilities being cut off. It was partly to call Mintoff's bluff that the British Government authorized a programme of withdrawal of personnel, some being taken off with their families on HMS *Bulwark*. Edward Heath, occupying 10 Downing Street as Conservative Prime Minister after 1970, recalled his dealings with Mintoff at this stage as 'perhaps the most curious foreign policy episode of my time as Prime Minister'.[171]

Part of the curiosity, apart from the sheer ebullience involved, was that although the Maltese leader's conflictual relationship with the British was now at its peak, it was always tempered by a residual attraction to Britain. Mintoff habitually went out of his way to emphasize that he was not anti-British, and that the old Mintoff of the 1950s – the one who had championed integration with the United Kingdom – had not entirely fled the scene. When HMS *Bulwark* was at work taking on departing Britons, for example, he made a point of going on board for a friendly chat with the Rear-Admiral overseeing the operation.[172] Heath and Mintoff also had one thing in common: a distaste for American power. Mintoff's attitude to the United States was one of loathing. His tactics always hinged on scraping the last ounce of advantage from Malta's status as a strategic pivot, whereas in Washington's Mediterranean policy the island counted for nothing. Apart from banning the United States navy from Valletta, therefore, one of Mintoff's key points in negotiating with Heath was that none of the facilities given to the British should be made available to the Americans.[173] Eventually, to the surprise and even disgust of some, Mintoff got most of what he wanted from the British Government during 1972 in a revised Military Facilities Agreement extending to 31 March 1979. British service personnel were now able to return to the island. The description of one of Mintoff's key civil service advisers of the 'demonstrations of joy all over the island' when news broke of the agreement suggests how much of the old psychology in the life of the island still prevailed.[174]

Nevertheless, the crisis over Malta during 1971–2 made Whitehall think again about the real value of maintaining vestigial responsibilities in the Mediterranean. The resulting risks emerged in much higher definition over Cyprus soon after Heath left office in March 1974. The independence settlement in Cyprus had fallen apart in the days leading up to the New Year of 1964, when constitutional proposals by Archbishop Makarios as President of the Republic led to bitter inter-communal fighting. On the urgent request of both Greek- and Turkish-Cypriot leaderships, some 3,000 British troops from the bases had managed to douse the disorder.[175] The 'Green Line' thereafter separating the Greek and Turkish quarters of Nicosia got its name from the fact that the British officer who designated it on the map had used a pen with green ink. Britain also provided a significant component in the United Nations peacekeeping force (UNFICYP) shortly sent to the island. Thereafter, however, the British disengaged themselves as much as possible from the internal problems of Cyprus, confining their interest to the Sovereign Base Areas at Dhekelia and Episkopi/Akrotiri. This inclination was all the more pronounced in the light of Turkish threats in 1964 and 1967 to invade Cyprus, ostensibly to protect the Turkish-Cypriots. On both occasions pressure from the United States was vital in dissuading Ankara from aggressive action. The inter-communal talks in the island in progress after 1968 provided a useful screen behind which the British could gradually taper off their unwanted exposure. Since the Greek-Cypriots did not recognize the legitimacy of the guarantees of 1960 it was quite conceivable that sooner or later they might be discarded, in which case any formal responsibility on Britain's part would conveniently come to an end.

The threat to such a transition was that the internal situation in the island might break apart while the guarantor status was still operative. By late 1973 this was the scenario that began to loom. The inter-communal exchanges were close to deadlock. Contingency plans were dusted off in Whitehall, though it was not clear they amounted to much.[176] The contingency envisaged was that of violence between Greek-Cypriots; that is, between the supporters of Archbishop Makarios, now more or less committed to the principle of an independent Cypriot state, and right-wing factions ('EOKA-B') clustered around the old ideal of union with Greece. The latter forces, acting as the instrument of the dictatorial junta then in power in Athens, launched a coup against the Archbishop on 15 July 1974. At first radio broadcasts announced that Makarios had been killed, but he escaped through a secret exit from his palace and sought refuge at a United Nations camp in Paphos. From there on 16 July he was whisked away by a Royal Air Force helicopter to the British base at Akrotiri, and taken to Malta – where he was personally greeted by Dom Mintoff – before going on to London. That the Archbishop, so long an opponent of the British, ended up owing his life to them, and reliant on their support to uphold the continuing legitimacy of his presidency of Cyprus, was one of the most acute ironies of a career filled with them.

With a thuggish EOKA regime taking a grip in Cyprus, the island was seemingly on the brink of *Enosis*. In Whitehall it had for some time been believed that Turkey, having twice drawn back from military invention in the midst of a Cypriot crisis, would next time carry it through. This is what now happened. First, however, the Turkish Prime Minister, Bülent Ecevit, tried to convince the British Government to act jointly with them in doing so on the basis of their shared guarantor status. To allow the Sovereign Base Areas to be used as the conduit for a Turkish descent on a Commonwealth country was wholly unacceptable in London. On 20 July Turkish seaborne and airborne troops therefore landed unilaterally and without warning in the north of the island, their first goal being to open out a corridor to the Turkish-Cypriot enclave north of Nicosia. Frantic diplomacy led to a fragile ceasefire on 30 July, and the British Foreign Secretary in a new Labour Government, James Callaghan, in the following days succeeded in convening talks among the various parties in Geneva. It was a forbidding experience – the last time that a British leadership was to find itself, whether it liked it or not, at the centre of a Mediterranean crisis. But the discussions were in large part a comedy of manners. The Turks, whose Foreign Minister periodically went missing in Geneva at crucial points, were no longer interested in negotiating a political solution in the island. They were bent on finishing the military action already undertaken, and on 14 August they launched a second phase of their invasion, leading to the seizure of one-third of the island and a de facto partition.

It has become a cardinal element in Greek and Greek-Cypriot understanding of these sequences that behind it all lay an Anglo-American conspiracy prompting and facilitating, if not actually controlling, Turkish actions.[177] Detailed research has rebutted such claims.[178] Britain's responses to the crisis were characterized by confusion, a growing parochialism and acute embarrassment. Confusion arose from the fact that there never had been any prior Whitehall planning to counter a Turkish attack on Cyprus. In London a kind of paralysis therefore set in as soon as news of the Turkish aggression arrived early in the morning of 15 July. The car sent to collect Callaghan at his home for an urgent meeting with Prime Minister Harold Wilson failed to arrive, and Callaghan had to wave down a milkman doing his round and persuade him to head straight for Downing Street.[179] Farce not conspiracy typifies a good deal of the British side of this story.

The acute embarrassment arose from Britain's transparent failure to carry out an obligation arising from the 1960 treaties, and, perhaps even more, a long-standing responsibility for Cypriot welfare. Callaghan clearly felt this embarrassment deeply. His first instinct was to do something rather than nothing. He raised the possibility with his own officials of Royal Navy and Sixth Fleet vessels interposing themselves between the Cypriot coast and Turkey, preventing Turkish reinforcements from disembarking.[180] Army reinforcements and Phantom fighter aircraft were rushed out to the island to convey an impression to the Turks that the obligation to repel an invader might be met. When Turkish troops seemed about to overrun Nicosia airport, it was the order from London to stand fast given to the British Lancers serving with the UN forces, and a direct warning by Callaghan to Ecevit that he would not let British troops be 'shot up', that stopped their advance.[181] Callaghan felt convinced, as this episode indicated, that ultimately the Turkish Government would not risk a serious confrontation with major powers. Before hostilities had been disastrously renewed, he pressed the Americans to give some 'prudent forethought' to a warning to Turkey, and complained that Kissinger 'was not facing up to the real problem on the military side'.[182] From very early in the crisis there was a divergence between London and Washington, and mutual frustration between Callaghan and Kissinger. In previous years the Americans had favoured a quick-fix solution in Cyprus by a partition negotiated through Athens and Ankara. This had proved impossible to bring about. But this new crisis, courtesy of Greek political blundering and Turkish use of force, presented Washington with the prospect of effecting the desired outcome, or something very like it. Anything or anybody getting in the way of this, Callaghan included, only aroused Kissinger's irritation. The British Foreign Secretary found his suggestions for concerted action swept aside. As Callaghan explained: 'I am convinced that Britain would have been courting military disaster if heavily outnumbered British troops, trained to guard a base, had taken the offensive in the face of opposition from the United States. The subsequent failure would have resembled a second Suez.'[183]

Callaghan's use of the Suez analogy indicates the degree of the tensions and risks involved. In a situation where the United States and the United Nations under Kurt Waldheim showed every sign of leaving the British in the lurch,[184] Callaghan and Wilson could hardly have acted in any other fashion than they did. This was certainly in line with their own military advice that British forces in the area were insufficient to prevent a determined Turkish onslaught (the shades here of the Chanak affair in 1922 were tangible). Probably, too, the calculated immobility of American policy and the paralysis of the United Nations only validated their own natural risk-aversion, though in Callaghan's case it was matched to a fierce resentment of Turkish exploitation – 'too close to Hitler for my liking', as he described it.[185] In these complicated circumstances any search for the 'smoking-gun' of crude conspiracy is misplaced. But it was painfully clear that the outcome exposed the hollowness of any pretence on Britain's part to offer guarantees and meaningful succour. Certainly Cyprus's last colonial Governor, Hugh Foot, now ennobled as Lord Caradon, afterwards felt that the United Kingdom's omission to act militarily in August 1974 had been 'shameful'.[186] Yet in thinking so he was perhaps expressing an old colonial morality.

It was therefore hardly surprising that those British actions that were taken in Cyprus at this time were dictated by an almost exclusive concern with narrow national interests. This did not always make for an edifying spectacle. Central to such a priority was the rescue of the many thousands of British tourists stranded at the height of the holiday season, and the safety of the 17,000 expatriate community and their properties. These matters were to the forefront of discussion in the House of Commons, along with the safety of the Sovereign Base Areas. HMS *Andromeda* and *Devonshire* took off 1,500 Britons and some other nationalities (including Russians) gathered on the beach at Kyrenia. Royal Navy vessels in the area also picked up survivors when the Turkish Air Force sank one of their own destroyers. The British High Commission organized a convoy of 1,000 cars for expatriates caught in Nicosia, escorted by military vehicles to Dhekelia.

Meanwhile the British army on the bases was overwhelmingly preoccupied with guarding perimeters and lending humanitarian assistance to the thousands of refugees crowding in. Many of these were Turkish-Cypriots previously living in the south of the island, and the eventual British decision in January 1975 to facilitate the movement of these families to the Turkish-occupied zone in the north aroused Greek-Cypriot anger as indicating complicity in the de facto realities now prevailing in an island devastated by the fighting and mass upheaval of the preceding summer. Approximately 3,000 had been killed, with more than 2,100 'missing', and 200,000 Greek-Cypriots and 40,000 Turkish-Cypriots were displaced from their homes.

The bases, indeed, hold a key to the tangled relationship between the United Kingdom and the Greek-Cypriots inevitably bequeathed by these events. This arises from the undoubted fact that in some sense at least the British have been beneficiaries of the disaster. After 1960, and even more after 1964, it had usually been assumed that the shelf-life of the British bases was limited, as it has been in most ex-colonies.[187] Before the crisis of 1974 Whitehall was contemplating giving them up.[188] During the crisis itself this prospect became wholly desirable. 'I see no future for us in Cyprus,' Callaghan told his officials. 'So let's not be long about getting out.'[189] But partition having been imposed at the point of Turkish bayonets, far from being evacuated the British Sovereign Base Areas have since been frozen into place as part and parcel of the whole Cyprus Problem, along with their trim lawns, excellent sports fields and a garrison life in miniature of a sort not even to be found any longer in Gibraltar. Greek-Cypriot attitudes to them have assumed an intense ambivalence, on the one hand seeing them as a point of stabilization should some new crisis erupt, and yet also considering they epitomize a continuing alien presence. Criticism of the bases has consequently become the surest barometer of the state of Anglo-Greek relations within Cyprus, and has occasionally threatened disorder, though the Republic of Cyprus has always exerted a calming influence. Relations between the United Kingdom and Greece, once again under democratic government with the fall of the junta, also bore part of the brunt of this sorry saga. One Foreign Office official remarked in November 1974 that 'our position as a major Western friend of Greece has slipped', and in essence that damage too has never quite been repaired.[190]

The most basic British instinct defined by the events of 1974 in Cyprus was to get off a hook consisting essentially of responsibility without power,[191] the dangers of which had been all too painfully demonstrated. But this imperative had wider Mediterranean connotations, accentuated by the inflationary and economic challenges facing the United Kingdom herself. Following a defence review completed in mid-1975 it was decided to liquidate virtually all military commitments outside the NATO area.[192] No Royal Navy surface vessels were to remain in the Mediterranean after 1976, and the base in Malta was to be abandoned in March 1979. The latter was a decision that Mintoff, having presided over Malta's emergence as a republic in 1975, and having won re-election the following year, was himself in no mood to try to reverse even if it had been feasible to do so.

In 1977 HMS *Ark Royal* visited Grand Harbour in Valletta and began a carefully staggered programme of taking off the army garrison, standing at 2,700 officers and men, plus their dependants. Then on 12 March 1979 Rear-Admiral Sir Oswald Cecil removed his flag as Commander of British Forces to HMS *London*, transferring the historic Fort St Angelo into Maltese hands for the first time. Negotiations had been proceeding for some time over the transfer of a range of assets, including Bighi Naval Hospital overlooking Kalkara Creek with its fabulous views across the knightly magnificence of the Maltese capital. The haggling – in keeping with the great tradition of Anglo-Maltese dealings – even extended to the bed allegedly once slept in by Nelson and Emma Hamilton, kept in St Angelo, which had been brought to Malta after the fall of Naples in 1943.

The only real British 'interest' in Malta at this late stage was to be allowed by its mercurial leader to get out on the designated day without an embarrassing incident. It would have been out of character if Mintoff had not kept the British anxious on this point.[193] What complicated matters was that he insisted on using the exit of the British as the excuse for a new Independence Day, as in Mintoff's eyes September 1964 had never been legitimate. As a result Malta became the only British colony ever to witness two such celebrations, fifteen years apart, each featuring a ceremonial lowering of the Union Jack. But this curiosity represented something more than mere symbolism. An informed Maltese comparison of the two occasions, September 1964 and March 1979, the former arising from a British constitutional departure and the latter a physical and military exit, concludes that if 1964 has pride of place in Malta's political evolution, the latter was far more radical in economic and social (and perhaps therefore also in psychological) terms.[194] To a degree not replicated in other British departures, what was disappearing in this case was not any kind of political or constitutional order but the last traces of a way of life.

In the week running up to 31 March 1979 the British military services in Malta held a series of farewell events in which local inhabitants and dignitaries participated. The island of Gozo was not forgotten – the Royal Marines Beat the Retreat in the capital of Rabat. The final broadcast of the local British Forces Broadcasting Service was of especial nostalgia, not least for the many Maltese for whom it had long been regular listening.[195] By the time the final day loomed, Michael Foot, Lord President of the Council, arrived from London to play his part as the British Cabinet's representative. Somewhat to Mintoff's disappointment, however, other foreign emissaries were mostly limited to serving ambassadors. The only head of state attending was Mintoff's collaborator and mentor in non-alignment and anti-Americanism, Colonel Gaddafi, whose coup in his own country on 1 September 1969 had been followed very shortly by the final departure of British troops from Libya. With Gaddafi on this occasion came a gaggle of pressmen and security 'heavies', plus 500 members of the Libyan Peoples Congress and some Arab horsemen. The latter, a Maltese witness recalled, 'held their own celebrations as if it had been their event'.[196] Certainly Gaddafi was determined to make the most of it. After a show by the English pop group Showaddywaddy, the formal proceedings unfolded. When Mintoff appeared on the podium as midnight, he was accompanied by the beshawled Libyan leader. 'Gaddafi,' the British High Commission reported to Whitehall, 'who was in his arrogant showman form, gave the thumbs down when the Union Jack was lowered.'[197] Of all British 'Independence Day' ceremonies, Gaddafi's assertive thumb helped to make this surely one of the most idiosyncratic.

Yet because the British and their warships had been such a large part of Maltese life, and its harbour the scene of so many historic events, there is probably a good deal of truth in the British High Commissioner's summary at the time that what aroused the interest of ordinary Maltese was not the staging of another ceremony in which politicians could hog the limelight, but rather the morning of the following day when, as he reported, 'they turned out in their tens of thousands to witness the departure of Rear Admiral Cecil in HMS *London.* Lined four deep along all the city's bastions, many unable to control their tears, they stood in eloquent silence as [HMS] *London* steamed out . . .'[198] Simultaneously, in a Royal Air Force farewell, a Nimrod aircraft flew over Valletta and dipped its wings above Fort St Elmo. Mention of tears had become a convention in the official *reportage* of British departures (though there had scarcely been any reference to them in Palestine in 1948, Egypt in 1954 or Cyprus in 1960). A more down-to-earth analysis was that most Maltese did not care greatly whether the British came or went in future.[199] But for many spectators overlooking Grand Harbour on that day the last exit of a navy whose comings and goings, sometimes in great strength, had been a part of their own upbringing and memories, must have struck home in a warm and personal way. Quite a few would have been able to conjure up such dramatic images as HMS *Illustrious* lit by flames as German bombs crashed down around it in December 1941, or the 'miracle' of the battered and limping ships of Operation Pedestal entering Grand Harbour on 14–15 August 1942. This book's narrative began with a British squadron entering Grand Harbour in September 1800, heralding a novel presence on the part of the British, but also an important turn in the life of the Mediterranean itself. It ends, appropriately, with the Royal Navy's departure from the same anchorage 178 years later, as HMS *London* turned west towards Gibraltar and back to a colder and now more introspective home.

# Postscript: Legacies, Residues and Continuities

During May 1964, on the name day of Constantine II, the Kingdom of Greece celebrated the centenary of the cession of the Ionian Islands by Great Britain. The British Ambassador, Sir Ralph Murray, attended the event in Corfu Town. He came away, however, somewhat disappointed, explaining to a colleague in the Foreign Office that

> There seems to be in Corfu faint traces of warmth towards the former Protecting Power . . . Nor has there been the slightest recognition in the press of this occasion as recalling our basic and historical relationship with Greece. Though I have received some private expressions of warmth . . . in the newspapers such articles as have been published on the subject have attempted to discredit our motives in transferring the Islands.[1]

The British had often expected gratitude for their actions and commitments in the Mediterranean, only to find that it was not forthcoming and that supposedly good intentions were impugned. The only saving graces on this occasion had been the opening by King Constantine of an exhibition of the paintings of the long-time Corfu resident Edward Lear, and a reception given at the Palace of St Michael and St George built by that despotic, slovenly, cynical but also highly effective architect of the old Ionian Protectorate, Sir Thomas Maitland.

In truth, gratitude is always best not looked for in political and social relations. But that Ambassador Murray did expect to find it in this case, in however small a quantity, suggests how episodes in British Mediterranean history were thought to have a considerable longevity and moral resonance. Oddly, nearing the hundred and fiftieth anniversary of Ionian cession, the *Guardian* newspaper reported the appearance of an autonomist party in Corfu, a spokesperson for which warmly declared 'that unification with Greece was the darkest day in our history'.[2] The cession of 1864 had become a road best not taken, as a good few discontented Englishmen had sourly prophesied at the time. Predictably, this said nothing at all about the 'real' history of British Protection in the Islands, or any desire to laud its achievements, and a lot about Corfiote complaints concerning their contemporary governance. The experiences we have described in this book, then, of which the Ionian 'gift' of 1864 was but one example, are part of an endless cycle of interpretation, digestion and reassessment.

But if the British did not leave gratitude behind them in their Mediterranean dealings, what did they leave? Did they, as the French observer René Pichon had once predicted about Malta, only bequeath some forts, a few tennis courts and a love of horse racing[3] – in other words, an at best marginal and glancing impact? This was too gloomy (or optimistic, depending on your vantage point) as even a casual experience of Valletta will reveal. Queen Victoria's statue still presides over Palace (now Independence) Square in the heart of the capital, minus a bit of arm, and Alexander Ball's memorial retains pride of place in the Lower Barracca Gardens overlooking the grandest harbour in Europe. During the evening a good place to eat in central Valletta, and open to all, is the King's Own Band Club, still revelling like other royal band clubs on the island in its name and tradition. Although Valletta is a quiet and dignified capital, a late-night drink can always be had in the Anglo-Maltese Union Bar, though the television will very likely be showing Italian football. These are small things, but small things are often revealing. Since language and education have always been intense Maltese concerns, we should note that the school system today is mostly on the British model and among the indigenous population more or less everybody speaks Maltese and 88 per cent speak English. The tuition at the University of Malta also remains largely in the English medium. René Pichon would be amazed and even disturbed to know that in the early twenty-first century hundreds of thousands of Britons come to the island every year. However, when Dom Mintoff's nationalization of the old British dockyard in 1975 finally came to grief in 2010, and the facilities were sold off to the private sector, they passed into the ownership of an Italian company.[4] An Italian dockyard in Grand Harbour must have made many old Admiralty souls shift uneasily in their graves.

Perhaps the most striking paradox of the legacy left by the British Mediterranean experience, however, is presented by Cyprus. There was clearly a great deal of ambivalence in this island's origins and development as a British possession. One might even go so far as to say that it never actually became a British colony mentally and emotionally, or at least did so only very partially. The struggle preceding independence underpinned a mutual rejection on the side of both Greek-Cypriots and the British. Few memoirs by ex-colonial civil servants carry the bitterness, for example, of that by John Reddaway, adviser to both the last two Governors; the title of his reminiscences, *Burdened with Cyprus*, is indicative.[5] Britain's failure – whether through sheer incapacity or otherwise – to stop the Turkish invasion of 1974 drove a wedge into this post-colonial relationship, and the ill feeling can still sometimes surge powerfully, as it did during the referendum in Cyprus on the 'Annan Plan' in 2004 for reunification of the island, a plan seen as yet another attempt at British (or Anglo-American) imposition oriented in favour of Turkey.

Yet for all this there are probably few 'ex-British' territories where, governmental relations apart, the tie with the United Kingdom is more intense than with Cyprus. Four of the first six post-independence Presidents of the Republic of Cyprus have been London-trained lawyers. The system of public administration in the island is British in derivation, and most Cypriots when trying to explain their prosperity despite massive political upheaval will often refer to that inheritance, not at all by way of gratitude but simply as an explanation for something that is otherwise often puzzling. Countless thousands of Cypriots have studied at British universities and continue to do so even when the island has its own expanding higher education sector. There are around 300,000 Cypriots in Britain, and in London keeping up with local Cypriot events is itself a full-time occupation. Leaving aside the annual wave of tourism, the expatriate British community in the island is growing, and beginning to take an active role (as are their counterparts on parts of the Spanish coast) in local and European elections.[6] A Cypriot writer refers to the British as the 'indigenous foreigner', and although this is meant not least in relation to the United Kingdom's role prescribed under the independence settlement of 1960, it also has a social meaning.[7] Of course, Englishness never got the better of Hellenism in Cyprus in the way that, generally speaking, it did with regard to Italianism in Malta. The 'atmosphere' in most of Cyprus remains indisputably Greek. But many Cypriots visit Greece and on return complain about strikes, train timetables and bureaucracy in the most English of ways. In short, to a degree inconceivable in the vast swathe of the former British Empire, there is a distinctive Anglo-Cypriot current present in Cyprus itself, and this interacts symbiotically with the Cypriot presence in Britain. Nor is this merely a residue, since it is dynamic and self-replicating, as the density of flights between British airports and Cypriot destinations testifies.

There is one place in the Mediterranean, of course, where Britishness still dares to speak its name with klaxon force: Gibraltar. 'Be careful over there,' a local cabbie advised a British journalist during 2004 as he dropped him by the Spanish border post. 'It's not like here.'[8] The man from the *Daily Telegraph* was there to observe the tercentenary of Rooke's capture of the Rock in 1704. On 4 August 2004 almost the entire population of Gibraltar joined hands in a line encircling its perimeter as a token of celebration. The occasion testified to the special place that the Gibraltarians had succeeded in acquiring within British public life, if only as an anti-model to often more disenchanting experiences elsewhere. Not only was the British Defence Secretary, Geoff Hoon, in attendance to watch 300 British soldiers (enough to gratify Gibraltarians, but not so many as to push Spanish patience beyond endurance) march down Main Street, but so was the First Sea Lord and the Conservative Shadow Foreign Secretary. Spanish opinion took particular umbrage at the twenty-one-gun salute fired by HMS *Grafton* as she sailed into port to join the festivities, along with two Royal Fleet Auxiliary ships. The Spanish Foreign Minister told the Madrid newspaper *El Pais*: 'It turns out to be very strange that in this twenty-first century, the military occupation of part of an EU member-state's territory is commemorated by another member state.'[9] But then the paradoxes of our subject have been almost without end.

In fact, over the years leading up to the Rock's tercentenary and since, Gibraltar's reputation has ebbed and flowed somewhat in the United Kingdom, as it always did. Its very rapid economic growth of up to 12 per cent per annum has been related to an off-shore finance industry that some view critically, as likewise with the more recent boom in online gambling. As post-Franco Spain has come in from the cold ideologically, especially after her entry into the European Union in 1985, sympathy for Gibraltar has been less marked. The celebration in 2004 also evoked this contrary aspect. 'The strategic significance of Gibraltar to Britain', the military writer Max Hastings commented, 'is rather less than that of Rockall';[10] and a certain impatience is occasionally expressed towards Gibraltar when its recurring spats with its neighbour impinge unhelpfully on relations between London and Madrid. Spanish protests when Princess Anne visited Gibraltar during 2009 to open a medical facility, described as an 'affront to Spain' by a member of the Spanish Parliament's Foreign Affairs Commission, provides an example of the costs and benefits involved.

According to some, then, Britain's clinging to the Rock has become, in Max Hastings' words, a saloon-bar folly.[11] Understood purely and simply as a foreign policy problem, or strategic consideration, such a critique seems rational enough. But the history we have covered in this book has not always proceeded according to entirely rational principles. Britain, and Britishness as a phenomenon, are scored indelibly into the Rock regardless of policies and governments, but in ways that are tied organically to the presence of Spain and Spanishness. The occasional mutual insults, deprecations and hindrances only prove the point. The progressive decline of an Anglo-Spanish blend of culture and commerce spanning the Rock and the adjoining *campo* has been a major change in the past sixty years. But the resilience of an underlying reality despite intense countervailing pressures is shown by its revival under rather different auspices. As Gibraltar's local economy has continued to grow, relatively impervious to economic downturns experienced across the land frontier after 2008, employment opportunities continue to suck in a changing and diverse workforce. Depending on the euro–sterling exchange rate, Spaniards and expatriates from such Andalusian towns as Sotogrande and Marbella flood into Gibraltar and trawl Main Street picking up bargains.[12] The bars in La Linea, slightly grubby but amiable as ever, are back in business.

The Rock's maritime tradition and strategic location have in 2010 taken it back into the top ten of world supply ports for bunker fuel, just as they did in the mid-nineteenth century.[13] This unique British enclave today has 30,000 residents. Here is yet another illustration of traits that always gave the British Mediterranean strength and ability to survive: hybridity, flexibility and responsiveness.

Had the old British maritime 'supremacy' in the Mediterranean been replaced by an alternative and equally compelling configuration of power, some at least of these various residues might have been erased. But in fact there has been nothing to replace it. The scare surrounding a Soviet push into the Mediterranean in the late 1960s and early 1970s faded quickly, though its echo can still sometimes be felt, as when in 2008 it was announced that the Russian navy would be making more visits to Syrian ports. Most telling, however, has been the enigma of the United States' presence. When American warships first started regular forays into the post-war Mediterranean in 1946–7, a formidable new force had clearly arrived. Certainly the United States has been a presence in the internal politics of various countries in the region and, perhaps because superpowers are even less popular than more traditional Great Powers, anti-Americanism has been a more sharply felt emotion than its forerunner of anti-Britishness. In broad regional terms, indeed, the American role – at least once the era of Marshall Aid was over – has been generally fragmented and episodic, except where Israel is concerned. Although the superior power of the Sixth Fleet was tangible, it was never part of any grand strategic conception particular to the region, remaining essentially a task force to be deployed away from the Mediterranean itself.[14]

By contrast, an integrated and rounded conception of the Mediterranean, a sense of its coherence as an entity, had long been embedded in British diplomacy and in naval power as it gradually came to assume a mature form. The British concentrated a good deal of their energies and scarce resources there, not to serve purposes in other theatres – and certainly not, as Sir Thomas Maitland's biographer underlined many years ago, for Indian purposes[15] – but to perform a specifically Mediterranean role, albeit of course one that suited British ends. We have seen how that role was first clearly defined in the 1830s and 1840s, assumed a classic shape in the 1870s and 1880s, survived two world wars in the twentieth century and finally broke up from the 1950s onwards. Latter-day theories of NATO's southern flank, and the institution of a Standing Naval Force Mediterranean (bearing the awful NATO acronym of STANAVFORMED), based in Naples in 1992, were never a substitute. The huge, brooding outline of a United States Navy aircraft carrier off the Lebanese coast in such crises as the war with Israel in 2006 is the Sixth Fleet's analogue to the British Mediterranean Fleet massing in Grand Harbour during, say, the war in the Crimea. The latter, however, had a lot to do with the Mediterranean world as a living organism, strategically, politically and even to some extent socially. The former was only coincidentally concerned with Mediterranean affairs, a mere appendix to superpower engagement in something called 'the Middle East'.

Finally, we come back to why the Mediterranean mattered so much to the British for so long. Churchill, with his facility for conveying something in a rhetorical flourish, famously referred to the region in relation to British preoccupations as 'the soft under-belly of Europe'. More prosaically, Sir Orme Sargent, Permanent Under-Secretary in the Foreign Office, reflected in March 1946 on the United Kingdom's involvement:

> Our position as a World Power and therefore as a Great Power depends surely on our maintaining our position in the Mediterranean, and this is not for strategic reasons, but on political grounds. In other words, the Mediterranean is of vital importance for us not so much because it is our direct link with the East but because if we abandon it in present circumstances the Russians will take our place there, with incalculable results . . . on Italy, France, Spain and Austria.[16]

These essentially continental concerns were also what principally lay behind the determination of Ernest Bevin as Labour Foreign Secretary through the later 1940s to maintain a strong physical presence by Britain in and around southern Europe. In this Bevin reflected what had long been an underlying imperative shaping British power overseas, together with its limits. From Napoleon to Hitler, through to the early phases of the making of what became the European Union with its Franco-German 'motor', the British repeatedly learned that they were not a continental power in the full sense of the phrase. Sometimes they forgot, and the lesson had to be painfully relearned, as it was during the Great War of 1914–18. But there was an alternative modus operandi, one initially discovered as it were by maritime instinct, and refined by trial and error through successive crises and challenges. This was to hammer into place a series of fixed points across the watery margins of southern Europe. From these vantage points British strength and influence could radiate in various directions according to need. The leverage thereby acquired was marginal and fluctuating, but usually enough for British requirements. In war, survival alone was a kind of victory. G. F. Leckie's vision of 1808 quoted in an epigraph to this book, with its ideal of the British Mediterranean as 'an insular empire, complete in its parts, and sufficient to itself', could never be fully realized. But even the mongrel version that emerged over time allowed British power to evolve a credible and resilient methodology, as well as defining an important interlude in the wider history of the Mediterranean.

Nor has the history of this special British relationship to southern Europe and its hinterlands, including its mediation between north and south, entirely lost relevance in the twenty-first century. The European Union now straddles the olive line as British power once did, most recently enhanced by the accession of Cyprus and Malta in 2004. Istanbul and the Straits, once so crucial in British diplomatic and naval considerations, beckon once more but now in the rather different form of the question of Turkey's accession to the EU, as ever with many difficulties and even dangers as well as opportunities. Yet the regional ramifications of the economic crash after 2008, initially most powerfully experienced in Greece but spreading steadily outwards, exposed the fault-lines between Europe's 'hard' north and 'soft' south only masked by European Union enlargement and a shared currency in the eurozone. The Mediterranean and its hinterland re-emerged in these early years of the twenty-first century as Europe's vulnerable rim in need of external reinforcement and patronage, just as it had been during much of the period of British maritime preponderance. How such weakness and permeability might unfold remains unclear, but it seems very probable that in this regard at least some of the themes in this book have a future as well as a past.

# *Notes*

## SOURCES

Acknowledgements and thanks are due to the institutions whose collections have proved indispensable in writing this book. In the United Kingdom these include the British Library, the London Library, the National Archives at Kew (designated TNA in the following notes) and Rhodes House Library in Oxford; in Greece, the Gennadion Library and the Library and Archive of the British School at Athens; in Gibraltar, the Garrison Library; in Valletta the National Library of Malta; in Nicosia the Library of the Archbishop Makarios III Foundation and the Cyprus American Archaeological Research Institute, which as usual provided the author with another home; and in the United States the National Archives in Washington. The *Oxford Dictionary of National Biography* (*ODNB* in these notes) is an invaluable source on many of the figures appearing in this book.

## INTRODUCTION: THE BRITISH AND THE MEDITERRANEAN

1. Robert Holland and Diana Markides, *The British and the Hellenes: Struggles for Mastery in the Eastern Mediterranean, 1850–1960* (2006), 78.
2. *The Scotsman*, 14 April 2005.
3. John Premble, *The Mediterranean Passion: Victorians and Edwardians in the South* (1987), 263.
4. Quoted ibid., 269.
5. James Barros, *Britain, Greece and the Politics of Sanctions: Ethiopia, 1935–1936* (1982), 119.
6. Roger Knight, *The Pursuit of Victory: The Life and Achievement of*

*Horatio Nelson* (2005), 463. Sardinia had been occupied by a British force for some time during the War of the Spanish Succession in 1708.

7. See Fernand Braudel, *The Mediterranean and the Mediterranean World in the Age of Philip II* (1972).
8. See Dominic Fenech, 'The Mediterranean Region during the Cold War and After', in John Hattendorf (ed.), *Naval Policy and Strategy in the Mediterranean Past, Present and Future* (2000), 235.
9. Julian Corbett, *England in the Mediterranean*, vol. 2 (1904), 314.

## CHAPTER 1. THE ORIGINS OF AN ANGLO-MEDITERRANEAN ORDER, 1800–1814

1. See W. Hardman, *A History of Malta during the Period of the French and British Occupations, 1798–1815* (1908), 310–11.
2. A. V. Laferla, *British Malta*, vol. 1: *1800–1872* (1938), p. xiii.
3. J. H. Holland Rose, 'The Conflict with Revolutionary France, 1793–1802', in *The Cambridge History of the British Empire*, vol. 2 (1940), 38.
4. Introduction by J. H. Holland Rose in Hardman, *A History of Malta*, p. ix.
5. Walter Frewen Lord, *England and France in the Mediterranean, 1660–1830* (1901), 63. The first British possession in the Mediterranean was Tangier, held between 1682 and 1684; Samuel Pepys, a great critic of the commitment, accompanied the expedition sent to oversee evacuation.
6. See Desmond Gregory, *The British Occupations of Minorca* (1990). When the Spanish regained the island in 1782, they had pulled down two key forts, reducing any attraction for fresh invaders. Although the British occupied the island for the last time in 1793, it was transferred to Spanish sovereignty in 1802 – though, as Nelson remarked, 'we can take it back whenever we want to'. Even at the end of the Napoleonic conflict the British Mediterranean Fleet was still wintering in Minorca.
7. Alfred C. Wood, *A History of the Levant Company* (1935) gives the commercial background. A recent related study is Christine Laidlaw, *The British in the Levant: Trade and Perceptions of the Ottoman Empire in the Eighteenth Century* (2010).
8. Roger Knight, *The Pursuit of Victory: The Life and Achievement of Horatio Nelson* (2005), 172.
9. See Desmond Gregory, *The Ungovernable Rock: A History of the Anglo-Corsican Kingdom* (1985).

10. Holland Rose, 'The Conflict with Revolutionary France', 61.
11. Quoted in Knight, *The Pursuit of Victory*, 202.
12. Ibid., 300.
13. Donald Sultana, *Samuel Taylor Coleridge in Malta and Italy* (1969), 185.
14. Knight, *The Pursuit of Victory*, 302.
15. Desmond Gregory, *Malta, Britain and the European Powers, 1793–1815* (1996), 256.
16. Piers Mackesy, *The War in the Mediterranean, 1803–1810* (1957), 12.
17. Patrick Staines, *Essays on Governing Malta, 1800–1813* (2009), 127–9.
18. Knight, *The Pursuit of Victory*, 441.
19. Laferla, *British Malta*, vol. 1, p. 28.
20. Harrison Smith, *Britain in Malta*, vol. 1: *Constitutional Development of Malta in the Nineteenth Century* (1953), 6.
21. Ibid., 124.
22. Mackesy, *War in the Mediterranean*, 22; also Sultana, *Coleridge in Malta and Italy*, 175.
23. Piers Mackesy, *British Victory in Egypt, 1801* (1998), 226–7.
24. See Fernand Beaucour, Yves Laissus and Chantal Orgogozo, *The Discovery of Egypt* (1990).
25. Mackesy, *War in the Mediterranean*, 42.
26. Ibid., 190.
27. John Marlowe, *Perfidious Albion: The Origins of Anglo-French Rivalry in the Levant* (1971), 136–7.
28. Wood, *The Levant Company*, 186.
29. N. A. M. Rodger, 'The Significance of Trafalgar: Seapower and Landpower in the Anglo-French Wars', in David Cannadine (ed.), *Trafalgar in History: A Battle and its Afterlife* (2006), 84–5.
30. Holland Rose, 'The Conflict with Revolutionary France', 92.
31. Quoted in Laferla, *British Malta*, vol. 1, p. 71.
32. Staines, *Governing Malta*, 188.
33. Ibid., 187.
34. Godfrey Pirotta, *The Maltese Public Service, 1800–1940: The Administrative Politics of a Micro-State* (1996), 66.
35. *Times of Malta*, 27 October 2009.
36. Sultana, *Coleridge in Malta and Italy*, 196.
37. Sam G. Benady, *General Sir George Don and the Dawn of Gibraltarian Identity* (2006).
38. Charles King, *The Black Sea: A History* (2004), 154.
39. Quoted Wood, *The Levant Company*, 180.

40. Noel Mostert, *The Line upon a Wind: The Greatest War Fought at Sea under Sail, 1793–1815* (2000), 522.
41. Ibid., 187–8.
42. Ibid., 181.
43. Emmanuel Rodocanachi, *Bonaparte et les îles ioniennes* (1899), 35.
44. Mackesy, *War in the Mediterranean*, 49.
45. Ibid., 35.
46. Ibid., 367.
47. Desmond Gregory, *Sicily: The Insecure Base. A History of the British Occupation of Sicily, 1806–1815* (1988), 77.
48. Mackesy, *War in the Mediterranean*, 230.
49. Gregory, *Sicily*, 37. See Ian Buruma, *Voltaire's Coconuts: Or Anglomania in Europe* (1999).
50. For Bentinck's stormy career in Sicily, see John Rosselli, *Lord William Bentinck: The Making of a Liberal Imperialist, 1774–1839* (1974), 114–79.
51. Gregory, *Sicily*, 33.
52. Ibid., 103.
53. Christopher Bayly, *Imperial Meridian* (1989), 103.
54. See the Introduction by J. Holland Rose in Hardman, *A History of Malta*.
55. Mackesy, *War in the Mediterranean*, 392.
56. Ibid., 58.
57. Ibid., 91.
58. George Hills, *Rock of Contention: A History of Gibraltar* (1974), 367. Nelson reflected a common view when he called Gibraltar 'an unsafe depot . . . which the Spaniards have always in their power to destroy'.
59. Quoted in Mackesy, *War in the Mediterranean*, 91.
60. Ibid., 357.
61. Patrick Louvier, *La Puissance navale et militaire britannique en Méditerranée, 1840–1871* (2006), 22.
62. Quoted in Lord Rosebery, *Napoleon: The Last Phase* (1909), 210.
63. Alfred Thayer Mahan, *The Life of Nelson: The Embodiment of the Sea Power of Great Britain* (1899), 317.
64. Knight, *The Pursuit of Victory*, 321.
65. Mostert, *Line upon a Wind*, 351–2.
66. Hugh Tours, *The Life and Letters of Emma Hamilton* (1963), 137.
67. C. K. Webster, *The Foreign Policy of Castlereagh, 1815–1822: Britain and the European Alliance* (1925), 333.

## CHAPTER 2. THE FORMATION OF A 'BRITISH LAKE', 1815–1841

1. Andrew Lambert, *The Last Sailing Battlefleet: Maintaining Naval Mastery 1815–1850* (1991), 4.
2. Even at the end of the war the number of French battleships was close to that of Great Britain. See Richard Glover, 'The French Fleet, 1807–1814: Britain's Problem and Madison's Opportunity', *Journal of Modern History*, 39/3 (1967), 233–52.
3. Today's Holland and Belgium.
4. R. C. Anderson, *Naval Wars in the Levant, 1559–1853* (1952), 480.
5. Glover, 'The French Fleet, 1807–1814', 242.
6. C. K. Webster, *The Foreign Policy of Castlereagh, 1812–1815: Britain and the Reconstruction of Europe* (1931), 260.
7. Ibid., 494.
8. Ibid., 162.
9. A. V. Laferla, *British Malta*, vol. 1: *1800–1872* (1938), 91.
10. John F. Beeler, *British Naval Policy in the Gladstone–Disraeli Era, 1866–1880* (1997), 17.
11. Desmond Gregory, *Malta, Britain and the European Powers, 1793–1815* (1996), 192.
12. Godfrey Pirotta, *The Maltese Public Service, 1800–1940: The Administrative Politics of a Micro-State* (1996), 73.
13. Laferla, *British Malta*, vol. 1, p. 100.
14. Gregory, *Malta*, 193.
15. Quoted in Webster, *Britain and the Reconstruction of Europe*, 352.
16. See A. E. Sokol, 'Nelson and the Russian Fleet', *Military Affairs*, 13/3 (1949), 129–37.
17. Webster, *Britain and the Reconstruction of Europe*, 410.
18. Gillian Weiss, 'Imagining Europe through Barbary Captivity', *Taiwan Journal of East Asian Studies*, 1 (2007), 49–67.
19. Roger Perkins and K. J. Douglas-Morris, *Gunfire in Barbary* (1982), 10.
20. Neville Gardner, *Bathurst and the British Empire, 1762–1834* (1999), 129.
21. Ibid., 128.
22. Perkins and Douglas-Morris, *Gunfire in Barbary*, 38.
23. Weiss, 'Imagining Europe', 59.
24. Ray W. Irwin, *The Diplomatic Relations of the United States with the Barbary Powers, 1776–1816* (1931), 184.

25. Edward Osler, *The Life of Viscount Exmouth* (1835), 399.
26. Perkins and Douglas-Morris, *Gunfire in Barbary*, 58.
27. Sp. D. Minotto, *La Cession de Parga* (1950), 17.
28. K. E. Fleming, *The Muslim Bonaparte: Diplomacy and Orientalism in Ali Pasha's Greece* (1995), 113.
29. Walter Frewen Lord, *Sir Thomas Maitland: The Mastery of the Mediterranean* (1897), 213.
30. Charles de Bosset, *Proceedings in Parga* (1821), 123.
31. Minotto, *La Cession de Parga*, 7.
32. B. R. Pearn, 'The Ionian Islands under the Administration of Sir Thomas Maitland, 1816–1824', MA thesis, University of London (1924), 146–7.
33. Lord, *Maitland*, 192.
34. Ibid., 263.
35. Ibid., 278.
36. Laferla, *British Malta*, vol. 1, p. 98.
37. Pearn, 'The Ionian Islands', 87.
38. Lord, *Maitland*, 210.
39. The intervention of St Spyridon – whose bones had been transferred from Constantinople to Corfu in 1453 – was credited with repulsing the great Turkish siege of 1716, leading to the cult of Spyridon in the island.
40. C. W. Dixon, *The Colonial Administrations of Sir Thomas Maitland* (1939), 240.
41. Christopher Bayly, *Imperial Meridian* (1989), 198–9.
42. See Gabrielle Paquette (ed.), *Enlightened Reform in Southern Europe and its Atlantic Colonies (1755–1830)* (2009), 209–19.
43. Dixon, *Colonial Administrations of Sir Thomas Maitland*, 181.
44. Lord, *Maitland*, 192.
45. J. M. Tumelty, 'The Ionian Islands under British Administration, 1815–1864', Ph.D. thesis, University of Cambridge (1952), 102.
46. C. K. Webster, *The Foreign Policy of Castlereagh, 1815–1822: Britain and the European Alliance* (1925), 326.
47. Pearn, 'The Ionian Islands', 78–9.
48. Dixon, *Colonial Administrations of Sir Thomas Maitland*, 190.
49. Colonel Charles James Napier, *The Colonies* (1837), 21.
50. Lord, *Maitland*, 228.
51. Pearn, 'The Ionian Islands', 159.
52. William St Clair, *That Greece Might Still Be Free: The Philhellenes in the War of Independence* (1972), 27–8.
53. See D. Wigley, *The Diplomatic Significance of Ionian Neutrality, 1821–31* (1988).

54. Pearn, 'The Ionian Islands', 170–73.
55. Ibid., 169.
56. Ibid., 176.
57. Dixon, *Colonial Administrations of Sir Thomas Maitland*, 138.
58. Quoted in Michael Pratt, *Britain's Greek Empire* (1972), 116.
59. Pirotta, *The Maltese Public Service*, 102.
60. George Finlay, *A History of the Greek Revolution*, vol. 2 (1861), 161.
61. Phanar (or Fener) was the neighbourhood midway up the Golden Horn which was the centre of Greek life in the city, and where the Eastern Orthodox Ecumenical Patriarchate still has its headquarters.
62. Webster, *Britain and the European Alliance*, 336.
63. As Ambassador in Constantinople Lord Elgin extracted a *firman*, or imperial edict, in 1801, under which he was enabled to remove and later export sculptures from the Parthenon and other buildings in Athens. In 1816 these 'Elgin marbles' were bought by the British Government and entrusted to the British Museum, where to date they remain.
64. See the entry on Byron in *Oxford Dictionary of National Biography* (hereafter *ODNB*).
65. St Clair, *That Greece Might Still Be Free*, 137–9.
66. Webster, *Britain and the European Alliance*, 271.
67. Wendy Hinde, *George Canning* (1973), 384.
68. See Stephen Minta, *On a Voiceless Shore: Byron in Greece* (1998).
69. St Clair, *That Greece Might Still Be Free*, 151–2.
70. Quoted in Stephen Minta, 'Letters to Lord Byron', Romanticism on the Web, No. 45, 2007, erudit.org.
71. Ibid.
72. Ibid.
73. Stanley Lane-Poole, *Stratford Canning*, vol. 2 (1888), 393.
74. Philip Mansel, *Levant: Splendour and Catastrophe on the Mediterranean* (2010), 75.
75. Lane-Poole, *Stratford Canning*, vol. 2, p. 483.
76. Ibid.
77. John Petropoulos, *Politics and Statecraft in the Kingdom of Greece, 1833–1843* (1868), 153.
78. Quoted in Pirotta, *The Maltese Public Service*, 108.
79. Alleged financial irregularities from his previous career in India dogged Hastings while he was in Malta and, broken in health, he died aboard a British warship in Naples during November 1826 on his way home. His body was returned to Valletta, where it remains interred in Hastings Gardens on the battlements.

80. Sir Gilbert Frankland Lewis (ed.), *Letters of Sir George Cornewell Lewis* (1870), 68.
81. Charles A. Price, *Malta and the Maltese* (1954), 104.
82. John Chircop, 'The British Imperial Network in the Mediterranean, 1800–1870', Ph.D. thesis, University of Essex (1997).
83. Athanasios Gekas, 'The Commercial Bourgeoisie of the Ionian Islands under British Rule, 1830–64', Ph.D. thesis, University of Essex (2004), 79.
84. Quoted in Pratt, *Britain's Greek Empire*, 127.
85. Eleni Calligas, 'The *Rizapastoi*: Politics and Nationalism in the British Protectorate of the Ionian Islands, 1815–1864', Ph.D. thesis, University of London (1994), 50.
86. Tumelty, 'The Ionian Islands', 136–7.
87. Lewis, *Letters of Sir George Cornewell Lewis*, 66.
88. Ibid., 64.
89. Quoted in Harrison Smith, *Britain in Malta*, vol. 1: *Constitutional Development in Malta in the Nineteenth Century* (1953), 130.
90. Donald Sultana, *Benjamin Disraeli in Spain, Malta and Albania, 1830–32* (1976), 110.
91. L. and J. Hamburger, *Troubled Lives: John and Sarah Austin* (1985), 118. Sarah was the mother of Lucie Duff Gordon, noted author of *Letters from Egypt* (1865).
92. G. P. Henderson, *The Ionian Academy* (1988).
93. See CO136/93, TNA.
94. Laferla, *British Malta*, vol. 1, p. 98.
95. Joseph Debono, 'The Language Problem and Educational Policy in Malta: 1800–1975', Ph.D. thesis, University of London (1981), 210.
96. F. Egerton, *Sir Geoffrey Phipps Hornby: A Biography* (1896).
97. Mary Sandars, *The Life and Times of Queen Adelaide* (1915), 275. In Valletta, the Queen inaugurated a new Anglican church, donating £10,000 herself. Far from antagonizing the Catholic hierarchy, an Anglican presence was tolerated as likely to combat the growth of more aggressive Protestant sects.
98. G. T. Garratt, *Gibraltar and the Mediterranean* (1939), 122.
99. Ibid.
100. Sam G. Benady, *General Sir George Don and the Dawn of Gibraltarian Identity* (2006), 98.
101. Stephen Constantine, *Community and Identity: The Making of Modern Gibraltar since 1704* (2009), 94.
102. Benady, *Sir George Don*, 99.
103. George Hills, *Rock of Contention: A History of Gibraltar* (1974), 372.

104. Garratt, *Gibraltar*, 124.
105. Benady, *Sir George Don*, 96.
106. Stephen Constantine, 'Monarchy and Constructing Identity in "British" Gibraltar, c. 1800 to the Present', *Journal of Imperial and Commonwealth History*, 34/1 (March 2006), 25.
107. See Gordon Ferguson, *Hounds are Home: The History of the Royal Calpe Hunt* (1979).
108. Gerald Graham, *The Politics of Naval Supremacy* (1966), 66–8.
109. When Ferdinand VII died without a male heir in September 1833, his eldest daughter, Isabella, became Queen under the so-called Pragmatic Sanction, with her mother, Queen Christina, as Regent. Ferdinand's brother, Don Carlos, challenged this outcome. What followed is known in Spanish history as the First Carlist War. The Carlists drew support from the fierce Catholic traditionalism of the Basque provinces and Navarre.
110. Major Francis Duncan, *The English in Spain* (1877), 4.
111. Barbara Wertheim, *The Lost British Policy: Britain and Spain since 1700* (1938), 58.
112. Ibid., 63.
113. C. K. Webster, *The Foreign Policy of Palmerston, 1830–1841: Britain, the Liberal Movement and the Eastern Question*, 2 vols. (1951), vol. 1, p. 440.
114. Duncan, *The English in Spain*, 27.
115. Webster, *Britain, the Liberal Movement and the Eastern Question*, vol. 1, pp. 422–4.
116. John Marlowe, *Perfidious Albion: The Origins of Anglo-French Rivalry in the Levant* (1971), 179–80.
117. Harold Temperley, *England and the Near East: The Crimea* (1936), 4.
118. Webster, *Britain, the Liberal Movement and the Eastern Question*, vol. 2, p. 629.
119. Ibid., 597.
120. H. Noel Williams, *The Life and Letters of Admiral Sir Charles Napier* (1927), 158–9.
121. Webster, *Britain, the Liberal Movement and the Eastern Question*, vol. 2, p. 623.
122. Noel Williams, *Sir Charles Napier*, 198.
123. Lambert, *Last Sailing Battlefleet*, 103.
124. Noel Williams, *Sir Charles Napier*, 182.
125. Ibid., 203.
126. See p. 82.
127. In 1830 Crete had been put under Egyptian administration. During the

following years Muslim domination within the island had become less pronounced.

128. Webster, *Britain, the Liberal Movement and the Eastern Question*, vol. 2, p. 772.
129. Harold Temperley, *England and the Near East*, 88–9.
130. Webster, *Britain, the Liberal Movement and the Eastern Question*, vol. 1, p. 206.
131. Patrick Louvier, *La Puissance navale et militaire britannique en Méditerranée, 1840–1871* (2006), 84.
132. Sultana, *Benjamin Disraeli in Spain, Malta and Albania*, 29.

## CHAPTER 3. THE BRITISH *PAX* IN THE MEDITERRANEAN, 1841–1878

1. G. M. Young, *Early Victorian England* (1934), 482.
2. The many thousands who turned out to catch a glimpse of Garibaldi constituted the biggest public demonstration in London for many years. The British Government was concerned that Garibaldi might visit northern cities with unsettling results, as he had in 1854, although it was denied in Parliament that he was encouraged to cut short his visit. See Countess Martinengo-Cesaresco, *The Liberation of Italy, 1815–1870* (1895), 353, and David Cannadine, *G. M. Trevelyan: A Life in History* (1992), 66.
3. See 'Stanley, Edward Henry, fifteenth earl of Derby (1826–1893)', in *ODNB*. Also see W. E. Moss, 'Queen Victoria and Her Ministers in the Schleswig-Holstein Crisis, 1863–4', *English Historical Review*, 78 (April 1963), 263–83.
4. Andrew Lambert, *The Last Sailing Battlefleet: Maintaining Naval Mastery 1815–1850* (1991), 7.
5. Augustus Phillimore, *The Life of Admiral Sir William Parker* (1880), 96. Intense Anglo-French rivalry over the marriage of Queen Isabella II of Spain was a feature of European diplomacy in 1845–6. The success of François Guizot, the French Premier, in arranging a union between the Spanish Queen's younger sister and the youngest son of King Louis Philippe of France revived old dynastic ties between France and Spain, and helped to repair French prestige in the Mediterranean after its setback in 1840–41.
6. F. Flournoy, *British Policy towards Morocco in the Age of Palmerston, 1830–1865* (1935), 112–28.
7. David Landes, *Bankers and Pashas* (1958), 80.
8. Sarah Searight, *Steaming East* (1991), 73.

9. A. V. Laferla, *British Malta*, vol. 1: *1800–1872* (1938), 184.
10. See entry on 'Hornby, Sir Geoffrey Phipps' in *ODNB*.
11. S. Eardley-Wilmot, *Life of Admiral Lord Lyons* (1898), 91.
12. V. Kofas, *International and Domestic Politics in Greece during the Crimean War* (1980), 6.
13. See David McLean, 'The Greek Revolution and the Anglo-French Entente, 1843–4', *English Historical Review*, 96 (January 1981), 117–29.
14. Stanley Lane-Poole, *Stratford Canning*, vol. 2 (1888), 120–21. Canning was undoubtedly thinking here of the earlier fate of Kapodistrias.
15. See 'Colborne, John, 1st Baron Seaton (1778–1863)', in *ODNB*.
16. Eleni Calligas, 'The *Rizapastoi*: Politics and Nationalism in the British Protectorate of the Ionian Islands, 1815–1864', Ph.D. thesis, University of London (1994), 104.
17. J. M. Tumelty, 'The Ionian Islands under British Administration, 1815–1864', Ph.D. thesis, University of Cambridge (1952), 178–9.
18. G. F. Bowen, *The Ionian Islands under British Protection* (1851), 49.
19. Phillimore, *Sir William Parker*, 554.
20. See Frank M. Turner, *The Greek Heritage in Victorian Britain* (1981).
21. Tumelty, 'The Ionian Islands', 193.
22. Phillimore, *Sir William Parker*, 295.
23. Ibid., 269–70.
24. Martinengo-Cesaresco, *Liberation of Italy*, 116.
25. Phillimore, *Sir William Parker*, 352.
26. Louis Napoleon, the nephew of Napoleon I, returned from exile in England when revolution broke out in Paris in February 1848, and was elected President the following December.
27. G. M. Trevelyan, *Garibaldi's Defence of the Roman Republic, 1848–9* (1908), 234.
28. R. M. Johnston, *The Roman Theocracy and the Republic, 1846–1849* (1907), 314.
29. Ian Buruma, *Voltaire's Coconuts: Or Anglomania in Europe* (1999), 131.
30. Cannadine, *Trevelyan*, 66.
31. Derek Beales, *England and Italy* (1961), 19.
32. J. P. Parry, 'The Impact of Napoleon III on British Politics, 1851–1880', *Transactions of the Royal Historical Society*, 11 (2001), 150.
33. Phillimore, *Sir William Parker*, 448.
34. For an account of the episode, see Donald Southgate, *'The Most English Minister': The Politics and Policies of Palmerston* (1966), 261–78.
35. Phillimore, *Sir William Parker*, 601–2.
36. Ibid., 623–4.

37. B. Kingsley Martin, *The Triumph of Lord Palmerston* (1924), 51–68.
38. Stefanos Xenos, *East and West* (1865), 11.
39. Hilda Lee, *Malta, 1813–1914* (1972), 110.
40. Godfrey Pirotta, *The Maltese Public Service, 1800–1940: The Administrative Politics of a Micro-State* (1996), 199.
41. Phillimore, *Sir William Parker*, 535–6.
42. Lee, *Malta, 1813–1914*, 125.
43. Calligas, 'The *Rizapastoi*', 159.
44. For the role of the dispute over the Holy Places see David Goldfrank, *The Origins of the Crimean War* (1994), 104–7, 141–2, 272–3.
45. Andrew Lambert, *The Crimean War: Britain's Grand Strategy, 1853–56* (1991), 39.
46. Charles King, *The Black Sea: A History* (2004), 179.
47. Eardley-Wilmot, *Admiral Lord Lyons*, 135.
48. Hew Strachan, 'Soldiers, Strategy and Sebastopol', *Historical Journal*, 21 (1978), 304.
49. Eardley-Wilmot, *Admiral Lord Lyons*, 160.
50. Christopher Hibbert, *The Destruction of Lord Raglan, 1854–55* (1961), 117.
51. Goldfrank, *The Origins of the Crimean War*, 265.
52. Dundas, as a young naval lieutenant, had served on Admiral Duckworth's expedition to the Dardanelles in 1807, and never forgot its cautionary lessons.
53. Eardley-Wilmot, *Admiral Lord Lyons*, 238.
54. James Merrill, 'British-French Amphibious Operations in the Sea of Azov', *Military Affairs*, 20 (Spring 1956), 21–2.
55. Eardley-Wilmot, *Admiral Lord Lyons*, 300.
56. Merrill, 'British-French Amphibious Operations', 24.
57. Nicolas Bentley (ed.), *Russell's Despatches from the Crimea, 1854–1856* (1966), 26.
58. Charles A. Price, *Malta and the Maltese* (1954), 107.
59. Carmel Cassar, 'Everyday Life in Malta in the Nineteenth and Twentieth Centuries', in Victor Mallia-Milanes (ed.), *The British Colonial Experience, 1800–1964: The Impact on Maltese Society* (1988), 91.
60. Quoted in F. Egerton, *Sir Geoffrey Phipps Hornby: A Biography* (1896), 86.
61. Patrick Louvier, *La Puissance navale et militaire britannique en Méditerranée, 1840–1871* (2006), 215.
62. Quoted in Robert Holland and Diana Markides, *The British and the*

*Hellenes: Struggles for Mastery in the Eastern Mediterranean, 1850–1960* (2006), 17.

63. Ibid.
64. Tumelty, 'The Ionian Islands', 292.
65. Quoted in Holland and Markides, *The British and the Hellenes*, 35.
66. Lawrence Durrell, *Prospero's Cell: A Guide to the Landscape and Manners of the Island of Corfu* (1945), 91.
67. Holland and Markides, *The British and the Hellenes*, 33.
68. Viscount Kirkwall, *Four Years in the Ionian Islands* (1864), 236.
69. Holland and Markides, *The British and the Hellenes*, 42.
70. Admiral Sir Rodney Mundy, *HMS Hannibal at Palermo during the Italian Revolution, 1859–1861* (1863), 27.
71. Beales, *England and Italy*, 94.
72. W. F. Reddaway, 'Great Britain and France, 1848–1870', in *The Cambridge History of the British Empire*, vol. 2 (1940), 557.
73. Martinengo-Cesaresco, *Liberation of Italy*, 232.
74. Ibid., 236.
75. Denis Mack Smith, *Cavour and Garibaldi, 1860* (1954), 8.
76. Beales, *England and Italy*, 149–50.
77. Ibid., 101.
78. Ibid., 127–8.
79. Ibid., 173.
80. The intervention, at Cavour's behest, had been by Sir James Lacaita, a crucial figure in Anglo-Italian society in both London and Rome. Lacaita had earlier served as Gladstone's secretary in the Ionian Islands.
81. Sir Henry Elliot, *Some Recollections and Other Diplomatic Experiences* (1922), 18, 95.
82. Mack Smith, *Cavour and Garibaldi*, 228.
83. Mundy, *HMS Hannibal*, 270–71.
84. Elliot, *Some Recollections*, 76–7.
85. Trevelyan, *Garibaldi's Defence of the Roman Republic*, 280–81.
86. Searight, *Steaming East*, 110.
87. K. D. Bell, 'British Policy towards the Construction of the Suez Canal, 1859–65', *Transactions of the Royal Historical Society*, 1 (1965), 136.
88. Searight, *Steaming East*, 120.
89. Quoted in Max Fletcher, 'The Suez Canal and World Shipping', *Journal of Economic History*, 18 (December 1958), 564.
90. Louvier, *La Puissance navale et militaire britannique en Méditerranée*, 322.

91. M. E. Yapp, *The Making of the Modern Near East, 1792–1923* (1987), 132–6.
92. Saint-Marc Girardin, *La Syrie en 1861: Condition des chrétiens en orient* (1862), 3, 49–50.
93. Ann Pottinger Saab, *Reluctant Icon: Gladstone, Bulgaria and the Working Classes* (1991), 40.
94. Girardin, *La Syrie en 1861*, 134.
95. Quoted in Holland and Markides, *The British and the Hellenes*, 59.
96. Quoted ibid., 51.
97. Phillip Sherrard, *Edward Lear: The Corfu Years* (1988), 213. There was a clear precedent, however, in the blowing up of the fortified Mole of Tangier, on which much money had been expended, when the British evacuated the town in 1684.
98. Holland and Markides, *The British and the Hellenes*, 72.
99. Ibid., 77.
100. Marquis of Zetland, *Lord Cromer* (1932), 31.
101. *The Times*, 14 June 1864.
102. 'The Last of the Ionian Protectorate', *Saturday Review*, 18 June 1864.
103. John Vincent (ed.), *Disraeli, Derby and the Conservative Party: Journals and Memoirs of Lord Stanley* (1978), 23.
104. See Kenneth Bourne, 'Great Britain and the Cretan Revolt, 1866–69', *Slavonic and East European Review*, 35 (1957), 74–94.
105. Saab, *Reluctant Icon*, 29.
106. Bismarck's encouragement of a Hohenzollern prince to the Spanish throne left vacant by Isabella II's deposition in 1868 lured Napoleon III into a fatal decision to declare war on Germany.
107. John F. Beeler, *British Naval Policy in the Gladstone–Disraeli Era, 1866–1880* (1997), 4.
108. 'Saunders Dundas Memorandum on the State of the Navy', June 1858, in *The Milne Papers, 1806–96*, vol. 1 (Navy Records Society, 2004).
109. Laferla, *British Malta*, vol. 1, p. 241.
110. Louvier, *La Puissance navale et militaire britannique en Méditerranée*, 332–8.
111. Lee, *Malta, 1813–1914*, 165.
112. Pirotta, *The Maltese Public Service*, 209.
113. Ibid., 265–6.
114. Price, *Malta and the Maltese*, 111.
115. Henry Frendo, 'Maltese Colonial Identity: Latin Mediterranean or British Empire?', in Mallia-Milanes, *British Colonial Experience*, 190.
116. Saab, *Reluctant Icon*, 151.

117. Theodore Ropp, *The Development of a Modern Navy: French Naval Policy, 1874–1904* (1987), 5.
118. Lee, *Malta, 1813–1914*, 78–9.
119. David Barchard, 'The Fearless and Self-Reliant Servant: The Life and Career of Sir Alfred Biliotti (1833–1915)', *Studi miceni*, 48 (September 2008), 38.
120. Hamilton Lang, *Cyprus* (1878), 190.
121. Sir George Hill, *A History of Cyprus*, vol. 4 (1952), 274–5.
122. Ibid., 265–6. In fact, at the time Hornby felt revulsion at the occupation of Cyprus, which he characterized as 'a sharing of the spoil with the other robbers [of Turkey]'.
123. Egerton, *Hornby*, 299.
124. Quoted in 'Stanley, Edward Henry, fifteenth earl of Derby (1826–1893)', *ODNB*.
125. Saab, *Reluctant Icon*, 195.
126. See p. 323.
127. Richard Millman, *Britain and the Eastern Question, 1875–1878* (1979), 412–13.
128. Hill, *A History of Cyprus*, vol. 4, p. 177.
129. Ibid., 257–89.
130. Whether the Archbishop raised union with Greece on this occasion is disputed in Rolandos Katsiaounis, *Labour, Society and Politics in Cyprus during the Second Half of the Nineteenth Century* (1997), 25–8.
131. Robert Blake, *Disraeli* (1966), 649.
132. Gladstone to Granville, 13 November 1870, in Agatha Ramm (ed.), *The Gladstone–Granville Correspondence* (1998), 156.
133. Egerton, *Hornby*, 247.

## CHAPTER 4. MESSAGES FROM THE MEDITERRANEAN, 1878–1914

1. Quoted in David Landes, *Bankers and Pashas* (1958), 84; also see John Darwin, *After Tamerlane: The Global History of Empire* (2007), 288–9.
2. Michael Reimer, 'Colonial Bridgehead: Social and Spatial Change in Alexandria, 1850–1882', *International Journal of Middle Eastern Studies*, 20 (1988), 531.
3. The 'Middle East', both as nomenclature and strategic notion, was essentially a construct of the 1914–18 war. See Roger Adleson, *London and the Invention of the Middle East: Money, Power and War, 1902–1922* (1995).

4. See Ronald Robinson and John Gallagher, *Africa and the Victorians: The Official Mind of Imperialism* (1961).
5. Ibid., 94.
6. Quoted in Peter Mansfield, *The British in Egypt* (1971), 33.
7. Robinson and Gallagher, *Africa and the Victorians*, 103.
8. Philip Mansel, *Levant: Splendour and Catastrophe on the Mediterranean* (2010), 120.
9. See Muriel Chamberlain, 'The Alexandria Massacre of 11 June 1882 and the British Occupation of Egypt', *Middle Eastern Studies*, 13/1 (1977), 14–39.
10. C. L. Seymour, 'The Bombardment of Alexandria: A Note', *English Historical Review*, 87/345 (October 1972), 793.
11. Quentin Hughes, *Britain in the Mediterranean and the Defence of her Naval Stations* (1981), 155.
12. John S. Galbraith and Afaf Lufti al-Sayyid-Marsot, 'The British Occupation of Egypt: Another View', *International Journal of Middle Eastern Studies*, 9/4 (November 1978), 486.
13. S. de Kusel, *An Englishman's Recollections of Egypt, 1863–1887* (1915), 209–10.
14. Ibid., 115.
15. A. G. Hopkins, 'The Victorians and Africa: A Reconsideration of the Occupation of Egypt, 1882', *Journal of African History*, 27/2 (1986), 374.
16. Admiral Lord Charles Beresford, *Memoirs* (1914), 182.
17. In Ceylon, Arabi Pasha took a strong interest in local education, and was patron of the first Muslim college, Zahira College, still situated in central Colombo. The Pasha was permitted to return to Egypt in May 1902, where he lived until his death in 1911. The square where President Nasser delivered his famous speech nationalizing the Suez Canal during July 1956 was named after him.
18. Charles Hallberg, *The Suez Canal: Its History and Diplomatic Significance* (1931), 288.
19. Colin Smith, *The Embassy of Sir William White at Constantinople, 1886–1891* (1957), 79.
20. See Maria Panayioutou, 'The Strategic Origins of the British Occupation of Cyprus and its Role during the Arabi Revolt and the Resulting Egyptian Campaign, 1876–1882', M.Phil. dissertation, University of Birmingham (2006).
21. Quoted in Tabitha Morgan, *Sweet and Bitter Island: A History of the British in Cyprus* (2010), 21.

22. Philip Magnus, *Kitchener: Portrait of an Imperialist* (1958), 23.
23. Sir George Hill, *A History of Cyprus*, vol. 4 (1952), 463–6.
24. Samuel White, *Cyprus As I Saw It in 1879* (1879), 265–6.
25. Quoted in Robert Holland and Diana Markides, *The British and the Hellenes: Struggles for Mastery in the Eastern Mediterranean, 1850–1960* (2006), 169.
26. Anne Cavendish (ed.), *Cyprus 1878: The Journal of Sir Garnet Wolseley* (1991), 56.
27. See p. 207.
28. Morgan, *Sweet and Bitter Island*, 11.
29. Quoted in Hill, *A History of Cyprus*, vol. 4, p. 418.
30. White, *Cyprus As I Saw It in 1879*, 415–20.
31. Quoted in George Georghallides, *A Political and Administrative History of Cyprus, 1918–1926* (1979), 59.
32. Holland and Markides, *The British and the Hellenes*, 167.
33. Sendall to Joseph Chamberlain, 23 April 1897, CO67/105, TNA.
34. Holland and Markides, *The British and the Hellenes*, 72.
35. Quentin Hughes, *Fortress: Architecture and Military History in Malta* (1969), 247–8.
36. Henry Frendo, *Party Politics in a Fortress Colony: The Maltese Experience* (1975), 30.
37. Harrison Smith, *Britain in Malta*, vol. 1: *Constitutional Development of Malta in the Nineteenth Century* (1953), 54–5.
38. A. V. Laferla, *British Malta*, vol 2: *1872–1921* (1938), 36–7.
39. Quoted in Frendo, *Party Politics in a Fortress Colony*, 44.
40. Smith, *Britain in Malta*, vol. 1, p. 25.
41. Ibid., 31.
42. Laferla, *British Malta*, vol. 2, p. 143.
43. James Glanville, *Italy's Relations with England, 1896–1905* (1934), 97.
44. *Times of Malta*, 9 November 1900.
45. Hilda Lee, *Malta, 1813–1914* (1972), 222.
46. Smith, *Britain in Malta*, vol. 1, p. 204.
47. René Pichon, *L'Empire de la Méditerranée* (1904), 426.
48. See Jeremy Boissevain, '*Festa Partiti* and the British: Exploding a Myth', in Victor Mallia-Milanes (ed.), *The British Colonial Experience, 1800–1964: The Impact on Maltese Society* (1988), 178.
49. Arthur J. Marder, *British Naval Policy, 1880–1905: The Anatomy of British Seapower* (1941), 222.
50. Theodore Ropp, *The Development of a Modern Navy: French Naval Policy, 1874–1904* (1987), 157.

51. Arthur Marsden, 'Britain and the Tunis Base, 1894–1899', *English Historical Review*, 79/310 (January 1964), 79.
52. Marder, *British Naval Policy, 1880–1905*, 197.
53. Quoted ibid., 178, 211.
54. Quoted ibid., 409.
55. Ibid., 20.
56. Marsden, 'Britain and the Tunis Base', 95.
57. See Stephen Constantine, 'Monarchy and Constructing Identity in "British" Gibraltar, c. 1800 to the Present', *Journal of Imperial and Commonwealth History*, 34/1 (March 2006), 23–44.
58. Quoted in Smith, *Britain in Malta*, vol. 1, p. 213.
59. See Thomas Bowles, *Gibraltar: A National Danger* (1903).
60. Marder, *British Naval Policy, 1880–1905*, 412; also Ropp, *Development of a Modern Navy*, 308–13.
61. For this aspect, see David Steel, *Lord Salisbury: A Political Biography* (1999), 107.
62. Holland and Markides, *The British and the Hellenes*, 100–105.
63. S. B. Chester, *The Life of Venizelos* (1924), 69.
64. Keith M. Wilson, *Empire or Continent? Studies in British Foreign Policy from the 1880s to the First World War* (1987), p. 210.
65. Marder, *British Naval Policy, 1880–1905*, 330.
66. The Kaiser's visit caused immense excitement. While in Jerusalem he laid the stone of a building named in honour of his consort, Augusta Victoria, later the residence of the first British High Commissioner in Palestine.
67. Sir Sydney Lee, *King Edward VII: A Biography*, vol. 2 (1927), 217.
68. Mansfield, *The British in Egypt*, 150–61.
69. See Roger Owen, *Lord Cromer: Victorian Imperialist, Edwardian Proconsul* (2004), 242, and Mansfield, *The British in Egypt*, 139–41. A programme of Anglicization was never attempted in Egypt.
70. See Gerard Noel, *Ena: Spain's English Queen* (1984), 94–5, 107.
71. Lee, *King Edward VII*, 537–8. The assassination of King Humbert of Italy at Monza in 1900 had underlined the risks surrounding European royalty.
72. Mansfield, *The British in Egypt*, 166.
73. Beresford, *Memoirs*, 513.
74. Mansfield, *The British in Egypt*, 404.
75. Lee, *King Edward VII*, 332.
76. Andrew Lambert, *Sir John Fisher's Naval Revolution* (1999), 5–6.
77. Holland and Markides, *The British and the Hellenes*, 138.
78. Philip Graves, *Briton and Turk* (1941), 152.

79. Paul Halpern, *The Mediterranean Naval Situation, 1908–1914* (1971), 41.
80. Lee, *King Edward VII*, 496; Magnus, *Kitchener*, 248.
81. John Lee, *A Soldier's Life: General Sir Ian Hamilton, 1853–1947* (2000), 112.
82. Frendo, *Party Politics in a Fortress Colony*, 136.
83. Chris Grocott, 'A Good Soldier, but a Maligned Governor: General Sir Archibald Hunter, Governor of Gibraltar, 1910–1913', *Journal of Imperial and Commonwealth History*, 37/3 (September 2009), 424.
84. Quoted in Mansfield, *The British in Egypt*, 180–81. See Peter Mellini, *Sir Eldon Gorst: The Overshadowed Proconsul* (1977).
85. Magnus, *Kitchener*, 248.
86. Sir Ronald Storrs, *Orientations* (1937), 126. 'Fellah' was a popular term for Egyptian peasantry.
87. Georghallides, *Political and Administrative History of Cyprus, 1918–1926*, 85.
88. Holland and Markides, *The British and the Hellenes*, 173.
89. Ibid.
90. Ima Christine Barlow, *The Agadir Crisis* (1940), 303.
91. Robert Holland, *The Pursuit of Greatness: Britain and the World Role 1900–1970* (1991), 47.
92. Ibid., 300.
93. See William Askew, *Europe and Italy's Acquisition of Libya, 1911–1912* (1942).
94. See P. J. Carabott, 'The Temporary Italian Occupation of the Dodecanese: A Prelude to Permanency', *Diplomacy and Statecraft*, 14/2 (July 1993), 285–312.
95. Holland and Markides, *The British and the Hellenes*, 175.
96. Anthony Sattin, *Lifting the Veil: British Society in Egypt, 1768–1956* (1988), 169.
97. Quoted in E. W. R. Lumby (ed.), *Policy and Operations in the Mediterranean, 1912–1914* (1970), 25–6.
98. Ibid.
99. Halpern, *The Mediterranean Naval Situation*, 15–16.
100. Lumby, *Policy and Operations in the Mediterranean*, 55.
101. Geoffrey Miller, *The Millstone: British Naval Policy in the Mediterranean, 1900–1914* (1999), 262.
102. Ibid., 86.
103. Halpern, *The Mediterranean Naval Situation*, 325.
104. Quoted in Michael Llewellyn Smith, *Ionian Vision: Greece in Asia Minor, 1919–1922* (1973), 13.

105. Holland and Markides, *The British and the Hellenes*, 158.
106. Halpern, *The Mediterranean Naval Situation*, 124.
107. Quoted in Miller, *The Millstone*, 557.
108. Ibid.
109. Winston Churchill, *The World Crisis 1911–1914* (1923), 225.
110. *Malta Herald*, 12 August 1914.

## CHAPTER 5. 'INDIFFERENT FRUITS IN THE SOUTH', 1914–1918

1. Sir Ronald Storrs, *Orientations* (1937), 150.
2. Arthur J. Marder, *From the Dreadnought to Scapa Flow*, vol. 2 (1965), 25.
3. Under the 1871 London Convention foreign warships were banned from appearing off Constantinople.
4. Marder, *Dreadnought to Scapa Flow*, 32.
5. The First Battle ('Miracle') of the Marne was fought 5–12 September 1914. Here the Franco-British forces brought the initial German offensive to a halt.
6. Quoted in Anthony Sattin, *Lifting the Veil: British Society in Egypt, 1768–1956* (1988), 168.
7. Vera Brittain, *Testament of Youth* (1933), 291. Ronald Storrs also remarked (*Orientations*, 302) after visiting wartime London how it felt 'besieged' compared to Cairo and Alexandria.
8. Sir Harry Luke, *Cities and Men*, vol. 2 (1953), 3.
9. Storrs, *Orientations*, 159.
10. Ibid., 163.
11. Mabel Caillard, *A Lifetime in Egypt, 1876–1935* (1935), 179.
12. Lieut.-Gen. P. G. Elgood, *Egypt and the Army* (1924), 115.
13. Caillard, *Lifetime in Egypt*, 189.
14. Marder, *Dreadnought to Scapa Flow*, 175.
15. Ibid., 211.
16. Paul Halpern, *The Mediterranean Naval Situation, 1908–1914* (1971), 58.
17. Marder, *Dreadnought to Scapa Flow*, 264.
18. Quoted in Alan Moorehead, *Gallipoli* (1960), 65.
19. Quoted ibid., 158.
20. Halpern, *The Mediterranean Naval Situation*, 159.
21. Marder, *Dreadnought to Scapa Flow*, 333.
22. Storrs, *Orientations*, 298.

23. Luke, *Cities and Men*, 17.
24. Ibid., 7.
25. Elgood, *Egypt and the Army*, 82–4.
26. Sir Valentine Chirol, *The Egyptian Problem* (1920), 130.
27. Mike Read, *Forever England: The Life of Rupert Brooke* (1997), 187.
28. Geoffrey Keynes (ed.), *The Letters of Rupert Brooke* (1968), 676.
29. A. V. Laferla, *British Malta*, vol. 2: *1872–1921* (1938), 168–9.
30. Albert G. Mackinnon, *The Nurse of the Mediterranean* (1916), 42.
31. Brittain, *Testament of Youth*, 308.
32. Storrs, *Orientations*, 232.
33. Quoted in Sattin, *Lifting the Veil*, 170.
34. Brittain, *Testament of Youth*, 332.
35. Quoted in Halpern, *The Mediterranean Naval Situation*, 180.
36. Robert Holland, *The Pursuit of Greatness: Britain and the World Role 1900–1970* (1991), 60–61.
37. Marder, *Dreadnought to Scapa Flow*, 288.
38. Quoted in Moorehead, *Gallipoli*, 307.
39. Sir George Hill, *A History of Cyprus*, vol. 4 (1952), 523; G. Glasgow, *Ronald Burrows* (1923), 226–31.
40. G. Leon, *Greece and the First World War: From Neutrality to Intervention, 1917–18* (1990), 29; also see George Georghallides, *A Political and Administrative History of Cyprus, 1918–1926* (1979), 101.
41. Georghallides, *A Political and Administrative History of Cyprus, 1918–1926*, 89.
42. Quoted in Alan Palmer, *The Gardeners of Salonica* (1965), 14.
43. Leon, *Greece and the First World War*, 240.
44. G. Ward Price, *The Story of the Salonica Army* (1918), ch. VII, p. 5.
45. Jean Karl Tannebaum, *General Maurice Sarrail, 1856–1929* (1974), 79.
46. Palmer, *Gardeners of Salonica*, 150.
47. Tannebaum, *Sarrail*, 89.
48. G. F. Abbott, *Greece and the Allies, 1914–1922* (1922), 130.
49. Leon, *Greece and the First World War*, 436.
50. Ibid., 371.
51. Ibid., 392.
52. Ibid., 154.
53. Eric Linklater, *Compton Mackenzie: A Life* (1987), 150.
54. Abbott, *Greece and the Allies*, 90.
55. Ibid., 154–5.
56. Ibid., 159. See Richard Clogg, 'Academics at War: The British School at

Athens during the First World War', in Michael Llewellyn Smith, Paschalis Kitromilides and Eleni Calligas (eds.), *Scholars, Travels and Archives: Greek History and Culture through the British School at Athens* (2009), 163–77.

57. Linklater, *Compton Mackenzie*, 166–7.
58. Abbott, *Greece and the Allies*, 19–20.
59. See Donald Bloxham, *The Great Game of Genocide: Imperialism, Nationalism and the Destruction of the Ottoman Armenians* (2005).
60. Halpern, *The Mediterranean Naval Situation*, 291–3.
61. Ibid.
62. Ibid.
63. Bloxham, *The Great Game of Genocide*, 142.
64. William A. Renzi, 'Italy's Neutrality and Entrance into the Great War: A Re-examination', *American Historical Review*, 73/5 (June 1968), 1421.
65. Ibid., 1416.
66. G. M. Trevelyan, *Scenes from Italy's War* (1919), 29; also David Cannadine, *G. M. Trevelyan: A Life in History* (1992), 80.
67. Trevelyan, *Scenes from Italy's War*, 30.
68. For a memoir of these batteries, see Hugh Dalton, *With British Guns in Italy* (1919). Dalton was awarded a military decoration by the Italian Government for his services. He was later Chancellor of the Exchequer in the British Labour government, 1945–51.
69. See John and Eileen Wilks, *The British Army in Italy, 1917–1918* (1998), 176–91.
70. Halpern, *The Mediterranean Naval Situation*, 126.
71. Ibid., 125.
72. Ibid., 234–6.
73. Brittain, *Testament of Youth*, 311–12.
74. *Malta Herald*, 6 August 1914.
75. Sir Charles Lucas, *The Empire at War*, vol. 5 (1926), 98.
76. Ibid., 11.
77. Anthony Zarb-Dimech, *Malta during the First World War, 1914–1918* (2004), 47.
78. Laferla, *British Malta*, vol. 2, p. 207.
79. Henry Frendo, *Party Politics in a Fortress Colony: The Maltese Experience* (1975), 161.
80. Laferla, *British Malta*, vol. 2, p. 213.
81. Zarb-Dimech, *Malta during the First World War*, 47.
82. Lucas, *The Empire at War*, 8.
83. Stephen Constantine, 'Monarchy and Constructing Identity in "British"

Gibraltar, c. 1800 to the Present', *Journal of Imperial and Commonwealth History*, 34/1 (March 2006), 31.

84. See Francisco J. Romero Salvado, 'The Great War and the Crisis of Liberalism in Spain, 1916–1917', *Historical Journal*, 46/4 (2003), 893–914.
85. Sir George Hills, *Rock of Contention: A History of Gibraltar* (1974), 402.
86. Salvado, 'The Great War and the Crisis of Liberalism in Spain', 908.
87. Halpern, *The Mediterranean Naval Situation*, 377.
88. See pp. 158–9.
89. Colonial Office minutes, 3 Nov. 1915, CO67/122, TNA.
90. Quoted in Andrekos Varnava, *British Imperialism in Cyprus, 1878–1915: The Inconsequential Possession* (2009), 265.
91. Georghallides, *A Political and Administrative History of Cyprus, 1918–1926*, 89.
92. Luke, *Cities and Men*, 43.
93. Quoted in Lucas, *The Empire at War*, 26.
94. Georghallides, *A Political and Administrative History of Cyprus, 1918–1926*, 88.
95. Luke, *Cities and Men*, 33. On the British role in Kyrillos's election, see material in the Luke Papers, Martin Laiki Bank Cultural Centre, Nicosia.
96. Hill, *A History of Cyprus*, vol. 4, pp. 522–4. There was anti-Greek feeling among British soldiers in the Mediterranean arising from the fatalities incurred in Athens a few months before.
97. C. W. J. Orr, *Cyprus under British Rule* (1918).
98. Sattin, *Lifting the Veil*, 216.
99. Elgood, *Egypt and the Army*, 114.
100. Ibid., 126.
101. Lucas, *The Empire at War*, 41–4, 235.
102. Holland, *Pursuit of Greatness*, 70–75.
103. Lawrence James, *Imperial Warrior: The Life and Times of Viscount Allenby, 1861–1936* (1993), 117.
104. A. P. Wavell, *The Palestine Campaign* (1929), 83.
105. Roberto Mazza, *Jerusalem: From the Ottomans to the British* (2009), 121.
106. Matthew Hughes, *Allenby and British Strategy in the Middle East, 1917–1919* (1999), 41.
107. Storrs, *Orientations*, 322.
108. Tom Segev, *One Palestine Complete: Jews and Arabs under the British Mandate* (2000), 19.
109. Ibid., 134.
110. Brian Gardner, *Allenby* (1965), 159; also Segev, *One Palestine Complete*, 51–4.

111. Mazza, *Jerusalem*, 136.
112. Ibid., 123.
113. Hughes, *Allenby*, 31–2.
114. Ibid., 78. David Lean's 1962 film *Lawrence of Arabia*, in novel Technicolor with Peter O'Toole in the starring role, helped sustain the Lawrence legend into the second half of the twentieth century.
115. For a discussion, see Avi Schlaim, 'The Balfour Declaration and its Consequences', in Wm. Roger Louis (ed.), *Yet More Adventures with Britannia: Personalities, Politics and Culture in Britain* (2005), 251–70.
116. The prime example was Edwin Montague, Secretary of State for India at this time and deeply anxious concerning Muslim disaffection in the Empire. See S. D. Waley, *Edwin Montague* (1964).
117. Elie Kedourie, *England and the Middle East: The Destruction of the Middle East, 1914–1921* (1956), 82–4.
118. Hughes, *Allenby*, 65.
119. Storrs, *Orientations*, 353.
120. Segev, *One Palestine Complete*, 94. The meetings of the Zionist Commission were conducted in English, since few of its members had enough Hebrew.
121. Storrs, *Orientations*, 324.
122. Kedourie, *England and the Middle East*, 155.
123. Charles King, in *The Black Sea: A History* (2004), states that 'The real fate of the Ottomans lay . . . in clashes with British forces in the Levant' (p. 214). In fact most Turkish troops had been withdrawn from the Syrian front by 1918, and it was the approach of *entente* forces from Macedonia that proved crucial. The fate of the Empire was therefore decided closer to the Turkish heartland.
124. Hughes, *Allenby*, 64.
125. Palmer, *Gardeners of Salonica*, 228–9. The recognition of Marshal Foch as Supreme Commander on the Western Front was key to this arrangement.
126. Ibid., 230.
127. Halpern, *The Mediterranean Naval Situation*, 563.
128. Ibid., 559.
129. Luke, *Cities and Men*, 30.
130. Halpern, *The Mediterranean Naval Situation*, 564.
131. Townshend had humiliatingly surrendered to the Turks with his army of 13,000 men at Kut in Mesopotamia in April 1916.
132. Halpern, *The Mediterranean Naval Situation*, 565.
133. Ian Lister (ed.), *Among the Ottomans: Diaries from Turkey in World War I* (2011), 67–9.

## CHAPTER 6. BETWEEN MASTERY AND ABANDONMENT, 1918–1939

1. E. H. Carr, *Great Britain as a Mediterranean Power* (1937), 6.
2. Basil Liddell Hart, *Paris or the Future of War* (1925), 130.
3. Philip Bell, *France and Britain: Entente and Estrangement, 1900–1940* (1996), 184.
4. Sir Harry Luke, *Cities and Men*, vol. 2 (1953), 79.
5. Philip Mansel, *Constantinople: City of the World's Desire, 1453–1923* (1995), 381–2.
6. Martin Gilbert, *Sir Horace Rumbold* (1973), 234.
7. A. J. Toynbee, minute, 11 July 1944, FO371/40842, TNA. Toynbee's analysis was part of a debate in 1944 about a looming occupation of Berlin. Germany after her defeat in 1945 had no inter-Allied zone precisely to avoid the precedent offered by Constantinople after 1919.
8. John Darwin, *Britain, Egypt and the Middle East: Imperial Policy in the Aftermath of War, 1918–1922* (1981), 173.
9. Quoted in Michael Llewellyn Smith, *Ionian Vision: Greece in Asia Minor, 1919–1922* (1973), 226.
10. Darwin, *Britain, Egypt and the Middle East*, 168.
11. N. Petsalis-Dimidis, *Greece and the Paris Peace Conference* (1978),108.
12. Llewellyn Smith, *Ionian Vision*, 80.
13. See Brig.-Gen. Sir James Edmonds, 'The Occupation of Constantinople, 1918–23', in WO161/85, TNA.
14. Gilbert, *Rumbold*, 282.
15. Abe Attrep, '"A State of Wretchedness and Impotence": A British View of Istanbul and Turkey in 1919', *International Journal of Middle East Studies*, 1 (January 1978).
16. Mehmed VI had succeeded to the Turkish Sultanate on the death of Mehmed V in July 1918.
17. Quoted in Darwin, *Britain, Egypt and the Middle East*, 177.
18. Stephen Roskill, *Naval Policy between the Wars*, vol. 1 (1968), 188.
19. Ibid., 233.
20. Winston Churchill, *The World Crisis: The Aftermath* (1929), 377.
21. Michael Finefrock, 'Atatürk, Lloyd George and the Megali Idea, June–August 1922', *Journal of Modern History*, 52/1 (March 1980).
22. D. Osborne, minute, 5 January 1922, FO371/369, TNA.
23. Llewellyn Smith, *Ionian Vision*, 253.
24. Henry Cumming, *Franco-British Rivalry in the Post-War Near East* (1938), 170–72.

25. Gilbert, *Rumbold*, 257.
26. Ibid., 251.
27. Llewellyn Smith, *Ionian Vision*, 300.
28. Ibid., 305.
29. Roskill, *Naval Policy between the Wars*, vol. 1, p. 197; see also Philip Mansel, *Levant: Splendour and Catastrophe on the Mediterranean* (2010), 219–22.
30. Gilbert, *Rumbold*, 278.
31. Cumming, *Franco-British Rivalry*, 178.
32. Edmonds, 'The Occupation of Constantinople'.
33. General Sir Charles Harington, *Plumer of Messines* (1935), 245–6.
34. Quoted in Patrick Kinross, *Atatürk: The Rebirth of a Nation* (1964), 385.
35. Cumming, *Franco-British Rivalry*, 210.
36. Gilbert, *Rumbold*, 281.
37. Ibid., 277.
38. Kinross, *Atatürk*, 193.
39. Gilbert, *Rumbold*, 266.
40. David Walder, *The Chanak Affair* (1969), 348.
41. Mansel, *Constantinople*, 380–414.
42. Sir David Kelly, *The Ruling Few: Or the Human Background to Diplomacy* (1952), 189.
43. Robert Holland, *The Pursuit of Greatness: Britain and the World Role 1900–1970* (1991), 102–3.
44. For background, see Ellis Goldberg, 'Peasants in Revolt – Egypt in 1919', *International Journal of Middle Eastern Studies*, 24 (1992), 261–80.
45. Darwin, *Britain, Egypt and the Middle East*, 69.
46. Peter Mansfield, *The British in Egypt* (1971), 223.
47. Steven Morewood, *The British Defence of Egypt 1935–1940: Conflict and Crisis in the Eastern Mediterranean* (2005), 13.
48. See Viscount Wavell, *Allenby in Egypt* (1943).
49. Lawrence Grafftey-Smith, *Bright Levant* (1970), 84.
50. Lanver Mak, 'The British Community in Occupied Cairo', Ph.D. thesis, University of London (2002), 64–6.
51. Quoted in Darwin, *Britain, Egypt and the Middle East*, 90.
52. P. N. Furbank, *E. M. Forster: A Life*, vol. 2 (1978), 33–4. Egypt never had for Forster the fascination he felt for India.
53. Mak, 'The British Community in Occupied Cairo', 242–52.
54. See material on the Council of the British Community of Alexandria in FO141/766, TNA.

55. Quoted in Mansfield, *The British in Egypt*, 302.
56. Darwin, *Britain, Egypt and the Middle East*, 77.
57. Richard Long, *British Proconsuls in Egypt, 1914–1929* (2009), 117.
58. Darwin, *Britain, Egypt and the Middle East*, 277.
59. Mak, 'The British Community in Occupied Cairo', 252.
60. Grafftey-Smith, *Bright Levant*, 46.
61. On Zaghloul in Gibraltar, see material in FO141/807, TNA.
62. P. J. Vatikiotis, *The Modern History of Egypt* (1969), 272–3.
63. Long, *British Proconsuls in Egypt*, 130.
64. John Charmley, *Lord Lloyd and the Decline of the British Empire* (1987), 127.
65. Grafftey-Smith, *Bright Levant*, 101–2.
66. Ibid.
67. Ibid.
68. Quoted in Charmley, *Lord Lloyd*, 140.
69. Ibid., 150.
70. Quoted in Long, *British Proconsuls in Egypt*, 156.
71. Vatikiotis, *Modern History of Egypt*, 280–82.
72. Grafftey-Smith, *Bright Levant*, 120.
73. Dominic Fenech, *Responsibility and Power in Inter-War Malta. Book One, 1919–1930* (2005), 42–3.
74. Report of June Disturbances Committee, 18 September 1919, WO32/9561, TNA.
75. Minute, 8 October 1919, WO32/9560, TNA.
76. Fenech, *Responsibility and Power in Inter-War Malta*, 38.
77. Harington, *Plumer*, 207.
78. Godfrey Pirotta, *The Maltese Public Service, 1800–1940: The Administrative Politics of a Micro-State* (1996), 380–87.
79. Quoted in Fenech, *Responsibility and Power in Inter-War Malta*, 230.
80. Ibid., 48.
81. Ibid., 243.
82. Ibid., 93.
83. Tito Benady, *The Royal Navy at Gibraltar* (1992), 126–30.
84. Henry Frendo, 'Britain's European Mediterranean: Language, Religion and Politics in Lord Strickland's Malta, 1927–30', *History of European Ideas*, 21/1 (January 1995), 51.
85. Joan Alexander, *Mabel Strickland* (1996), shows how Stricklandite politics in Malta drifted unerringly towards irrelevance, despite or because of its orientation towards the crustier forms of English Toryism.

86. Fenech, *Responsibility and Power in Inter-War Malta*, 192.
87. Frendo, 'Britain's European Mediterranean', 49.
88. Harrison Smith, *Lord Strickland: Servant of the Crown* (1954), 351.
89. D. B. Swinfen, 'Lord Strickland, the *Ultra Vires* Cases and the Maltese Constitution, 1924–1939', *Journal of Imperial and Commonwealth History*, 17/3 (May 1989), 416.
90. For the Vatican, see P. Kent, *The Pope and the Duce: The International Impact of the Lateran Treaties* (1981).
91. Pirotta, *The Maltese Public Service*, 435.
92. Fenech, *Responsibility and Power in Inter-War Malta*, 284.
93. Ibid., 430.
94. Frendo, 'Britain's European Mediterranean', 61.
95. Stephen Constantine, *Community and Identity: The Making of Modern Gibraltar since 1704* (2009), 325.
96. Ibid., 329.
97. General Sir Arthur Godley, *Life of an Irish Soldier* (1939), 321.
98. Gareth Stockey, *Gibraltar: 'A Dagger in the Spine of Spain'* (2009), 49.
99. Constantine, *Community and Identity*, 295–6.
100. Quoted in Stockey, *'Dagger in the Spine of Spain'*, 18–19.
101. Gilbert, *Rumbold*, 300.
102. Tabitha Morgan, *Sweet and Bitter Island: A History of the British in Cyprus* (2010), 97.
103. James McHenry, *The Uneasy Partnership, 1918–1939: The Political and Diplomatic Interaction between Great Britain, Turkey and the Turkish-Cypriot Community* (1987), 115.
104. Sir George Hill, *A History of Cyprus*, vol. 4 (1952), 503.
105. George Georghallides, *A Political and Administrative History of Cyprus, 1918–1926* (1979), 329.
106. T. E. Lawrence, *Seven Pillars of Wisdom* (1926), 57.
107. McHenry, *Uneasy Partnership*, 137–8.
108. Fenech, *Responsibility and Power in Inter-War Malta*, 229.
109. George Georghallides, *Cyprus and the Governorship of Sir Ronald Storrs: The Causes of the 1931 Crisis* (1985), 67.
110. Rory Miller, 'Sir Ronald Storrs and Zion: The Dream that Turned into a Nightmare', *Middle Eastern Studies*, 36/3 (2000).
111. Georghallides, *Sir Ronald Storrs*, 383.
112. 'His great desire as an administrator', it was recalled, 'was to please everybody, and this quality tended to his undoing both in Palestine and later in Cyprus . . .'. See Norman and Helen Bentwich, *Mandate Memories, 1918–1948* (1965), 36.

113. McHenry, *Uneasy Partnership*, 95.
114. Georghallides, *Sir Ronald Storrs*, 365.
115. Ibid., 355.
116. Sir Ronald Storrs, *Orientations* (1937), 534.
117. Bentwich and Bentwich, *Mandate Memories*, 45.
118. Ibid., 90.
119. Quoted in Tom Segev, *One Palestine Complete: Jews and Arabs under the British Mandate* (2000), 147.
120. Bernard Wasserstein, *The British in Palestine: The Mandatory Government and the Arab-Jewish Conflict, 1917–1929* (1991), 77–8.
121. Bernard Wasserstein, 'Herbert Samuel and the Palestine Problem', *English Historical Review*, 91/361 (October 1976).
122. Wasserstein, *The British in Palestine*, 134.
123. Ibid., 131.
124. Segev, *One Palestine Complete*, 147, 198.
125. Quoted in Wasserstein, *The British in Palestine*, 127–8.
126. Naomi Shepherd, *Ploughing Sand: British Rule in Palestine, 1917–1948* (1999), 64.
127. Ibid., 131.
128. Ibid., 36.
129. Before 1939, however, most of Britain's oil needs were supplied from the United States.
130. Shepherd, *Ploughing Sand*, 106.
131. Geoffrey Powell, *Plumer: The Soldier's General* (1990), 316.
132. Segev, *One Palestine Complete*, 315.
133. Ibid., 325.
134. Quoted in A. J. Shermann, *Mandate Days: British Lives in Palestine, 1918–1948* (1997), 81–2.
135. Simon Ball, *The Bitter Sea: The Brutal World War Two Fight for the Mediterranean* (2009), 18.
136. Morewood, *British Defence of Egypt*, 72.
137. Reynolds Salerno, *Vital Crossroads: Mediterranean Origins of the Second World War, 1935–1940* (2002), 38.
138. Ibid., 106.
139. Douglas Austin, *Malta and British Strategic Policy, 1925–43* (2004), 15.
140. Trefor Evans (ed.), *The Killearn Diaries, 1934–1946* (1972), 58.
141. Ibid., 41.
142. M. E. Yapp (ed.), *Politics and Diplomacy in Egypt: The Diaries of Sir Miles Lampson, 1935–1937* (1997), entry for 25 May 1935.
143. See Laila Morsy, 'The Military Clauses of the Anglo-Egyptian Treaty of

Friendship and Alliance, 1936', *International Journal of Middle East Studies*, 16/1 (March 1984), 67–85.

144. Ibid., 74.
145. Evans, *Killearn Diaries*, 77–8.
146. Viscount Cunningham, *A Sailor's Odyssey: The Autobiography of Viscount Cunningham* (1951), 207.
147. Yapp, *Politics and Diplomacy in Egypt*, 29–32.
148. Hoda Nasser, *Britain and the Egyptian Nationalist Movement, 1936–1952* (1994), 24.
149. Evans, *Killearn Diaries*, 71.
150. Ibid., 109.
151. John Manduca (ed.), *The Bonham-Carter Diaries: What the British Governor Thought of Malta and the Maltese* (2004), 65, 82.
152. Lawrence Pratt, *East of Malta, West of Suez: Britain's Mediterranean Crisis, 1936–1939* (1975), 121.
153. Manduca, *Bonham-Carter Diaries*, entry for 16 December 1936.
154. Swinfen, 'Lord Strickland, the *Ultra Vires* Case and the Maltese Constitution', 419.
155. Manduca, *Bonham-Carter Diaries*, entry for 25 March 1939.
156. Pratt, *East of Malta*, 24.
157. Salerno, *Vital Crossroads*, 36.
158. Pratt, *East of Malta*, 86–7.
159. Manduca, *Bonham-Carter Diaries*, entry for 1 November 1937.
160. Ibid., entry for 14 September 1938.
161. Ibid., entry for 1 October 1938.
162. Ibid., entry for 12 April 1939.
163. Stockey, *'A Dagger in the Spine of Spain'*, 90.
164. Quoted ibid., 96.
165. See pp. 187–8.
166. See Jill Edwards, *The British Government and the Spanish Civil War, 1936–1939* (1979), and Tom Buchanan, *Britain and the Spanish Civil War* (1997).
167. Cunningham, *A Sailor's Odyssey*, 185–6.
168. Roderick Macleod (ed.), *The Ironside Diaries 1937–1940* (1962), 17.
169. Benady, *Royal Navy at Gibraltar*, 147–9.
170. Quoted in Alexis Rappas, 'The Elusive Polity: Social Engineering and the Reinvention of Politics in Colonial Cyprus, 1931–1941', Ph.D. thesis, European University Institute (2008), 70.
171. Ibid., 143–50.

172. Anastasia Yiangou, *Cyprus in World War Two: Politics and Conflict in the Eastern Mediterranean* (2010), 110.
173. Quoted in Robert Holland and Diana Markides, *The British and the Hellenes: Struggles for Mastery in the Eastern Mediterranean, 1850–1960* (2006), 173.
174. Yiangou, *Cyprus in World War Two*, 21.
175. Segev, *One Palestine Complete*, 414, 442.
176. Sir Hugh Foot, *A Start in Freedom* (1964), 40.
177. Segev, *One Palestine Complete*, 377.
178. Shepherd, *Ploughing Sand*, 112–18.
179. Gilbert, *Rumbold*, 423.
180. Ibid., 428.
181. The Chief of Staff in London considered that at best Haifa had the capacity to act as a base for light naval forces. See Pratt, *East of Malta*, 125.
182. Evans, *Killearn Diaries*, 94.
183. Segev, *One Palestine Complete*, 436.
184. Shepherd, *Ploughing Sand*, 193.
185. See Charles Townshend, 'The Defence of Palestine: Insurrection and Public Security, 1931–1941', *English Historical Review*, 103 (October 1988).
186. Matthew Hughes, 'The Banality of Brutality: British Armed Forces and the Repression of the Arab Revolt in Palestine, 1936–1939', *English Historical Review*, 124 (April 2009).
187. Shepherd, *Ploughing Sand*, 202.
188. Hughes, 'The Banality of Brutality', 353.
189. Pratt, *East of Malta*, 125.
190. Segev, *One Palestine Complete*, 442.
191. Pratt, *East of Malta*, 29.
192. Salerno, *Vital Crossroads*, 97.
193. Ibid., 136.
194. Morewood, *British Defence of Egypt*, 224.
195. Salerno, *Vital Crossroads*, 97.
196. Pratt, *East of Malta*, 174.
197. Salerno, *Vital Crossroads*, 141.
198. HMSO, *East of Malta, West of Suez: The Admiralty Account of the Naval War in the Eastern Mediterranean, September 1939–March 1941* (1943), 9.
199. Manduca, *Bonham-Carter Diaries*, entry for 6 October 1939.
200. Morewood, *British Defence of Egypt*, 208.
201. Pratt, *East of Malta*, 260.

## CHAPTER 7. BRITAIN'S FIRST BATTLEFIELD, 1939–1945

1. Quoted in Robert Holland, *The Pursuit of Greatness: Britain and the World Role 1900–1970* (1991), 177.
2. HMSO, *East of Malta, West of Suez: The Admiralty Account of the Naval War in the Eastern Mediterranean, September 1939–March 1941* (1943), 7.
3. John Manduca (ed.), *The Bonham-Carter Diaries: What the British Governor Thought of Malta and the Maltese* (2004), entry for 27 August 1939.
4. Ibid., entry for 1 January 1940.
5. Steven Morewood, *The British Defence of Egypt 1935–1940: Conflict and Crisis in the Eastern Mediterranean* (2005), 138.
6. Viscount Cunningham, *A Sailor's Odyssey: The Autobiography of Viscount Cunningham* (1951), 218–19.
7. HMSO, *East of Malta, West of Suez*, 9–10.
8. Cunningham, *A Sailor's Odyssey*, 221–3.
9. Trefor Evans (ed.), *The Killearn Diaries, 1934–46* (1972), 110.
10. Hoda Nasser, *Britain and the Egyptian Nationalist Movement, 1936–1952* (1994), 44–7.
11. Laila Amin Morsy, 'Britain's Wartime Policy in Egypt, 1940–1942', *Middle Eastern Studies*, 25/1 (January 1989), 65.
12. Ibid., 66.
13. Morewood, *British Defence of Egypt*, 119.
14. Lord Wilson, *Eight Years Overseas, 1937–1947* (1948), 27.
15. Quoted in Nicholas Bethell, *The Palestine Triangle: The Struggle between the British, the Jews and the Arabs, 1935–1948* (1979), 74.
16. Moshe Dayan was later a senior figure in the Israeli Defence Force, and was Defence Minister during the 1967 Six Day War. In 1941 he served in an Allied unit during the occupation of Syria.
17. Ronald W. Davis, 'Jewish Military Recruitment in Palestine, 1940–1943', *Journal of Palestine Studies*, 8/2 (Winter 1979).
18. Countess Ranfurly, *To War with Whitaker* (1994), entry for 4 March 1940.
19. Ibid., entry for 8 October 1941.
20. Quoted in Anastasia Yiangou, *Cyprus in World War Two: Politics and Conflict in the Eastern Mediterranean* (2010), 25.
21. Ibid., 34.
22. Reynolds Salerno, *Vital Crossroads: Mediterranean Origins of the Second World War, 1935–1940* (2002), 196.

23. Ibid., 189.
24. Cunningham, *A Sailor's Odyssey*, 221–2.
25. Ibid., 230–32.
26. Salerno, *Vital Crossroads*, 209.
27. James Holland, *Fortress Malta: An Island under Siege, 1940–1943* (2003), 28–9.
28. Charles Jellison, *Besieged: The World War II Ordeal of Malta, 1940–44* (1984), 72.
29. Ibid., 59.
30. Ibid., 37.
31. T. J. Finlayson, *The Fortress Came First* (2000), 5.
32. Ibid., 7.
33. Joseph Garcia, *Gibraltar: The Making of a People* (2002), 19.
34. Tito Benady, *The Royal Navy at Gibraltar* (1992), 151.
35. Quoted in Denis Smyth, *Diplomacy and Strategy of Survival: British Policy and Franco's Spain, 1940–41* (1986), 4.
36. Ibid., 42.
37. H. Goda, 'Franco's Bid for Empire: Spain, Gibraltar and the Western Mediterranean in World War Two', in Raanan Rein (ed.), *Spain and the Mediterranean since 1898* (1999), 173.
38. Smyth, *Diplomacy and Strategy of Survival*, 49.
39. Ibid., 70–71.
40. Ibid., 60–64.
41. Goda, 'Franco's Bid for Empire', 179.
42. Philippe Lasserle, 'Could Admiral Gensoul have Averted the Tragedy of Mers-el-Kebir?', *Journal of Military History*, 67 (July 2003), 835–44.
43. Martin Thomas, 'Mers-el-Kebir: The Armed Neutrality of the Vichy French Navy, 1940–44', *English Historical Review*, 112 (June 1997), 650.
44. Stephen Roskill, *Churchill and the Admirals* (1977), 151–2.
45. Ibid., 213. Admiral Godfroy did not surrender control of his fleet to the Allies until North Africa had been cleared of Axis troops in May 1943.
46. Ibid., 157.
47. Colin Smith, *England's Last War against France: Fighting Vichy, 1940–42* (2009), 86.
48. Douglas Porch, *Hitler's Mediterranean Gamble* (2004), 67.
49. Thomas, 'Mers-el-Kebir', 651.
50. Artemis Cooper, *Cairo in the War* (1989), 146.
51. Morsy, 'Britain's Wartime Policy in Egypt', 73.
52. Cooper, *Cairo in the War*, 101.
53. Jellison, *Besieged*, 88.

54. Porch, *Hitler's Mediterranean Gamble*, 111.
55. Ibid., 69.
56. Charles Cruickshank, *Greece, 1940–1941* (1976), 106.
57. David Dilks (ed.), *The Diaries of Sir Alexander Cadogan, 1940–1943* (1971), 358.
58. Roskill, *Churchill and the Admirals*, 182.
59. Cruickshank, *Greece, 1940–1941*, 112.
60. Lord Wilson, *Eight Years Overseas*, 69.
61. Ibid., 117.
62. Antony Beevor, *Crete: The Battle and the Resistance* (1991), 40.
63. Cruickshank, *Greece, 1940–1941*, 146.
64. Beevor, *Crete*, 42.
65. Wilson, *Eight Years Overseas*, 74.
66. Stewart Perowne, *The Siege within the Walls: Malta 1940–1943* (1970), 83.
67. Beevor, *Crete*, 112.
68. Selina Hastings, *Evelyn Waugh: A Biography* (1994), 425, 430.
69. Donald Macintyre, *The Battle for the Mediterranean* (1964), 73.
70. Quoted in Beevor, *Crete*, 217.
71. Porch, *Hitler's Mediterranean Gamble*, 173.
72. Andrew Lambert, *Admirals: The Naval Commanders who Made Britain Great* (2008), 403.
73. Ranfurly, *To War with Whitaker*, entry for 31 May 1941.
74. Porch, *Hitler's Mediterranean Gamble*, 174.
75. Quoted in Yiangou, *Cyprus in World War Two*, 44.
76. Ibid., 69.
77. Quoted in C. Svolopoulos, 'Anglo-Hellenic Talks during the Axis Campaign against Greece', *Balkan Studies*, 23/1 (1982), 201.
78. Yiangou, *Cyprus in World War Two*, 69–71.
79. Holland, *Fortress Malta*, 92.
80. Perowne, *Siege within the Walls*, 64–6.
81. R. Leslie Oliver, *Malta Besieged* (1944), 16–17.
82. Jellison, *Besieged*, 25, 40, 78.
83. Ibid., 61.
84. Oliver, *Malta Besieged*, 24.
85. Porch, *Hitler's Mediterranean Gamble*, 283.
86. Jellison, *Besieged*, 143.
87. Porch, *Hitler's Mediterranean Gamble*, 158–9.
88. Quoted ibid., 7.
89. Lambert, *Admirals*, 406.

90. Macintyre, *The Battle for the Mediterranean*, 119.
91. Cooper, *Cairo in the War*, 168–72.
92. Ibid., 173; Morsy, 'Britain's Wartime Policy in Egypt', 84–7.
93. Holland, *Pursuit of Greatness*, 182.
94. Porch, *Hitler's Mediterranean Gamble*, 278.
95. Cooper, *Cairo in the War*, 195.
96. Macintyre, *The Battle for the Mediterranean*, 164.
97. Jellison, *Besieged*, 154–5.
98. 'What Caused Sir Ugo Mifsud's Death?', *Times of Malta*, 8 October 2009.
99. Jellison, *Besieged*, 172.
100. Perowne, *Siege within the Walls*, 157; Jellison, *Besieged*, 212–14.
101. Jellison, *Besieged*, 134.
102. Holland, *Fortress Malta*, 345.
103. Oliver, *Malta Besieged*, 90.
104. Ibid., 97.
105. Holland, *Fortress Malta*, 358.
106. Ibid.
107. Lawrence Mizzi, *The People's War: Malta, 1940–43* (1998), 94.
108. Perowne, *Siege within the Walls*, 234.
109. Matthew Jones, *Britain, the United States and the Mediterranean War, 1942–44* (1996), 29.
110. Ibid., 63.
111. Alistair Horne, *Macmillan, 1894–1956* (1988), 160.
112. See the entry on Macmillan by H. C. G. Mathew in *ODNB*.
113. Horne, *Macmillan*, 229.
114. Alan F. Wilt, 'The Significance of the Casablanca Decisions, January 1943', *Journal of Military History*, 55/4 (October 1991), 528.
115. Porch, *Hitler's Mediterranean Gamble*, 410.
116. Sarah Bradford, *King George VI* (1985), 351–2.
117. S. W. C. Packer, *Cunningham: The Commander* (1974), 253.
118. Bradford, *King George VI*, 350.
119. Simon Ball, *The Bitter Sea: The Brutal World War Two Fight for the Mediterranean* (2009), 216.
120. Elena Agarossi, *A Nation Collapses: The Italian Surrender of September 1943* (1991), 38.
121. See Carlo d'Este, *Bitter Victory: The Battle for Sicily, 1943* (1988).
122. Porch, *Hitler's Mediterranean Gamble*, 504.
123. Ibid., 547.
124. Ibid., 551.
125. Jones, *Britain, the United States and the Mediterranean War*, 192.

126. Ibid., 93–4.
127. David Williams, *A Most Diplomatic General: The Life of General Lord Robertson* (1996), 60.
128. Agarossi, *A Nation Collapses*, 89.
129. Packer, *Cunningham*, 270.
130. Bruno Arcidiacono, 'The "Dress Rehearsal": The Foreign Office and the Control of Italy, 1943–1944', *Historical Journal*, 28/2, June (1985), 422.
131. See I. C. B. Dear, *The Oxford Companion to the Second World War* (1995), 572–80.
132. Roskill, *Churchill and the Admirals*, 216.
133. Jones, *Britain, the United States and the Mediterranean War*, 123.
134. Ibid., 156.
135. See Jeffrey Holland, *The Aegean Mission: Allied Operations in the Dodecanese, 1943* (1988).
136. Quoted in Robert Holland and Diana Markides, *The British and the Hellenes: Struggles for Mastery in the Eastern Mediterranean, 1850–1960* (2006), 189.
137. Ibid., 193.
138. Roskill, *Churchill and the Admirals*, 220.
139. Dilks, *Diaries of Sir Alexander Cadogan*, 576.
140. See Mark Mazower, *Inside Hitler's Greece: The Experience of Occupation, 1941–1944* (1993).
141. C. M. Woodhouse, *The Struggle for Greece, 1941–1949* (1976), 26.
142. Elizabeth Barker, *British Policy in South-eastern Europe* (1978), 166–7.
143. Ibid., 56.
144. Nigel Clive, *A Greek Experience, 1943–1948* (1985), 74.
145. Ibid., 40.
146. Dimitris Livanios, *The Macedonian Question: Britain and the Southern Balkans, 1939–1949* (2009), 227.
147. Harold Macmillan, *The Blast of War, 1939–1945* (1967), 580–84.
148. Barker, *British Policy in South-eastern Europe*, 146.
149. David Close, *The Origins of the Greek Civil War* (1995), 138.
150. Quoted in Woodhouse, *Struggle for Greece*, 101.
151. Close, *Origins of the Greek Civil War*, 139.
152. Ibid., 141.
153. Andrew Thompson, '"In a Rather Emotional State"? The Labour Party and British Intervention in Greece, 1944–1945', *English Historical Review*, 121/493 (September 2006).
154. Dear, *Oxford Companion to the Second World War*, 507.

155. Harold Macmillan, *War Diaries: Politics and War in the Mediterranean. January, 1943–May, 1945* (1964), 604–5.
156. Directive for SOE Field Commander, Cyprus, 27 July 1942, HS3/120, TNA.
157. Yiangou, *Cyprus in World War Two*, 91.
158. Ibid., 148.
159. See Meir Chazan, 'The 1943 Reconstruction Plan for Mandatory Palestine: The Controversy within the Jewish Community', *Journal of Imperial and Commonwealth History*, 38/1 (March 2010), 101–2. On air raids, see Nir Arselt, '"Haifa is Still Burning": Italian, German and French Air-Raids on Palestine during the Second World War', *Middle Eastern Studies*, 46/3 (May 2010).
160. Chazan, 'The 1943 Reconstruction Plan for Mandatory Palestine', 105.
161. Ibid.
162. Tom Segev, *One Palestine Complete: Jews and Arabs under the British Mandate* (2000), 465.
163. Joseph Heller, *The Stern Gang: Ideology, Politics and Terror, 1940–1949* (1995), 137.
164. Bethell, *Palestine Triangle*, 184.
165. Ibid., 183.
166. Ibid., 187–8.
167. Heller, *The Stern Gang*, 139–40.
168. Bethell, *Palestine Triangle*, 186.
169. Nasser, *Britain and the Egyptian Nationalist Movement*, 59–60.
170. Killearn to Admiral Rawlings, 10 August 1947, ADM1/18521, TNA.
171. 'The War at Sea in the Mediterranean', in ADM223/695, TNA.
172. Ibid.
173. Ball, *The Bitter Sea*, 294.
174. Dominic Fenech, 'The Mediterranean Region during the Cold War and After', in John B. Hattersdorf (ed.), *Naval Policy and Strategy in the Mediterranean: Past, Present and Future* (2000), 227.

## CHAPTER 8. THE PASSING OF THE BRITISH MEDITERRANEAN, 1945–1979

1. Eric Grove, *Vanguard to Trident: British Naval Policy since World War Two* (1987), 3.
2. See Richard Clogg (ed.), *Bearing Gifts to Greeks: Humanitarian Aid to Greece in the 1940s* (2008).

3. C. M. Woodhouse, *The Struggle for Greece, 1941–1949* (1976), 148.
4. Ibid., 142.
5. Quoted in David Close, *The Origins of the Greek Civil War* (1995), 163.
6. Ibid., 164.
7. Simon Ball, *The Bitter Sea: The Brutal World War Two Fight for the Mediterranean* (2009), 297.
8. Robert Holland, *The Pursuit of Greatness: Britain and the World Role 1900–1970* (1991), 213.
9. H. McNeil to Bevin, 4 December 1946, FO800/468, TNA.
10. Note on the Straits, 23 August 1946, FO371/59228; also CAB121/672, TNA.
11. Close, *Origins of the Greek Civil War*, 214.
12. Greece – Publicity for Military Mission, WO32/15547, TNA.
13. Quoted in Robert Holland and Diana Markides, *The British and the Hellenes: Struggles for Mastery in the Eastern Mediterranean, 1850–1960* (2006), 212.
14. Ibid., 218.
15. This ship is much better known as having carried the first batch of Jamaican migrants to Britain in 1948, providing a landmark in the history of multi-racialism in Britain.
16. H. Wolstan-Weld to Norton, 3 February 1950, FO371/187754, TNA.
17. The British Police Mission, in fact, did not leave Greece entirely till 1951.
18. Wm. Roger Louis and Robert W. Stookey (eds.), *The End of the Palestine Mandate* (1986), 11.
19. For these camps, see Stavros Panteli, *A Place of Refuge: A History of the Jews in Cyprus* (2004).
20. Fritz Liebreich, *Britain's Naval and Political Reaction to the Illegal Immigration of Jews to Palestine, 1945–1948* (2005), 166.
21. Ibid., 168.
22. Ninian Stewart, *The Royal Navy and the Palestine Patrol* (2002), 168.
23. David Charters, *The British Army and Jewish Insurgency in Palestine, 1945–1947* (1989), 150.
24. Nicholas Bethell, *The Palestine Triangle: The Struggle between the British, the Jews and the Arabs, 1935–1948* (1979), 290.
25. Norman Rose, *'A Senseless and Squalid War': Voices from Palestine, 1945–1948* (2009), 167.
26. Charters, *The British Army and Jewish Insurgency in Palestine*, 109.
27. For a comparative treatment on this theme, see Robert Holland, Carl Bridge and H. V. Brasted, 'Counsels of Despair or Withdrawals with

Honour? Partitioning in Ireland, India, Palestine and Cyprus, 1920–1960', *Round Table*, 342 (1997), 257–68.

28. Sir Henry Gurney to John Martin, 24 January 1947, CO967/102, TNA.
29. Gurney to Martin, 17 April 1947, CO967/102, TNA.
30. Gurney to Martin, 24 January 1947, CO967/102, TNA.
31. Directive and Administrative Instructions to General Officer Commanding, Palestine PREM8/860, TNA.
32. Gurney to Martin, 26 March 1947, CO967/102, TNA.
33. Benny Morris, *1948 and After: Israel and the Palestinians* (1987), 11.
34. Martin Jones, *Failure in Palestine* (1986), 321.
35. Cunningham to Colonial Office, 23 April 1948, PREM8/860, TNA.
36. Stewart, *The Royal Navy and the Palestine Patrol*, 166.
37. Motti Golani (ed.), *The End of the British Mandate for Palestine, 1948: The Diary of Sir Henry Gurney* (2009), 148–9.
38. Rose, *'A Senseless and Squalid War'*, 202.
39. Ibid., 210–11.
40. Golani, *The End of the British Mandate for Palestine*, 41.
41. For the definitive study of this policy, see Wm. Roger Louis, *The British Empire in the Middle East, 1945–1951: Arab Nationalism, the United States and Post-War Imperialism* (1984).
42. Quoted in Hoda Nasser, *Britain and the Egyptian Nationalist Movement, 1936–1952* (1994), 175.
43. Ibid., 128.
44. Peter Mansfield, *The British in Egypt* (1971), 287.
45. Ibid., 288.
46. Sir David Kelly, *The Ruling Few: Or the Human Background to Diplomacy* (1952), 261.
47. General Headquarters to Ministry of Defence, 20 November 1951, PREM 11/632, TNA.
48. See pp. 256–7.
49. Quoted in David Williams, *A Most Diplomatic General: The Life of General Lord Robertson* (1996), 161–2.
50. Robertson, Appreciation of Egyptian Situation, 12 February 1952, WO 216/754, TNA.
51. Eden to Churchill, 11 July 1952, PREM11/632, TNA.
52. Williams, *A Most Diplomatic General*, 164.
53. John Kent (ed.), *Egypt and the Defence of the Middle East: Part 1. 1945–49* (1998), p. xciii.
54. Quoted in Mohamed Heikal, *Cutting the Lion's Tail: Suez through Egyptian Eyes* (1986), 43.

55. Richard Worrall, 'Britain and Libya: A Study of Military Bases and State Creation, 1945–1956', D.Phil. thesis, Oxford University (2008), 108–9.
56. Ibid., 121.
57. Ibid., 183.
58. Ibid., 194.
59. General Keightley to General Harding, 13 May 1954, WO216/799, TNA.
60. Evacuation of British Subjects from Egypt, March 1954, PREM11/632, TNA.
61. See material in FO371/10830 and FO371/10842, TNA.
62. Kent, *Egypt and the Defence of the Middle East*, 416.
63. Ibid., p. lxxxvi.
64. Keith Kyle, *Suez* (1991), 62–3.
65. Ibid., 127.
66. Trevelyan to Foreign Office, 19 June 1956, FO371/118980, TNA.
67. Trevelyan to Selwyn Lloyd, 23 June 1956, FO371/118980, TNA.
68. See p. 138.
69. Trevelyan to Selwyn Lloyd, 29 June 1956, FO371/118980, TNA.
70. Note on Civilian Population of Gibraltar, CO968/94/9, TNA.
71. Nigel Lawson, *The View from No. 11: Memoirs of a Tory Radical* (1993), 13–14.
72. F. A. von Hayek, 'Report on Economic Conditions in Gibraltar', CO91/522/1, TNA.
73. Ibid.
74. Arthur Whitaker, *Spain and the Defense of the West: Ally and Liability* (1961), 22–3.
75. Minute on Gibraltar and the Neutral Zone, 28 March 1946, FO371/60414, TNA.
76. Quoted in Joseph Garcia, *Gibraltar: The Making of a People* (2002), 45.
77. Ibid., 62.
78. CO minute, 19 November 1954, CO926/280, TNA.
79. Whitaker, *Spain and the Defense of the West*, 37–8.
80. John Balfour to Foreign Office, 12 May 1954, CO926/239, TNA.
81. Ibid.
82. Notes of Interview with Spanish Consul-General, 17 April 1954, CO926/239, TNA.
83. Quoted in Yiorghos Leventis, *Cyprus: The Struggle for Self-Determination in the 1940s* (2002), 16.
84. Quoted in Robert Holland, *Britain and the Revolt in Cyprus, 1954–59* (1998), 16.

85. Holland and Markides, *The British and the Hellenes*, 134.
86. Tabitha Morgan, *Sweet and Bitter Island: A History of the British in Cyprus* (2010), 198–9.
87. Director of Plans, 30 December 1944, ADM1/1852, TNA.
88. Note of meeting, 24 July 1948, AIR20/7374, TNA.
89. Quoted in Holland, *Britain and the Revolt in Cyprus*, 38.
90. *Sunday Times*, 4 July 1954.
91. Anthony Montague-Brown, *Long Sunset: Memoirs of Winston Churchill's Last Private Secretary* (1995), 183.
92. Holland, *Britain and the Revolt in Cyprus*, 56.
93. Memorandum of conversation, 25 June 1954, Box 3602, RG59, State Department Records, United States National Archive.
94. Quoted in Peter Catterall (ed.), *The Macmillan Diaries, 1950–1957* (2003), 466.
95. Holland, *Britain and the Revolt in Cyprus*, 86.
96. Ibid., 118–19.
97. *Spectator*, 17 March 1956.
98. Lawrence Durrell, *Bitter Lemons* (1957), 214–15.
99. For Durrell, Seferis and Cyprus, see Jim Potts, *Corfu Blues* (2006), 124–46.
100. Christopher Pollaci, *An Outline of Socio-Economic Development in Post-War Malta* (2003), 5.
101. Simon C. Smith (ed.), *British Documents on the End of Empire: Malta* (2006), 12.
102. Ibid., 43.
103. Joan Alexander, *Mabel Strickland* (1996), 181, 210.
104. Dennis Austen, *Malta and the End of Empire* (1971), 110.
105. Smith, *Malta*, 33.
106. Catterall, *Macmillan Diaries*, 443.
107. Simon Smith, 'Integration and Disintegration: The Attempted Incorporation of Malta into the United Kingdom in the 1950s', *Journal of Imperial and Commonwealth History*, 35/1 (March 2007), 49–71. Also see Stephen Howe, 'British Decolonization and Malta's Imperial Role', in Victor Mallia-Milanes (ed.), *The British Colonial Experience, 1800–1964: The Impact on Maltese Society* (1988), 135–58.
108. Smith, *Malta*, 64.
109. Ibid., 129.
110. Joseph M. Pirotta, *Fortress Colony: The Final Act, 1945–1964*, vol. 2 (1991), 134.
111. Ibid., 146.
112. Ibid.

113. Ibid., 274; Kyle, *Suez*, 131.
114. Heikal, *Cutting the Lion's Tail*, 122–6.
115. Ibid., 130.
116. Kyle, *Suez*, 131.
117. Ibid., 234–5.
118. Worrall, 'Britain and Libya', 248–59.
119. Ibid.
120. Peter Elliott, *Cross and the Ensign: A Naval History of Malta, 1798–1979* (1980), 219.
121. Kyle, *Suez*, 441.
122. Ibid., 482.
123. Philip Mansel, *Levant: Splendour and Catastrophe on the Mediterranean* (2010), 280.
124. See Dionysios Chourchoulis, 'High Hopes, Bold Aims, Limited Results: Britain and the Establishment of the N.A.T.O. Mediterranean Command, 1950–1953', *Diplomacy and Statecraft*, 20/3 (September 2009).
125. Quoted in Philip Ziegler, *Mountbatten* (1985), 508.
126. Kyle, *Suez*, 411–12.
127. Holland, *Britain and the Revolt in Cyprus*, 208–9.
128. The official was John Reddaway. See his *Burdened with Cyprus* (1989).
129. Holland, *Britain and the Revolt in Cyprus*, 306.
130. Ibid., 313.
131. Ibid., 326–7.
132. See Hubert Faustmann, 'Independence Postponed: Cyprus 1959–1960', *Cyprus Review*, 14/2 (2002).
133. Smith, *Malta*, 174.
134. Ibid., 166.
135. For an excellent coverage, see Pollaci, *Socio-Economic Development in Post-War Malta*.
136. Ibid., 203.
137. Smith, *Malta*, p. xiv.
138. Henry Frendo (ed.), *Maltese Political Development, 1798–1964* (1993), 813–29.
139. Ibid., 283.
140. Note to the Prime Minister, 27 July 1964, PREM11/4912, TNA.
141. Smith, *Malta*, 333–4.
142. 'Malta: The Political Future', in FO371/182888, TNA.
143. See CAB163/34 and CO1035/153, TNA.
144. See CAB 21/5099; also Smith, *Malta*, 350.
145. Edith Dobie, *Malta's Road to Independence* (1967), 258–9.

146. Smith, *Malta*, 310.
147. Ibid., 388–9.
148. Godfrey Pirotta, *The Maltese Public Service, 1800–1940: The Administrative Politics of a Micro-State* (1996), 430–31.
149. Smith, *Malta*, 388–9.
150. Pollaci, *Socio-Economic Development in Post-War Malta*, 241–2.
151. See James Craig, 'Escape from the Fortress Colony: The Politics of Economic Diversification in Malta', in James Mayall and Anthony Payne (eds.), *The Fallacies of Hope: The Post-Colonial Record of the Commonwealth Third World* (1991), 129–42.
152. Quoted in Whitaker, *Spain and the Defense of the West*, 62–3.
153. *Gibraltar Chronicle*, '40 Years On: The Closure of the Gibaltar/Spain Frontier', 21 August 2009.
154. For a slightly later example, see J. N. Henderson to A. B. Davidson, 25 January 1968, FCO9/461, TNA.
155. Quoted in Whitaker, *Spain and the Defense of the West*, 352.
156. Garcia, *Gibraltar*, 149.
157. Gibraltar and Rhodesia had already been linked in 1966 when Wilson chose to hold talks with Ian Smith, the rebel Rhodesian leader, on HMS *Tiger* at Gibraltar. Any supposition that Smith might be mellowed by the sight of such an imperial symbol as the Rock proved mistaken.
158. In some quarters there was even wild talk of some kind of coup against Wilson in May 1968. See Holland, *Pursuit of Greatness*, 336.
159. Peter Gold, *Gibraltar: British or Spanish?* (2005), 19.
160. Grove, *Vanguard to Trident*, 297.
161. Keith Hamilton and Patrick Salmon (eds.), *Documents on British Policy Overseas: The Southern Flank in Crisis, 1973–1976* (2006), 385.
162. Charles Powell, *King Juan Carlos of Spain* (1996), 194–5.
163. Grove, *Vanguard to Trident*, 297.
164. A. Cecil Hampshire, *The Royal Navy since 1945* (1975), 246.
165. Evelyn Shuckburgh to Michael Stewart, 16 April 1968, FCO16/224, TNA.
166. For an astute comment on this theme, see 'British Interests in the Mediterranean in the Long-Term', minute by M. Tesh, 15 April 1970, FCO49/300, TNA.
167. Paul Gore-Booth to Shuckburgh, 9 July 1968, FCO46/2, TNA.
168. Grove, *Vanguard to Trident*, 297–8.
169. Edgar Mizzi, *Malta in the Making, 1962–1987* (1995), 97.
170. See entry on Sir Maurice Dorman Smith in *ODNB*.
171. Edward Heath, *The Course of My Life* (1998), 498.

172. Mizzi, *Malta in the Making*, 128.
173. Ibid., 101, 121.
174. Ibid., 130.
175. James Ker-Lindsay, *Britain and the Cyprus Crisis, 1963–1964* (2004).
176. A. C. Goodison to S. Olver, 17 October 1973, FCO9/1683, TNA.
177. Brendan O'Malley, *The Cyprus Conspiracy: America, Espionage and the Turkish Invasion* (1999).
178. See Jan Asmussen, *Diplomacy and Conflict during the 1974 Crisis: Cyprus at War* (2008), and Andreas Constandinos, 'America, Britain and the Cyprus Crisis of 1974', Ph.D. thesis, University of East Anglia (2008).
179. James Callaghan, *Time and Chance* (1987), 342–3.
180. Hamilton and Salmon, *The Southern Flank in Crisis*, 99.
181. Ibid., 195. For a detailed account of the UN (including British) military involvement, see Brigadier Francis Henn, *A Business of Some Heat: The United Nations Force in Cyprus before and during the 1974 Turkish Invasion* (2004).
182. Callaghan, *Time and Chance*, 351–2; also Hamilton and Salmon, *Southern Flank in Crisis*, 195. The Cyprus crisis was simultaneous with the climax of the Watergate affair in the United States.
183. Callaghan, *Time and Chance*, 356.
184. Hamilton and Salmon, *Southern Flank in Crisis*, 248–51.
185. Ibid., 247.
186. Parliamentary Debates, House of Commons, vol. 405, 20 February 1980, col. 774.
187. See 'Cyprus: Sovereign Base Area' by J. L. Bullard, 15 June 1979, FCO9/2828, TNA.
188. Constandinos, 'America, Britain and the Cyprus Crisis of 1974', 107.
189. Hamilton and Salmon, *Southern Flank in Crisis*, 265–6.
190. Ibid., 318. The nadir of this 'slippage' was the assassination of Brigadier Stephen Saunders, the British military attaché in Athens, on 8 June 2000, allegedly as revenge for the NATO bombing of Serbia in 1999. The murder was carried out by the terrorist group November 17. Co-operation between British and Greek police forces later led to the conviction of the culprits.
191. Ibid., 209.
192. Ibid., 327.
193. Norman Aspin to David Owen, 17 April 1979, FCO9/2849, TNA.
194. Mizzi, *Malta in the Making*, 325.
195. Ibid., 326.
196. Ibid., 327.

197. R. M. Purcell to David Owen, 17 April 1979, FCO9/2849, TNA.
198. Norman Aspin to David Owen, 6 April 1979, FCO9/2849, TNA.
199. 'Rundown Ceremonies: Background Note', 19 March 1979, FCO9/2849, TNA.

## POSTSCRIPT: LEGACIES, RESIDUES AND CONTINUITIES

1. R. Murray to Rohan Butler, 25 May 1964, FO371/174838, TNA.
2. 'Neglect and Disrepair Leads Corfu Dissidents to Seek Split from Greece', *Guardian*, 26 September 2008.
3. See pp. 123–4.
4. *Times of Malta*, 3 June 2010.
5. John Reddaway, *Burdened with Cyprus* (1990).
6. See, for example, 'Expats a Political Force in Spain', BBC News, 12 May 2007.
7. Andreas Avgouti, 'The Indigenous Foreigner, 1963–1965', *Cyprus Review*, 21/1 (Spring 2009).
8. 'Gibraltar: The View from the Other Side', *Daily Telegraph*, 31 July 2004.
9. 'Hoon in Gibraltar Despite Protest', BBC News, 4 August 2004.
10. 'The Saloon Bar Follies that Keep us Clinging to Gibraltar', *Guardian*, 5 August 2004. Rockall is a small and uninhabited island in the north-west Atlantic. Under a 1972 British Act of Parliament it is part of Inverness-shire, though ownership has been disputed by Ireland, Denmark and Iceland.
11. Ibid.
12. 'Good Times on Main Street for Thriving Gibraltar', *Guardian*, 24 August 2009.
13. 'The Rock Carves out a New Identity', *Financial Times Special Report*, 18 October 2010.
14. Simon Ball, *The Bitter Sea: The Brutal World War Two Fight for the Mediterranean* (2009), 326–7.
15. Walter Frewen Lord, *Sir Thomas Maitland: The Mastery of the Mediterranean* (1897), 133–4.
16. Quoted in Matthew Jones, *Britain, the United States and the Mediterranean War, 1942–44* (1996), 233.

# *Index*